Law and Language

The Italian Analytical School

Law and Language

The Italian Analytical School

edited by

Anna Pintore and Mario Jori

translations by

Zenon Bankowski, Simona Stirling and Anne Pirrie

Deborah Charles Publications

LEGAL SEMIOTICS MONOGRAPHS (ISSN 1360-1652)

1. Bernard S. Jackson, *Law, Fact and Narrative Coherence*
2. David R. Papke, ed., *Law, Narrative and the Legal Discourse* (out of print)
3. Dragan Milovanovic, *Postmodern Law and Disorder*
4. Bernard S. Jackson, *Making Sense in Law. Linguistic, Psychological and Semiotic Perspectives*
5. Bernard S. Jackson, *Making Sense in Jurisprudence*
6. Kaarlo Tuori, Zenon Bankowski and Jyrki Uusitalo, eds., *Law and Power, Critical and Socio-Legal Essays*
7. Anna Pintore and Mario Jori, eds., *Law and Language. The Italian Analytical School* (1997)
8. Bernard S. Jackson, *Semiotics and Legal Theory* (reprint)

This title first published in 1997
by Deborah Charles Publications
173 Mather Avenue, Liverpool L18 6JZ, U.K.

Published with support from the
Ministero italiano dell'Università e della Ricerca Scientifica.

Typesetting by Deborah Charles Publications
Printing by Antony Rowe Ltd., Chippenham

British Library Cataloguing-in-Publication Data
A catalogue record for this book is available from the British Library.

ISBN 0-9513793-5-6 (cased)

Contents

Andrea Belvedere teaches civil law at Pavia. Among his works on the analytical theory of law: *Il problema delle definizioni nel codice civile* (Milano: Giuffrè, 1978); *Definizioni giuridiche e ideologie* with M. Jori and L. Lantella (Milano: Giuffrè, 1979).

"Some Observations on the Language of the Italian Civil Code" first appeared as "Il linguaggio del codice civile: alcune osservazioni", in *Trattato di diritto civile diretto da Pietro Rescigno*, vol.21 (Turin: UTET, 1985), 1-44.

Norberto Bobbio is an emeritus professor of the philosophy of law and a Life Member of the Italian Senate. Among his immense theoretical-juridical production, see: *Teoria della norma giuridica* (Torino: Giappichelli, 1959); *Teoria dell'ordinamento giuridico* (Torino: Giappichelli, 1960), and the collections of essays *Studi sulla teoria generale del diritto* (Torino: Giappichelli, 1955); *Studi per una teoria generale del diritto* (Torino: Giappichelli, 1970); *Diritto e potere. Essays on Kelsen* (Napoli: ESI, 1992); *Contributi per un dizionario giuridico* (Torino: Giappichelli, 1994).

"The Science of Law and the Analysis of Language" first appeared as "Scienza del diritto e analisi del linguaggio", *Rivista Trimestrale di Diritto e Procedura civile* IV (1950), 342-367.

Gaetano Carcaterra teaches philosophy of law in Rome. Among his works: *Le norme costitutive* (Milano: Giuffrè, 1974); *La forza costitutiva delle norme* (Roma: Bulzoni, 1979); *Norme giuridiche e valori etici. Saggi di filosofia del diritto* (Roma: Bulzoni, 1991).

"The Rules of the Pickwick Club. A Model for the Theory of Law" first appeared as "Le regole del circolo Pickwick (un modello per la teoria del diritto", in *Nuova civiltà delle macchine* III/3-4 (1985), 16-25.

Alfonso Catania teaches philosophy of law at Salerno. Among his works: *Argomenti per una teoria dell'ordinamento giuridico* (Napoli: Jovene, 1976); *Decisione e norma* (Napoli: Jovene, 1979); *Il problema del diritto e l'obbligatorietà. Studio sulla norma fondamentale* (Napoli: Esi, 1983); *Analisi del diritto. Studi di teoria generale* (Napoli: Jovene, 1992); *Manuale di filosofia del diritto* (Napoli: Esi, 1995).

"Acceptance in the Thought of H.L.A. Hart" first appeared as

"L'accettazione nel pensiero di Herbert L.A. Hart", *Rivista internazionale di filosofia del diritto* XLVIII (1971), 261-279.

Amedeo G. Conte teaches philosophy of law at Pavia. Among his works: *Primi argomenti per una critica del normativismo* (Pavia: Tipografia del libro, 1968); *Saggio sulla completezza degli ordinamenti giuridici* (Torino: Giappichelli, 1962); *Nove studi sul linguaggio normativo* (Torino: Giappichelli, 1985); *Filosofia del linguaggio normativo. I. Studi 1965-1981* (Torino: Giappichelli, 1989).

"Eidetic-Constitutive Rules" first appeared as "Regole eidetico-costitutive", in *Nuova civiltà delle macchine* III/3-4 (1985), 26-33.

Luigi Ferrajoli teaches philosophy of law at Camerino. Among his works: *Teoria assiomatizzata del diritto* (Milano: Giuffrè, 1970); *Democrazia autoritaria e capitalismo maturo*, with D. Zolo (Milano: Feltrinelli, 1978); *Diritto e ragione. Teoria del garantismo penale* (Roma-Bari: Laterza, 1989).

"The Semantics of the Theory of Law" first appeared as "La semantica della teoria del diritto", in U. Scarpelli, ed., *La teoria generale del diritto* (Milan: Edizioni di Comunità, 1983), 81-130.

Letizia Gianformaggio teaches philosophy of law at Ferrara. Among her works: *Gli argomenti di Perelman: dalla neutralità dello scienziato all'imparzialità del giudice* (Milano: Comunità, 1973); *Studi sulla giustificazione giuridica* (Torino: Giappichelli, 1986); *In difesa del sillogismo pratico ovvero alcuni argomenti kelseniani alla prova* (Milano: Giuffrè, 1987); *Filosofia e critica del diritto* (Torino: Giappichelli, 1995).

"On Moral and Legal Justification" first appeared as "Sul senso della giustificazione morale e giuridica", in L. Gianformaggio and E. Lecaldano, eds., *Etica e diritto* (Roma-Bari: Laterza, 1986), 151-172.

Giacomo Gavazzi teaches general theory of law at Pavia. Among his works: *Delle antinomie* (Torino: Giappichelli, 1959); *Norme primarie e norme secondarie* (Torino: Giappichelli, 1967); *Elementi di teoria del diritto* (Torino: Giappichelli, 1970); *Studi di teoria del diritto* (Torino: Giappichelli, 1993).

"In (Partial) Defence of a Predictive Conception of Legal Obligation" first appeared as "In difesa (parziale) di una concezione predittiva dell'obbligo giuridico", *Rivista di Filosofia* LVII (1966), 165-174.

Riccardo Guastini teaches general theory of law and constitutional law in Genoa. Among his works: *Lezioni di teoria analitica del diritto* (Torino: Giappichelli, 1982); *Le fonti del diritto e l'interpretazione* (Milano: Giuffrè, 1993); *Il giudice e la legge* (Torino: Giappichelli, 1995).

Mario Jori teaches philosophy of law in Milan. Among his works: *Il metodo giuridico tra scienza e politica* (Milano: Giuffrè, 1976); *Il formalismo giuridico* (Milano: Giuffrè, 1980; *Saggi di metagiurisprudenza* (Milano: Giuffrè, 1985); *Il giuspositivismo analitico italiano prima e dopo la crisi* (Milano: Giuffrè, 1987); *Manuale di Teoria generale del diritto,* with Anna Pintore (Torino: Giappichelli, 1995, 2nd ed.).

"The Object and Method of Legal Science" first appeared as "Oggetto e metodo della scienza giuridica", in U. Scarpelli, ed., *La teoria generale del diritto* (Milan: Edizioni di Comunità, 1983), 177-230.

Giorgio Lazzaro taught philosophy of law in Turin. Among his works: *Storia e teoria della costruzione giuridica* (Torino: Giappichelli, 1965); *L'interpretazione sistematica della legge* (Torino: Giappichelli, 1966).

"Law and Ordinary Language" first appeared as "Diritto e linguaggio comune", *Rivista trimestrale di diritto e procedura civile* XXXV (1981), 140-181.

Enrico Pattaro teaches philosophy of law in Bologna. Among his works: *Il pensiero giuridico di L.A. Muratori tra metodologia e politica* (Milano: Giuffrè, 1974); *Il realismo giuridico scandinavo: I. Axel Hägeström* (Bologna: CLUEB, 1975); *Lineamenti per una teoria del diritto* (Bologna: CLUEB, 1985); *Introduzione al corso di filosofia del diritto* (Bologna: CLUEB, 1986-87).

"Towards a Map of Legal Knowledge" first appeared as "Per una mappa del sapere giuridico", in U. Scarpelli, ed., *La teoria generale del diritto* (Milan: Edizioni di Comunità, 1983), 249-279.

Uberto Scarpelli (1924-1993) taught philosophy of law in Milan. Among his works: *Esistenzialismo e marxismo* (Torino: Taylor, 1949); *Filosofia analitica, norme e valori* (Milano: Comunità, 1962); *Semantica, Morale, diritto* (Torino: Giappichelli, 1969); *L'etica senza verità* (Bologna: Il Mulino, 1982); *Contributo alla semantica del linguaggio normativo* (Milano: Giuffrè, 1985, 2nd ed.).

"Ethics, Language and Reason" first appeared as "Etica, linguaggio, ragione," in U. Scarpelli, ed., *L'etica senza verità* (Bologna: Il Mulino, 1982), 49-72.

Giovanni Tarello (1934-1987) taught philosophy of law in Genoa. Among his works: *Il realismo giuridico americano* (Milano: Giuffrè, 1962); *Teorie e ideologie nel diritto sindacale* (Milano: Comunità, 1967); *Diritto, enunciati, usi* (Bologna: Il Mulino, 1974); *Storia della cultura giuridica moderna. Vol. I: Assolutismo e codificazione del diritto* (Bologna: Il Mulino, 1976); *L'interpretazione della legge* (Milano: Giuffrè, 1980); *Cultura giuridica e politica del diritto* (Bologna: Il Mulino, 1988).

"Philosophical Analysis and the Theory of Legal Interpretation" first appeared as "Orientamenti analitico-linguistici e teoria dell'interpretaz-ione giuridica", in U. Scarpelli, ed., *Diritto e analisi del linguaggio* (Milan: Edizioni di Comunità, 1976), 375-396.

The permissions of authors and publishers to publish the translations in this volume are gratefully acknowledged.

INTRODUCTION

by

ANNA PINTORE

1. *This Book*

The purpose of this collection is to offer the English-speaking public a selection of writings by the Italian analytical school of legal philosophy and general theory of law. I hope that the essays translated here will help in promoting an interest in Italian analytical legal thinking among legal scholars in English-speaking countries, an interest that up to now has not been proportionate to the undoubted good quality of much of the Italian work in this area.

I suspect that the language barrier has been the main obstacle to a wider diffusion of Italian analytical-legal writings in English-speaking philosophical circles, particularly those influenced by philosophical analysis. Indeed, this introduction proposes to show that there is an extensive common area of themes and problems discussed by both English-speaking writers and in Italian analytical legal philosophy and that much the same authors are commented upon, criticized or taken as the starting point of further research. Themes and problems will be mentioned further on; as for the common authors, suffice it to say that Italian analytical-legal philosophy, from its very origins, has expended much energy in dealing with Wittgenstein, J.L. Austin, Searle, Hare and the other fundamental authors of philosophical analysis. With regard to legal philosophy itself, the major point of convergence is represented by the ideas of Hart, the author most widely discussed and criticized by second-generation analysts (in this anthology Hart is central to the essays by Gavazzi, Catania and Jori).

The essays presented herein are all by Italian authors deeply influenced by the exceptional figure of Norberto Bobbio, spiritual guide of the school and a philosopher deeply engaged in Italian scientific and political life. The essays were not chosen for having a similar or connected

Law and Language, The Italian Analytical School, ed. A. Pintore and M. Jori (Liverpool: Deborah Charles Publications, 1997).

subject. On the contrary, I have tried to offer a cross section, as representative as possible, of this philosophical approach. In this way we can see, through the writings of its most prominent advocates, just how vast are the interests, and how varied are the ways of understanding and practising analytical philosophy, present in Italian legal culture today.

This introduction gives a mere sketch of the history and salient features of Italian analytical legal philosophy. I hope thereby to give the reader a better understanding of the contributions in this volume.[1]

2. *Bobbio's School*

The birth of the Italian analytical school is usually said to take place in 1950, the year in which *Scienza del diritto e analisi del linguaggio* by Norberto Bobbio, the first of the essays herein, was published.[2] Enrico Pattaro has called it the "programmatic manifesto" of the new trend.[3] In this 1950 essay, Bobbio dealt with the venerable problem of the scientific nature of doctrinal jurisprudence and gave it a positive answer. In fact, in

1 The idea for this anthology came from Bernard S. Jackson and Mario Jori. The essays were chosen together with Mario Jori. Many thanks to both.

2 More details concerning the history of the Italian analytical legal school, can be found in E. Pattaro, "Il positivismo giuridico italiano dalla rinascita alla crisi", *Politica del diritto* III (1972), 821-852, now reprinted in U. Scarpelli, ed., *Diritto e analisi del linguaggio* (Milan: Comunità, 1976), 469-76; U. Scarpelli, *La filosofia. La filosofia dell'etica. La filosofia del diritto di indirizzo analitico in Italia*, Introduction to U. Scarpelli, ed., *Diritto e analisi del linguaggio, op. cit.*, at 7-35; A. Baratta, "Il positivismo e il neopositivismo", in R. Orecchia, ed., *La filosofia del diritto italiana nel XX secolo. Atti dell'XI Congresso Nazionale della Società di Filosofia Giuridica e Politica* (Milan: Giuffrè, 1977), vol. II, 21-57; U. Scarpelli, "Filosofia e diritto", in F. Tessitore, ed., *La cultura filosofia italiana dal 1945 al 1980 nelle sue relazioni con altri campi del sapere* (Napoli: Guida, 1982), 173-199; E. Pattaro, *Per una mappa del sapere giuridico*, in U. Scarpelli, ed., *La teoria generale del diritto. Problemi e tendenze attuali. Studi dedicati a Norberto Bobbio* (Milan: Comunità, 1983), 249-279; M. Jori, *Il giuspositivismo analitico italiano prima e dopo la crisi* (Milan: Giuffrè, 1988); M.A. Barrere Unzueta, *La escuela de Bobbio. Reglas y normas en la filosofía jurídica italiana de inspiracíon analitica*, (Madrid: Tecnos, 1990); M. Barberis, *Introduzione alla storia della filosofia del diritto* (Bologna: Il Mulino, 1993), ch.VII. In particular, on Bobbio and the Italian analytical theory of law, see P. Borsellino, *Norberto Bobbio metateorico del diritto* (Milan: Giuffrè, 1991), esp. ch.I.

3 See Pattaro, *Diritto e analisi del linguaggio, supra* n.2, at 455.

his opinion, the work performed by the jurist on law could in many ways be compared to that of the empirical scientist, provided that a neo-empiricist model of science be adopted. Twenty years later, Bobbio re-examined the same problem and came up with a different answer which repudiated many points of his "seminal" thesis of 1950.[4] But by that time the 1950 essay had already accomplished its role as the manifesto of the new school; a manifesto not so much in that it was taken as a definitive solution to the specific problems dealt with, but because Bobbio's essay had approached the age-old problem of legal science in a new way which set the agenda for all further discussions on this subject among Italian legal philosophers of the analytical bent. Bobbio's essay was the first, in Italian legal culture, to consider law as a language and legal science as a meta-language having as its object the language of law. For the first time in Italy the epistemological model formulated by neo-empiricism was used as a parameter in assessing the scientific nature of jurists' work on law. Bobbio thus introduced into the climate of Italian legal philosophical studies, which idealistic fogginess had made rather stale, the disciplines of epistemology and semiotics.

The novelty of Bobbio's approach was even more profound and evident if we consider that he applied the new tools of linguistic analysis and neo-positivist epistemology to a conception of law that was substantially Kelsenian.[5] Pattaro, in describing this operation, used another felicitous image, in speaking of the grafting of logical empiricism and analytical philosophy on to the legal positivism of Kelsenian inspiration.[6] Bobbio's

4 See his "Essere e dover essere nella scienza giuridica", *Rivista di Filosofia* LVIII (1967), 235-62, reprinted in his *Studi sulla teoria generale del diritto* (Turin: Giappichelli, 1970), 139-73.

5 Bobbio has always seen his own role in all modesty simply as an importer of Kelsen into Italy. What he actually did is much more important. Kelsen's thought has been central in the discussion of first-generation Italian analysts, up to the crisis of Italian analytical legal positivism (see *infra* in the text).

The last decade have seen a revival of interest in Kelsen, but in different, more detached terms: from the viewpoint of "Kelsenologists" rather than that of "Kelsenians". Thanks to Letizia Gianformaggio, several seminars on Kelsen have been held. The proceedings of these are now being published: see L. Gianformaggio, ed., *Hans Kelsen's Legal Theory. A Diachronic Point of View* (Turin Giappichelli, 1990); L. Gianformaggio, ed, *Sistemi normativi statici e sistemi dinamici. Analisi di una tipologia kelseniana* (Turin: Giappichelli, 1991); L. Gianformaggio and S. Paulson, eds., *Cognition and Interpretation of Law* (Turin: Giappichelli, 1995).

6 See *Il positivismo giuridico italiano, supra* n.2, at 451.

essay was followed in the next few years by some fundamental works by Scarpelli, which were devoted to the problem of defining the concept of law and to the semiotics of normative language.[7] Since then, several generations of legal philosophers, and also some adventurous jurists, have been influenced by Bobbio's and Scarpelli's works. The essay by Andrea Belvedere, a professor of civil law, on the 1942 Italian Civil Code, is an excellent example of the use of analytical tools by a scholar of positive law and has every right to be included in this anthology .

These brief observations on the birth of the Italian analytical school of philosophy and theory of law are, I think, sufficient for the aims I have set myself. Those who wish to learn more should consult the essay by Pattaro in this volume, as well as the works cited in the footnotes.

Summing up in a few lines the history of Italian analytical-legal philosophy from 1950 to the present is a nearly impossible task. In order to make things as simple as possible, we may use another date, 1965, the year in which Bobbio's collected essays *Giusnaturalismo e positivismo giuridico*, and Scarpelli's volume, *Cos'è il positivismo giuridico* were published.[8]

According to many analysts, the year 1965 represents the watershed between two periods: a first period of the Italian school of analytical philosophy of law, characterized by its legal-positivism (a legal positivist phase) and a second period, when many of the basic theses of the first period came under heavy criticism, but were not forgotten. This has been called a phase of "post legal-positivism".[9] We know that the Italian analytical school was born, with Bobbio, as a (legal)positivistic approach. This must not, however, lead us to believe that different orientations were

7 The works are: U. Scarpelli, *Filosofia analitica e giurisprudenza* (Milan: Nuvoletti, 1953); U. Scarpelli, *Il problema della definizione e il concetto di diritto* (Milan: Istituto Editoriale Cisalpino, 1955); U. Scarpelli, *Contributo alla semantica del linguaggio normativo* (Turin: Memorie dell'Accademia delle Scienze di Torino, 1959; latest edition: Milan: Giuffrè, 1985). As a matter of naked chronological fact, it was Scarpelli who first in Italy mentioned analytical philosophy in connection with legal philosophy. This was in a brief note bearing the same title as Bobbio's essay: "Scienza del diritto e analisi del linguaggio", *Rivista trimestrale di diritto e procedura civile* 4 (1950), 342-67, repr. in U. Scarpelli, ed., *Diritto e analisi del linguaggio* (Milan: Edizioni di Comunità, 1976), 287-324, and in U. Scarpelli and P. Di Lucia, eds., *Il linguaggio del diritto* (Milan: Ledi, 1994), 87-93.

8 N. Bobbio, *Giusnaturalismo e positivismo giuridico* (Milan: Comunità, 1965); U. Scarpelli, *Cos'è il positivismo giuridico* (Milan: Comunità, 1965).

9 See Jori, *supra* n.2.

not present within it almost from the beginning. A group sympathetic to the North American and Scandinavian legal realist movements appeared early and immediately occupied a central position in analytical discussions. This especially owed to the works of Tarello and Pattaro, but even of scholars, such as Gavazzi,[10] who cannot be classified as legal realists *tout court.* Nonetheless, on the whole the first period of the school can be correctly labelled as that of legal positivism, since this orientation was preponderant, and above all since the problem of legal positivism represented the unifying element of the analytical debates in those years.[11]

The two works published by Bobbio and Scarpelli in 1965 turned analytical discussions in another direction and, in the eyes of some, went so far as to sign the death warrant of analytical legal positivism. In any case, Bobbio abandoned his old positions when he concluded that a scientific and value-free approach to the study of law led inevitably to emphasising the evaluative and political nature of positivistic legal science: therefore adhesion to legal positivism in its most acceptable sense of a value-free position towards each legal system led inevitably, in Bobbio's opinion, to the discovery that the work of jurists is neither scientific nor value-free.[12] As for Scarpelli, he declared himself a legal positivist but, in contrast with Bobbio, he thought that being such meant taking a *political* standpoint. Scarpelli's thesis is that legal positivism is not a purely descriptive and theoretical approach but rather presupposes a prior political choice in favour of a certain definition of law as the object of description (in Kelsenian terms, this is the choice of a basic norm). Far from being a value-free and scientific approach, legal positivism even as a method of legal description is thus for Scarpelli the rationalisation of a political involvement in favour of, firstly, a certain notion of positive law

10 See for example his criticism of the Hartian normative conception of legal obligation in the essay in this volume.

11 Discussion of the works of Bobbio and Scarpelli of the first period culminated with a *Tavola rotonda sul positivismo giuridico,* the proceedings of which were published as a monographic issue of *Il Politico* (Milan: Giuffrè, 1967). For the reconstruction of this stage of the debate, see in particular Jori's work cited in note 2.

12 See Bobbio, *supra* n.4. Bobbio distinguishes three main senses of "legal positivism": as a value-free approach to law; as a legalistic theory of law and state; as an ideology of justice affirming the duty to obey the law as such. See N. Bobbio, *Il positivismo giuridico* (Turin: Giappichelli, 1960; latest edition: 1996).

and, secondly, those legal systems which correspond to this notion, i.e. systems which are, on the whole, effective. In a nutshell, Scarpelli considers legal positivists as those who choose, whether as judges or as doctrinal jurists, to bow to the legal powers which are in force in a given territory at a given time. Scarpelli holds that this position is ethically acceptable and preferable to other theoretical positions in the field of law, but only when such obedience is paid to morally acceptable legal systems, which for him means a constitutional and democratic legal system.

I do not mean to give the impression that after 1965 all Italian analysts were suddenly converted to legal realism. However, many are of the opinion that the very founder of the school, Bobbio, came nearer to the positions of the legal realists because of the interest he has taken in the problem of the function of law in his more recent works.[13]

In any case, few Italian legal philosophers of the analytical persuasion would at present call themselves legal positivists;[14] furthermore, today's analytical positions certainly appear less definite and less easily circumscribed than they were in the past. Nonetheless, within the Italian analytical school the age-old legal-philosophical conflict between legal positivism and legal realism is still in full swing. It is now mostly fought on the semiotic ground, in terms that differ only partly from those of the past, and are closely connected with the analysis of law conceived as a language. We can thus describe it as a conflict between those who think that norms or rules are central to a semiotic analysis of law and those who believe that rules or norms, beyond appearances, play no real role in the workings of legal language (a normativistic semiotics versus an anti-normativistic semiotics).

3. *A Divisionist Philosophy*

We now turn to a more precise indication of the principal features and problems now being discussed by the Italian analytical legal school. This

13 See N. Bobbio, *Dalla struttura alla funzione* (Milan: Comunità, 1977). Bobbio has since then devoted his time more and more intensely to the study of political philosophy and political science, to the neglect of the theory of law.

14 It is not clear whether Scarpelli in his last works still adheres to legal positivism, even in the political version that he himself theorised. See his "Dalla legge al codice, dal codice ai princìpi", *Rivista di Filosofia* LXXVIII (1987), 3-15, and "Il positivismo giuridico rivisitato", *Rivista di Filosofia* LXXX (1989), 461-475.

is by no means an easy task. Indeed, the very notion of "analytical philosophy" is quite controversial. Debate on this very theme is lively today, in Italy as elsewhere. From it have emerged different characterisations of this philosophical orientation. As I see it, three families or notions of "analytical philosophy" have been advanced thus far among Italian analytical legal philosophers. In a first, quite weak sense, it has been said that analytical philosophy is for the most part a "philosophical style" characterised by a preference for analysis rather than synthesis, by a propensity for distinctions rather than for the great conceptual *rassemblements*, and by a preference for rigorous argumentation.[15] In a second sense, analytical philosophy has been characterized as a philosophy asserting the total reducibility of thought to language: an analytical philosopher is one who holds that language is the indispensable vehicle of thought.[16] In a third sense, which is certainly the strongest of the three, analytical philosophy is connected with certain basic metaphysical ideas or ultimate principles not susceptible to further justification (discussed in what follows as "divisionism" and "neo-empiricism"); they condition its proceeding and distinguish it from that of all other philosophical orientations.[17]

It would be out of place in this context to abandon the description of the Italian analytical-legal school in order to embark on a general discussion of these and other possible definitions of analytical philosophy. I shall therefore limit myself to a brief exposition of my opinion on this subject. I take it for granted that analytical philosophy is not merely a *technique* to be used in the analysis of language. To reduce it to this is tantamount to mistaking the menu for the meal.[18] The dishes served at

15 See U. Scarpelli, "La critica analitica a Kelsen", in *Rivista di filosofia* LXXII (1981), 481-490; *idem* , "Filosofia e diritto", *supra* n.2, at 177-79; R. Guastini, *Dalle fonti alle norme* (Turin: Giappichelli, 1990; 2nd ed., Turin: Giappichelli, 1992), 296ff. Scarpelli and Guastini both mention this weak sense, but they have always understood and practiced linguistic analysis in the strongest sense indicated in the text.

16 Thus V. Villa, "Sulla nozione di "filosofia analitica"", in M. Jori, ed., *Ermeneutica e filosofia analitica. Due concezioni del diritto a confronto* (Turin: Giappichelli, 1994), 163-181. Villa refers to the ideas of Dummett. See also M. Barberis, "Vincoli e strumenti. Sulla filosofia analitica del diritto", *Analisi e diritto* 6 (1995), 7-26.

17 See M. Jori, *Filosofia del diritto*, in M. Jori and A. Pintore, *Manuale di teoria generale del diritto* (Turin: Giappichelli, 1988; latest edition: 1995), 111ff.

18 Here I have adapted P.G. Monateri's witty metaphor in *Giurisprudenza,* entry

the analytical banquet are full of quite demanding principles and philosophical options, so much so that many consider them indigestible and turn to lighter, and faster, philosophical food. To continue with the gastronomic metaphor, we may add that the table of analytical philosophy is set with a rich variety of dishes capable of satisfying different tastes, even though they are all prepared with the same basic ingredients.

The analytical philosopher undoubtedly considers that one cannot transcend language. This would, however, be insufficient to characterise him or her, for many contemporary philosophers would in fact be willing to subscribe to this idea. It is also beyond doubt that analytical philosophy has an unmistakable "style", although it is difficult to translate this impression into words and into a list of distinctive elements. Concerning the analytical philosophy that deals specifically with *law*, it has rightly been said that, compared to other philosophical orientations, its style and approach is no less influenced by legal thinking, problems and style than by general philosophical ideas. Nevertheless, it is to be stressed that to practice a philosophy closer to jurists does not imply adopting indiscriminately their language and concepts; much less ignoring the philosophical problems of law. Within Italian analytical-legal philosophy, the coexistence of a theory of law *from above* with a theory of law *from below* has rightly been pointed out.[19] This distinction does not coincide with the distinction between a more and a less philosophical theory: rather it is useful in distinguishing between a theory more oriented towards logical, methodological and even metaphysical problems and one that is more interested in the "concrete problems of conceptual arrangement as they arise in this or that legal discipline".[20] An excellent example of a theory *from below* is supplied in this anthology by Lazzaro's essay on the relationship between legal and common language. A paradigmatic example of a theory *from above* is to be found in Conte's essay on constitutive rules.

We can already see that the Italian analytical approach to legal philosophy is by no means representative of a compact and homogeneous school with univocal ideas and positions. However, it is possible to find

---

in the *Digesto delle Discipline Privatistiche. Sezione civile* (Turin: Utet, 1993), 165.

19 See G. Gavazzi, *L'onere. Tra la libertà e l'obbligo* (Turin: Giappichelli, 1970, now in his *Studi di teoria del diritto*, Turin: Giappichelli, 1993), 318.

20 Gavazzi, *ibid.*

within it certain common characteristics that are not simply questions of style or due to the importance attributed to language. These characteristics are rather philosophical principles that Italian analysts consider *fundamental* and that must be taken into consideration, even if only for the purpose of rejecting them. One characterisation of the analytical method in this sense has been attempted by Jori and Guastini, and it is significant that both of them — the former, a normativist, and the latter, close to legal realism — consider the same two principles as constitutive of the analytical attitude: the principle of the "Great Division" between prescriptive and descriptive language and the principle of the distinction between analytical and synthetic judgements.[21]

With the distinction between *prescriptive* and *descriptive,* a first, fundamental and distinctive feature of the analytical school can be identified, that is, *divisionism.*; with the distinction between *analytical* and *synthetic* it is possible to single out the second, which is *empiricism.*

These two characteristics, although indicative of the peculiar position of the Italian analytical school in contemporary legal culture, are at the same time quite general and problematic. Therefore they serve to explain not only the points of convergence, but also the disagreements to be found within the analytical school.

Let us begin with divisionism: this is a complex ethical conception, within which one must distinguish between three logically independent theses. Firstly, there is the *semiotic* thesis of the Great Division in the strict sense, that is, the semantic-pragmatic distinction between types of discourse and linguistic functions, both descriptive and prescriptive. Secondly, there is the *(meta)ethical* thesis, known as *Hume's Law,* which prohibits going from descriptive premises to prescriptive conclusions and vice versa by purely logical-linguistic means. Thirdly, there are two *ontological* and *epistemological* theses, known as *ethical non-objectivism* and *non-cognitivism* respectively; these deny that the prescriptive is the dominion of the true or the false, or of any other objective and knowable value.

Their divisionism causes Italian analysts to be critical of both old and new versions of natural law theories: indeed, whatever Italian analysts are today, they are certainly *not* natural lawyers. They are not so with regards to the substance, since they refuse all confusion between the concept of law as it is and the concept of law as it ought to be; they do not want to adulterate the description of law with value judgements. Nor are

21 See Jori, *supra* n.17; Guastini, *supra* n. 15, at 286ff.

they natural lawyers in the methodological sense, since they deny that moral judgements can be objectively true and knowable.[22]

A fundamental test of membership to the analytical school is thus represented by acceptance of the distinction between descriptive and prescriptive. This is obviously not a distinction between two spheres of reality, but between two kinds of discourse. It should not appear surprising that analysts get along quite well with those philosophers who claim they can overcome the Great Division, but still take quite seriously the distinction between the prescriptive and the descriptive and problems connected with such a distinction. Gaetano Carcaterra is an analyst in this sense. He is the author of a powerful work on the naturalistic fallacy in which, after a profound and careful examination of the problem, he concludes by rejecting the Great Division in the strong sense of the impossibility of going from the descriptive to the prescriptive.[23]

With a brevity appropriate to these rather blunt periodisations, three main stages in the discussions amongst Italian analysts concerning meta-ethics can be distinguished. In a first stage the implications of divisionism were examined in depth, both as metaethical and ethical problems, and as semiotic problems.[24] The next stage was dominated by the need to refine theoretically and to defend from attacks the divisionistic thesis; attacks, especially with regards to criticisms coming from within *philosophical analysis* itself, and based mainly upon Austin's theory of performatives and Searle's theory of institutional facts.[25] A significant text on this point is the essay by Scarpelli in this volume, which shows that it is possible to be both a divisionist and a fierce critic of radical emotivism and other forms of ethical irrationalism. The most recent stage is characterised by a deep change in the way in which the divisionist thesis is practiced and applied to practical problems within the field of the law.

Italian legal philosophy is today part of what has been called the

22 According to Bobbio this thesis is at the core of a theory of natural law: Bobbio, *supra* n.8, at 185ff.

23 G. Carcaterra, *Il problema della fallacia naturalistica* (Milan: Giuffrè, 1969).

24 See especially Scarpelli, *Contributo, supra* n.7.

25 An important document at this stage is represented by a debate that took place in the 1970s on the *Is-Ought* question, with the participation of Scarpelli, Carcaterra and Lecaldano. The proceedings are to be found in U. Scarpelli, ed., "La logica e il dover essere", a monographic issue of the *Rivista di Filosofia* LXVII (1976).

"rediscovery of practical reason" in ethics and law.[26] Several and diverse factors have contributed to the creation of the new atmosphere; among them, the shifting of interest among analytical philosophers from metaethics to normative applied ethics, a shift that is usually related to Rawls' *A Theory of Justice;* interest in Perelman's new rhetoric and, more recently, in Habermas' and Apel's ethics of discourse and the theories of rational argumentation of Alexy, Aarnio and Peczenick; the diffusion of the so-called post-positivistic theories, proposing less rigorous criteria of empirical scientificity.

A most significant aspect of this recent stage in the discussion, which well exemplifies the new course in analytical debates, is documented by the proceedings of an analytical meeting on moral and legal justification[27] which took place in 1984. Within the Italian school of analytical legal philosophy, the subject of practical reason in law has been closely studied, particularly by Letizia Gianformaggio (see the essay in this volume), who was led from Perelman to a weak and divisonistic concept of practical reason. The most recent, and at the same time most remarkable, contribution supplied by the Italian analytical school to the "rediscovery" of normative ethics is *Diritto e ragione* by Luigi Ferrajoli, a powerful book that will certainly make a long-lasting mark on legal culture. *Diritto e ragione* is a treatise on the philosophy of criminal justice inspired by the defence of a refined normative model of minimum criminal law in support of the rule of law.[28]

This divisionistic, and accordingly anti-natural law attitude shared by Italian analysts accentuates the impression of their apparent sharp differentiation from theorists of other schools, and their apparent closeness of opinion *inter* se. In effect, anti-divisionism makes all possible

26 The reference is to N. MacCormick, "Contemporary Philosophy: the Rediscovery of Practical Reason", *Journal of Law and Society* 10 (1983), 1-18. See C. Faralli and E. Pattaro, eds., *Reason in Law* (Milan: Giuffrè, 1985-88, 3 vols.), which is a collection of the proceedings of an international meeting held in Bologna in 1984. *Ragion Pratica* (Practical Reason) is also the title of a recent journal which is the result of interdisciplinary collaboration between jurists and legal and moral philosophers, both of analytical and other orientations.

27 Published in L. Gianformaggio and E. Lecaldano, eds., *Etica e diritto* (Milan: Angeli, 1986).

28 L. Ferrajoli, *Diritto e ragione. Teoria del garantismo penale* (Roma-Bari, Laterza, 1989). See also L. Gianformaggio, ed., *Le ragioni del garantismo. Discutendo con Luigi Ferrajoli* (Turin: Giappichelli, 1993).

dialogue with adversaries difficult, certainly not because either position is intolerant of debate, but because they bring about many subtle differences in the use of language. The Italian natural lawyer devotes his efforts prevalently to the philosophy of justice and the history of legal philosophy, two branches of study that he appears to see as largely coincident, as the philosophy of justice is equated to the study of the concretisation of the idea of justice throughout history. The naturalists show scant interest for legal theory: only rarely do they deal, for example, with the problem of the norm, of the legal order, of interpretation, of legal reasoning and so on. Up to now, current Italian legal theory has been prevalently analytical. Nonetheless, also in Italy, a hermeneutic theory of law is now developing a close-knit dialogue with analytical theory. I suspect, however, that the reciprocal interest shown by hermeneuts and analysts does not arise so much from a convergence of principles or the existence of common problems, but from an extrinsic factor, that is, from the fact that both orientations are interested in language and law as a language.[29]

4. *An Empiricist School*

Divisionism is thus a first fundamental feature of the Italian analytical school, a position accepted and defended not only for epistemological but also for ethical-political reasons. Divisionism in fact is seen as a precondition for defending the space of a scientific, or at least neutral, description of the law and to preserve the clarity of moral criticisms of law.

The approach of Italian analysts to law is characterised by another principle: the distinction between analytical and synthetic judgements, and thus empiricism, in its special version of neo-empiricism.[30]

In fact, Italian analysts today on the whole still accept the neoempiricist model of the natural and social sciences, just as Bobbio had

29 See Jori, *Ermeneutica e filosofia analitica, supra* n.15. The hermeneutic scholars closest to the Italian analytical school are Francesco Viola and Giuseppe Zaccaria.

30 The distinction between analytic and synthetic, as is well known, has been defined as a dogma of empiricism by its detractors and as a cornerstone of empiricism by its supporters. See W.V.O. Quine, "Two Dogmas of Empiricism" (1951) and G. Bergmann, "Two Cornestones of Empiricism" (1953), both reprinted in F. Zabeeh, E.D. Klemke and A. Jacobson, eds., *Readings in Semantics* (Urbana: University of Illinois Press, 1974).

done in the 1950s. The essays by Ferrajoli and Jori published in this collection are an example of the persistence of neoempiricist influence on Italian legal analytical philosophy. As both these essays show, this model is used to examine closely the several discourses concerning law, and especially those of jurists, purporting to be part of a "legal science".[31] I suspect that this is the part of Italian analytical discussions that English-speaking readers will find furthest from their own interests. For often discussed historical and cultural reasons, the question of the epistemological nature of legal science and the very notion of "legal science" are not among the problems studied by jurisprudence in common law countries. Significantly, one fault Hart's Italian critics have repeatedly found in his much appreciated theories is that of having neglected to account for the position of the doctrinal jurist when making his celebrated opposition between the external and internal point of view. A criticism of this kind is expressly formulated in Jori's essay on legal science, and it is clearly suggested in Alfonso Catania's essay on the concept of "acceptance" in Hart.

Among Italian analytical-legal philosophers, adhesion to a common epistemological model has not given rise to a unitary conception of science and the theory of law. Two main facts explain this. Firstly, this shared epistemological model (according to the present fashion, it should perhaps be called a *paradigm*) has its roots in rather divergent versions of empiricism. These different opinions will be briefly discussed below, where mention will be made of the simultaneous presence within the Italian analytical school of different semiotic conceptions, which point to rather different versions of empiricism. Secondly, the intervention of the other analytical principle (the distinction between descriptive and prescriptive) further complicates things. In fact, when applying this distinction to the problem of legal science and cognition, one immediately realises that the question is actually composed of three problems. Firstly, the problem of whether legal science-as-it-is really is a genuine science; secondly, the problem of whether legal science-as-it-is, although not a true science, *can* be transformed into a scientific undertaking; finally, the

31 Conversely, two analytical scholars of the latest generation, Barberis and Villa, are openly critical towards the neo-empiricism of the analytical school: see V. Villa, *Teorie della scienza giuridica e teorie delle scienze naturali* (Milan: Giuffrè, 1984), *idem*, *Conoscenza giuridica e concetto di diritto positivo* (Turin: Giappichelli, 1993); M. Barberis, *Il diritto come discorso e come comportamento* (Turin: Giappichelli, 1990).

problem of whether it is *opportune* for the jurist to become a scientist. The various answers to these problems can intersect in rather complicated ways.

Italian analysts have thus applied the neo-empiricist model of science first and foremost as a descriptive model, as a yardstick for ascertaining whether or not the arguments effectively produced by jurists are consonant with the model and can consequently be considered scientific. Today, almost all Italian analysts refuse to grant the status of scientificity to legal science.[32] Nevertheless, this convergence turns out to be rather shallow, once the much different reasons advanced in justifying such a conclusion are spelled out. In fact, it is one thing to say, with Scarpelli, that legal science is not a science since it identifies its object (the law) through the preliminary choice of a basic norm, which is a politically biased choice and therefore a methodologically inadmissible move in the light of neo-empiricist scientific criteria. It is another thing to say, as does Tarello (see the essay published in this volume), in the tradition of interpretative scepticism, that legal science is not a science since mere cognition of norms, through mere *cognition* of legal prescriptive meanings, is impossible.[33]

These divergences resound on the second question, whether legal science can be turned into a genuine scientific discourse. For some analysts, legal science, as practised by contemporary jurists, is not a science. But it could become one without undergoing radical changes, or could at least be made into a controllable rigorous discourse. This was Bobbio's position in the 1950s and was substantially shared by Scarpelli and Jori, that is to say by the normativist branch of the analytical school.[34] On the sceptical-realist side, we find the opposite thesis, implicit above all in the ideas of Tarello, Pattaro and Guastini, that so-called legal

32 On the contrary, from a post-positivist standpoint Vittorio Villa refers to a much weaker model of scientificity and consequently is able to reach the conclusion that descriptive jurisprudence, after all, belongs to the realm of scientific discourse. See the works by Villa mentioned *supra* n.31.

33 See especially G. Tarello, *Diritto, enunciati, usi* (Bologna: Il Mulino, 1974); *L'interpretazione della legge* (Milan: Giuffrè, 1980).

34 Bobbio's conception in the 1950s was rightly criticised (by Pattaro: see the essay published herein) because he judged rigour to be a *sufficient* requisite to turn so-called legal science into a scientific enterprise. Ferrajoli, on the other hand (see his essay herein), states that juristic discourse may, under certain conditions (precision of normative meanings, faithfulness in interpreting the law), become a science in the fullest sense and be endowed with truth value.

science as such could never become a true science nor a rigorous (univocal) discourse, without a radical change in its very nature. Jurisprudence is seen by these sceptics as the activity of creating norms, and thus of producing law, which can never be reduced to a pure recognition of pre-existing law. The essays in this volume by the authors just mentioned show these differences.

We now come to the third point, whether or not it is opportune to transform jurisprudence into a scientific discipline. Disagreements on this point would appear to be the simplest to examine and to resolve, by reaching a philosophical agreement as to the prescriptive model of legal science to adopt, which could then be recommended to jurists. However, the questions of opportunity are at least as troublesome as those of fact, perhaps because, as history shows, legal philosophers have little chance of success when they venture onto the field of *prescriptive meta-jurisprudence* (the term was coined by Bobbio) and start prescribing how jurists should behave, particularly when their proposals aim at innovation in actual legal practices. Perhaps the near impossibility of influencing reality explains why so few legal theorists (basically only Alf Ross) have dared to propose openly a radical transformation of legal science and its adaptation to the canons of neo-empiricism.[35] None of the Italian analytical theorists has taken such a stance. They have elected not to try to induce *soi-disant* legal science to change its course, limiting themselves to propound a greater rigour and intellectual honesty in not hiding the choices made. They recognise that the need for a properly empirical and scientific description of law can be satisfied by the sociology of law and the other empirical sciences of law (anthropology, psychology and so on); these disciplines might avail themselves of the conceptual clarifications performed by analytical legal theory, when constructing their own network of theoretical concepts which, in the well-known image of Hempel, must be placed in contact with reality through empirical investigations.[36]

35 The theoretical reformer must face up to another awkward problem: that of distinguishing between the new empirical legal science and some "old" empirical approach to legal facts, in particular the sociology of law. The question did actually embarrass Ross, who answered it in a rather unconvincing way: see A. Ross, *On Law and Justice* (London: Stevens & Sons 1958), ch.I.

36 Tarello's position is peculiar: he criticises the normativistic attempt to separate the sociology of law from legal science, and favours socio-juridical investigations that jurists already perform within the single legal disciplines

5. *Analytical Semiotics*

Divisionism and empiricism, of course, deeply influence the legal semiotics elaborated by the Italian analytical legal school. Thus, such legal semiotics is divisionistic and empiricist; this means firstly that the analyst considers the prescriptive nature of legal language to be its most important semiotic feature, as befits a discourse aimed at guiding human conduct. Second, it means that the analyst attributes crucial importance to relations between language and extra-linguistic empirical reality, even when dealing with a prescriptive language such as that of law. These two ideas prove that the legal semiotics of the Italian analysts belongs to the family of so called prescriptivistic semiotics, to the development of which they have made some substantial contributions, although this is unfortunately little known. Semiotic prescriptivism is in fact animated by two basic convictions: that prescriptive language no less than descriptive language contains a semantic component representative of reality (the *phrastic,* in R.M. Hare's terminology); and that prescriptive language is semantically different from descriptive language, since it is meant to function as a guide to behaviour. These two features may be used to distinguish the semiotics practised by the analytical legal philosophers from other kinds of semiotics which may be considered not analytical, since they are not motivated by analogous empiricist and divisionistic preoccupations.[37] As usual, this is a very rough division; the least "orthodox" thinkers from this standpoint are Carcaterra and Conte, whose essays included in this volume deal with the puzzling subject of

---

for practical reasons: a sociology *within* law, or better, within legal doctrine, rather than a sociology *of* law. See G. Tarello, "La sociologia nella giurisprudenza", *Sociologia del diritto* I (1974), 40-51.

37 The leading texts of semiotic prescriptivism are: R.M. Hare, *The Language of Morals* (Oxford: Oxford University Press, 1952); U. Scarpelli, *Contributo*, *supra* n.7; *idem* , *Semantica, morale, diritto* (Turin: Giappichelli, 1969); A. Ross, *Directives and Norms* (London: Routledge & Kegan Paul, 1968).

See M. Jori, "Tendances en semiotique juridique", *International Journal for the Semiotics of Law / Revue Internationale de Sémiotique Juridique* 2 (1989), 277-300, in which a description of the main tendencies in contemporary legal semiotics is given, together with criticism of non-analytical semiotics, especially that of B.S. Jackson. See B.S. Jackson, *Semiotics and Legal Theory* (London: Routledge & Kegan Paul, 1985, repr. Liverpool: Deborah Charles Publications, 1997); see also B.S. Jackson, *Law, Fact and Narrative Coherence* (Merseyside: Deborah Charles Publications, 1988).

constitutive rules. Both these authors have devoted long years of study and have made important contributions to this argument, which represents a crucial test for prescriptive semiotics, insofar as constitutive rules are norms but appear to prescribe no action. Carcaterra upholds a kind of ontological productivity of language (language shapes reality), while Conte, the most enigmatic of the Italian analytical philosophers, draws a typology of the constitutive rules behind which we may perhaps glimpse the thesis that language and the world are really not separable at all.

Thus, within the Italian analytical legal school a common basis of semiotic ideas coexists with quite different conceptions of the further objectives of the semiotic investigation of legal discourses. Since semiotic ideas never represent the ultimate foundation of legal philosophical positions, we should not be surprised at discovering that the tendencies we find at the level of semiotics represent the restatement of more traditional positions of legal philosophy. Today, the main orientations of Italian legal analytical theory dispute on semiotic ground, rather than directly by arguments of general legal philosophical positions. In fact, the corrosive criticism of analytical reason has rather made the traditional labels used in the legal theory to differentiate among general positions, such as (legal) positivism, naturalism and realism, outmoded. This is because of their uncertain capacity to designate definite standpoints. It has not, however, been able to do away entirely with what they stand for.

It is therefore possible in semiotics to distinguish between a normativistic (formerly legal positivistic?) tendency and an anti-normativistic (legal realistic?) tendency within the Italian analytical school. The former is characterised by the central place accorded to the notion of rule or norm defined as a meaning-content and of a normative order or system, and by its favouring an approach to law seen as an abstract set of such normative meanings. Conversely, the anti-normativistic tendency assigns a central place to the problem of interpretation, embraces a quite sceptical conception of this activity and for the most part devotes itself to the study of actual interpretative activities and of their results. This approach doubts that an abstract normative description of law is admissible, unless it is seen merely as a part of historical or sociological discourses about the law; one that purports to describe and explain what produces certain normative meanings, seen as jurists' ideological positions, and what cultural and social effects the adoption of specific laws might have.[38]

On the other hand, the abstract normativistic description is admissible for its advocates insofar as they accept a more liberal version of empiricism, one that has learned Saussure's structuralist lesson; while for its detractors, normativism is tantamount to a theory of natural law *en travesti* as it represents a departure from strict empiricism, which (they believe) is bound to reject abstract notions such as "meaning", "structure" and "system" (both legal system and perhaps even linguistic system).[39] Jori has proposed resorting to another basic principle for explaining the conflict between these two analytical tendencies, the distinction between the sociological context and the context of justification, which normativistic semiotics certainly accepts but anti-normativistic semiotics tends to reject.[40]

Albeit not because of any logical or theoretical necessity, the legal realist approach usually goes with a greater propensity for the study of *descriptive meta-jurisprudence,* for an approach *from below* to legal problems and in general for lexical investigations, descriptions of arguments actually produced by jurists, of the history of legal culture and of juristic ideologies. Significantly, Guastini, a disciple of Tarello, indicates, as the main objectives of the analysis of language, the recording of linguistic usages, the discovering of syntactic and semantic ambiguities and uncertainties, the unveiling of value elements hidden in legal discourses, and the systematic definition of the terms used.[41]

On the other hand, the normativistic semiotic approach is accompanied (it too certainly not because of any logical-theoretical necessity) by a greater propensity towards *prescriptive meta-jurisprudence* (the expression is again Bobbio's), towards the theory *from above* and in general towards reconstructive analysis, and the development and use of models, in the sense of ideal-typical reconstructions of actual legal discourses.

These different semiotic tendencies within the Italian analytical

38 Significantly, the principal exponent of this tendency, Giovanni Tarello, devoted himself to studies of legal history and the history of legal culture. See especially G. Tarello, *Storia della cultura giuridica moderna. Vol. I: Assolutismo e codificazione del diritto* (Bologna: Il Mulino, 1976).

39 For the distinction between *performance-oriented* and *competence-oriented* semiotics, see Jori, "Tendances en semiotique juridique", *supra* n.37.

40 See Jori, *supra* n.37.

41 See Guastini, *supra* n.15, at 286-288.

school obviously influence the choice of themes that receive the greatest attention, and the two semiotic orientations end up by being attracted by rather different areas of investigation, as stated previously. But all legal-theoretical problems are inextricably interwoven, so that in dealing with one problem it is inevitable that many others must be tackled at the same time. The differences in semiotic formulation we have just mentioned are often perceptible only if one examines the merits of the solutions found for the various problems, rather than in the choice of the areas to be studied.[42]

42 An excellent view of the most recent analytical themes and interests is to be found in the volumes of *Analisi e diritto,* edited by P. Comanducci and R. Guastini. These publications have been issued since 1990 and include both legal and philosophical papers, by authors from several countries.

THE SCIENCE OF LAW AND THE ANALYSIS OF LANGUAGE

by

NORBERTO BOBBIO

1. *Introduction*

With this essay I would like to draw the attention of legal theorists, and of all those engaged in scientific research in general, to a new conception of science which, stemming from recent methodological approaches of logical positivism, may help understand the nature of the jurist's research, and may contribute to a new and more adequate foundation of legal science. This is an area which has attracted relatively little attention to date, especially in Italy, and has been addressed, so far, neither by jurists nor by logicians.[1] What follows has therefore no pretence of being a completed enterprise and is to be read as a mere research outline, almost a blueprint for the job ahead. Only future research will, in fact, tell if the approach which is here proposed has been productive and valid.

2. *"True" Science of Law and Jurisprudence*

I shall make my first move by tackling the problem which has become a traditional starting point for all research on legal methodology, namely the extent to which jurisprudence can be considered a science. This is an issue which, although at times relegated in importance or neglected does occupy jurists and legal theorists. It is an issue that comes up every time comparisons are drawn between research in legal theory and research in mathematics, physics or biology, disciplines which are traditionally

Law and Language, The Italian Analytical School, ed. A. Pintore and M. Jori (Liverpool: Deborah Charles Publications, 1997).

1 The only exception is U. Scarpelli's note bearing the same title as the present essay, in *Rivista di Diritto Commerciale* (1948), 212-16. Even outside Italy, specific literature is limited: see Glanville Williams' essay, "Language and the Law", *Law Quarterly Review* 61 (1945), 71-86; 179-95; 293-303; 384-406; 62 (1946), 387-406; and the few references, in this essay, to American writings.

considered "scientific" by common consent. The question of whether or not jurisprudence is a science is one which has long plagued those working in this field. This is not merely a matter of words, or of the professional dignity of those concerned. If we define science as research conducted with some rigour (in the sense that will be explained below), it is then a matter of ascertaining whether the results of legal theoretical enquiry have equal validity in their own sphere as those in physics, biology, etc. This is a debate that has been going on for a long time in the history of jurisprudence. It came to a head during the last century, at a time when scientific knowledge was progressing at a tremendous rate both in the old and new fields of inquiry. The wide gap between the development of the old natural sciences and of the new social sciences on one side, and on the other side a comparatively unchanging jurisprudence, which only found its identity by latching on to a past two thousands years older, made it more difficult for jurists to carve out a position for their researches in the general advancement of sciences.

In giving thought to the long standing disquiet jurists have always felt in comparing their own inquiry with what, at different times, has been acknowledged as science, a plain observation can be made. To this day, of all the subsequent images of what is scientific, offered ever since a theory of science existed, jurist have not been able to find any with which to identify their role and their work. In other words, until today jurisprudence has never fully recognised itself in any of the definitions of science that have been put forward by the various theories of science. To summarise again: jurists have not been able, however regretfully and against their best judgement, to fit their inquiry into any of the conceptions of science and knowledge produced so far. This is what caused that feeling of discomfort and uneasiness which one may be tempted to define icastically as an inferiority complex of the jurist with regard to other scientists. Such a complex does end up producing the melancholy conclusion of the "lack of value of jurisprudence as a science", to phrase it as a famous essay did.

This leads us immediately to another point and allows us to throw some light upon another characteristic of the domain of legal experience viz. the "duplication" of knowledge. The jurist is driven by the inferiority complex described above to adopt the following line of reasoning: granted that jurisprudence is not a science because it does not fit into the official concept of science, this does not preclude the possibility, however, of imagining and constructing a type of research in law that would meet all the requirements and methodological canons of science in the official sense. It may be possible to construct a science of law which is also a science in the true sense, even if this *true science* does not coincide with the research of the jurist, that is with jurisprudence. The line of argument which I sketched here has had the following consequences: alongside jurisprudence, considered non-scientific in all times, but strikingly so in the modern age, a different kind of legal knowledge emerged. Modelled on the methodological schemes of the true sciences it differed totally from jurisprudence and was regarded much more highly because supposedly more scientific. This new kind of legal knowledge represented the ideal model to which jurisprudence must aspire and of which the latter is merely a caricature. This is what I referred to above as the "duplication" of knowledge in the field of legal experience. As we saw before, at a specific historical moment a gulf has opened up between the conception of science and the practice of jurists. This has led to the development of, on the one hand, *a jurisprudence which is not science* and on the other hand, *a science which has nothing to do with jurisprudence* (and which jurists usually dismiss as useless for them). In other words, acknowledging the incompatibility between science and jurisprudence, far from producing an attempt to reduce jurisprudence to science, had the effect of relocating the scientific ideal beyond jurisprudence and hence of creating a science of law which was wholly severed from jurisprudence.

3. *Jurisprudence in the Rationalistic Conception of Science …*

History provides us with two good examples of this development. Let us consider the two dominant conceptions of science in the modern era: the rationalistic conception of the 17th century and the positivistic of the 19th. I shall attempt to demonstrate two things. Firstly, that both these conceptions put forward a theory of science which could lend jurisprudence no arguments supporting its claim for a scientific status (if jurisprudence had remain faithful to its own task). Secondly, in the legal domain both conceptions have resulted in the creation of a legal science which has nothing at all to do with jurisprudence and the actual work of jurists.

The rationalistic conception, which derives its abstract, mathematical character from the mentality of the Enlightenment, is characterised by two fundamental assertions: 1) the world is an ordered system governed by universal and necessary laws (objective and metaphysical rationalism);

2) man is a rational being endowed with the faculty for understanding these laws (subjective and methodological rationalism). It is upon these two assertions that the conception of science as the adaptation of the subjective reason of man to the objective reason of the universe is based. All scientific activity, then, revolves round the discovery and formulation of rules which are given in nature and are as such immutable and necessary. The fruits of scientific inquiry, scientific truth, thus have a definitive quality. This way of understanding science and the function of the scientist seem destined to disconcert the jurist and to show up the fragility of his constructs. The natural scientist is concerned with the uncovering of universal and necessary laws. And since when has the jurist ever had to do with laws of this kind? Indeed it would seem that changeableness, temporariness, temporal and spatial limitation, conventionality, contingency, the total absence of universality and necessity are characteristic features of the world of jurists. Also, the truths with which the natural scientist are concerned are definitive truths. But is there anything definitive about jurisprudence? Has there ever been universal consensus among scholars on a legal question, or have the ideas of a jurist, albeit great, been considered as an established acquisition by all legal scholars who came after him, as it is the case with scientific discoveries? Jurisprudence is fertile ground for unresolved disputes. It is indeed an area in which "opinion" in the sense that it is traditionally opposed to "science" holds sway.

If we go back to the time when the rationalistic conception of knowledge dominated culture, then the contrast between the ambitiousness of scientific endeavour and the much more modest claims made by jurisprudence is even more striking. The situation is different nowadays, when laws have found a principle of unity in the State and a principle of system in the codes. At that time, however, there was a complete absence of any unifying principle or any notion of system: the legal material was a confused and chaotic, venerated by tradition and therefore difficult to change. It appeared more than ever strikingly antithetical to the ordered world of nature. The rationalists felt a profound need for some kind of system. It is easy to imagine how the proponents of a universal and immutable order were mortified and offended by such an intractable disorder in the world of law. They reacted by diminishing the status of jurisprudence to that of a practical art, thus condemning it to remain forever outwith the realm of science.

However, precisely this rationalistic attitude, that had discredited *real* jurisprudence, provided a strong impetus for the development of an *ideal* jurisprudence based on the canons of scientific rationalism, which could be accepted within the ranks of the true sciences and could bring its contribution to the universal system of knowledge. Jurists and philosophers joined forces to create this ideal jurisprudence, which would emancipate the world of jurists, so that they too could claim their contribution to scientific renewal. This is how that vast and complex phenomenon, the *natural law* movement, was born. What the natural law movement represented in essence was the extension of the rationalistic conception of science to the field of human laws: in short, legal experience was reduced to a science. Natural law was to represent the "true" science of law, the definitive knowledge of human laws that could not be constituted by jurisprudence (due to the very nature of its object). It is worth noting that natural law, like the rationalist conception described above, is also based upon two presuppositions: (1) there exist universal and necessary laws which regulate human behaviour. These are natural laws on a par with all the other laws which govern the universe; (2) it is the task of the science of natural law to discover and articulate these laws; the source of these laws is human nature itself, and the aim is to establish once and for all valid and immutable rules to govern social behaviour and to lay down the principles of the optimal society. All of the above is well known, and yet it is worth toiling over again not just as a good example of what we were referring to but also as a reminder of those methodological characteristics of natural law theory which tend to be overlooked in favour of the ideological ones. These vary considerably from author to author (one only needs to compare the ideology of the Hobbes with that of Leibniz) so that they do not help us identify the unity of the natural law movement as a whole. The unity of the so called natural law theory is thus not ideological but methodological. This methodological unity is largely due to the fact that ethical-legal research has been successfully integrated into the dominant rationalistic conception of science and mechanistic theories of the world. The gulf that came to separate the conception of science and the reality of jurisprudence at a particular point in time is amply exemplified by the rich development of natural law. It is also a conspicuous example of the so called duplication of knowledge in the field of law. The rationalistic conception of science gave rise to a type of legal research which differed from jurisprudence. This was because the research of the jurists would not fit into its schemes. The effect of this was that the world of legal knowledge was split in two. It is not too much to say that on the one hand there arose a new form of knowledge, which, for all that it was "true" was not "legal" (natural law). On the other, the traditional form of knowledge was maintained, which, for all that it was "legal" was not "true" (jurisprudence).

4. ... *And in the Positivistic Conception of Science*

Something similar happened during the period in which the positivistic conception of science predominated. It rejected the presuppositions of the rationalistic conception and tried to purge it of any metaphysical residue. According to the positivists, the world was neither a rational system, nor was man in possession of the faculty of reason which would allow him knowledge of the absolute truth. The world, for the positivist, was not a depository of absolute and predetermined laws. Rather, it was the sum of a collection of occurrences, events, or, to use the term that is generally favoured, of facts. In order to be admitted to the scientific system these facts have to be subject to experimental verification. The prime task of the scientist is to register facts. He can no longer act as legislator of the universe, but is assigned a more humble role, that of explorer of a small part of this world. It is only by registering and exploring events in the world in this way that he is able to make up constant conjunctions or general laws. These in turn are destined to be overturned as new facts are put to the test.

But the positivist and the rationalist have this much in common. Neither is prepared to abandon the idea that through the testing of facts science can attain the true law of nature, even if by a process of trial and error. Indeed the positivist thinks that only he is capable of attaining this goal. In his view, the metaphysician, having set himself beyond the realm of facts, is incapable of becoming acquainted with them, however hard he tries. The positivistic conception of science and the metaphysical one are thus pursuing the same goal: both are aiming towards the true law of nature. They merely adopt different means to this end. As Ardigò puts it "while the metaphysician is condemned to remain forever in a vicious circle, the positivist ends up by finding what he was looking for: *the true law of observed facts*".[2] The positivist is opposed to metaphysics, but he shares with the metaphysician the idea of total knowledge. He disagrees on how to get there. For the positivist, total knowledge can only be

2 *Opere*, I.49 (italics have been added).

attained through a steadfast and laborious registration of facts and a process of trial and error, and not through pure speculation. The positivist's final goal, just like the metaphysician's, is true science, total science; absolute science.

For the positivist, facts are the presupposition and the guide to scientific analysis. What cannot be reduced to facts, i.e. subject to verifiable occurrences is not scientific. And since, for the positivist science is the only possible form of knowledge, anything that cannot be reduced to fact cannot even be known. Even the laws of thought, which constitute the traditional object of logic defined as the study of the rules which precede experience have to be reduced to experience in order to become a legitimate object of a positivistic system of knowledge. Logic thus transforms itself into psychology. The same thing happens with moral laws. Ethics becomes the science of moral behaviour, of custom, etc. In short, it becomes sociology. And jurisprudence? How does jurisprudence fit into the positivist conception of knowledge? The fact is it doesn't. It remains a thing apart. Jurisprudence is not concerned with facts which can be tested but with given propositions (legal norms) which cannot be interfered with. These remain valid even when they are contradicted by facts. According to the official philosophical doctrine, and this is a view which became widely shared, jurisprudence is not a true science and can never be one. Jurisprudence is *dogmatics*. In my view, this description is a perfect illustration of the conflict between jurisprudence and official science in the positivist era. To say that jurisprudence is dogmatics means that it has nothing to do with science as it is officially defined; it means, in short, that it cannot be reduced to scientific knowledge. But the moment the laws of thought and the laws of morality are reduced to facts, so that it becomes possible to talk of a science of logic and a science of ethics, what is there to prevent the same happening to legal laws? Nothing whatsoever. Indeed there have been several attempts to do just this. The bases of the psychology and sociology of law were laid in the 19th century and achieved currency even among jurists from Jhering onwards. But what else are these but forms of the empirical science of law, that is of a science of law conducted according to the prescribed canons of a positivist methodology? Clearly, legal laws could also, like logics and ethics, be reduced to empirical fact and the process would be no different. In fact, it could be reduced to empirical facts, namely to psychic facts, if we were to discount the abstract legislative form and regard law as the product of the will and the intelligence; or to a social fact in the broad sense of the term, if we were to consider it as part of the network of human relations which gives rise to it in the first place, and within which it develops and declines. It goes without saying that the science of a law understood as a psychic or social fact was a science on a par with all the other sciences accepted as such by the dominant conception, and was considered a true science. But this could do little to bridge the gulf between science and jurisprudence; if anything, it only recognized it openly and widened it, making it insurmountable. Precisely the same thing which happened when the true science of natural law was being devised. The reduction of law to fact had made the foundation of an empirical science of law possible. But, once again, it ceased to be jurisprudence, as it no longer held any resemblance to the work of the jurist, directed at achieving doctrinal settlement or the practical application of the normative propositions in force in a given order. Just as natural law was the only science of law that could be conceived in a rationalist conception of science, so sociology and legal psychology were the only possible sciences of law conceivable in the positivist conception. Jurisprudence, however, did not fit either of these categories. Inevitably, though, it moved forward. But it was held in disdain by scientists who considered it as no more than a technique or art with regards to law, and as dogmatics with regards to the empirical study of legal facts. Once again the jurists who reflected on legal science found themselves confronted by a science that was not jurisprudence or a jurisprudence that was not science.[3]

3 One recent aspect of the duplication of legal knowledge is the common distinction between legal science and legal technique. Whatever the formula used, this distinction aims at relegating to the technical field lawyers' proper research. Its aims overlay it with a true science, which has nothing to do with legal science but is nearer, according to how the various authors deal with it, to natural law, to sociology, to pure logic, or to phenomenology. This latter example includes the thesis which I defended in my youth, in the essay *Scienza e tecnica del diritto* (*Memorie dell'istituto giuridico dell'università di Turin*, series II, Memoria XXIX (Turin: Istituto della Regia Università, 1934), which clearly illustrates the psychological and conceptual motives of the duplication described above. Starting from a phenomenological conception of science and recognising the difficulty of including legal science in it, I was lead to conclude, on one hand, that legal science was not a science — and was therefore a technique — and on the other that in order to build a legal science, it was necessary to lay the foundations of a phenomenological study of law. Recently, D. Barbero has rightly recognised that a lawyer pursues a scientific activity even when he deals with technical research: "Empirismo e dogmatica nel

5. *Kirchmann's Critique*

This is the context in which Kirchmann's famous little book about 'the lack of value of jurisprudence as a science' which is still a thorn in the heart of legal science, should be understood. We can now see clearly why Kirchmann was lead publicly and honestly to express his dissatisfaction with the methods and the achievements of jurisprudence. Kirchmann subscribed to the traditional and conventional view of science according to which the task of science, is to discover the eternal and immutable laws of nature. One can understand why jurisprudence, measured with such standards, seemed to perform very poorly indeed. Some of Kirchmann's basic criticism of jurisprudence is based upon this type of comparison.[4] In blaming legal science for the mutability of its object, Kirchmann is, no doubt, drawing a comparison with the object of natural sciences: nature itself, or rather that hypostatized concept of it which is the natural scientist's rather naive realistic view of nature as something which is eternally fixed, complete in itself: "The sun, the moon and the stars appear to us now as they did in past millennia. Plants and animals live and grow just as they did in Pliny's time, but the law of that period has changed fundamentally".[5] Later he goes on to complain that jurisprudence is forced to make positive law its object, but this type of law is contingent, arbitrary and often erroneous (in that it no longer corresponds to the underlaying natural law), full of gaps and so on. Again, Kirchmann contrasts this negatively with the object of the natural sciences: allegedly, what necessary and eternal. It is clear that Kirchmann shares the conceptions his age had of science; today we would call them preconceptions and could be stated as follows: the object of science must have some objective existence and be true in itself beyond the inquiring subject; the starting point of scientific inquiry must not be arbitrary; it has to correspond to the true and immutable nature of the object. Now, then, given that jurisprudence does not match any of these criteria, its scientific pretensions must be rejected, and thus, incontrovertibly, it can not be considered a science. According to Kirchmann, one can only talk of science in the field of law if one abandons the treacherous terrain of positive law and

diritto", *Rivista trimestrale di diritto e procedura civile* III (1949), 310-31.

4 See B. Leoni, "Il valore della giurisprudenza e il pensiero di J.H. von Kirchmann", *Rivista internazionale di filosofia del diritto* XVIII (1940), 343-59; XIX (1941), 64-95.

5 Leoni, *supra* n.4, at 69.

embraces the quest for natural law (even though no longer understood in the rationalist sense). This inquiry will be a science of law different from jurisprudence insofar as it has the traits of true science.

But, we may ask ourselves, if Kirchmann were alive today and were as willing to accept the current concept of science as he was to accept that of his own day, would he still be right in retaining his inferiority complex as a jurist towards the other scientists? To put it another way, if he had espoused today's conception of what constitutes a true science, would he have dared to claim with such assertiveness? Perhaps there has been a loss of faith in the principles of absoluteness and necessity of the scientific object against which Kirkmann used to evaluate jurisprudence and which appeared as the incomparable virtue of natural sciences. This is the problem. They are now considered as prejudices, the last vestiges of a metaphysical conception of science, quite unable to explain what the scientific enterprise actually entails. No-one nowadays would claim that the natural sciences were superior because they are based on the study of nature which remains unchanged, rather than on the study of unpredictable human activities. No-one would claim today that natural sciences are based upon absolutely evident and non-arbitrary presupposed propositions. Indeed it is possible to claim that natural science, considered by some to be the "true" science and model and paradigm of all sciences, has itself destroyed the traditional concepts of nature, of fixed laws and evident propositions and has substituted them with more flexible ones such as a system of relativity, operative principles and conventional points of departure. In the light of these changes, perhaps it is time to reassess the traditional view of jurisprudence. Up until now the difference between jurisprudence and science was based on the affirmation that jurisprudence was not a true science. But if the scientific attributes jurisprudence is considered to lack are no longer considered the attributes of science, but rather of pseudo-science or metaphysics, then Kirchmann's position is no longer tenable. Indeed some of the very characteristics which according to Kirchmann made jurisprudence unscientific do not deny natural science its credibility today. In the light of this, it is perhaps time to reevaluate whether or not the science of law can in fact be considered a "true" science. Perhaps it was wrong to deny jurisprudence the accolade of a true science because it did not fit into the canons of the true conception of science. It may be that the existing conception of science was false because, among other things, it could not account for jurisprudence.

6. *The Present-Day Conception of Science*

The present-day conception of science was formed gradually as scientists themselves became more aware of precisely what the pursuit of scientific research was about. It received further impetus from the new discoveries in physics which shook the foundations of the mechanistic conception which had dominated for several centuries. For a long time, philosophers and scientists had tended to the mechanistic conception as the only possible expression of the true laws of nature. The best philosophical expression of this approach was logical positivism. According to modern methodologies, scientific propositions are not unconditionally true in the sense that they reproduce an alleged truth-of-reason or truth-of-experience, respectively by intuition (an idea) or by a process of trial and error (a fact). Rather, they are rigorous propositions. The emphasis has shifted from truth to rigour or, to put it another way, truth has come to be understood in terms of rigour. What makes an argument scientific is not whether or not it is true, whether or not a statement corresponds to an objective reality. Rather its truth value lies in the rigorousness of the sentence in which it is expressed, that is in the consistency of that sentence with the other sentences belonging to the same system. In order for any investigation to have any scientific value, it must be expressed in rigorous language. Science is not possible if it is not expressed in a language that is essentially more rigorous than ordinary language. Language can be said to be rigorous a) when all the words in the primitive propositions of the system are defined, so that all the rules for their use have been established and they are never used unless these rules are respected; b) when rules have been established on the basis of which it is possible to derive other propositions from the primitive ones and only these rules are used. In other words, rigorous scientific language is characterised by the fact that there are rules for the *formation* of the initial propositions and rules of *transformation* which make it possible to pass from the initial propositions to subsequent ones. Science can thus be seen as a closed and consistent system of propositions. Indeed the extent to which a system of propositions can be said to be scientific is directly related to its degree of internal consistency. The transition from ordinary language to mathematical language is effected through a series of increasingly consistent systems, that is increasingly rigorous languages. However, this certainly does not amount to reaching the paradoxical conclusion that a science is merely a scientific language and can be wholly reduced to its own language. All that we are saying here is that all types of research, empirical (for example, physics) and formal (mathematics) are recognised as sciences the moment their propositions constitute a consistent system of sentences which can be communicated effectively between subjects without great risk of misunderstandings, that is sentences formulated in a rigorous language. It is not a question of reducing science to a pure and simple linguistic fact. It is a matter of recognising that we can only claim that science, this highest form of objective knowledge, or rather inter-subjective knowledge, is fully constituted when I am able to express my observations (which are a matter of perception) in conventional signs. This enables me to communicate them to others without the slightest risk of being misunderstood. To put it another way: the degree to which a piece of research can be said to be scientific is in direct proportion to the level of rigour that characterises the language in which it is expressed. Ordinary language is rendered more rigorous and less flexible, or indeed entirely supplanted by, scientific language.

Science starts with the development of a scientific language, that is with a language which renders purely subjective knowledge (my perception) as inter-subjective as possible. This is evident with regard to the science of mathematics. Mathematics is a discourse, or a collection of discourses conducted in a particular language. The language of mathematics lays down its own rules of formation and transformation. We can see the importance of the linguistic element in the empirical sciences as well. Scientific inquiry starts on the basis of an observation. This results in the formulation of a proposition (protocol) which is expressed in a particular language. This proposition gains validity as a scientific proposition to the extent that it can be fitted in to the linguistic system of the science concerned, or that it permits the development of a new scientific language. An observation which is not expressed in scientific proposition, that is in a proposition that can be accommodated in a scientific language, does not have the value nor the character of a scientific observation.

Having established the general premises, we can now turn to the more interesting question. How, if at all, does jurisprudence fit into this new way of understanding science? We shall see that jurisprudence fits perfectly, and we shall try and establish in a general way how this is possible. We shall be able to conclude that, unlike its predecessors, the neo-positivist conception of science allows the work of the jurist to be included among the sciences. Thus, it also allows the jurist to become more aware of exactly what he is doing when he constructs that consistent system of propositions which is the general and particular theory of a positive legal system, that is to say, jurisprudence.

7. *The Object of Jurisprudence*

Our first step is to determine the object of jurisprudence. The jurist is concerned with a group of *rules of behaviour*. We shall not go into how these are to be distinguished from many other types of rules. This is a sociological and historical issue which falls outwith the scope of the present essay. As we are primarily interested in methodological issues, it is not particularly important to determine what type of rules are at issue here. Studies which focus upon groups of rules of behaviour are methodologically similar. They are distinct from both the formal sciences in the proper sense of the term, such as mathematics and logic, and the empirical sciences, such as physics, biology, psychology and sociology. At the most we can ask whether there are other types of research besides jurisprudence which are concerned with rules of behaviour. Or is jurisprudence, because of the nature of its object, a unique mode of inquiry which has nothing in common with all the other types of science? There is undoubtedly at least one other discipline which is concerned with the same issues, namely moral theology. Jurisprudence has much to learn from the way the casuists go about things. It is worth remembering that old treatises such as *De legibus*, which were written by theologians, were as much concerned with legal rules as moral ones. They are of interest to all those concerned today with rules of behaviour, irrespective of the distinction between different types of rule.

With regard to rules of behaviour, which make up the object of his studies, the jurist is faced with a choice: he can either analyze *rules as such*, or he can focus on their content, i.e with *what is regulated*. As I have pointed out elsewhere,[6] the study of rules as such constitutes what is commonly known as the *general theory of law*, but which, in my view, would be more appropriately termed the *formal theory of law*. The true object of *jurisprudence* proper is the study of the content of the rule, of the abstract kind of the legally regulated fact (the "*fattispecie giuridica*").

6 "Francesco Carnelutti, teorico generale del diritto", in *Giurisprudenza italiana* IV (1949), 113-127, repr. in N. Bobbio, *Studi sulla teoria generale del diritto* (Turin: Giappichelli, 1955), 1-26.

This definition of what constitutes the object of legal research is accepted by most jurists, at least in those continental countries where the principle of a single source of law and thus of the closed order, is in force. However, it was the normative theory of Kelsen and his school that was primarily responsible for having introduced it into the field of legal studies and eliminating some dangerous confusions and wrong presuppositions that had bedeviled it. Yet, now and again, from the works of the jurists, a complex and confused picture of a jurist allegedly standing above the law and able to ascertain its social and ideological basis in order to capture the spirit of the time, still lurks out. This jurist would be able to determine the extent to which the law matches up to current ideals of justice. This view is rather frequent among those primarily concerned with the history of institutions, such as Roman lawyers, or among constitutional lawyers, whose subject matter is less conceptually elaborate and more open to political influences. The same can be said for those for whom the study of law is also a vehicle for the expression of their own political and moral preoccupations (and indeed there are times when it is not easy to suppress them). In the face of these reckless viewpoints it is necessary to keep hold of the fact that jurisprudence is concerned only with rules and what is regulated. Everything that pre-exists the rule (both its basis or its origin) falls outwith its scope. This is to stop jurisprudence being overcome by the "true" sciences of law, natural law on the one hand (the search for the ideal basis of the rule) and sociology (the search for its real origin) on the other. Such a confusion may cause jurisprudence to lose its scientific status, as happened in the past. We can see how normative theory has played an important part in defining the object of jurisprudence. In so doing, it has excluded the ethical-political dimension and the investigation of facts from the domain of legal research. These are the principal concerns of natural law and sociology respectively, which, in turn, have been the two main culprits for the mistaken conclusion that jurisprudence is not a science.

8. *Jurisprudence as Linguistic Analysis*

In the following pages we are not concerned with the general theory of law. We shall focus our attention on what constitutes the real work of the jurist proper. Rules are expressed in propositions which may be described as normative, since they have ideal rather than actual validity. The object of the jurist's research is a set of these normative propositions. It should be noted, however, that the jurist does not observe phenomena like the empirical scientist, nor is he interested in verifying the truth of normative propositions through experience. It is precisely because these propositions are normative, that is they regulate future behaviour and do not represent something that has already happened, that they have a purely ideal rather than an actual truth. Their truth value does not reside in the fact that they can be verified, but in that they correspond to certain ethical principles accepted as criteria to regulate action in a particular society. This distinguishes jurisprudence from an empirical science such as sociology. The sociologist studies social facts in order to determine those rules which the jurist takes as given, without being able to change them or deny their existence. Jurisprudence is not a formal science like mathematics or logic either. Its object is not the form of every possible discourse, but the particular content of a particular discourse (the discourse of the legislator or of laws). It is perhaps the general theory of law which is more like a formal science in that it operates with norms as such, that is with the form of every possible legal content. Jurisprudence, on the other hand, operates with the abstract kind of legally regulated fact and is thus neither an empirical nor a logical science. It has something in common with both, however, exactly because it is research. Any inquiry which aspires to the status of science, is constituted not only by a research part, either empirical, as is the case with empirical sciences, or formal, as is the case with formal sciences; it is also constituted by a *critical* part which consists in the construction of a rigorous language. This only will bestow on the research work scientific validity. The two parts are closely linked and are, except heuristically, indistinguishable. A scientific system is usually constructed from both of them. Jurisprudence differs in that it is concerned with already given normative propositions, which have emerged from previous empirical research, and which must be regarded by the jurist, however absurd or even patently unjust they may be. Jurisprudence is exclusively concerned with the critical part of a scientific system, the construction of a rigorous language which allows to fully communicate predetermined experiences. That critical element which is common and necessary to all science, is what is called *linguistic analysis*. Jurisprudence is thus essentially an analysis of language, more precisely of the language through which the legislator expresses himself through normative propositions. Faced with the legislative language it behaves like any other science faced with the language of physics, mathematics, etc. It has to transform legislative language into a rigorous language in the sense described above. It is only upon this basis that it becomes science. Exactly in that jurisprudence fundamentally operates by constructing a rigorous, hence scientific language, is it to be considered as science on a par with any other science, be it formal or empirical. Its operations match exactly that core of operations which are crucial and unforsakeable in any other science and which mark any research as scientific. This core of operations, in the case of jurisprudence is but the *interpretation of the law*, the job, by long standing tradition, of the jurist. And what is the interpretation of law if not the analysis of legislative language, of the language in which legal rules are expressed? But if the analysis of legal language and legal interpretation are one and the same thing, and if the analysis of language is indeed the scientific part of the work of the jurist, we would have to conclude that the jurist in the traditional way, by doing his job of interpreting the law, in fact constructs the science of law. In other words, there is no such thing as a science of law outside the activity of the interpreting jurist. Precisely in his role of interpreter he will perform that very linguistic analysis which no science can forsake and will construct that rigorous language which forms the essence of any research claiming scientific status. This he will do in full accordance with the modern conception of science which shifted the issue of scientificity from truth to rigour.

9. *The First Phase of Legal Science: The Purification of Language*

A detailed analysis of jurisprudence as linguistic analysis falls outwith the scope of this introductory essay. We shall limit ourselves here to a brief sketch of what in my view might be considered the three phases of the development of jurisprudence. If jurisprudence is understood here as the linguistic analysis of the normative propositions of a particular legal system, (*a*) The language of the legislator is not necessarily rigorous: the first task of the jurist is to make it more so; (*b*) the language of the legislator is not necessarily complete: the second task of the jurist is to try to make it as complete as possible; (c) the language of the legislator is not necessarily ordered: the third thing the jurist has to try to do is to reduce it to a system. The customary work of the jurist can be reduced to these three phases: the first is one of *purification*, the second of *completion*, and the third of the *ordering* of legal language. This is certainly the case for legal orders founded upon the monopolization of law by the legislative norm where the activity of the legislator is clearly distinct from that of the judge and, consequently, where the activity of the jurist who interprets the laws can also be distinguished from that of the judge who applies them.

Let us take a brief look at the first phase. The legislator expresses himself in a language that is not necessarily rigorous. To say that this language is not necessarily rigorous does not mean to say that it is a language without sense, nor that it is vague and ambiguous like ordinary language. The language used by the legislator has traditionally been elaborated and constructed by jurists. For this reason, at least in modern legislation, normative propositions are no longer formulated in common, everyday language. Legislative language has become technical, to a certain degree. This degree of rigour is dependent upon how developed jurisprudence is in different countries and upon the extent to which legislation is able to assimilate the work of jurists. If we look at how the jurist operates when faced with normative propositions, we shall see that his first concern is to bring some degree of rigour to the legislator's language. The jurist usually begins his analysis by determining the meaning of the words making up the normative proposition or group of normative propositions which constitute the specific object of his research. The aim of this analysis is to establish the set of rules which determine the use of a particular word. The group of rules which determine the use of a particular word constitutes the *concept* corresponding to that word. The concept of ownership, of mandate, loan, etc, emerges from the group of rules which determines the use of the word mandate, ownership, loan, etc.

This way of understanding the concept allows us to clear up a methodological misunderstanding that crops up rather frequently. Let us suppose that the concept of property has no point of reference in a real or true property, whose essence or nature the concept should be able to capture. If the concept is not a copy of reality but merely a means of communication, then jurists are wasting their time trying to determine (as they often do) whether a particular concept corresponds to a presupposed reality. As if the degree to which a concept matched reality made it any more true. A concept is fixed once and for all only when the rules which determine the use of the word which corresponds to it have been established. Therefore a concept is not more or less true but more or less usable depending upon the degree of rigour used to establish the rules of its use. We can see how it is possible to move from a conception of science as a means of getting at the truth to one which aims at a systematic and rigorous reordering of concepts for practical ends. Legal research on property can be described as rigorous when all the rules which we consider necessary in order to be able to use the word have been established. The research is only valid when these rules are respected and when the word is used respecting these rules without inadvertently introducing any new ones. There are often disputes between jurists which are presented as being ones about the truth or falsehood of a concept of property, for example. In fact, they very often come down to differences in the rules governing the use of that word. It is thus impossible to resolve these differences, since it is not a question of getting at the reality of property. In this case, and only in this case, one could talk of one concept being nearer to the truth than another and the concept which did not correspond to the presupposed reality could not be turned into the true concept and one of the jurists would be right and the other wrong. On the contrary, it should be established at the outset how the word is to be used. If no agreement is reached on this, there is no way of getting over the problem. Those involved are speaking two different languages; the problem is that they think they are speaking the same one. They believe that the origin of their dispute lies in the nature of the thing they are talking about, whereas the problem is that they are talking about it in two different languages. Because they are speaking different languages there is no way they will ever understand each other, however hard they try. However, as long as they believe they are speaking the same language, they will continue to argue as if there were a remote possibility of coming to an understanding. The fact is that such an understanding is only possible if right from the start they agree to adopt the same rules of formation and transformation. In the same way it is only possible to have a game if both players adopt the same rules. What seems a matter of course to those engaged in playing a game seems to elude scholars, who often behave just like players who wanted to play together but insisted on each following different rules. It is easy enough to understand the difference in approach. Players are perfectly aware of the conventionality of the rules of the game. They make no claims that the game in which they are engaged is the true game whereas the others are playing a false one. Scholars and scientists, on the other hand, are consumed with the idea that there is such a thing as the one possible science and thus find it more difficult to accept that scientific rules, just like the rules of a game, entail a good deal of conventional agreement at the moment of their foundation.

The fact that many disputes between jurists are insoluble from the outset does not mean that they are pointless. They are only pointless if they move beyond the conditions under which a science is possible. This is why an awareness of methodology is so important, as it alone allows us to establish the terms within which a dispute is meaningful. Is it possible, after what we have said, to establish these terms? We have seen that research can call itself scientific when it uses a scientific language. A scientific language is one in which all the words are defined and the use of such words does not contravene the rules used to define them in the first place. In short, scientific language is a set of rules and a set of operations conforming to these rules. For a dispute between two jurists to make sense, therefore, it must have as the object of contention either one or the other of these two prime constitutive elements of all theoretical research. It must, that is *a*) carry out a critique of the logical-grammatical rules used by the opposition for his research; this critique can start from the point of view that the rules in question are either too complicated (in which case they can be simplified), or that they do not conform to the researcher's purpose (i.e. they are inappropriate), or that they cannot easily be adapted to the rules that apply for other related concepts (i.e. they are incompatible). Or *b*) the disputant must show that his adversary has not taken heed of the established rules in the use of a particular word, that is that he has made an ambiguous statement or even directly contradicted himself. It is clear that in both cases it is not a lack of truth that puts paid to the research but a lack of rigour. It is clear that the jurist does not need such methodological rules to address his thoughts in this direction rather than in the one criticised above, which is vain and sterile. There is no kind of logic that can teach people to think; no kind of methodology which would enable one to conduct scientific research. It is enough to consider the types of argumentation most frequently used in legal disputes to realise that the most common forms of argumentation are those two described above. This is further evidence of the methodological approach which sees in theoretical research a move not so much towards absolute objective truth but towards increased rigour.

All this gives us the opportunity to take a critical look at the concept of interpretation. The activities of the jurist which we have described so far constitute what is commonly known as "legal interpretation". However, what we have said above shows that there is some misunderstanding surrounding this term. An accurate critical analysis of the concept is needed to dispel these misunderstanding. In talking of interpretation, I am thereby assuming that behind the normative propositions which, as we have seen, are the object of legal research, there is something which cannot be entirely reduced to the propositions themselves. This "something" I have described variously as the spirit, will, thought and intention of the legislator, all terms which betray a naive realism. Thus, interpretation is commonly regarded as an intellectual process which allows us to look beyond propositions, to move beyond language. Is this a legitimate way of understanding the work of the jurist? What meaning can I attribute to the word interpretation, understood as the search for what lies behind normative propositions? Certainly, if this is a legitimate process, then jurisprudence cannot be reduced to the analysis of language. However, there are strong reasons for believing that there is something fundamentally wrong with the notion of interpretation as it is commonly understood. If I endeavour to find the meaning of a proposition by looking beyond it, I merely come upon other propositions. If I move beyond these propositions, I find yet more. If I finally reach a point where there are no other propositions to give sense to the original one, I cannot go further. There is nowhere else to go. What I call will, thought, spirit or intention can only be grasped at the moment it expresses itself in words or signs, that is becomes part of inter-subjective communication. A will which is not signified, a thought which is not expressed, a psychic act which is not communicated, cannot be inserted into any cognitive system and consequently not into any scientific system either.

It is possible to raise the following objection. How is it possible to explain the distinction jurists have always made, and continue to make, between the study of the meaning of the words themselves and the intention which lies behind them, between the interpretation of the *verba* and the interpretation of the *mens legis*? To explain the distinction there is no need to stop regarding jurisprudence as the analysis of language. For even the so-called interpretation of the *mens* is in effect an interpretation of the *verba*. Interpretation is not restricted to the words expressed in the proposition itself, but includes all the words outside it which can be used to clarify its meaning. The passage from the interpretation of the letter to the interpretation of the spirit is no more than the broadening of the enquiry into the use of the word in question to an ever increasing number of propositions which bear an increasingly tenuous relation to the initial context. The study of contexts, which allows us to broaden our knowledge of the use of a word, and thus to determine with a greater degree of certainty the rule, is one of the most difficult. And, as every jurist knows, the discovery of a new context can represent a new area of research. The fact that in this case we use the expression "to discover the intention" or other equivalents is of no importance. It does, however, matter that this discovery of the intention in fact amounts to a discovery of new propositions which help us determine the meaning of a particular word or proposition. By interpretation of intention we mean the use of all the means at our disposal to determine the meaning of a word or a group of words. And, it should be remembered, all these means are linguistic. What is known as historical interpretation is the analysis of normative propositions that were in force in the past; systemic interpretation studies the connection between the normative propositions of the institution under examination and others which relate to similar institutions which can be subsumed in the same general category. Indeed, the interpretation of intention, which is now habitually described as logic, is also essentially grammatical interpretation, given that the jurist in this early stage of his inquiry uses all the means at his disposal, which are inevitably linguistic, to determine the rules governing the use of certain words. In other words (using an expression now common among logical positivists), the jurist is concerned with defining the *grammar* of the particular language which is the language of that particular legislator.[7]

7 The same criteria should influence the study of the theories of the interpretation of contract or contractual intention. The distinction between declarative and will theories is ambiguous. Will theories are also declarative theories though different, of course, from that theory properly so called. According to those theories, a contractual declaration should be read not only by taking into account the contractual declaration in its usual meaning; all other parallel declarations should also be taken into account if they are liable to clarify the specific meaning that the words have in the contract. This means that they do not necessarily have to have the meaning they would in technical or common language, which would be the case if the contractual declaration alone were to be taken into consideration. The will theory, in other words, requires words in a contract not to be given the meaning which they have in the general language (this could be a technical one or simply the common one) but the meaning which they have according to a specific language, used by one or both the authors of the declaration in the specific case. In using the word "sale", for example, the authors might have wanted to imply an unwritten rule such as: "Each time the word sale appears in our contract it will correspond to that which in common language is called donation." The declarative theory knows only one language (it is a useful simplifying device, used in many primitive legal orders); the theory of the will knows a variety of languages and therefore knows a corresponding variety of rules determining their uses. It

10. *The Second Phase: Completion*

As we have already seen, not only is the language of the legislator lacking in rigour, it is also incomplete. There is a sense in which the very lack of rigour by itself generates incompleteness: a proposition expressed in a non-rigorous language is such that not all the rules governing the use of the words occurring in the proposition are laid out. This incompleteness, however, can be disposed of by means of the grammatical analysis of language, we have already mentioned. The incompleteness of which we now speak is understood in a different and more specific sense, or at least one nearer to traditional legal use. What we mean by incompleteness in juridical language is that the legislator does not derive from the normative propositions expressed all the possible normative consequences which can be derived by simple combination of propositions on the basis of the accepted rules of transformation. We will not go into the reasons why the legislator himself lays bare only a minimal part of the consequences implied by his language. It is not difficult to imagine why this is so. On the other hand, it is important to establish *a*) that the language of the legislator is, in the specific sense of the term, *incomplete*; *b*) and that, like any other language that is gradually made more rigorous, it can be made *more complete*. And this is precisely what jurists set out to do in this second phase of their work.

It is possible to derive one proposition from another by applying certain rules governing the transformation of propositions, i.e. the logical rules. As we have already seen, a language can be said to be scientific not only when all the rules governing the use of the words have been made clear, but also when it is clearly established which rules are to be used in the transformation of propositions and discourse is produced solely by using these convened transformation rules and no others. Scientific discourse, hence, contains within itself the possibility of its own development, never stepping out of itself, but keeping within the boundaries of the rules which govern it. When a language develops within itself, making explicit the implications which are contained in its constitutive rules it can be described as a *closed language*. The most obvious example of this type of language is mathematical language.

---

knows, therefore, that there is not only one meaning to a word but there are as many meanings as there are languages which make use of that word. For each word and context therefore, one has find the distinctive language which has used them.

Juridical language, or more precisely the language of a particular legal system interpreted by the jurist, can also be described as a closed language. At the basis of every legal system there is a fundamental rule according to which the group of normative propositions making up the system constitutes a *closed whole*. Jurists know this rule as the norm of closure of the legal system. Indeed in the view of jurists it is this norm that transforms a set of propositions into a system. On the basis of this fundamental rule, the only propositions that can be properly termed juridical are the ones laid down by the legislator through the required formalities and those which are implicit in them and thus can be deduced from them through the rules of transformation given by the legislator himself. It thus follows that the only normative proposition that can be considered part of the legislative system is one put forward by the legislator or one derivable from it by the rules of transformation which apply within a particular juridical language. Consequently legal analysis is conducted within the narrowly circumscribed limits of a particular language. The rules of transformation are determined in advance, independently of the jurist's will. This is what we mean when we say that legal language is a closed language.

This is not the place to delve further into whether or not it is beneficial that such a norm of closure exists. There are those, for example, in the free school of law and in the sociological approach to law who have frequently denied it. Here we take it that such norms do exist, indeed that they are one of the fundamental canons upon which our legal systems are constructed. These systems are founded upon the total absorption of legislative law. Faced with this fundamental rule of the closure of the legal system, the jurist does two things when striving to complete the law. On the one hand he integrates a particular proposition into the normative system using the rules of transformation admissible for that system. On the other he removes from the system those propositions which are not deducible. This does not mean that the work of the jurist is purely mechanical and that the solutions he comes up with are always sufficient. The normative system is not perfect (cf. the problem of gaps in the law). Often the process of deduction opens the way to two contradictory solutions (the problem of antinomies). But we will return to these issues later.

If, then, we accept the rule of closure, the legal system appears as a whole which, although incomplete, is capable of completion. It falls to the jurist to perform this work of completion. This task is the most important and interesting part of his researches. It is this which permits the development of juridical discourse, provided, of course, that this development is in accordance with the rules. This brings us to what is commonly known as extensive interpretation, in the broad sense of term, as it was used by jurists in the Middle Ages. It would be a fascinating topic in legal logic to spell out the implicit rules which govern the operation of extension. The jurists and the logicians of the Middle Ages traditionally attempted it for a long time. Today, however, we would have to use the tools that modern logic puts at our disposal. Let it suffice for now to point out that the rule of analogical extension is one of the rules of transformation of juridical discourse. It is admitted, explicitly or implicitly, in all modern legislation (with noted exceptions in particular branches of the law). The importance of this rule resides in the following. It lends a particular character to legal language, distinguishing it from others which do not admit of such a rule, or only within certain limits, as to my knowledge is the case the languages of the physical and biological sciences. This is further evidence of the element of conventionality which is inherent in every specific language. It is a convention of juridical language that like be treated alike. There is no reasoning by analogy which is valid in itself and for itself. It is valid in situations where the fundamental rules of a particular language permit and indeed demand it. For the physicist reasoning by analogy is a weak form of reasoning; for the jurist, on the other hand, it is perfectly sound, since it is, so to speak, one of the rules of the game.

Some people may find it surprising that analogical extension is mentioned in connection with extensive interpretation, given that jurists usually consider extensive interpretation and analogy to be two different things. I have outlined my reasons for disagreeing with this view elsewhere.[8] Incidentally, the view of legal science as the process of purifying and completing a closed language, accepted here, only serves to reinforce my point. Analogical extension is an operation admitted by the rules of transformation of the legal language, that is the rules which make the development of the language possible. But this development coincides with what jurists call extensive interpretation. Analogical extension is thus a form of extensive interpretation. Viewed in this way, being an operation governed by the rules of legal discourse, analogy is not, as some jurists would have us believe, a creative act. It is an operation which is in

8 *L'analogia nella logica giuridica* (Turin: Istituto Giuridico dell'Università, 1938), 139ff.

the strictest sense logical and compatible with the view of legal science as the analysis of language. Thus one of the instruments with which one does that analysis of language which we call jurisprudence.

11. *The Third Phase: Ordering*

The second stage of legal research (completion stage) is followed by a third and last stage, that of systematization. As we have already seen, legal language is not necessarily rigorous or complete. In the same way it is not necessarily *well ordered*. The normative propositions which make up a legal order have been produced over a long period of time. There is no general overarching plan bestowing an order upon them. Even if some kind of overall scheme has evolved, it bears too many of the marks of its own history to be able to provide systematicity according to purely logical requirements. Legal science has for centuries been totally overpowered by the great weight of the authority of Roman law: great, both as a juridical experience and as a juridical culture. Roman law has played the same role in legal science as Aristotle's *Organum* in logic and Euclide's *Elements* in geometry in that it has assumed the historical significance of an ideal model and acquired paradigmatic value. For a long time Roman law was held to be not merely a historical legal system, even though the richest and more perfect historical legal system which had ever existed. Many believed it law *par excellence* just as Aristotelian logic was "the" logic and Euclidean geometry was "the" geometry. In the natural law period Roman law was considered the *ratio scripta* of law, a kind of natural law eternally valid. Looking beyond, and indeed at the counter-productive effects of the Roman law tradition, in no way detracts from the valuable, renewed interest juridical science is taking in Roman law at its best. The idealization of Roman law has come to the stage where it hampered the development of legal science, slowed it down and rendered it overcautious. Modern jurisprudence started moving towards becoming a science when it freed itself of the categories and divisions of Roman law, perhaps driven in this by the very requirements of its own quest. It then set about constructing new categories and divisions over the foundations of the traditional ones. These new categories and divisions were more in tune with the drive towards a more systematic approach of the new law which was just then being established.

Legal science has, almost unconsciously, gradually freed itself of the influence of Roman law. This process, though never explicitly acknowledged, has indeed taken place. A tangible change has taken place: if one compares the works of jurisprudence written today with those written not longer than fifty years ago, one will notice there has been a perceptible decline in the number of references to Roman law. Developments in the historical sciences in the previous century have made this process easier by expanding our knowledge of the history of Roman law, which thus has increasingly come to be viewed as a stage in the history of law and the Roman lawyer seen as a legal historian. It was not long ago that the Roman lawyer and the civil lawyer were seen to be carrying out essentially the same researches and writing the same books. Whereas formerly there was a sort of relaxed contiguity between the institutions of civil law and those of Roman law, nowadays there is a considerable difference between a Roman lawyer and a civil lawyer. The first is a historian, the second a systematiser. The development of legal science will demand of jurists enough courage to construe a new systematization of law which draws nothing from tradition merely *qua* tradition, and which takes into account how the meaning of words is dependent upon the context and language in which they are used. The only rules they should adhere to in this systematization will be those pertaining to the language under scrutiny. They would thus be able to develop a consistent and unitary language which would reduce the misunderstandings to the minimum — with obvious advantages for the practical application of law. These developments are not without their historical precedents. The impetus for the development of modern logic and geometry came when there was a break with tradition and people realised that Aristotelian logic was not the ideal form of logic, but just one of many possible logics. It began to be seen in its historical context, as a form of logic which corresponded to the particular conception of the world which prevailed among the ancient Greeks. The same applies to geometry. People began to realise that Euclidean geometry was not the only possible geometry. Others could be built, which were perhaps more suited to resolving the problems which the advancement of knowledge had brought to light.

12. *Legal Antinomies*

There is, however, one grave objection to which I will have to respond right away. As anyone who is acquainted with legal discussions knows, many such discussions are inconclusive. Both sides of the argument are equally acceptable, as both are sustained by valid arguments which, by conflicting, neutralize each other and don't allow for a definitive conclusion. How, then, is it possible to reconcile the uncertainty of the outcome with the rigour which has up until now been considered an inherent part of a scientific system? How is disputability, which is a feature of so many jurisprudential propositions, to be reconciled with the *scientific* approach? It goes without saying that this question addresses a different problem; in fact disputes due to lack of rigour are commonplace in each and every science. That jurisprudence should be ridden by this kind of disputes only proves that it has made as yet only little progress in the direction of rigour, but certainly not that jurisprudence cannot be rendered rigorous at all. If anything, on the contrary, it encourages us to pursue the enterprise further. The type of objection alluded to above is of a different order. The disputes referred to here are thought to be grounded not in a lack of rigour, rather, in the fact that the structure of the system lacks the very rules that should provide a solution for them. In effect these disputes are proved insoluble by the very rigour deployed to try and solve them.

Those same logicians who helped develop a new conception of science as the construction of a rigorous language discovered that such insoluble questions within the limits of a particular language are to be found in all sciences, that is in all languages.[9] These are known as "antinomies", as "unresolved propositions", and are to be found even in mathematics and logic. Geymonat described these as propositions "whose very linguistic structure makes it impossible for us to come up with either a positive or a negative response".[10] We can add that such antinomies, or unresolved propositions, are also to be found in law. We have already seen that there are questions to which both the positive and negative solutions are valid. Both are legitimate according to the canons laid down by legal language. I am not saying that this need not worry us, merely that these problems are shared by all scientific researchers. And if, as Geymonat has pointed out, "a system does not break down just because it contains unresolved propositions",[11] we then have good reason to believe that the legal system too is safe. The future of legal science is not in jeopardy just because within its theories it is possible to arrive through deduction at two

9 See Gödel's theory in L. Geymonat, "La crisi della logica formale", in *Fondamenti logici della scienza* (Turin: F. De Silva, 1947), 132.

10 Geymonat, *supra* n.9, at 133.

11 *Op. cit.*, at 133.

mutually exclusive propositions.

But is legal science like all the other sciences which can support antinomies, as logicians say, without collapsing? This is where the objection gets close to a raw nerve. We can accept that the presence of a few antinomies does not lead to the collapse of a scientific system. There is, however, a condition attached to the maintenance of the system. Among the fundamental and constitutive rules which govern the system there has to be one which states that such antinomies are permitted. The question we must now ask ourselves is whether legal science permits antinomies. Or is there perhaps a rule which prohibits them among the basic rules of legal language? And if indeed there is such a rule, how is it possible to construct a legal science which permits them? How could a jurisprudence still be considered scientific, which allows antinomies in total defiance of the rule which bans them? How could such a research be considered scientific if it does not comply with the constitutive rule of its own language? There are two possible answers to this question. We must consider which of them offers the better way round this difficulty. Either, *a*) the rule which prohibits antinomies is a constitutive rule of legal language; or, *b*) this rule is not constitutive of legal language.

In the first case antinomies are not permitted. This means that some sort of solution has to be found. As we have seen already, antinomies arise when the terms for a solution are lacking in the scientific language itself. Thus in order to find a solution in a situation where an antinomy has arisen, it is necessary to insert a proposition taken from a different language (that is, another sphere of experience). This will then have the effect of eliminating the undecidable proposition. But it is not quite as straightforward as that. The insertion of a new proposition violates another fundamental rule of legal language, that of the closure of the system, which, as we have seen, prescribes that legal language be considered a closed whole, completable by itself and in itself. Instead of being resolved, the antinomy is thus merely displaced. Indeed in many respects it is made worse, because the antinomy is no longer located in the propositions but in the constitutive rules of the language itself. In the end, then, once there is a rule prohibiting antinomies, the antinomy can only be eliminated by contravening the rule of closure. But if I respect the rule of closure, I am no longer able to resolve the antinomy. Respecting the first rule implies violating the second and *vice versa*. It is not possible to obey both at the same time because they contradict each other. If I remain inside the limits prescribed by the rule of closure, I cannot avoid the antinomies. If I obey the rule against antinomies, I violate the rule of closure. We are presented with a thorny problem indeed. Is the qualification of "scientific" still warranted for jurisprudence if the scenario we have presented holds true? And precisely, if it is not just single propositions that contradict each other, but it is the very constitutive and foundational rules of this science that contradict each other and are therefore mutually exclusive?

Let us then look at the second alternative. There is no rule against antinomies embedded in the structure of legal language. Antinomies are thus permitted. This means that two propositions which exclude each other in turn can still be legally valid, provided that both can be deduced from the same normative system, that is that they are equally valid in the given system, that is they are equivalent in that system. But what, legal operators may ask, is to become of legal certainty? One response is that legal certainty is an ethical and political requirement which will be fulfilled only by drafting new laws, laws which are more precise and rigorous than the existing ones, and not by pretending to find in them what is not there. Secondly, however rigorous a language is, there will always be cases that are unpredictable, and which have thus never been clearly defined, precisely because they have not been predicted. There will always be uncertainty as to which rigidly defined terminological category into which these cases should be subsumed into. The problem of gaps is one which affects every system. Every system has its gaps, that is it does not provide, and cannot provide, all the necessary means to eliminate antinomies. Moreover, the elimination of gaps (and therefore of antinomies) is a legislative rather than a jurisprudential problem. We may assume that where a gap arises the legislator does not mind which way the case is resolved. What matters to him is that the case is resolved, the manner of its resolution does not concern him. In fact it is possible to argue that as far as antinomies are concerned, the principle of legal certainty is continually being violated, for, in practice, the judge opts for either alternative when it comes to an undecidable proposition. There is nothing that can be done to make him opt for the same one consistently. Judging from what goes on in legal practice, it would appear that the presence of antinomies and thus of mutually exclusive answers is not so serious an inconvenience as to make us renounce the principle of the closed system. Thus, on balance, given the present situation of our legal systems, it is difficult to imagine that we could admit as a fundamental rule of the system itself one which prohibits antinomies.

This is an issue which deserves to be gone into in greater depth. Here it has been used to illustrate the type of problems which arise when legal science is viewed as being primarily about the analysis of language. As we said from the beginning, we were concerned with a different issue; namely to show that the research activities of the jurist are at base scientific, whether or not he is aware of it and even if he is at pains to demonstrate its very lack of scientific rigour. Molière's Monsieur Jourdain speaks prose without realising it. In the same way, the jurist's activity is basically scientific, however much he denies it and claims merely to be a dogmatist or a technician. This conclusion teaches us a general lesson. In order to produce a science the jurists does not have to go outside his own domain. He does not has to look for a true legal science within natural law; to develop a science of natural law as a surrogate of the unsatisfactory science consisting in the interpretation of positive law. Today, nobody would write yet another treatise of natural law. The history of natural law is the history of a grand evasion and diversion. The history of jurisprudence started the day this came to an end. Once back home, jurists realised that they could easily do within the walls of home what they had sought to achieve in a long journey away. Further, they realised that within these walls, long neglected, there was much still to be done, almost everything, in fact. The rigour which was used to construct an ideal law would have been better employed to construct a system out of the existing positive law. And this would give the jurist the satisfaction of being able to make, through the analysis of law, a practical and direct contribution to the immediate task of social construction.

ETHICS, LANGUAGE AND REASON

by

UBERTO SCARPELLI

I

Is a rational ethics possible? This is the fundamental problem of moral philosophy. My purpose here is to offer a solution suggested by contemporary linguistic philosophy.

The name of linguistic philosophy is given to a philosophy which approaches and tries to solve philosophical problems through the analysis of language and an enquiry into meaning. It also looks at logical structures, the functions and uses of language. It is through this that it approaches the problems of ethical philosophy. My argument will be closely connected to my understanding of linguistic philosophy. We shall not here explore fully the many strands, which all share a common approach, though they produce different answers concerning philosophy in general, moral philosophy and the very possibility of a rational ethics.

My solution mainly follows linguistic philosophy of the logico-empirical sort. This logical empiricism had, for many years, to answer difficult and penetrating criticisms from various areas of linguistic philosophy and from areas of non-linguistic philosophy. It thus produced new answers and problems and overcame the "reductionism" of its beginnings. I start with a brief note about my own intellectual history, for those interested in using it as an interpretative tool. I came to philosophy through idealism and, like many others in the immediate after-war period, lived through its transformation into existentialism. These philosophical misadventures of a youth living difficult times, were followed by an encounter with linguistic philosophy and in particular with logical empiricism. This path has lead me through marvellous countries (in the meaning of Alice, at least). It opened up new horizons and I never contemplated abandoning it. It is from this perspective that I have dedicated the most important part of my studies and of my activities to

Law and Language, The Italian Analytical School, ed. A. Pintore and M. Jori (Liverpool: Deborah Charles Publications, 1997).

law. This has made me intensely aware of the conflict between the ethical non-rationalism of primitive logical empiricism and the rational web which law appears to introduce into ethical life. My deepest and most long-lasting philosophical preoccupations stem from my experience of such conflict and the need to dissolve it.

II

A necessary step on the way to solve the problem as to whether a rational ethics is or is not possible is to look at the concept of reason. A definition of the concept of reason cannot be a "lexical" one. This would seek to collect the meanings, in a definite, more or less wide, historical context, which the word "reason" and its synonyms (or near-synonyms) has assumed in the Italian language and eventually in other languages. This record of different meanings would not help theoretical purposes. Nor can such definition be a "stipulative" one. A pure and simple convention as to the theoretical use of the word "reason", independent of previous uses of the same word and its synonyms. A solution to our problem reached with the help of such an arbitrarily fabricated instrument, would become private, without roots in philosophical tradition and would have no effects on it.

As is the case for the definition of any philosophical concept essential to philosophical theorising, our definition of the concept of reason can only be an "explicative" one or, one might say, a "re-definition". An explicative definition remains in the area of meaning which a word or its synonyms have historically acquired. Within this area it endeavours to extract and explain with precision a meaning which serves theoretical aims. The explicative definition relates to the philosophical tradition and allows us to intervene in it.

The definition of the concept of reason which can be extracted from linguistic philosophy of the logico-empirical kind relates in particular to the nominalistic tradition. With Hobbes, we can say that reason is calculation. Reason involves a discourse in which it is possible to make propositions and to check them by criteria proper to that universe of the discourse. The result is expressed by way of positive or negative values given to propositions (truth-untruth, validity-invalidity). Propositions with a positive value are kept in the discourse, and are seen to conform to its function, those with a negative value are deleted because they do not conform to it. Determination of the concept of reason by reference to the discourse does not prevent us from speaking of the rationality of individuals, things, situations, non linguistic events (for example, of rational beings, of non-linguistic rational behaviour, etc.). But individuals, things, situations and events will appear to be rational in virtue of their relations with rational discourses (for example the ability to produce a rational discourse, a structure in accordance with the structure of a rational discourse, etc.).

The explicative definition of the concept of reason, of which I have suggested the essential elements, has the advantage that it does not establish a necessary relation between the concept of reason, and rationality of a discourse, and the value of truth and untruth. It might be that values of truth or untruth suit the proposition of a rational discourse. But there might be a rational discourse the propositions of which will not agree with values of truth and untruth. This is important to the question as to whether ethics has a rational basis or not. This concept of reason is wide if compared with precedents, particularly important for logico-empiricists. Hume's definition of reason, for example, was the discovery of truth and untruth. Wherein lies the advantage of our wider definition of the concept of reason? The narrow definition would reduce the problem of the rationality of ethics to the question of whether truth and falsity can be attributed to ethical propositions. The wider definition makes the problem much richer. It becomes one of whether ethical discourse is possible where the criteria for the acceptance for its propositions come from the discourse itself. We do not have to consider the question as to whether these criteria should be of truth or falsity or of some other value.

III

Linguistic philosophy, of the logico-empirical strand, in its attempt to determine forms and structures of rational discourse as well as criteria of control of propositions therein, has spent most of its time and energy seeking to extract a model for it from the logical and empirical science. We must remind ourselves of two main results which stem from this. Firstly, the demonstration that criteria of the control of propositions are in fact just that, criteria of *control*. Here we see an ever finer clarification of the distinction between "context of invention" and "context of control". The context of invention is the context of discourse operations by which scientific propositions are established. Inventing propositions is an act of intellectual fantasy stemming from the scientist's personality (trying to explain the scientist's intellectual fantasy and his actions pertains to psychology). The context of control or justification is that of discursive operations with which propositions, invented on the basis of criteria specific to the universe of the scientific discourse where they are generated, are justified.

Secondly, logical empiricism came to conclusion that the criteria for the justification of scientific propositions are either logical or empirical verification. Logical verification takes place when a proposition is justified by looking to the validity of the logical derivation or derivations which lead from premises, accepted as true, to that proposition. A proposition justified in such a way will be logically true or false. Empirical verification is when a proposition is justified by way of a comparison with recorded data of experience. A proposition so justified will be empirically true or false. This is but a brief summary of a complex and subtle analysis. The analysis has gone a long way from the narrow verificationist position of early logical empiricism. The intertwining of logical verification and empirical verification is accepted. Empirical verification can take place not in respect of individual propositions but in respect of theoretical systems by comparing propositions logically true within those systems with recorded data of experience.

The criterion of empirical verification has been stretched in various directions ending up as the criterion of empirical falsification. Propositions or theories are empirically true if they cannot be falsified.

What we should emphasise and retain is the strong central thesis, characteristic of logical empiricism. Truth and falsity can be predicated of propositions, and it can be predicated in two senses, that of logical truth and that of empirical truth. Logically true propositions are analytic. They contain nothing that is not implied in the premises and definitions, in the rules of formation and transformation which allow the formation of premises and the logical derivation of the propositions themselves. Empirically true propositions are synthetic and require experience to confirm them. Logical empiricism does not allow the synthetic *a priori*.

IV

Whoever attempts to speak of ethics or religion comes up against the very limits of language. Rattling the bars of a cage is a desperate action. Ethics arises from a desire to express something about the ultimate meaning of life, about the absolute good, and about absolute value. It cannot, therefore, be a science. It can add nothing to knowledge, it cannot make use of the language with which we know facts. These are Wittgenstein's positions which he expressed in a lecture on ethics, the only public one he ever held.

Linguistic philosophy, though deeply influenced by Wittgenstein in his different attitudes, has not shared his mysticism. Therefore, it has not made its own the mystical feature of this philosophy of ethics according to which ethics is nonsense for aiming further than the language, beyond the bars of the cage, towards the ultimate meaning of life, at absolute good, at absolute value. In linguistic philosophy, as everyone knows, there has been in the long run an acceptance of Wittgenstein's idea that the scope of discourse coincides with the scope of acquaintance with fact. Not only is the criterion of empirical verification used as a justificatory criterion for propositions in the world of empirical science, but it has been raised to the rank of general semantic criterion (only those discourses which generate empirically verifiable propositions have sense). Beyond the limits of sense, however, ethics remains something wholly and thoroughly human, not to be transmogrified through mystical interpretations. The language, or better, the non-language of ethics is nothing but the expression and stimulation of emotions.

The emotivist conception of ethics, which Ayer expresses with provocative radicalism, is best developed by Stevenson.[1] By using concepts such as "descriptive meaning" (meaning determined by linguistic rules, specific and exclusive to cognitive language) and "emotive meaning" (the capacity of language to express and stimulate emotions), Stevenson has advanced the study of the relations and reciprocal influences between meanings determined by linguistic rules and emotive meanings or the capacity of language to express and stimulate emotions. This is an important contribution (one should remember his theory of persuasive definition). But, as we have seen, he identifies meanings determined by linguistic rules with descriptive meanings, specific and exclusive to cognitive language. Precepts and ethical judgments possess only emotive meanings. For Stevenson, as well as for Ayer, they are expressions of satisfaction or dissatisfaction aiming at provoking reactions of desire or repulsion. The reduction of ethical judgments to expressions and stimulations of emotions, appears quite unreasonable when dealing with

1 See *Ethics and Language* (New Haven: Yale University Press, 1945) and his collection of essays: *Facts and Values. Studies in Ethical Analysis* (New Haven and London: Yale University Press, 1963).

the elaborate and complex precepts and ethical judgments such as those encountered in morality and law, for example. But here linguistic philosophy, still limited by its equation of discourse to knowledge, explores another way of interpreting ethical judgments. One close to great names of the past such as Hume and Bentham. Ethical judgments are significant insofar as they can be interpreted as cognitive propositions. Their ethical character consists of the content of the meaning of the propositions, as they now become statements about psychological states of approval or disapproval, or about the consequences, certain or probable, of behaviour.

Up till now linguistic philosophy has given two solutions to the question of the rationality of ethics. Though, at first sight different, they are similar on an important and essential point. On one hand, Wittgenstein and the emotivists tell us that a rational ethics, is not possible, as even an ethical discourse is impossible. On the other hand, we are told that a rational ethics is possible. But, since it is a cognitive discourse, then its potential rationality is that of a cognitive discourse, the rationality of science.

I have emphasised above the drawbacks, in these questions, of a narrow definition of the concept of reason. One which has a necessary connection between the concept of reason, the rationality of a discourse and the truth and or falsity of the propositions of the discourse. As we have seen, early on linguistic philosophy had not only a narrow definition of the concept of reason alone, but of the very concepts of language, meaning, discourse. They were all connected with the criteria of truth and falsity specific to cognitive discourse. In consequence of this the problem of the rationality of ethics has turned into the problem of whether ethics consists of a cognitive discourse or whether it is a discourse at all. The answer of Wittgenstein and the emotivists is that there are no ethical propositions to which one can predicate truth or falsity and therefore ethics is not a discourse. Reductionists have answered that one can call ethical propositions true or false because the are part of the only possible discourse, the cognitive one. The assumptions of both force them to deny that ethics exists as a rational discourse with propositions justifiable by criteria specific to it. They deny that ethical discourses could have a different function than cognitive discourse with other justificatory criteria than truth or falsity.

V

The preceding belongs to the history of linguistic philosophy. No one denies today that a discourse with a different function than the cognitive one is possible. There is no logical empiricist who is so obstinate as to deny the existence of discourses whose criteria of justification or not truth and falsity.

The crucial turning point came with Hare and what is called prescriptivism. In particular with his most important work, *The Language of Morals.*[2] Hare cannot be called logical empiricist, though in some aspects he is near to it. The work of Hare and his followers in the theory of language and meaning has radically modified the picture that I have given so far.[3]

As we have seen, the verification principle was transformed by linguistic philosophy from justificatory criterion in empirical sciences to a general semantic criterion. We now turn to the distinction between a semantic criterion (discourses are meaningful when their references are sufficiently determined in relation to their functions) and a justification criterion such as the verification principle, which is still the case for the empirical sciences. The combination of the semantic criterion and the justificatory criterion still gives the same result in the empirical sciences as did the verification principle seen as a semantic criterion. In empirical sciences, the only meaningful propositions are those which, sufficiently determined in relation to their function, provide propositions empirically verifiable. At this point, it is possible to accept the sense of discourses whose propositions are sufficiently determined in relation to their function. But, because they do not perform a cognitive function, not accept the verification principle as the criterion whereby the propositions are justified.

The function of language consisting in recording, elaborating and transmitting empirical knowledge is usually designated, in a way not wholly felicitous or well chosen, as its "descriptive function". How many other functions of language are there beside the descriptive function? The solution to this fundamental problem, one which strongly characterises

2 Oxford: Clarendon Press, 1952.

3 See my *Contributo alla semantica del linguaggio normativo* (Turin Academy of Sciences, 1959, 2nd ed. Milan: Giuffrè, 1985).

the prescriptivistic phase of the linguistic philosophy of ethics, is that there is only one other function, the "prescriptive" (or directive as I prefer to call it) function of language. This involves considering that value judgements, in so far as they do not have a descriptive function and are not a pure and simple expression or stimulation of emotions, perform, in an oblique way, a prescriptive, or directive, function.

This is the way the "great division" between descriptive and prescriptive (or directive) function comes to be introduced into the theory of language and meaning. Any sentence, in either of the two functions, must satisfy the semantic reference criterion in order to be meaningful. Its references must be adequately determined by reference to its function. There will be, in every sentence, an indicator of function (we refer here to complete sentences; of course, in certain linguistic contexts and non-linguistic situations, sentences with unsaid implicit elements can be found). Hare calls the part of the sentence which carries the reference "phrastic" and the part indicating function "neustic".

It is in the distinction between the two functions of language and between phrastic and neustic that we find the theoretical key to our problem. Through this we can go beyond the old logical tradition, an ancient tradition in logic, firmly rooted in the primacy of "truth" and "falsity", and we can set up a system of logical relations between propositions performing the two functions. The acknowledgement that discourses with a "directive" function are possible, followed by appropriate theoretical development, represent an introduction to the study of the logics of those discourses. Thus in contemporary philosophy deontic logics, logics of normative systems, logics of value or preference, etc. arise and are developed in different forms and directions. The logic of the relations between propositions of the two functions can be approached by using the distinction between phrastic and neustic. The possibility of logical relations between them depends on the relations between their phrastics, but logical derivations are permitted or not by reference to the nature of their neustics.

The supreme rule here concerns the "logical jump" from descriptive to directive (or *vice-versa*, that there is a "logical jump" from directive to descriptive, but we shall not deal with this problem here). From descriptive premises, no conclusion in the form of a directive proposition can be logically derived. The logical derivation of a directive proposition is admitted according to conditions to be explained later. By and large it requires that a directive premise should be available. A logical rule which, to the contrary, allowed the logical derivation of a directive proposition from descriptive premises would be more than a logical rule (one relating to the logical derivation of propositions from propositions). It would be a norm with a meta-logical directive content or, more exactly, a meta-norm establishing the norm so derived, together with its specific directive content. It would not be a good thing for norms with directive meta-logical contents to dress up as logical rules.

VI

Thus the central problem is now, borrowing a current expression of English philosophical jargon, the *is-ought question*. Let us first of all summarise the position of the "divisionists" position regarding the *is-ought question*. It contains three main theses. Firstly, a distinction should be made between the two language functions, the descriptive function and the directive one. Such a distinction is exhaustive, even though each function should then be further distinguished and developed within its respective category. Secondly, truth and falsity assigned by the verification principle are only suited to the propositions with a descriptive function. Different values pertain to propositions with a directive function. Thirdly, there is a "logical gap" between descriptive and directive proposition. In particular, no directive conclusions can be derived from descriptive premises. The logical derivation of a directive proposition requires there to be a directive proposition among the premises.

My summary expresses the nub of the thesis. This is sometimes expressed differently; for instance some authors conceive the object of meta-discourses in a different way, and use "sentence" where I use "proposition". These views have generated some of the most subtle and sophisticated arguments of the entire history of philosophy. At stake are very important issues, as the meta-ethical dispute hides not only intellectual but also ethical disputes. Anti-divisionists attack divisionists with various strategies. Firstly we have the hidden directive premise. This consists in deriving a directive conclusion from apparently descriptive premises but in which a directive is hidden. As an example of such a strategy is the following disingenuous argument. It is maintained that from the (apparently) descriptive locution by James, "I promise" one can, with the addition of a few more phrases, quickly reach the conclusion that James must therefore give or execute whatever he has promised.

Apprentice linguistic philosophers could practice their skills by trying to spot when the conjurer surreptitiously inserts the directive premise. This happens in the example of reasoning above, when the key-term "promise" is made to shift from a descriptive to a directive use.

This operation comes under the heading of "naturalism". "Naturalism", in the jargon of linguistic philosophy, is the fiction of a continuum from the descriptive to the directive. This is done by definitions and other linguistic connections which hide the logical jump. For instance, naturalism claims that the word "good" is used ethically in the following way. To call x morally good is to say that x is good when it presents the observable characteristics a, b, c. This means that something bearing the observable characteristics a, b, c, is good. In order to overcome the "naturalistic fallacy", the divisionists use Moore's so-called argument of the "open question". One can always sensibly reopen the question as to whether characteristic so described really are good. Or, more generally, whether they represent the suitable reference of a judgment of value or of a prescription.

Moore used such arguments to hold that goodness is a non natural property of natural objects. This allowed him to call such ethical judgements true or false. There is, for Moore, a second class of ethical judgments which can also be true or false. These are judgements stating that certain things have good effects. They are ultimately based (as far as the goodness of the effects is concerned), on the ethical judgments of the first sort. These are the prime principles of ethics, not deducible from other propositions and self-evident. If we ask: "what are we to do?" the answer comes from the second class of ethical judgments. To ask what actions we are to perform, or what behaviour is right, is equivalent to asking what will the effects of certain actions or a certain behaviour be. It is the function of the second class of ethical judgements, based upon ethical judgement of the first class, i.e. on ethical principles, to tell us which action and behaviour will produce good effects.

Though he does not admit to it, Moore (I refer here to the Moore of *Principia Ethica*, and not his later views) makes too casual a jump here from the descriptive to the directive. As if those true or false descriptive propositions carried with them as a logical necessity, the directive propositions prescribing the actions able to lead towards natural objects with the non-natural property of goodness. The argument of the open question can be used again. I might know that the non-natural property of goodness is present in certain natural objects, and know that certain actions are able to produce good effects, i.e. they can lead to natural objects with the non natural property of goodness. But must I thereby really commit myself to produce good effects? The linguistic philosophy of ethics surmounts that fallacy, if such it be, because of the total eclipse of Moore's platonism and his conception of goodness as a non-natural property of natural objects. The proposition that an object is good is not a true or false statement that it has a non natural property. But it is to make (a more or less oblique) directive about that object.

VII

A second strategy against divisionism consists in widening the idea of derivation of conclusions from premises. Within a society of communicators, linguistic rules determining the meanings of linguistic signs, their possible combinations and logical transitions are usually complemented with ethical rules as to language communications. For example, the ethical norm, generally accepted (with limits and exceptions not relevant in our context) that one should assert only what one believes to be true. Liars assert what they do not believe, but pay respect to that ethical norm by trying to conceal it. Thus the strangeness of the statement, "it rains, but I don't believe it" (the very banality of the example enhances the paradox). While, in the absence of an ethical norm forbidding the assertion of things others do not believe in, the sentence "it rains, but James doesn't believe it" does not sound strange. The relation between a proposition or a set of propositions and the contrary proposition to that which, when joined with the first, would result in a similar oddity, has been named "pragmatic implication".

Pragmatic implication has been used in deriving directive propositions from descriptive propositions. The argument is that, given certain conditions, a descriptive proposition or set of descriptive propositions pragmatically imply a directive proposition. An ethical norm, parallel to the one stated above, (also with limits and exceptions) that the value of something can be asserted only when that something is actually valued in that way. Moral liars, that is hypocrites, assert values which they do not value, but pay respect to this ethical norm by hiding their real attitude. Hence the oddity of the sentence, "such an act is good, though I don't believe it to be good". This oddity shows that a value judgment (directive) pragmatically implies an assertion (descriptive) as to the corresponding attitude, when the attitude is that of the author of the value judgment.

Vice versa, it shows that an assertion (descriptive) as to one's own attitude, pragmatically implies the same value judgment.

On the basis of the above, at a congress on the *is-ought question* held in Turin beginning of May 1975, a brilliant attempt was made to exhume, and re-present in analytical form, a substantially naturalistic ethics. It was claimed that it was possible, by pragmatic implication, to derive a value judgement from a descriptive proposition stating a trans-cultural universal law about an attitude which also concerned its assertor. Such an attempt has been opposed by the argument that a trans-cultural universal law is not a scientific law, verifiable or falsifiable. Furthermore, the model of a universal trans-cultural law suggested at the congress favours the concealment of a directive premise on which to hook the directive conclusion. Finally, my objection was that, even if we were to accept descriptive propositions asserting universal trans-cultural laws relating to attitudes, and the derivation therefrom of value laws by pragmatic implication, this would not make it a logical derivation. Thus the logical gap between description and direction would remain as would the divisionist thesis that a logical jump is necessary to bridge it.

We must conceive logical derivation as a derivation which is valid and cogent on the sole basis of the syntactic and semantic rules of the language which is used for the derivation itself. Without entering into details, I can refer here to the theory of logic, best formulated within linguistic philosophy by Strawson. We may call it "linguistic-conventionalism". To the moral philosopher, such a perspective (which has of course other justifications) has a clear advantage. It makes a clear distinction between conclusions which, given certain premises, presume only linguistic obligations towards syntactic and semantical rules of the language used, and conclusions, which, given certain premises, suppose more than linguistic obligations. They also presuppose obligations going beyond the syntactic and semantic dimensions of language, such as obligations towards ethical norms concerning language communication. Such a distinction allows to pinpoint and highlight the moment when, and the way in which, anyone recognises and accepts ethical bonds.

At this point, it should be clear how the most dangerous of all the attacks launched against divisionism is that which questions the very idea of language rule. The conception of language as a system of signs with applications and functions governed by rules. The distinction (which especially Carnap and Morris have turned into theory, now classical) between the syntactic, semantic and pragmatic dimensions of language.

And, as a consequence, the distinction between logical connections and transitions solely on the basis of syntactic and semantical rules, and connections and transitions between combinations of signs within the pragmatic dimension, by reference to the cultural and social contexts where the language is used. Those who deny or go beyond that conception of language often refer (though not always relevantly) to J.L. Austin. They use a range of concepts which depart from or modify the tradition in which Carnap and Morris were the leaders. Among these is the idea of a "speech act" and the "force" of such an act within a given context.

Learning the lessons of Austin, does not mean one has to abandon the primary role of the linguistic rule in the analysis of language. Consider Searle's case: He acknowledges his "obvious debt" to his teacher Austin (associated with Strawson), and devotes a book to "speech acts". He argues that speech acts are generally allowed by, and performed according to, rules as to the use of linguistic elements. It is only by their relation to linguistic rules, in fact, that speech acts can be performed and recognised as significant and not only just sounds and gestures etc. It is only due to the generating potential of a system of linguistic rules that original speech acts can take place, that is acts never previously seen or heard, yet significant and comprehended (the Chomskian school has insisted on this aspect of linguistic experience, by defining language as a finite or infinite set of sentences which a regulative grammar is able to generate). It is thus possible to initiate and develop a pragmatic study of speech acts and their force in each context, distinguishing, with Austinian patience, each single nuance. At the same time it is still possible to hold on to the concept of linguistic rule and to an idea of language as system of signs with applications and functions governed by rules. To continue to talk of logical derivation on the basis of syntactic and semantics rules and of the logical jump from descriptive and directive.

Like other rules, linguistic rules can be described as rules accepted and effective within a social group (their indeterminacies and fluctuations, if any, shall also have to be reported) or they can be laid down through acts of linguistic legislation, constructed as "perfect languages" or as partial reconstruction of ordinary languages. Linguists contrast also, a descriptive grammar, one which describes the rules followed by the language users, with a normative grammar. As far as the identification of linguistic rules accepted and effective within a social group is concerned, it has been emphasised how the linguistic dispositions of each individual belonging to the group, if able to use and understand the language, can be taken as evidence of the existence of these rules. Hence the existence of the method of linguistic inquiry often used by linguistic philosophers (the "open question" argument is an example of this). This method consists in looking at language by devising linguistic contexts perceived as normal and contexts perceived as abnormal or paradoxical. Through the careful study of these examples, it is thought that one will be able to discover and explain the actual rules of language use.

We can look at and defend the rule which says there is a logical gap between the descriptive and the directive on two levels; that of exposition and that of construction and reconstruction. At the first level one demonstrates (by the method of linguistic inquiry just sketched or some other method) that the rule is in fact one of the accepted and effective linguistic rules within a social group. I assume (though, of course, this may be false) that this can be demonstrated in Italian as well as in other natural languages. At the second level, the question is whether to recommend the introduction of this rule for inclusion among the rules of the constructed or reconstructed language. In this, we look to the pragmatic dimensions of the constructed or reconstructed language and also to ethical values.

The main argument for the rule is that referred to at the end of section 5. If we accept that, given a descriptive proposition or a plurality of descriptive propositions, no directive proposition derives logically from them, then an ethical attitude consisting in the formulation of a directive is expressed at the first level of the language, the level of language which refers to things and behaviour. A directive can be logically derived from premises of which at least one is a directive premise. As we go back, from directive premise to directive premise, we arrive at one not derived logically from premises. Here the ethical attitude is laid bare and must rest on meta-logical bases.

If, on the contrary, we accept that, given a descriptive proposition or a plurality of descriptive propositions, a certain directive proposition derives logically from them, then the ethical attitude hides behind the logical rule. This acts as a meta-logical meta-norm and bases the derived directive proposition on its specific directive content. The meta-logical bases of the attitude do not get expressed. There is therefore, in favour of the rule that there is a logical gap, an ethical attitude requiring that we should be ethically aware.

VIII

We can finally ask what answer linguistic philosophy, or rather linguistic philosophy as I have described it, gives to the question of whether a rational ethics is possible? We can condense what has been said above in a series of points.

(a) A fundamental distinction must be made and maintained among the functions of language, between the descriptive and directive functions. Ethical propositions perform, directly and indirectly, a directive function.

(b) Because of their directive function, ethical propositions cannot be justified by criteria and procedure of logical and empirical verification. They cannot, therefore, be said to be true or false. The rationality of ethical discourse cannot be the same as that of scientific discourse.

(c) Because of their directive function, ethical propositions cannot be logically derived from descriptive propositions. They cannot therefore be justified by verifying whether the logical derivation from descriptive propositions is correct. The rationality of ethical discourse cannot be a rationality secondary to the rationality of scientific discourse.

(d) The logical derivation of a directive proposition requires a directive premise. The fundamental schemata of ethical systems can be seen by looking at the structure of directive propositions able to serve as premises for the logical derivation of directive propositions and the logical form taken by the relations between the first and the second ones. Complex ethical systems result from the repetition, from one level to another, of the same schemata, or from the combination of different schemata.

Recently, linguistic philosophy has undertaken the analysis of logical and semantic structures of ethical systems, obtaining remarkable results. One only has to think of Hare's work on the "universalizability" of ethical propositions; of Hart's work on rules and their relation in legal orders; of the clarification, using utilitarianism seen through the optic of a linguistic philosopher, of the logical organisation of ethical systems founded on purposive directives.

Philosophy of law has the ability to link logical and semantic analysis of ethical systems to the great European tradition of legal theory and to studies of the legal norm and the legal order within that tradition. This is the field where, in Italy, linguistic philosophy has achieved the best results.

(e) Ethical systems can be classified into three main types. First, where directive propositions are logically derived from higher directive propositions, with the structure of "norms of behaviour", on the basis of relations between the contents of the propositions (Kelsen's "static systems"). This is the fundamental schemata of moral systems. Secondly, where directive propositions are logically derived from higher directive propositions, with the structure of "norms of competence", by the mediation of descriptive propositions stating the position of the directive propositions derived within the areas of competence (Kelsen's "dynamic systems"). This is the fundamental schemata of legal orders. Thirdly, where directive propositions are logically derived from higher directive propositions, with the structure of "teleological norms", by the mediation of descriptive propositions stating the efficacy to reach the set aims of the behaviour constituting the object of the directive propositions derived. This is the fundamental schemata of systems of political ethics.[4]

(f) A directive proposition derived logically in an ethical system can be qualified as "valid" (within the system). Validity is to directive propositions what truth is to descriptive propositions. Values of truth and validity are values attributed, within the context of justification, respectively to descriptive and directive propositions. They are justified by criteria of justification appropriate to the discourse in where they are generated.

(g) Qualifying a directive proposition as valid supposes the logical derivation of the proposition itself by virtue of a directive premise. One reaches, in every ethical system, one or more directive propositions which cannot be logically derived from further directive premises and therefore are not valid in the system (I leave open, for the time being, the question of whether an ethical system can be founded on several directive propositions, not valid in the system itself, or whether the concept of "system" implies that the system can be based on only one directive proposition). Directive propositions founding ethical systems can be called "ethical principles" (the founding principle of a legal order is called, in the theory of law, the "fundamental norm").

(h) Ethical principles can be qualified as valid according to higher ethical systems (thus the fundamental norms of a legal order can be valid according to a moral system). But the ethical principles, or the one ethical principle, which one reaches at the end, ground the validity of all those below and are themselves not valid.

4 For a more detailed explanation on this topic, see my essay "Dovere morale, obbligo giuridico, impegno politico", now in U. Scarpelli, *L'etica senza verità*, (Bologna: Il Mulino, 1982), 165-175.

(i) In conclusion, a rational ethics is possible. Better still, several rational ethics are possible. Each ethical system of the three types describes above is rational. But rational ethics rests on principles which cannot be rationally assumed.

IX

Beyond rational ethics, ethical discourse consists of persuasion, from the call of blood to the argumentative techniques of Perelman and Olbrechts-Tyteca's *Traité de l'argumentation.*[5] Even where there is no room for calculation and where it is only a matter of what may be possible and plausible, human beings, when decisions have to be taken in such contexts, use their ability to bring and weigh evidence. For Perelman and Olbrechts-Tyteca, both the use of that ability and that of calculating can be given the name of "reason". It appears to me, that we should, for the sake of clarity, limit the use of "reason" to the world of calculation. To qualify argumentation with a term of praise related to the word "reason", we should speak of reasonable argumentation, as a civilised alternative to verbal or non verbal violence.

It is possible to argue in favour and in defence of a rational ethics. It is possible to induce somebody to accept ethical reason by civilised persuasion, and it is also possible to enforce ethical reason (enforcement of ethical reason is typical of legal orders; when analyzing the structures of legal orders, theorists of law identify the species of sanctioning norms alongside that of the norms of competence and norms of behaviours). However, where the peculiar cogency (for whoever accepts the principles and the rules of calculation) of the logical operations within a calculation does not obtain, then there is always room for choice. This is true both in the face of argumentation and enforcement.

A rational ethics, an ethical principle grounding the validity of directive propositions within an ethical system but not itself valid, have their roots in an existential choice, however much justified by arguments or reinforced with sanctions. There is a deep affinity between the linguistic philosophy ethics and the ethics of existentialism. This has been shown by Iris Murdoch in her collected essays *The Sovereignty of Good.*[6] Those values which were once written in the sky and guaranteed

5 Paris: Presses Universitaires de France, 1958.

6 London: Routledge and Kegan Paul, 1970.

by God have now fallen to the human will. The supreme ethical concept is that of freedom. Its roots lie in an act of freedom, to be renewed and confirmed in ever-opening possibilities, of an existence rules by way of the directive propositions of a rational ethical discourse.

PHILOSOPHICAL ANALYSIS AND THE THEORY OF LEGAL INTERPRETATION

by

GIOVANNI TARELLO

1. *Interpretation (Activity and Product)*

"Interpretation", as used in practical or doctrinal juridical contexts, has two main lexical meanings. This is also true of corresponding words in other languages. In the first meaning, "interpretation" refers to an activity. In the second meaning, it refers to the product of such an activity. I use "interpretation" in the first meaning when I say that art. 40 of the Italian Constitution is subject to interpretation. I use "interpretation" in the second meaning when I say that the interpretation, given to art. 40 of the Constitution by Italian doctrine for many years, is mainly restrictive. Or when I say that gaps in Italian law have been filled by juristic interpretation.

Survey of these two meanings, both widely used in technical juridical language, pertains to semantics. As such, this has been made use of by those lawyers who proceed analytically. But they are not the only lawyers who survey meanings. Such surveys have always been done and they are not a distinguishing feature of analytical lawyers. It simply helps to distinguish those lawyers and historians who are precise from those who are not.

I will give an example of how research in semantics from an non-analytical approach will be perfectly acceptable to whoever adopts an analytical approach. It will also show that semantics do not necessarily imply, from an analytical point of view, any particular interpretative doctrine. I deal here with the work, in historical jurisprudence, of Gino Gorla. He came to the conclusion that during the XVIIIth century, in many European countries and particularly in Italy, the word "interpretation" (*interpretatio*) was mainly used in its second meaning. In particular, it was used to refer to a certain stock of maxims and rules found in the

Law and Language, The Italian Analytical School, ed. A. Pintore and M. Jori (Liverpool: Deborah Charles Publications, 1997).

works of "interpreters" and "doctors", in tribunals decisions, and in particular in those of Higher Tribunals. He demonstrated that it was generally held not to be an interpretation of the law but a body of norms which was used to fill lacunae in the law; how, therefore, the doctrine of the division of powers would work, together with other factors, to discredit "interpretation" as a procedure which incompetent organs would use for creating law. He showed how the prohibition of interpretation was limited to the creation of an interpretation-object; how, in spite of the general prohibition on considering an interpretation-object as law, art. 4 of the Code Napoléon would be used to allow the judges interpretation-activity. He further demonstrated how, historically, many articles of recent codes, among which art. 12 of the preliminary provisions of Italian Civil Code have been reformulations of art. 4; how, therefore, art. 12 should be understood not as a norm about norms, or a second level norm, but as a first level norm addressed to the judges.[1] Here, a semantic distinction (concerning the actual usage of the word "interpretation" in the XVIIIth century and at the beginning of the XIXth century) is added a particular theory as to the nature of a rule (art. 12 understood not as a second order rule, i.e. a general norm about norms, but as a first order norm addressed to the judges). From this Gorla draws, or purports to draw, a precept for interpretational practice.

Now, from the point of view of an analytical approach, the vocabulary survey (it is useful to know that at a certain period a certain meaning of "interpretation" has prevailed) is immediately acceptable. The rest will not immediately be accepted. Other questions have to be asked. What reasons are there to attribute this function to art. 12 on the basis of a vocabulary survey? How could one back this understanding of art. 12 by a factual statement relative to the vocabulary use or by a theory relative to the structure of a system? Gorla's conclusion cannot be accepted without presupposing a norm according to which interpretation-activity should not interrupt the historical continuity of a traditional interpretation-object. But this assumption is not an outcome of the analysis, but comes from a particular doctrine or ideology of interpretation.

This latter consideration gives me the opportunity for a clarification which I think useful. The emphasis that the analytical approach puts on the language has, in particular, to do with lexical meanings. Within semantics one can see the work of those analytically inclined and those

1 G. Gorla, "I precedenti storici dell'articolo 12 delle disposizioni preliminari del codice civile del 1942", *Foro italiano* XCII/V (1969), 112-32.

historically inclined converging. Both pay attention to meaning and the history of meaning. But the analytic school does not draw normative consequences from the study of lexical meanings. Those of an analytic bent do not believe that vocabulary (historical or actual) represents an accepted norm.

This introduces a further level. Before I deal with this, I propose some therapeutical semantics (in Scarpelli's sense).[2] We must accurately distinguish the two meanings in lawyers' discourses, and therefore use the terms "interpretative activity" or "product of the interpretation" respectively.

2. *Interpretation and Application*

Having distinguished these two meanings of "interpretation", we can proceed to other clarifications. These will not be solely of a lexical nature. In respect of lexical meaning it can be based on the comparison between the respective semantic extensions of the two words "interpretation" and "application".

We sometimes say indifferently that "the Court of Cassation applies law A in a restrictive way" or that "the Court of Cassation interprets law A in a restrictive way"; that "there is a clear tendency to apply law B in a certain way 'x'" or that "there is a clear tendency to interpret law B in a certain way 'x'". We would not, however, consider as interchangeable the expressions "Law P is not applied anymore" and "Law P is not interpreted anymore". We would not consider as interchangeable the expressions: "I apply this law" and "I interpret this law" if a professor of law were to say them. We would consider them interchangeable if they were pronounced by a judge or by an official of the public administration. We can thus say: (a) "interpretation" and "application" have a common area of meaning but there is no total coincidence between the two; (b) the common meaning is particularly evident when the words are used to refer to the activity of judges or officials. So much so that, when "application" is used as "application by the judges and/or officials", one might suspect that application is included within interpretation.

The survey of the partial coincidence of meaning between "interpretation" and "application" can commonly be found in the works of European

2 I refer to U. Scarpelli, "Semantica giuridica", *Novissimo Digesto Italiano* XVI (1969), 978-999.

lawyers and theoreticians of this century. This is irrespective of their theoretical and philosophical position. We consider this a relatively general position. What is not so general is the analysis of the reason or meaning of this coincidence. This is in some sense cultural. In modern legal European culture, it is generally held that every application of laws (or, as it is too often referred to, of "norms") implies an interpretation of those laws. No lawyer, nowadays, seems to believe that it could be possible for a lawyer or for an official to apply a law without interpreting it. If the two operations are not separated then it is assumed that the interpretation is implied in the application or that it consists of the application itself. No one today seems to believe, for example, that there exist laws which are so clear that they do not require an interpretation in order to be applied. Any book or chapter on interpretation starts with mocking the Latin maxim *"in claris non fit interpretatio"*.[3] Thus the assumption is that, when the judges apply, they interpret at the same time.

The belief according to which it is not possible to interpret a law without "applying it" is not general. This explains why the two meanings do not totally coincide. On the contrary, the opposite belief, that it is quite possible to interpret a law without applying it, is the general one. At the same time lawyers hold that the only persons unable to interpret the law for no other purpose but that of applying it are judges and civil servants.

We have emphasised a relatively general and constant relation between the meanings of "interpretation" and "application". We have put forward an equally general underlying concept according to which every application-activity supposes an interpretation-activity while not every activity of interpretation supposes an activity of application. We must now take another step and pinpoint how, in general, the word "application" also has two meanings. These are "application-activity" and "application-product". This enables us to see how, when the word "interpretation" is given the meaning of "interpretation-product", reference is made to interpretations for the purpose of applications. Here this is the interpretation of the judges, of the officials and of all those persons whose interpretations and applications bear important consequences on other subjects' situations. Whose continuous operations carry with them important consequences for the stability and the transformation of the legal system.

3 Its original meaning was not the same as the one usually given by modern lawyers.

These lexical points have come to the attention of formalist and normativist theoreticians of law, as well as to those of a realist or analytic persuasion. All of them have recognised the necessity to draw carefully a distinction not only between interpretation-activity and interpretation-product but also between interpretation-activity and the interpretation-application operated by organs such as judges and officials. Such a distinction gives rise to some therapeutical semantics. It is aware of the fact that the application of the laws by judges and officials is a different operation than the mere attribution of a meaning to the law which is applied. It always implies, however, the attribution of a meaning to the law which is applied. The difference lies in the fact that the application carries consequences for the legal system of the kind that an intellectual interpretation does not carry.

We can go thus far with linguistic and therapeutical semantics. To proceed further, one must enquire into legal doctrine and ideology. Here we are not just surveying language use but also qualifying it. It must be noted, though, that the survey in itself carries with it great ideological importance, however negative that may be. For a survey of the distinction in current legal language and acknowledgement that such a distinction corresponds to a distinction which can somehow be verified through the facts, though not in itself a (legal) ideology, can be used to discredit a certain ideology. In fact, the above distinction discredits the ideology according to which, while applying the law, a judge (and in some cases the officials also) performs a mere intellectual operation and simply behaves like a machine. The distinction between interpretation-activity and application-activity expresses at least the belief that the judge does not always behave like a machine. That application is not always a merely intellectual operation. Contemporary legal theorists usually proceed beyond mere linguistic surveys. They try theoretically to qualify the distinctions found therein. We go on to discuss some of these theories.

Kelsen sees the application of law by legal organs as creation of law. To the product of that application he gives the name "norm" (individual norm). While doing this he uses the same name ("norm") to designate the object of the interpretation (i.e. "general norms") and the product of the interpretation-application. This gives the legal order the appearance of a set of norms which are the object of a continuous process of production: the result of an ever creative production where the internal consistency is provided by a hierarchical relation between norms, according to which the hierarchical superior norm simultaneously delegates the authority to create lower norms and gives legal force to these.

The American realists see the application of law by the judges as being the mode of creation of all law. They deny the name of "law" to documents which are the object of activity-interpretation. They reserve the term "law" for the product of applications which have been verified in the past or which can be foreseen in the future.

Alf Ross also sees the product of application as valid law. Because he gives great value to the underlying motives behind the document's object of interpretation, he builds a particular interpretation theory. Having noted how every interpretation-activity is an activity aiming at elucidating the meaning of a sentence, he sees that there are two methods of elucidation. The first is an elucidation through words ("interpretation through meaning"). The second consists in elucidation through observation of whether «a certain factual course of events "fulfils" the meaning of the utterance so that it may be confirmed that we are confronted with such facts as the utterance refers to» ("interpretation by reference").[4] Or Ross, the "factual course of events" able to verify a sentence designated as a norm is the application-product. Ross's aim is to account simultaneously for two facts. Firstly that the activity of application is always creative and proceeds from a decision, according to which the application-product is "valid law". Secondly that normative documents are a motivating element in the activity of application and, as objects of interpretation-activity, they allow for more or less safe statements about what counts as valid law.

Hart, an analytic theorist, explains the relation between interpretation-activity and interpretation-product through J.L. Austin's theory of performatives. In given circumstances the role of some utterances is not so much that of "saying" as that of "doing". In particular, the purpose of the technical terminology of juridical statements would be to do a particular thing, that is to attribute rights, obligations, powers, faculties. The only purpose of the interpretation-activity is to say that a right, an obligation, a power, a faculty is attributed to someone. The purpose of the application-activity is to allow the attribution of a right; and the application-product is the fact that a right is (has been) attributed.

Except for the American realists, these theoretical considerations confirm the fact that, on one hand, "application" of law by legal organs creates law; on the other hand, the creation of law is set within pre-existing rules and is therefore controllable and somehow foreseeable. Again with the exception of the realists, these considerations go towards

4 A. Ross, *On Law and Justice* (Berkeley: California University Press, 1959).

the representation of a legal order as a "system of norms" (eventually of different kinds). It still remains a "system" and "consistent" however creative is the activity identified with the name of "application".

3. *Traditional Doctrines, or Ideologies, of Interpretation, in Continental European Culture*

Up to now, we have identified four meanings (if this is how we want to call them) of "interpretation": interpretation-activity; interpretation-product; application-activity; application-product. We must now proceed further to clarify some uses not only of the word "interpretation", but also of the phrase "theory of interpretation".

It is common to mock those who, when speaking of Chinese literature, look up, in an encyclopaedia, the two entries, China and Literature. Such procedure appears to me quite sensible. Provided the two entries are well compiled, it could bring very useful results. I therefore think that in this case too it would be useful first of all to note that the expression "theory of interpretation" could prima facie be used to designate four different theories, i.e. that of interpretation-activity; that of interpretation-product; that of application-activity; that of application-product. One should then see whether in fact the expression "theory of interpretation" has been used in these four ways. Would also at least one use of "theory" suit each of the meanings of "interpretation" which have been identified? Before we do that, we must say something about the word "theory".

There is a technical-philosophical use of "theory". According to this a theory is a system of propositions, relating to one object, linked to each other in such a way that if some of them (called assumptions) are true, then all the others are also true. If some of them (assumptions or otherwise) are false, it is likely that the others are also false. Or at least, not necessarily true according to the theory, and that the theory is thereby discredited.

This use of "theory" is not frequently encountered in association with "interpretation" in the European legal tradition of the XIXth and XXth centuries. Here the expression "theory of interpretation" often does not designate theories but doctrines, representations, ideologies. These relate to the nature of the activity of interpretation, and are mainly directed to singling out a strange entity which would be the "correct", or "exact", or "right" method for the performance of interpretative activity. When "theory of interpretation" is used in the context of such doctrines etc., "theory" is not used in the technical-philosophical sense.

We now turn to ideological theories of interpretations or doctrines of "correct" interpretation. The modern doctrines of interpretation have their origin in two schools of jurisprudence which existed at the beginning of the XIXth century; the exegetical school and the historical school. Most professional ideologies of the continental lawyers in the XIXth and the beginning of the XXth century find their origin here. This is certainly true for Italy. In any case, lawyers accept the vocabulary of these schools and, with that vocabulary, a series of unconscious beliefs.

The historical school is the richest example of the way description and prescription are conflated when talking of interpretation. Both schools considered law as a preconstructed reality preceding interpretation. They thought of interpretation as an activity consisting in finding the "true" meaning of such preconstructed reality. For the lawyers of the exegetical school, this preconstructed reality was but the code. For the lawyers of the historical school that reality was a much more complex historical phenomenon, the whole consistent system of the "real" regulation covering all of the legal relations.

The exegetical lawyers were interested in explaining and interpreting the Napoleonic code. Now, such explanation and interpretation were carried out following the order of materials in the code. The order of the books was followed and, within them, the ordering of the titles. This occurred to such an extent that the order of the articles within the title was followed. The work would thus take the literary form of a "commentary". On the other hand, where the order of the titles and not that of the articles were followed, the work was considered nearer to a "treatise" (which was the literary form specific to the dogmatic school). The choice of the treatise form in preference to that of the commentary appeared as a concession to the "dogmatic" method. Better, it was seen as a "mixed" method, somewhere between the strictly exegetical or analytical and the dogmatic.[5]

Preference for the commentary form, or at least techniques close to it, was justified by the principle of the closest possible (or, as it was thought possible, total) adherence to the letter of the code. Where such adherence

5 Writers who chose the pure "commentary" as a literary genre are, for example, Demante and Colmet de Santerre, Marcadé, Troplong. Writers who modify the order of the articles, though maintaining the order of the titles are, for example, Touiller, Duranton, Taurlier and above all Demolombe.

resulted in contradictions (which anyway were considered only apparent), one could, with caution, make an interpretation or explanation according to the intention of the historical legislator. This involved an inquiry into the preparatory works and made use of the technique, born in this context, of the so called "*combinato disposto*" of several articles. Such combination had to be somehow justified. The only possible way of justifying it was, once again, to make sure of the will of the historic legislator, through an inquiry into the preparatory works. This should not be confused with what dogmatic-rationalistic trends called, or should have called, "the abstract will of the law", nor with the historicist "spirit of the law."

The examination of concrete cases was considered not only useful but necessary. The exegetical school's literature presents (contrary to the one of the dogmatic school) abundant case surveys which, as one moves away from the codification, are more and more drawn from the jurisprudence of the courts. As long as the school's activities lasted this was how this attitude towards the jurisprudence of the court did not change. However, the practice changed deeply.

The exegetical school denied categorically that the judgements of the courts and even those of the Court of Cassation could have any wider value than that of *res judicata*. It could not be a binding precedent and therefore a general norm. They also denied any particular authority to a line of cases, however clear. Confronted with the codified will of the legislator, all the interpreters could do was use their skill to carry out historical-psychological research into the will of that legislator. In practice, however, they found themselves to be more and more in agreement with the line steadily adopted by the Court of Cassation. Such agreement, however surprising, was considered to prove simultaneously that the judges' opinion was correct and that the truth was shared by all.

One must make clear, however, that these references to concrete cases, some of which do not come from the jurisprudence of the courts, are not presented "raw". On the contrary, the concrete cases are described in terms of the articles of the code. What the reader is presented with is simply minor premises of syllogisms, the major premise of which is a disposition or the combination of several dispositions of the Napoleonic Code. Thus the case survey, however abundant, conducted by the French lawyers whom we are thinking of, appears, on close scrutiny, to be very poor. It consists not so much of a series of clarifications of real situations, made to explain the field of application of a legal disposition. Rather, it consists of a monotonous repetition of the descriptive part (i.e., the fact-situation or "fattispecie") of the articles of the code. The exegetical lawyers use the following language: "grammatical interpretation"; "logical interpretation" (which is, however, psychological); "restrictive" and "extensive interpretation" (this distinction refers to grammatical interpretation).

The historical school's attitude to interpretation is far more interesting and influential, though more complex. We can reconstruct the broad lines of the attitude, using as a basis the *System des heutigen Römischen Rechts* of Friedrich von Savigny, chapter IV, volume I of which deals with the interpretation of laws.

First of all, Savigny represents interpretation *(Auslegung)* as apprehending the meaning of a law constituted before the act of apprehension (para. 36). Thus he does not see interpretation itself as a group or a system of rules which would fill gaps in the law. On the contrary, he sees it as an activity whose object is the laws. He also denies that the reason for the act of apprehension as well as the social role of those who interpret are of any relevance.

This is extremely important because it determines and conditions all doctrines of interpretation which pandectist lawyers and nearly all the modern schools have been successively fighting over. Savigny writes:

> if this (legal) rule must be translated in practical life...it is necessary that we somehow apprehend its meaning. Such apprehension of its meaning can lead to the most varied applications: for the academic lawyer, to the elaboration of the science in various forms; for the judge, to the pronouncement of sentences and their execution; for private individuals, to guiding in a determinate way their daily relations. The characteristic particularities of such special applications are outside our purpose; but they all share as a common base a determined way of understanding the content of the sources of law ...

namely

> an intellectual operation, that is ... a scientific work, starting point and foundation of the science of law.

This excludes from interpretation and its study any enquiry as to the aims and motives of the various interpretations, and as to the role of the interpreter. It denies validity to study of interpretation unless carried out by "legal science". Just as Savigny entrusts to doctrine the elaboration of the law in force, he also gives to legal doctrine the work of interpreting such law. He also says that interpretation is a work of science, carried out through the use of concepts elaborated by it. This is clearly an ideology. One according to which the right interpretation, or even the true one, is that of science. Such an ideology presupposed, or helped create, a substantial identity of attitudes between legal doctrine (which was in a pre-eminent position), judges and the bar. Finally, one should note that to assign interpretation to a legal doctrine liable to condition judges and lawyers, means to assign it to a particular professional group. A group which, in Savigny's time, was marked with a precise social identity. This meant that any study of law outwith that professional group would be discredited as non scientific.

To accomplish his work, Savigny needed to dissolve the differences between the various methods of interpretation. He needed to discredit those methods which more easily eluded the control of the "doctrine". Firstly therefore, Savigny examined the traditional threefold distinction of interpretation into authentic or statutory, judicial and doctrinal. He excludes authentic interpretation as being something more than a mere intellectual operation. He sees judicial and doctrinal interpretation as doing identical work in so far as they are "scientific". Secondly, Savigny examines the presuppositions, historically recognised, on which to ground the legitimacy of interpretation. These are that there are gaps in the law and that the law is obscure. He denies that there can be gaps in the law. For him however, since the law requires an intellectual apprehension, it must always be interpreted through legal science. Thirdly, Savigny examines the traditional methods of interpretation. These were (a) grammatical interpretation; (b) logical interpretation; (c) historical interpretation; (d) interpretation according to the purpose of the law. Savigny attacks (d). The aims of the historic legislator can be many and anyway are very difficult to discover. He wants the actual legislator to be ignored for the sake of historical continuity. He accepts the other methods but sees them as being aspects and elements of one intellectual process.

To the various methods of interpretation he adds a further method, the systematic. One should rather see this as a further element of the "unitary intellectual" activity, which he names "systematic element". The systematic element "relates to the intimate link which binds all the institutes and all the legal rules into a large unity." This interpretative criterion sets legal doctrine as the arbiter of an operation consisting of attributing meaning to the laws, constructing and reconstructing them according to its own categories. It is being presented by Savigny - one could justly say hypocritically — as being subservient to the legislator, because "such connection came to the mind of the legislator" [para. 33].

It is to the grammatical, logical, historical, systematic elements of interpretation that Savigny reduces his famous unitary intellectual operation. But to this he adds two dogmas derived from what he considers to be the nature of the law. These determine the truth of the result of the interpretation and are that the law must present "these two characters: unity and completeness"[para. 42]. Therefore interpretation eliminates antinomies and fills lacunae. How? By using the "system". Once more the procedure is handed over to the categories of legal science. They establish relations of inclusion and exclusion among the institutes and parts of law (in order to determine the hierarchy of conflict resolving rules) and areas of similarity between relations and institutes (in order to make use of the *analogia legis* and *iuris*).

From all this the following scheme can be established: interpretation is a "scientific" intellectual operation. It makes use (for each law) of the following "elements":

a. grammatical (meaning of the words: technical meaning);
b. logical (meaning of the connections of words);
c. historical (the context of the rule: the motives and purposes of the legislator are excluded);
d. systemic (meaning given by the system, i.e. by the classification of the relations into institutes).

Such a scheme supposes that all the law is consistent and complete. Therefore for every law, interpretation is nothing else but the systematization (devised by science) of all the law in force. Therefore the system of the institutes and parts of the law constitute both the presuppositions and conclusions of interpretation.

The interpretation, or the attribution of meaning, which satisfies all these elements or moments of the interpretation is considered "scientific", "correct", "true". In cases of conflict it must satisfy the hierarchical ordering of these elements. These are: the system of the parts, the system of the institutes, the system of each single institute, the systemic, historical, logical, grammatical element of interpretation, according to a hierarchy which subordinates the legislator to doctrine.

This ideology of interpretation covers what we have called application-product, application-activity, interpretation-product, each coinciding with what we have called interpretation-activity. We are therefore dealing with an ideology which presupposes, or wants to produce, (a) a univocal legal doctrine which gives a system acceptable to all, (b) a jurisprudence dependent on doctrine, (c) negligible law making.

Such a view of interpretation (or, as it has been in the past, the professional ideology of the lawyers) is plunged into crisis whenever there are conflicts within legal doctrine or between doctrine and jurisprudence. Its utility becomes problematic whenever, through new legislation, the sources of law have been badly mishandled. All the so-called sources of the interpretation of the modern times, in continental Europe, are the expression of one or the other of these crises. This is particularly true of the teleological schools, of the 'jurisprudence of interests' and so on, in cases where there is conflict within doctrine or loyalty to a new legislator rather than the old systematization. It also occurs in evolutionary interpretation. Today also, for a whole series of reasons, an analytical attitude, particularly of the neo-positivistic kind, leads to a bullish fight against what remains of the old pandectist army.

4. *Analysis and Theory of Interpretation*

We turn again to our discussion as to the use of "theory". For some time now, "theory", in relation to interpretation, has been used in its technical-philosophical meaning and not as a learned name for doctrine. In particular, one encounters "theory" in this meaning in writings of lawyers. This is especially so if they are neo-positivist, inclined towards an analytical approach. It is often found in the works of lawyers calling themselves neo-positivist, but engaged in propounding a personal ideology of interpretation, or putting new clothes on some old ideology. We will not concern ourselves with these self appointed analysts here. We will instead go on to see if, in relation to interpretation, a "theory" in the technical sense is possible. How and if "theory" is possible in respect of the four meanings of "legal interpretation" that we talked about. These were, interpretation-activity, interpretation-product, application-activity, and application-product. This would involve a system of propositions, linked together according to rules of derivation and transformation which all have as a reference something called "legal interpretation".

In my view, this is possible provided we accept an important limitation. The object of a theory in this sense can only be a phenomenon (simple or complex) capable of empirical study. It could not consist therefore of a duty to interpret unless such "duty" were defined empirically. It could not be the interpretation of the law in general, or that of the rule, unless the words "law" or "rule" were used to designate the actual written form of it, that is a sentence or set of sentences collected in a document or a set of such documents. It would not therefore refer to deciding or attributing meaning but rather to the fact that some determinate person or body had given a meaning to a law or rule. "Theory" here then applies only to interpretation-product or to application-product. The activity of interpretation and application cannot be the object of theory but only, eventually, the aim of ideology.

The need to construct genuine theories, which manifests itself among those of a neo-positivistic and analytical bent, does not embody any particular ideology, but serves to discredit many. This will not directly engender new knowledge, but will help to produce unprejudiced knowledge, unhindered by traditional legal culture. Let me explain. Firstly, the need to construct genuine theories makes it necessary to distinguish between the descriptive and the normative. How interpretation and application do take place (the objects of theory) and how they should take place (the aim of ideology). Thus traditional ideologies of interpretation are discredited in so far as they present themselves as descriptions of a particular (legal) reality. They become objects of research in so far as they are beliefs shared by groups of legal actors. They are therefore *facts*, namely beliefs which produce certain effects in some of the activities of interpretation and application. They are thus internal elements of certain interpretation-products and application-products. But once these ideologies cease to be analytical tools and are reconstructed and studied empirically and theoretically, they have less and less effect on interpretation-activity and the interpretation-product. They become less and less internal elements of interpretation-products and application-products. The scientific attitude has always had liberating effects. In this case it frees one from the belief according to which the job of a legal actor consists, both *de facto* et *de jure*, in following particular methods for the attribution of meaning to documents called laws. While it calls ideological the adoption of any particular method, it submits that choice to the question "for what reasons"?

Secondly, the need to construct genuine theories stimulates empirical research and the theoretical application of such empirical knowledge. Thus there is an increase in the sciences which study legal phenomena as facts. They have little to do, from the point of view of method, with what is traditionally called legal science (though they might have objects of study in common). This latter was a normative science in the sense that it could be reduced to a set of prescriptions or to the professional ideology of lawyers rather than having as an object something constituted by norms. The empirical sciences, on the contrary, come about from the analytical necessity to operate a distinction between description and prescription. They are applied linguistics, applied psychology, and above all sociology of law. On this view, the spreading of analytical attitudes, in particular when inspired by neo-positivism, runs parallel to the need to allot a large portion of legal studies (hence of law Faculties and Departments) to disciplines such as sociology, cultural anthropology, psychology, linguistics, and the history of ideas.

One cannot conclude an essay on the tendencies and influences of an analytical approach to studies of legal interpretation, without mentioning, at least in passing, its tendency to introvertedness (I acknowledge that there is a value judgement here) whenever the historico-cultural context is objectively favourable to such an approach. This tendency consists in using conceptual tools that are analytical only in appearance, in order to remake the old dogmatics or to give them "scientific" legitimacy. This happens in two different ways which differ only in appearance. The first consists in using the symbolic tools of logical theory to formalise old arguments, grounded upon the acceptance of a given system of concepts (the mere fact of presenting in symbolic form a proposition on the necessary content of the right of property does not change the essential character of that proposition). The second consists in carrying out "field-specific" sociological enquiry, where the field is defined by reference to a legal concept belonging to a traditional dogmatic system rather than being defined through stipulating a convention functionally adapted to the research. A "sociological" enquiry into the tendency to increasing length of "interlocutory procedures" would not stop being a dogmatic discourse through the mere fact of being empirical in style.

TOWARDS A MAP OF LEGAL KNOWLEDGE*

by

ENRICO PATTARO

1. *Philosophy and Science*

> The philosophy of law which I have cultivated, and to which I have chosen to devote my university courses, is made up of three parts which I call: a) Theory of law, b) Theory of justice and c) Theory of legal science. If one day I were ever to write a treatise on the philosophy of law (something which is unlikely to come about) I think that it would be divided into these three parts.[1]

These are Bobbio's words in an essay on the nature and tasks of the philosophy of law. Let us briefly see what features Bobbio ascribes to the three disciplines he outlines.

The *theory of law* has the task of analyzing the concept of law. Treading in Kelsen's footsteps, it must be a theory of law understood as legal system, i.e., a set of norms, for "only by understanding the legal system as a whole can we grasp the characteristics of the legal phenomena which are usually called into play to distinguish law from morals or from custom".

The theory of law comprises the following six parts: the composition of the legal system, i.e., the concept of norms and different types of norms, given the fact that the legal system is made up of norms (theory of legal norms); the formation of the legal system, i.e., the theory of the sources of law; the unity of the legal system, i.e., gaps in law and how they can be filled; the consistency of law, i.e., antinomies and how to get rid of them; and spatial, temporal and material relations among legal systems. Bobbio's theory of law is a formal theory as it is concerned with the form of law, that is, the structure of norms and legal systems, not of their

Law and Language, The Italian Analytical School, ed. A. Pintore and M. Jori (Liverpool: Deborah Charles Publications, 1997).

* Translated by Anne Collins and Timothy Endicott.

1 N. Bobbio, *Giusnaturalismo e positivismo giuridico* (Milan: Edizioni di Comunità, 1965), 46.

content.[2]

In contrast, the *theory of justice* is often seen as akin to the theories of natural law abstractly defined *a priori*. For Bobbio, however, the task of the theory of justice is b.1) a comparative study of the criteria adopted by different civilizations in different periods of history to judge right and wrong. In this sense he speaks of the phenomenology of justice within which "justice" signifies a set of values or property or interests which man seeks to protect or augment by making recourse to the social technique we commonly call law.

Alongside Bobbio's historical comparative study of justice we find b.2) an analytical view (carried out with the techniques of analytical philosophy) of the value judgements formulated in terms of justice, developed in the hope that these methods might be used to renew the criticism of the traditional doctrines of natural law.

Bobbio has also claimed that the theory of justice is b.3) the philosophy of law *stricto sensu*, arguing that, since every philosophy is ideological in the sense that it is a system of values on which reality is judged, the philosophy of law is the law's theory of justice, i.e., the determination of the "value at the very basis of legal reality".[3]

Lastly, in Bobbio's view the *theory of legal* science must study the intellectual processes legal scholars adopt to ascertain, interpret, integrate and reconcile the rules of a legal system. It is not just a question of building an abstract model of the science of law to impose on legal scholars, but of analyzing the different types of argument used by legal scholars to draw up a new legal logic, applying the tools of modern logic, from symbolic logic to Perelman's *nouvelle rhétorique*.[4]

To complete the picture, two more disciplines must be added to the first three: legal science and the sociology of law.

Legal science deals with the content of law, i.e., the content of norms and legal systems, whereas the theory of law, as we have seen, is concerned with their form:

> With regard to rules of behaviour, which make up the object of his studies, the jurist is faced with a choice: he can either analyze *rules as such*, or he can focus on their content, i.e with *what is regulated*. The study of rules as such [...] constitutes what is commonly known as the *general theory of law*, but

2 Bobbio, *supra* n.1, at 46-47.

3 Bobbio, *supra* n.1, at 47, 72, 71; *idem*, *Studi sulla teoria generale del diritto* (Turin: Giappichelli, 1955), v-vi, 7-8, 49ff.

4 Bobbio, *supra* n.1, at 55ff., 71.

which, in my view, would be more appropriately termed the *formal theory of law*. The true object of *jurisprudence* proper is the study of the content of the rule.[5]

Lastly, the *sociology of law* is concerned with law as a social phenomenon; in particular, the discipline investigates the historical origin of law, the different stages of its evolution, the function of law as a means of social control, the relation between social development and legal development, the mutual relations between law and society, etc.[6]

Let us now introduce a higher-level conceptual scheme. Bobbio writes: "in Italy at the turn of the century much favour was accorded the idea that the philosophy of law had three tasks: *deontological*, or the theory of what the law should be; *ontological*, or the theory of what law is; and *phenomenological*, or the theory of the evolution of law in society". "This division into three", Bobbio adds, "failed to include a whole series of problems usually considered to belong to the philosophy of law; problems which philosophers of law have appropriated over the years and, in Italy at least, have made their prime subject of study: I refer, here, to the *methodological* problem of legal science [...]. Here, the philosopher of law makes use of the theory of knowledge and logic".[7]

This scheme contains four of the five legal disciplines identified above.

According to Bobbio, the theory of law fulfils its ontological task, but is not philosophy: Bobbio considers, or better, used to consider the theory of law a science,[8] and as such it fulfils the methodological task.

More complicated is his view of the theory of justice, which fulfils three of the above tasks: the phenomenological task, in so far as historical and sociological enquiry pinpoints the criteria and ideals of justice at

5 N. Bobbio, "Scienza del diritto e analisi del linguaggio", *Rivista Trimestrale di Diritto e Procedura civile* IV (1950), 342-367, reprinted in U. Scarpelli, ed., *Diritto e analisi del linguaggio* (Milan: Edizioni di Comunità, 1976), 287-324, at 303, italics in text. English translation: "The Science of Law and the Analysis of Language", in this volume, *supra* pp.21-50, at 33.

6 Bobbio, *supra* n.1, at 46, 53, 38, 72; *idem* ,*supra* n.3, at vi.

7 Bobbio, *supra* n.1, at 53, 54.

8 N. Bobbio, *Teoria della scienza giuridica* (Turin: Giappichelli, 1950), 12-13; *idem* , *supra* n.3, at vi, 8, 34ff., 40ff.; *idem* , *supra* n.1, at 72. Bobbio devoted two university courses to the theory of law: *Teoria della norma giuridica* (Turin: Giappichelli, 1958), and *Teoria dell'ordinamento giuridico* (Turin: Giappichelli, 1960). His more recent writings on legal science and the general theory of law include "Essere e dover essere nella scienza giuridica", in *Studi sulla teoria generale del diritto* (Turin: Giappichelli, 1970), 139-73.

different times in different societies;[9] the methodological task, in so far as it analyzes value judgements, their logical status and the relations between value judgements and factual judgements; and the deontological task *stricto sensu* (which Bobbio also calls ideological), in so far as it determines the values and takes a stand with respect to positive legal systems.[10]

Legal science does not fall directly within the conceptual scheme outlined above.

According to Bobbio, the sociology of law fulfills the phenomenological task. We are faced with *five* disciplines (the theory of law, the theory of legal science, the theory of justice, legal science and the sociology of law), one of which, the theory of justice, comprises *three* parts (sociological, analytical and ideological). This makes *seven* disciplines in all in addition to *four* types of research (deontological, ontological, phenomenological and methodological). I suggest this number be reduced, and the disciplines and types of research allocated between the two fields of philosophy and science. In doing so, I shall pursue some hints involved in Bobbio's works. Philosophy shall include:

(1) the theory of legal science, which studies the concepts and processes of legal science (a methodological task);
(2) that part of the theory of justice which studies value judgements from a logical-analytical standpoint (a methodological task);
(3) that part of the theory of justice which produces judgements and takes a stand on questions of positive law (a deontological task).

Science shall include:

(1) the theory of law, which studies rules, i.e. the form of law (an ontological task);
(2) legal science, which studies what the rules require, i.e. the content of law (a task awaiting definition);
(3) the sociology of law, which studies the evolution and the functions, etc. of the law (a phenomenological task);
(4) that part of the theory of justice which studies the values historically pursued by different legal systems (a phenomenological task).

9 Cf. Bobbio, *supra* n.1, at. 55ff., 71, 73.

10 Cf. Bobbio, *supra* n.3.

2. *Ethics and Philosophy*

In this section I shall tackle some issues in Bobbio's thought concerning legal disciplines falling within philosophy. In the following sections I shall do the same in more detail for some of the disciplines falling within science.

Bobbio ascribes two very different functions to philosophy: methodology and deontology. Strictly speaking, the branch of the theory of justice which applies a logical-analytic, and hence methodological, approach to the study of value judgements should deal with the other philosophical branch of the theory of justice which deontologically formulates judgements and takes a stand on questions of positive law. The two philosophical functions of the theory of justice appear radically different; so different as to give rise to disciplines which are not merely distinct, but which fall within different spheres, to the extent that the deontological function becomes the object of the methodological function.

As is well known, Bobbio takes the idea of philosophy as analysis from neoempirical thought. Most would agree that the deontological branch of Bobbio's theory of justice is ethics or, at least, a part of ethics: legal ethics. The notion of ethics (in the deontological aspect of the theory of justice) as philosophy dates back to a period in Bobbio's thought in which he was yet to be influenced by neo-empiricism, and is found in his university lectures given from 1945 to 1948.[11] From a neo-empiricist standpoint, this concept, found in the neo-empiricist Bobbio, seems difficult to uphold.

Rudolf Carnap, for example, in his *Logical Syntax of Language*, divides the problems arising in any theoretical field into "objective problems" and "logical problems". Objective problems concern the topics of the field under investigation, their properties and their interrelations. For example, in the field of zoology, objective problems are those which concern the properties of animals, the relations among them, etc. Logical problems concern the propositions, terms and theories which have to do with the given subjects: in zoology, for example, the propositions of zoology, the logical connections between them, the logic of the definitions of zoology or of its theories and hypotheses, etc.

Dividing philosophy into objective and logical problems, Carnap reaches the following conclusions.

11 Cf. N. Bobbio, *Lezioni di filosofia del diritto* (Turin: Giappichelli, 1946), 10ff., *idem, Introduzione alla filosofia del diritto* (Turin: Giappichelli, 1948), 44ff., 111ff.

(a) In many philosophies, there are objective problems concerning imaginary topics not found in the sciences: for instance, things in themselves, the absolute, the ultimate purpose of the world, the categorical imperative, ultimate values, etc. These imaginary topics constitute the subject matter of those branches of philosophy known as metaphysics, the philosophy of values, ethics and the like. Thorough analysis shows that these problems are pseudoproblems, in the same way as the subjects they deal with are imaginary topics. The propositions by which such problems are treated are meaningless, i.e. they are pseudopropositions. The statements interwoven in metaphysics, value philosophy, ethics, etc. are simply expressions of feelings which in turn arouse feelings and desires on the part of those who perceive them. Sometimes imaginary objective issues raised by philosophy are poorly formulated questions of logic.

(b) In philosophy, there are also objective problems concerning the subjects studied by the empirical sciences, for example humanity, society, history, language, space, time, nature, etc. These are the subjects of those branches of philosophy known as the philosophy of history, the philosophy of language, natural philosophy, etc. Many philosophers have claimed that philosophy studies some of the topics studied by science, but from a special viewpoint, a philosophical viewpoint. As Carnap observes, however, the specifically philosophical viewpoint from which the subjects of science ought to be studied proves illusory. In point of fact, the study of subjects remains strictly within the confines of science while philosophy provides a logical analysis of science itself and of its propositions, terms, concepts, theories and the like. This means that once again philosophy is left with logical rather than objective problems.

(c) Finally, in philosophy there are logical problems: in logic, applied logic and the theory of knowledge (or epistemology).

From the above considerations it emerges that philosophy can and indeed must be confined to the study of logical problems. Philosophy is the logic of science: as Carnap has it: "the logic of science takes the place of the inextricable tangle of problems which is known as philosophy".[12]

Carnap treats the philosophies of values and ethics as on a par with metaphysics, that is as a set of meaningless pseudopropositions or statements. More generally, neo-empiricism is characterized by a non-cognitivist notion of evaluation and an emotive conception of values.

12 R. Carnap, *The Logical Syntax of Language* , English trans. Amathe Smeaton (London: Kegan Paul, Trench, Trubner & Co. Ltd., 1937), 279.

We may observe that, since Carnap, neo-empiricism has made great advances on the nature of ethical propositions. This is true. I recall, for example, the works of Scarpelli in Italy.[13] Yet the evolution of neo-empiricist thought only allows Carnap's exclusions to be changed in part, and allows Bobbio's inclusive position to be entertained only in part, as far as the relations between philosophy and ethics are concerned.

According to Carnap, ethics is neither a branch nor a subject of philosophy: it is not a branch because it is not logical; it is not a subject because it is not science.

According to Bobbio, ethics (deontology) is a branch of philosophy and is also a subject of philosophy (a subject of its methodology).

For their part the developments of neo-empiricism mentioned above claim that ethics is a subject of philosophy, but not a part of it: ethics is not philosophy.

The evolution of neo-empiricism on the nature of ethical propositions with respect to Carnap's position reveal that ethical propositions have some meaning. More exactly, they do not have only an expressive and emotional meaning, but also a preceptive significance. On the other hand, the distinction, which dates back to Hare, between phrastic and neustic shows that ethical propositions also have a representative semantic meaning.[14] (It remains true, however, that ethical propositions are neither true nor false).

Carnap's distinction between objective problems and logical problems in any theoretical field can be, and in fact has been, reformulated by neo-empiricism in more general terms as follows.

Discourses on extralinguistic topics (things, facts, people, behaviour) are distinguished from discourses on linguistic topics (words, terms, phrases, discourses). Extralinguistic discourses are first degree discourses, whereas linguistic discourses are discourses of (at least) the second degree. It is also said that first degree discourses constitute uses of language or discourses *simpliciter*, while second degree discourses are uses of metalanguage or metadiscourses, or uses of language to talk about language, discourses about discourses.

Developments in neo-empiricist thought have led to a recognition that

13 Cf. U. Scarpelli, *Filosofia analitica, norme e valori* (Milan: Edizioni di Comunità, 1962); *idem*, *L'etica senza verità* (Bologna: il Mulino, 1982).

14 I drafted a new version of the classification of the meanings in "Diritto oggettivo, norme e precetti", *Rivista trimestrale di diritto e procedura civile* XXXII (1978), 690ff.

ethics is a first-degree discourse with preceptive and semantico-representative meaning (as well as being expressive and emotive). It is a discourse which can give rise to logical problems, despite the fact that it is not a scientific discourse, and is thus a discourse on a par with science and can be the *subject* of philosophical clarification. Nowadays, philosophy which has ethics as its subject-matter is commonly called metaethics. Metaethics is also the methodological part of Bobbio's theory of justice which adopts a logico-analytic standpoint to study the value judgements which, in terms of justice, are formulated about positive legal systems.

By contrast, neo-empiricism denies that philosophy can ever be a first degree discourse, as it never deals with extralinguistic matters (things, facts, people or behaviour), but is solely concerned with linguistic entities (words, terms, phrases and discourses). Philosophy is made up of a metalanguage, discourses of at least the second degree, discourses on discourses. In contrast, ethics (Bobbio's deontology) is a first degree discourse on extralinguistic matters: its statements represent (phrastic) behaviours and prescribe them or proscribe them (neustic).[15] Ethics, then, not unlike science, is not philosophy: it is the subject of philosophy, not a *branch* of philosophy or a philosophical discipline.

On the side of philosophy, there thus remains only methodological, logico-analytical and metatheoretical research. When philosophy concerns science it is called the philosophy of science or metascience; when it concerns ethics it is known as the philosophy of ethics or metaethics.

3. *Legal Science Between Hermeneutics and Axiomatics*

Just as Bobbio ascribes numerous disciplines and tasks to philosophy, so he does to science: the ontological task to the theory of law, the phenomenological task to the sociologies of law and justice; and a further, different task (which is not given a specific name) to legal science.

It is the task of legal science which I shall deal with here, following in Bobbio's footsteps in an attempt to define the task or tasks which this discipline fulfils. Bobbio, we must recall, tackled legal science explicitly on many occasions at different times, changing his thought in this regard

15 In the sphere of preceptive discourses ethics qualifies as a further discourse in terms of absolute unconditional duty, establishing ends or asserting (with the naturalistic fallacy, that is to say with moral value judgements) objective values. Cf. E. Pattaro, "Presupposti metafisici e metaetici di un'etica della responsabilità", *Rivista di filosofia* LXXIV (1983), 117-41.

as he came to appreciate the changes which affected the issues which legal science is called upon to resolve. To begin with, I shall refer to Bobbio's views in the Fifties.[16]

In his *Theory of Legal Science*, Bobbio's extensive historical and critical analysis rids the field of a series of classifications of science — of nature and of the spirit, depending on the subject (Wundt, Dilthey, Rothacker); natural and historical, depending on the method (Windelband, Rickert, Croce) — which can hardly be reconciled with a neo-empiricist epistemology. Moreover, these classifications do not serve to define a category of sciences other than natural sciences in which legal science can scientifically be inserted.[17] With this clarification completed, Bobbio then sets himself the arduous task of ascribing to legal science a scientific nature, adopting the tools of neo-empiricist philosophy, i.e. the distinction between empirical (or real) sciences and formal sciences dating back to Carnap, and enhancing the value of the axiomatic method.

Bobbio writes: "The sciences of facts, or, if you like, of reality as far as it is empirically conceived: physics, biology, psychology, sociology, etc. are empirical sciences". By contrast, the analytical propositions of the formal sciences "make no claim on the empirical world", they are tautologies (e.g., "A=A", "2+2=4"), "they tell us how to use certain symbols", once certain conventions have been established.[18] Plainly, since the formal sciences

16 In other words, for the moment I concentrate on Bobbio, "Scienza del diritto e analisi del linguaggio", *supra* n.5, and *idem*, *Teoria della scienza giuridica*, *supra* n.8. Bobbio held different views (later rejected) in "Scienza e tecnica del diritto", in *Memorie dell'istituto giuridico dell'università di Torino*, series II, memoria XXIX (Turin: Instituto della Regia Università, 1934), 1-53; and, subsequently, yet other views, for example in "Essere e dover essere nella scienza giuridica", *Rivista di filosofia* LVIII (1967), 235-62, reprinted in his reprinted *Studi sulla teoria generale del diritto* (Turin: Giappichelli, 1970), 139-73; and "Diritto e scienze sociali", in N. Bobbio, *Dalla struttura alla funzione. Nuovi studi di teoria del diritto* (Milan: Edizioni di Comunità, 1977), 43-61. Cf. R. Guastini, "Norberto Bobbio: analisi del linguaggio e teoria formale del diritto. (I) 1949-1960", *Materiali per una storia della cultura giuridica* VIII (1978), 294-300, 302-305; *idem*, "Norberto Bobbio teorico del diritto. (II) 1961-1965", *Materiali per una storia della cultura giuridica* IX (1979), 535-36; *idem*, "Norberto Bobbio teorico del diritto. (III) 1966-1980", *Materiali per una storia della cultura giuridica* X (1980), 483-91.

17 Cf. Bobbio, *supra* n.8, at 78 et seq., 101-3, 104 et seq., 120 et seq.

18 Cf. N. Bobbio, *supra* n.8, at 137, 138; A. Pasquinelli, *Nuovi principi di epistemologia* (Milan: Feltrinelli, 1974), 58ff., and *Introduzione alla logica simbolica* (Turin: Boringhieri, 1965), 10ff.; R: Carnap, *Formal and Factual*

consist only in analytical propositions, they furnish no concrete knowledge, nor do they have a cognitive function; as Carnap would have it, they lack subjects, they have no objective point of reference, they have no real content. Yet the formal sciences do have an important auxiliary or instrumental function with respect to the empirical sciences, to which they supply the instruments of inference and calculation: logic supplies qualitative instruments of inference, mathematics quantitative instruments of inference.

According to Carnap, the use of synthetic and analytic propositions in scientific research is the following. "Science uses synthetic and analytic statements in the following manner. The factual science establishes synthetic statements, e.g. singular statements for the description of observable facts or general statements which are introduced as hypotheses and used tentatively. From the statements thus established the scientists try to derive other synthetic statements in order, for instance, to make predictions concerning the future. The analytic statements served in an auxiliary function for these inferential operation. All of logic includes mathematics, considered from the point of view of the total language, is thus no more than an *auxiliary calculus for dealing with synthetic statements*. *Formal science* has no independent significance but is an auxiliary component introduced for technical reasons in order to facilitate linguistic transformations in the *factual science*.[19]

Basically, Bobbio agrees with Carnap's thesis, recognizing the instrumental nature of the formal sciences and commenting that "the fact that there exist formal sciences as well as empirical sciences in no way detracts from the empirical nature of science, since they [the formal sciences] do not have a subject matter of their own, but constitute a system of propositions which operate on the sole subject matter of science, of every non-instrumental science, which is an empirical subject".[20] Bobbio then goes on to demonstrate cogently — in very keen and helpful pages, given the confusion which usually surrounds the "form" and "formalism" of legal disciplines — that legal science is *not* a formal science.[21]

Science, in Herbert Feigl and May Brodbeck, eds., *Readings in the Philosophy of Science* (New York: Appleton-Century-Crofts, 1953), 121-28.

19 Carnap, *supra* n.18, at 127 (my italics).

20 Bobbio, *supra* n.8, at 138.

21 Cf. Bobbio, *supra* n.8, at 136-60.

There is not enough space here to retrace Bobbio's demonstration--and this is not really necessary. What is noteworthy is that his theory entails that legal science does not consist of analytical propositions and its task is not one of calculation secondary to the synthetic propositions of logic and mathematics. Having accepted this view, which coincides with common opinion, the only path left open to Bobbio to consider legal science "true science" is that of reducing it to empirical science. Yet Bobbio does not take this path in these essays, but tries to blaze a new trail which leads him to a *special outline of the empirical nature of legal science* and a *special enhancement of its axiomatic method*. I shall tackle both these points.

Indirect confirmation of the problems raised by the notion of empirical science Bobbio proposed for legal science emerges from the fact that he goes so far as to claim that legal science "is not an empirical science", and yet that it is part of the "great family of empirical sciences".[22]

According to Bobbio, legal science "is not an empirical science" because the rules the legal scholar is concerned with "are expressed in propositions which may be described as normative, since they have ideal rather than actual validity. The object of the jurist's research is a set of these normative propositions. It should be noted, however, that the jurist does not observe phenomena like the empirical scientist, nor is he interested in verifying the truth of normative propositions through experience. It is precisely because these propositions are normative, that is they regulate future behaviour and do not represent something that has already happened, that they have a purely ideal rather than an actual truth. Their truth value does not reside in the fact that they can be verified, but in that they correspond to certain ethical principles accepted as criteria to regulate action in a particular society."[23] Two arguments emerge from this passage: (a) legal scholars are concerned with language (the language of rules of behaviour), not facts; (b) moreover, they are concerned with a prescriptive language which cannot be verified. These are two interesting arguments typical of a neo-empiricist approach, which I will return to later.

On the other hand, Bobbio tells us that legal science is part of the

22 Bobbio's two cited claims can be found respectively in *supra* n.5, at 305, and *supra* n.8, at 201.

23 Bobbio, "Scienza del diritto e analisi del linguaggio", *supra* n.5, at 304-6 [Engl. transl., *supra* at 33-34]; cf. *Teoria della scienza giuridica*, *supra* n.8, at 158ff., 168ff.

"great family of empirical sciences". This is because although legal scholars deal with rules of behaviour, normative propositions and hence linguistic entities, their activity presupposes "reference to real behaviour [extralinguistic entities] from which [...] the statement is extracted". Bobbio explains thus:

> that in the case of legal scholars, the language [of the legislator], expressing a given reality, has come between reality [facts, behaviour] and research. What is being studied is not reality per se, but a certain judgment of reality: it is not a question of knowing the real facts, but interpreting the meaning of certain statements [preferably, prescriptions] on reality.

He concludes as follows:

> It is an old prejudice that understanding statutory law requires nothing more than what the statutes themselves furnish and hence that legal dogmatics has no need of experience but is a kind of pure formal deduction from statutes. To understand the meaning of a rule prescribing a given form of behaviour, the interpreter observes real behaviour, just as the historian or sociologist does, and from this knowledge extracts elements that are indispensable to his function as interpreter. Today, this need is commonly acknowledged by legal scholars; they are willing to recognize, as a hermeneutic means to be adopted by the good interpreter, recourse to the so-called 'nature of facts' or 'nature of the regulated relationship', etc. All these expressions reflect the requirement ... that the presumed behaviour envisaged in legal norms be based on the observation of real behaviour.[24]

I can endorse Bobbio's remarks on a legal scholar's way of proceeding. From a neo-empiricist standpoint, what I cannot endorse is the idea that by proceeding in this way, a legal scholar works in the manner of an empirical scientist: that the statements in which he formulates the results of his interpretive activity are the statements of an empirical science.

The empirical scientist works on two levels: observation and theory. By observing individual phenomena, he takes his cue pragmatically "to formulate universal hypotheses and conjectures which he then elaborates rationally, by deductive and inductive inference with the aid of additional satisfactory premises and, if necessary, definitions of the *predictions* consisting in possible results of specific observed or experimental processes [...]. If the results of such processes are positive in many cases, inductively they ensure an adequate degree of confirmation of the hypotheses themselves, allowing the same to be stated as laws or theories. Lastly, once such laws and theories have been established, and after

24 Bobbio, *Teoria della scienza giuridica*, *supra* n.8, at 162, 163, 200, 202, 168, 171, 174, 170, 176, 177 (quotes taken from pp. 201, 169, 177).

having identified the relevant initial conditions, the scientist can use them to *explain* or *predict* phenomena within the field of investigation by inferring them from this or that set of nomological principles at the level of observation or theory."[25]

In legal science, Bobbio claims that the level of observation is displaced by the fact that both the legislator and the interpreter are, so to speak, immersed in society and in history. Here Bobbio broadly distinguishes between two types of empiricism: on the one hand the empiricism of the statements of the natural or social sciences, which describe facts; on the other, the empiricism of the statements of hermeneutic, interpretative disciplines, which do not describe facts, but make reference to past or future events to justify or endorse the interpretations which such disciplines put forward for certain precepts or rules of behaviour.

In contrast, as far as the level of theory is concerned, Bobbio makes much of the method of legal science, depicting it as a model which resembles, as I have already mentioned, the (non formal) axiomatic method.

In this regard, Bobbio drew attention to the fact that the methodology of logical neo-positivism had shifted the emphasis from truth to rigour, construing truth in terms of rigour:

> What makes an argument scientific is not whether or not it is true, whether or not a statement corresponds to an objective reality. Rather its truth value lies in the rigorousness of the sentence in which it is expressed, that is in the consistency of that sentence with the other sentences belonging to the same system.

Bobbio warns that the rigour of scientific language can be achieved only if the rules governing the formation of the system's initial propositions and the transformation rules governing the passage from the initial propositions to subsequent ones are properly established. Rigour can be achieved:

(a) when all the words of the primary propositions of a system are defined, i.e. when all their rules of usage have been established, and the words are never used without respecting such rules;

(b) when the rules by which derivative propositions can be deduced from primary propositions have been established, and no rules other than those established can be used.[26]

25 Pasquinelli, *supra* n.16, at 152, italics mine.

26 Bobbio, *Scienza del diritto e analisi del linguaggio*, *supra* n.8, at 299ff. [above,

In relation to legal science, Bobbio notes that the legislator's language is not necessarily rigorous, and it is the task of legal scholars to make it so by "purifying it", that is determining the meaning of the words which are found in legal precepts. The meaning of a word is determined by establishing rules of usage:

> the set of rules governing how a word is used constitutes the concept corresponding to that word. The concepts of property, writ, mortgage and the like, are given by the set of rules establishing how the words writ, property, mortgage and the like should be used.

Secondly, Bobbio notes that the legislator's language is not necessarily complete, and it is the legal scholar's task to make it so. By assuming that legal propositions (preferably, legal prescriptions) are only those enacted under certain rules by the legislator and those implicit in such prescriptions and hence deducible by means of the rules of transformation allowed by the legislator itself, Bobbio defines the legal scholar's task of "completion" as tracing back to the legal system those precepts which can be traced back (by the rules of transformation allowed) and at the same time getting rid of those which cannot correctly be so deduced. The rules available to the legal scholar include extensive interpretation and analogical extension (which for Bobbio is a form of extensive interpretation).

Lastly, Bobbio observes that the legislator's language is not necessarily orderly, and it is the legal scholar's task to make it systematic: "The development of legal science will demand of jurists enough courage to construe a new systematization of law which draws nothing from tradition merely *qua* tradition, and which takes into account how the meaning of words is dependent upon the context and language in which they are used. The only rules they should adhere to in this systematization will be those pertaining to the language under scrutiny. They would thus be able to develop a consistent and unitary language which would reduce the misunderstandings to the minimum — with obvious advantages for the practical application of law."[27]

Bobbio, it seems, tends to put forward a model of legal science carried out according to the non-formal axiomatic method whose terms are thus

---

31ff] (quotes are taken from p. 300) [31]; *idem* , *supra* n.8, at 213-14, 215-16.

27 Bobbio, *supra* n.5, at 307, 308, 315, 316-17 (quotes taken from pp. 308 [31] and 319 [45]); *idem*, *Teoria della scienza giuridica*, *supra* n.8, at 218, 220, 229-30, 231ff.

endowed with meaning *ab initio*. Moreover, with respect to Euclidean non- formal axiomatics, for example, the method requires that the rules of formation and transformation of discourse be stated, and proposes primary terms and conventional axioms (rather than immediately understandable or self-evident as the primary terms and axioms, as those of Euclidean axiomatics were held to be).[28]

Following this portrayal of the nature of the legal scholar's work at the theoretical level and the considerations outlined above on how legal scholars work at the level of observation, Bobbio reaches the conclusion that legal science *stricto sensu* is neither a formal science nor an empirical science, "yet in some sense, it has something of each". In fact, Bobbio claims, any inquiry which purports to have the value of science "is composed of a part which constitutes the research which makes it an empirical science if the research concerns the events of experience, or a formal science if the research concerns the formal elements of the universe to be investigated and also of a truly *critical* part which consists in the construction of a rigorous language through which alone the research acquires the value of science. The two parts are closely linked and are not, except in abstract terms, distinguishable. A scientific system is usually made up of one and the other. In contrast, the subject matter of jurisprudence [legal science] consists of enacted normative propositions (which are themselves the outcome of prior empirical research which legal

28 As is well known, a distinction is made between non-formal, semiformal and formal axiomatic systems. Euclidean axiomatics is non-formal axiomatics, which briefly comprise the following four operations, of which the first two constitute the basis and the others the development of the axiomatic system: (1) Identifying a class of primitive concepts or terms which would be immediately comprehensible by an act of direct intuition, for example the concept of "point"; (2) Stating axioms or postulates, that is propositions, whose truth is self-evident, for example the axiom that there is one and only one straight line passing through two given points; (3) Defining new terms or concepts on the basis of undefined primitive terms. For example, the definition of "plane" (on the basis of the primary terms "point" and "line") as the set of points enclosed within a line; (4) The demonstration of theorems on the basis of undemonstrated axioms. For example, the demonstration that the sum of the internal angles of a triangle is equal to 180°. The definition of new terms and the demonstration of theorems are done according to rules which, in the case of Euclidean axiomatics, were implicitly the grammar rules of Greek and Aristotelian logic. Cf. S.F. Barker, *Philosophy of Mathematics* (Englewood Cliffs, N.J.: Prentice-Hall, 1964); William Calvert Kneale and Martha Kneale, *The Development of Logic* (Oxford: Clarendon, 1962).

scholars must respect to the point of outright absurdity or scandalous injustice). As such, legal science consists solely in the critical part pertaining to every scientific system, that is to say, the construction of a rigorous language aimed at the fullest possible communication of experience fixed beforehand".

Although it lacks the constituted part, legal science for Bobbio is science "on a par with every other science", for the very reason that its operations "coincide perfectly with the operations, or at least a vital, irreplaceable part of the operations of every other science, and without which no research can claim to have the value of science. These operations, note, are quite simply that complex activity which traditionally constitutes the legal scholar's work, that is, *the interpretation of law*".[29]

This suggestive portrayal of the scientific nature of legal interpretation runs into the objection that was raised by Moritz Schlick when the problem of the importance empiricism and rigour have for the scientific nature of research was posed in general terms:

> anyone seriously taking consistency as the sole criterion of truth must take an arbitrarily invented fable to be as true as an historical account or the laws of a chemistry treatise as long as the fable is so well thought up that there is never any contradiction.[30]

Assuming that the legal scholar's interpretation builds up an axiomatic system, such a system could be taken as science in that it is the product of the axiomatization of either a formal science, made up of analytic propositions, or an empirical science, made up of synthetic propositions, in relation to which it is the function of the axiomatic method to introduce rigour. In contrast, the subject matter of the legal scholar's interpretation, as Bobbio remarks, is neither the analytic propositions of a formal science nor the synthetic propositions of an empirical science, but the prescriptive language of the legislator: this is why the legal scholar's inquiry lacks the "constitutive" part which establishes any research as science.

Just as a rigorous fable is not science, neither is science a rigorous system of prescriptions. Besides, as far as the interpretation of the law is concerned, the opposite thesis leads to a paradox. If rigour (in this case

29 Bobbio, *supra* n.5, at 305-306 (from which all quotes are taken, italics in text); *idem*, *Teoria della scienza giuridica*, *supra* n.8, at 17-18.

30 M. Schlick, "Über das Fundament der Erkenntnis", *Erkenntnis* IV (1934), 79-99.

achieved by means of the axiomatic method) were a sufficient condition to make a universe of discourse scientific, then on completion of the task of purification, completion and systematic arrangement involved in the jurist's work of interpretation, the legal system of a state would present itself as a rigorous linguistic universe. We would paradoxically obtain a system of laws that, being rigorous, would also be scientific, but this would not suffice to make it a rigorous and thus scientific legal science. The axiomatic method alone does not produce science. Quite the contrary: it does not even achieve its secondary scientific potential if the universe of discourse to which it is applied is not the "constitutive", underlying, part of an empirical or formal science.

The two tasks which Bobbio assigned to legal science in his writings dating back to the Fifties, on the one hand to keep the legislator's language in touch with society and with history, and on the other to make the language rigorous, are in fact the tasks legal scholars carry out in interpreting the law. Savigny, for example (in another context, removed from legislation) referred to the first as the "political element" and the second as the "technical element" of law.[31] The point criticized here is simply their being placed in the realm of science: the technical element is not sufficient to make the legal scholar's interpretative activity scientific, while the political element which Bobbio held as (a substitute for) the empirical, observational, element predominates and equates it with the legislator's activity.

In later writings, Bobbio put forward a different definition and classification of legal science and was inclined to claim that legal scholars do *not* know but *make* law, or at least contribute to the process. He writes:

> Together with judge and legislator, the legal scholar is one of the leading figures in the formation and transformation [...] of a legal system; once jurisprudence [the science of law] has been rid of improper models, a critical, or as has been said, realistic reflection on the work of legal scholars shows that despite these models jurisprudence [science of law] has carried out a primary or secondary function to a greater or lesser extent in all legal systems as a *source of law*.
>
> The laws of a system are the tools of the legal scholar's trade, the instruments with which he fulfills his social function, which is to determine certain forms of behaviour as compulsory, prohibited or allowed, and hence to

31 F.C. von Savigny, *Vom Beruf unserer Zeit für Gesetzgebung und Rechtswissenschaft*, in J. Stern ed., *Thibaut und Savigny, Wissenschaftliche Buchgesellschaft* (Darmstadt: Wissenschaftliche Buchgesellschaft, 1959), 79.

> assign rights and duties. Not unlike a craftsman who is part artist, the jurist does not simply find his tools there in front of him, ready for use. To use them he must first go and find them (and sometimes they are far away and hidden), then mould them to his purpose and sometimes even fashion them from scratch with his own hands. Where he does not face all this preliminary work, it is a sign that some other craftsman, that is, some other legal scholar, has already done it.[32]

The most significant novelty to emerge from Bobbio's latest views on legal science is the assumption that legal norms are not bestowed "ready to use", but are moulded, created by the legal scholar "with his own hands". This brings to mind Tarello's distinction between the two meanings of "interpretation": interpretation as an interpretative *activity* and interpretation as the *outcome* of interpretative activity.[33] We have legal texts, documents on which legal scholars carry out their interpretative activity; and we have interpretation, the outcome of that interpretative activity, which consists in stating the existence of certain legal norms.

In point of fact, wishing to establish what, when and where legal norms are and who produces them, we can stretch our horizons further and proceed with our analysis from a wider perspective. It is obvious, for example, that there is a distinction between those who draft and prepare laws (civil servants and expert committees, etc.) and legislators: the former draw up the wording of the law; the latter participate in the formal procedure which leads to the enactment of the law. The fact that legislators may or may not have contributed to drafting the text and the fact that they may or may not know the wording are irrelevant; their task in the complex mechanism of law is essentially that of endowing legal texts with the formality required to make them psychologically operative, that is, so they can be implemented as legal precepts.[34] However, the model of behaviour which ordinary citizens will abide by is not prescribed by the drafters of legal texts alone, or by legislators alone.

A myriad of legal scholars (lawyers, judges, senior civil servants, etc.) interpret the legal texts and even the legislative preparatory materials (interpretative activity) and thus establish that: "this is the legal rule, the norm, the model of behaviour to follow!" (interpretative outcome), thus

32 Bobbio, *supra* n.8, at 146-47, 151, 154 (from which the quotes are taken, my italics); *idem* , *Diritto e scienze sociali*, *supra* n.16, at 47ff. On Bobbio's latest views see Guastini, *supra* n.16, at (II) 535-36, (III) 483ff.

33 Cf. G. Tarello, *Diritto, enunciati, usi* (Bologna: il Mulino, 1974), 403ff.; *idem*, *L'interpretazione della legge* (Milan: Giuffrè, 1980), 39-42.

34 K. Olivecrona, "L'imperativo della legge", *Jus* (NS) V (1954), 451-467.

helping to define and make legally binding the model of behaviour to be followed by society.

Interpreting the language (the legislator's wording in the case in point), ascribing meaning to it, resorting, *inter alia*, as inevitably happens in legal science, to the nature of facts and hence adopting a teleological interpretation (not to mention the infinite expedients of the legal scholar's interpretative activity), is not a scientific, empirical activity. It is not the same as sociological or psychological research into given linguistic uses in a given community, or predicting the impact of certain preceptive statements on the activity of judges (according to Ross's legal science model, for example, irrespective of its inadequacy for the purposes of legal practice).

Interpreting is not describing. Not only is it not describing facts, but neither is it describing the meaning of statements. Interpreting is proposing, *prescribing*, on the basis of given arguments and with a view to certain ends, that certain meanings shall be accorded to certain statements. It is prescribing, as legal scholars do, that new statements be included within the class of statements (in the legal system) of which it determines (prescribes) the meaning.

In particular, in legal science interpretation is interpretation of prescriptive statements (of the legislator's language): it thus consists in prescribing prescriptions. This means that the criterion regulating the proposed interpretation cannot be an empirical criterion. The proposal to accord a certain meaning to a statement may be weighed up by verifying whether the statement, interpreted in the proposed sense, is true or false. The same cannot be said for the proposal to accord a certain meaning to a prescription, because however a prescription is interpreted, it is neither true nor false, but incapable of verification and falsification.[35]

In conclusion, legal science, which studies — as Bobbio remarks — what the rules require, i.e., the content of the law, is not a science which investigates its subject matter by formulating hypotheses and laws from which to infer predictions and explanations that can be subjected to empirical verification or falsification; nor is it a secondary formal science which supplies the tools for the operations mentioned above. It is a science which creates, or shares in creating its subject matter, i.e. the content of legal rules. Because "it is not natural to say that a norm *exists*

35 This seems to me a way of reproposing the arguments Bobbio previously pinpointed. Cf. *supra* n.23 and the relevant passage in the text.

in the same sense as do the objects of physical reality",[36] they are not outside the legal science which studies them, but are to a large extent the product of the legal scholar's activity.

This means that legal science is not a science, even though this term will not readily be ousted; it is too enshrined in current linguistic usage, although there are those who prefer the term "legal doctrine" or "legal dogmatics". *Cum de re constat*, in any case, *de verbis non est litigandum*. Legal science is a practical discipline, more akin to ethics than science in its concepts and method. This will suffice to support the claim that in an attempt to draw a map of legal knowledge, legal science can be classified neither among the sciences nor (plainly) within philosophy.

4. *The General Theory of Law from the World of Science to the World of Politics: "Sociology of Law is Knocking at the Door"*

Until 1966, Bobbio's theory of law was a theory inspired by Kelsen and legal positivism. Yet Bobbio has always maintained a critical position towards legal positivism in a global sense. In this section I shall discuss the scientific nature of Kelsen-inspired theories of law and the appropriateness of placing formal ontological *scientific* research alongside phenomenological *scientific* research. This issue has much in common with the debate between legal positivism and legal realism.

In one of his celebrated courses, Bobbio noted that legal positivism "introduces into the definition [of law] only the element of validity, considering legal norms as all the norms enacted in a given way established by the same legal system", while legal realism takes law to be a "complex set of norms which are actually followed in a given society", introducing the requirement of efficacy into the definition of law.[37] In point of fact, legal positivism cannot, in the long run, avoid the issue of efficacy: in Kelsen's theory, for example, efficacy, if not a requirement for the formal validity of law, is nonetheless a *sine qua non*.[38] In other words, legal positivists must recognize that rules issued strictly according to the

36 Cf. A. Aarnio, *On Legal Reasoning* (Turku: Turun Yliopisto, 1977), 15; but also Hans Kelsen, *Pure Theory of Law*, English trans. M. Knight (University of California Press, Berkeley: 1967), 193.

37 N. Bobbio, *Il positivismo giuridico*, philosophy of law lectures collected by N. Morra (Turin: Giappichelli, 1960-61), 175-76.

38 Cf. M.G. Losano, "Il rapporto tra validità ed efficacia nella dottrina pura del diritto", *Sociologia del diritto* 2 (1981), 5-23.

criteria laid down by a legal system would be nothing more than empty formulae, albeit by hypothesis theoretically consonant with the system, if they were not obeyed by society.

Nonetheless, the champions of legal positivism accuse legal realists who adopt a phenomenological-descriptive standpoint of having an improper or inadequate approach for a theory of law. As Bobbio writes, a legal scholar "in carrying out his activity, approaches law from a *normative* standpoint; before he can study the content of a norm or legal institution, he must ask himself if they are valid, but he does not ask himself if they are effective, that is if and to what extent they have been, are and will be implemented"; instead, the legal positivist theory of law "adapts itself and faithfully reflects the operative approach the legal scholar actually adopts".[39]

Here lies the crux of the debate between legal positivism and legal realism. Do legal positivist theories of law aim to describe the current way legal scholars (whoever they be) conceive of law? Or do they claim, instead, to tell us what law really is (ontological task)? When, for example, Kelsen writes that to say a norm "is 'valid' means that it is binding", is his aim to describe the way in which the average legal scholar "sees" and considers legal prescriptions to be? Or does he aim to explain what a legal prescription is, depict its "reality" and tell what "to be binding" entails.[40] The answer, plainly, is the latter.[41]

The underlying flaw in Kelsen's theory of law is the assumption that validity (conformity in enactment of a prescription to another prescription) makes a norm binding, and the endorsement of the view that bindingness is the distinctive feature of certain prescriptions (of legal prescriptions), or the conceptual generalization of a reality (possibly non-empirical: of the norm as ought) rather than a notion derived from the mental conditioning an individual undergoes in society by means of hypostatization and rationalization. Because of this underlying flaw, Kelsen's legal positivist theory of the validity of law "adapts itself and faithfully reflects the operative approach the legal scholar actually adopts" (even though it is not his aim to illustrate such an approach), but it does not describe the reality of law, which is an empirical social reality. This description is offered, instead, by the realist legal theories which assume a

39 Bobbio, *supra* n.37, at 177, my italics.

40 Kelsen, *supra* n.36, at 193.

41 Cf. E. Pattaro, *Per una critica della dottrina pura*, in AA.VV., *Contributi al realismo giuridico*, I, ed. E. Pattaro (Milan: Giuffrè, 1982), §§2.3 and 3.3.

phenomenological task to be carried out through sociological and psychological research.

Bobbio's position here is quite peculiar. He searches legal positivism for a scientific appraisal of law by distinguishing between ideology, theory and method (approach) in the study of law as follows.

Legal positivist *ideology* is the belief that law, by the mere fact that it exists, constitutes a value and implies that "legal norms must be obeyed per se, as such; in other words, obeying legal norms is a moral duty, moral duty being construed as an internal obligation or according to conscience, that is, due out of respect for the law, as opposed to external obligation or fear of sanctions".

Legal positivist *theory* is what "links the legal phenomenon to the formation of a sovereign power capable of exercising coercion: the state". Concerning the definition of law, such a theory appears as a theory of coercion; concerning the definition of legal norm it appears as an imperative theory; concerning the sources of law it appears as a theory placing statute as the source of law hierarchically above all others; concerning legal system it appears as a theory which considers legal norms united in a consistent and complete system; concerning the method of legal science and interpretation it appears as a theory which considers the activity of legal scholars and judges to be essentially logical.

The legal positivist *method*, on the other hand, implies "a certain approach to the very function of research". This, Bobbio notes, is a "scientific" approach, referring to "the descriptive and explicative sciences", which is why he makes a clear-cut distinction between real law and ideal law, "between law as fact and law as value", between law as it is and law as it ought to be, abstaining from any stance towards observed reality and from any assessment. This approach has much in common with *philosophical* positivism, as it consists in adopting the "positive" method of the descriptive and explicative sciences in the study of law.[42]

Bobbio defends all three of these ways of presenting legal positivism. Faced with having to adopt one as his own, he has this to say: "faced with a clash of ideologies, where no prevarication is possible, then I confess, I still stand for the doctrine of natural law; with regard to method, I am equally positivist, but as far as the theory of law is concerned, I am neither one nor the other".[43]

Legal positivism and analytical philosophy (neo-empiricism) claim the

42 Bobbio, *supra* n.1, at 104-10.

43 Bobbio, *supra* n.1, at 146.

method of *philosophical* positivism as their own. Bobbio claims to be a convinced positivist only insofar as "positivism" concerns method, that is the epistemological orientation which does not really belong to legal positivism, but to philosophical positivism, for instance the contemporary neo-positivist and analytical currents.

The legal positivist theory of law is not a theory of real law, law as it is, a scientific theory as neo-empiricist epistemologists would have it. It may appear to be so, especially if legal positivism is reappraised and corrected, in particular by those who admit the separation between the ideological and theoretical aspects of legal positivism. Here, Bobbio goes further: making reference to the fact that legal positivist theorists distinguish between l*aw as it is* and *as it ought to be*, between positive law and natural and moral law, he even claimed to be able to ascribe the scientific method to the methodology entailed in the research program of legal positivism.

In so doing, Bobbio further revealed that over and above the terms adopted, he essentially favoured a non-evaluative method in the study of law, a method able to produce a theory of law not compromised by ethical or ideological contamination of any kind. That such contamination inevitably intrudes on a legal positivist theory of law emerged when the debate on legal positivism was at its height in Italy: Uberto Scarpelli, Bobbio's most authoritative follower, revealed the ideological position underlying the theory and emerging through the notion of validity and *Grundnorm*.

Scarpelli writes:

> Legal positivism is not only the determination of a criterion of validity for law, the criterion regarding the way laws are produced [...]: the determination of the criterion of validity goes hand in hand with a legitimation of positive law.

Legal positivism "does not lead to knowing the law as it is, law as fact, real law, but only knowing how the formal aspect of law can and must be when certain premises are accepted; it has very close links with dogmatic legal disciplines" which reach "propositions and sets of propositions whose logical nature is not easy to discern, but which are certainly not propositions describing facts". The conditions of the legal positivist model of operations depend "on a decision which is not justifiable within a legal system and cannot be based on ascertaining the efficacy of the system, and implying a political decision, linked to moral and ideological values". The model of the legal positivist theory of law should be shifted away "from the world of science to the world of political activity aimed at building some form of political organizations".[44]

Within the debate which led Scarpelli to make these statements, it is significant that Bobbio admitted that all aspects of the legal positivist model were on the rocks: he declared, "I note that legal positivism is in difficulty not only as an ideology and as a theory, [...] but also as a way of approaching the theory of law".[45] In later years, as is well known, Bobbio went on to put forward a functionalist theory of law which is variously construed as a sociological or phenomenological theory and hence — unlike the formal legal positivist theory relating to the structure of law — a theory which can be reconciled with the neo-empiricist model of descriptive and explicative sciences.[46]

Generally speaking, Bobbio saw the radical social and political changes which led to the transformation from the "laissez-faire" liberal state to the "dirigisme" of the welfare state as responsible for the change of course from the formal theory to the functionalist theory of law. Moreover, Bobbio has not disavowed the recent contribution "to widening and deepening the structural analysis which gave birth to a fascinating new discipline, deontic logic". Instead, Bobbio considers the functionalist theory of law "in addition, rather than in opposition to the structuralist [formal] theory".[47]

These comments, interwoven in Bobbio's writing in favour of a functionalist theory of law, merit some analysis.[48] They are not directly relevant here, but it is noteworthy that in Bobbio's new theoretical perspective "law is not a closed independent system"; it is "a subsystem which lies alongside, partly overlapping, partly clashing with other subsystems, such as the economic, the cultural and the political": "what

44 U. Scarpelli, *Cos'è il positivismo giuridico* (Milan: Edizioni di Comunità, 1965), 77 (see also pp. 53-89, 127-34); *idem*, *Risposta di Uberto Scarpelli* , in AA. VV. *Tavola rotonda sul positivismo giuridico* (Pavia, May 2, 1966) (Milan: Giuffrè, 1967), 81-83, 84. Cf. E. Pattaro, *Il positivismo giuridico italiano dalla rinascita alla crisi*, in Scarpelli, *supra* n.5, at 469-76.

45 N. Bobbio, "Intervento di Norberto Bobbio", in AA.VV., *supra* n.44, at 73.

46 Cf. N. Bobbio, "Teoria sociologica e teoria generale del diritto", *Sociologia del diritto* I (1974), 9-15, and his essays collected in *Dalla struttura alla funzione, supra* n.16; R. Guastini, "Norberto Bobbio teorico del diritto. (III)", *supra* n.16, at 496ff,. and bibliography cited at 498.

47 Bobbio, *supra* n.16, at 7-8.

48 Cf., for example, V. Ferrari, "L'analisi funzionale in sociologia del diritto. Problemi terminologici e problemi metodologici", *Sociologia del diritto* 1 (1980), 43-70.

distinguishes this subsystem from other subsystems with which it constitutes the social system as a whole, is its function".

This view of law, insofar as it is the subject of a general functionalist theory, is plainly different from the theory which led Bobbio to claim in the Sixties that the pure, formal, Kelsen-inspired theory has — as an inquiry about the concept of law — an ontological task (which is nonetheless scientific) in dividing up legal knowledge. The move towards functional analysis "did not come about without the direct contribution of sociology" wrote Bobbio in 1977. The passage from the structural theory to the functionalist theory of law in Bobbio's thought in the wake of the expanding welfare state "is also the passage from a formal (pure!) theory to a sociological (impure?) theory": "you can hear sociology of law knocking at the door".[49]

5. *Law Restored to Ethics*

At first sight, tracing a map of legal knowledge, as I have attempted to do in these pages in Bobbio's footsteps, may leave an impression of having impoverished the world of legal discourse. I have expunged deontological research from the philosophy of law and banned legal science and the general (formal) theory of law from the realm of the sciences. The sociology of law lies ready, lurking in the wings, coveting the aspirations of Eighteenth century positivists, to appropriate the tasks and research areas of ancient and noble disciplines.

On a more thorough analysis, it should be clear that far from being reductive in the name of an abstract methodological rigour or a flat empiricism, the marking out of boundaries in these pages has taken another discipline, ethics, away from philosophy and from science and restored it to its rightful place: ethics, the discipline which legal positivism and neo-positivism had compressed and usurped at one time or another.

If the formal theory of law decides to moor in the harbour of deontic logic or some logic of normative discourse, it will be a discipline instrumental to ethics in the same way as logic is instrumental to the empirical sciences.

Law and legal science, only in part divergent, belong to the great realm of ethics, ethics construed in the broad sense as the whole of all

49 Bobbio, *supra* n.16, at 8-9.

discourses (moral, political, legal, etc.) whose prescriptions are aimed at practice, that is, behaviour. To attain their practical ends, law and legal science can make use of logical instruments without becoming scientific discourses by so doing, but rather making such logical instruments contribute to the practical preceptive function of law.

Whenever the general theory of law, which claims to be formal and yet to fulfil a purely ontological task, fails to explicitly take the guise of a discipline instrumental to ethics, especially to law and legal science to achieve their practical aims, it will nonetheless carry out the same function in disguise and doubtless with less rigour: the function which, albeit concealed, places the theory of law within the world of political activity, to use Scarpelli's expression. This presumably pure formal theory, neither sociological nor ideological, in Kelsen's sense, but specifically legal, has nothing in common with the descriptive and explicative sciences. It is not affected by the results which are obtained, nor does it influence them; it has its own method, which is not that of the descriptive and explicative sciences; it has its own subject, the *Sollen*, which does not belong to the empirical world of phenomena, but, as its most consistent followers would have it, to the world of the spirit. "Ich bin nicht Monist", Kelsen wrote, "sehe Ich keinen Weg der über den unleidlichen Zwiespalt hingwegführt zwischen Ich und Welt, Seele und Leib, Subjekt und Objekt, Form und Inhalt": law belongs to the dimension of the id, soul, subject, form.[50]

To deal further with legal positivism, which is what we are mainly concerned with, because it conceives as "true" science both legal science and the formal theory of law, other well-known statements by Kelsen spring to mind:

> the definition of law as norm and ought is not [...] without a certain ideological element [...]. The pure theory of law makes every effort to rid this definition of such elements, that it tries to separate totally the concept of legal norm from that of the moral norm from which it arose and guarantee the autonomy of law vis-à-vis moral law: by defining law as a norm [...] and by limiting the science of law to the cognition and description of legal norms [...] the law is delimited against nature, and the science of law as a science of norms is delimited against all other sciences that are directed toward causal cognition of actual happenings; [...] uncritically the science of law has been mixed up with psychology, sociology, ethics, and political theory. This adulteration is

50 H. Kelsen, *Hauptprobleme der Staatrechtslehre. Entwickelt aus der Lehre vom Rechtssatz* (Tubingen: Mohr, 1911), v-vi. Cf. Pattaro, *supra* n.41, at LXII-LXX.

> understandable, because the latter disciplines deal with subject matters that are closely connected with law. The Pure Theory of Law undertakes to delimit the cognition of law against these disciplines, not because it ignores or denies the connection, but because it wishes to avoid the uncritical mixture of methodologically different disciplines (methodological syncretism) which obscures the essence of the science of law and obliterates the limits imposed upon it by the nature of its subject matter.[51]

Kelsen's thesis that a pure, normative, specifically legal and yet *scientific* theory and science of law can be created is an epistemological error, because these disciplines do not contemplate "potential falsifiers", that is particular propositions to be accepted following empirical observation contradicted by universal propositions within the system: the dogmatic legal positivist theory of law and legal science cannot be confuted and are thus not scientific.

The mistake in believing them to be "true sciences" also leads to conclusions incompatible with non-cognitivist metaethics, such as that adopted by Kelsen himself and by so-called analytical legal positivism which after Kelsen coincided with neo-empiricism, especially in Italy. Some of the important effects of this error are a notion of positive law as the only ought, that is to be objectively verifiable and, at the same time, the exclusion of law from the realm of ethics.[52]

In contrast, consistent non-cognitivist metaethics cannot admit values which are objectively verifiable as values: even less can it admit values which are objectively verifiable as values because, being "positive", they are somehow linked to facts. To admit this would be to contradict divisionism, which is the central tenet of ethical non-cognitivism: one cannot consistently be a non-cognitivist and subjectivist with regard to ethics and a cognitivist and objectivist with regard to law, and even less so with regard to positive law, if law is construed normativistically as ought as opposed to being.

Law and its normative disciplines, like hermeneutic-dogmatic legal science and the general-formal theory, trace back to that part of the theory of justice which Bobbio termed ideological because they too are preceptive, deontological, broadly speaking ethical universes of discourse: the domain of neither science nor philosophy.

51 Kelsen, *supra* n.36, at 75.

52 Cf. Pattaro, *supra* n.41, at LXXIff., LXXX-LXXXI; as regards positivist morals, *ibid.*, LXXIV n.60.

THE RULES OF THE PICKWICK CLUB: A MODEL FOR THE THEORY OF LAW

by

GAETANO CARCATERRA

§1

One advantage offered to the theoretician by legal pluralism, is that it allows him to study the general structure of law in borderline cases represented by extremely simple models. For example, in the case of a small club, provided with legal instruments totally independent of State law, unable to use physical coercion, its ultimate sanction being expulsion. Let us consider one of these elementary cases. To help us identify it with a familiar name and a familiar appearance, let us call it the Pickwick Circle (PC).

What would be the minimum amount of rules needed for such a circle?

To form such an entity, it is first necessary to determine its membership, what the behaviour will be required of that membership and what sort of sanctions to introduce. Sanctions are either behaviour demanded of the membership, or in the last resort consist of expulsion. They thus have an effect on the *status* of members of the club. The fundamental dimensions of the club appear to be two, its *social structure* and its *code of conduct*. Two corresponding groups of norms are therefore necessary, in line with the two dimensions. There is a clear parallelism between them. By the norms of social structure, we establish which subjects become members of the Circle and under which conditions their membership ends (an expulsion rule, for example). Equally, with the code of conduct we establish what behaviour is prescribed within the Club and under what conditions it ceases to be so prescribed (an abrogation rule, for example). Within the constitution itself, one can prescribe some aspects of membership or behaviour, or leave it to the future decisions of appointed organs, such as the members' General Assembly.

The parallelism between the two groups of norms stops here. Should

Law and Language, The Italian Analytical School, ed. A. Pintore and M. Jori (Liverpool: Deborah Charles Publications, 1997).

one wish to limit as much as possible the content of the constitution, as far as the code of conduct is concerned, we can delegate the power to prescribe conduct to the Assembly. This cannot be done as far the social structure is concerned. Before we can delegate the nomination of new members and the establishment of the code of conduct to the members' General Assembly, we will have to establish directly a minimum number of members (say three) allowing the initial functioning of the Assembly.

We can now imagine that the PC enters into history by way of a Statute made of few essential provisions, laid down by Samuel Pickwick himself. We can also imagine that Pickwick has introduced the Statute itself with a simple declaration, a sort of article O, which, though not a presupposition of legal science but an utterance positively expressed, assumes the role of basic norm of the order. Or at least, it has one of the most important functions of a basic norm, that of serving as an identifying and unifying principle for all the valid rules of the system.

art. 0: the rules of PC are the following(this declaration is then followed by the text of the Statute in five articles)

art. 1: the members of PC are Samuel Pickwick (P), Joseph Smiggers (S) and Tracy Tupman (T);

art. 2: whoever is declared a member by the members' General assembly is also member of the CP;

art. 3: whoever refuses to abide by the rules giving the obligatory code of conduct and is declared by the General Assembly as not belonging anymore to the CP, will cease to be a member;

art. 4: conduct which the Assembly declares as such is obligatory;

art. 5: conduct which the Assembly declares not to be such anymore, is not obligatory.

Art. 0 should be interpreted as referring not only to articles 1-5, but also to the rules logically implied, either immediately (for instance: "Tupman is a member of the PC") or on the basis of given facts (for instance: "Winkle is a member of the PC" if he has been declared as such by the Assembly). Art. 5 is a rule for explicit abrogation. The hypothesis of implicit abrogation is disregarded (this is a highly complex matter, as C.E. Alchourrón[1] and E. Bulygin have demonstrated). Other minor norms are also disregarded, though, in fact, necessary for the actual functioning of

1 C. Alchourron and E. Bulygin, *Normative Systems* (Wien: Springer Verlag, 1971).

the association (for example norms regarding the nomination of the President of the Assembly, the voting system which we suppose here to one of majority, when the Assembly is first to be convened, etc.).

Articles 1, 2 and 3 are the structural norms, direct or delegating (art. 3 should be interpreted as a discretionary sanction which the Assembly can, but is not compelled to, apply when the necessary conditions are fulfilled). Articles 4 and 5 are norms of behaviour, purely delegating. Art. 3, however, is somehow a hinge norm between the two groups, being a structural norm and yet the supreme sanction for all behavioral norms, in addition to the sanctions which the Assembly establishes for each behavioral duty according to art. 4. The Statute could have been limited to articles 1 and 4 though its social structure would have been rigid and temporally limited. Its code of conduct could, at the very most, be widened by accumulation: articles 2, 3 and 5 secure, in principle, its future existence and give it the widest capacity for change.

What has not been expressed in the Statute but is usually referred to in the preamble is the context of values within which the Club is located, the beliefs, attitudes and dispositions which those part of that world share. This includes, besides its founder and the present members, others who by virtue of sharing the same values and expectations are potential members. It is only by reference to these values that expulsion has any meaning. It is only the wide gap existing between the actual and the potential members that constitutes a permanent source of vitality for the Club.

§2

What is the nature of the Statute's norms? When considered one by one, they reveal a clear difference between behavioral norms and norms of social structure, or even between behavioral norms and all the other norms. The case of art. 4, *prima facie* at least, is simple. Assembly decisions adopted on its basis aim at setting obligations and can therefore be conceived of as imperatives or prescriptions. Learning, prescribing, setting duties and obligations appear to be correlative acts. As art. 4 sets these obligations indirectly it can then be seen, in its turn, as a rule setting a duty to comply with the obligations set by the Assembly. As a prescription to abide by its prescriptions (obey the Assembly's prescriptions). Such a prescription is clearly generally addressed to the Club's members.

Though a behavioral norm, art. 5 is not aimed at setting obligations but at abolishing them. It cannot, therefore, be explained in the same way. We have pointed out the analogy between art. 5, excluding obligations, and art. 3, excluding members. One can also note that art. 3 is a rule of social structure, homogeneous with articles 1 and 2 which create members. "Such a disposition is abrogated", "such a person has ceased to be a member of the Club", "Tupman is a member of the Club" have all the same nature. The question that has to be asked then is what is the nature of art. 1.

Art. 1 says "Tupman is a member of the PC", though this does not set any obligations and therefore does not prescribe anything either for Tupman or for the others. It is true that by becoming a member of the circle, Tupman takes on a commitment to observe certain rules of conduct. But these are other rules and not art. 1 which in itself cannot be either obeyed or disobeyed. It could not be said, either, that art. 1 is a prescription because together with other rules, for example with art. 4, it does produce obligations. This would be a confusing argument (as if one could say that the sentence "potatoes contain starch" is a prescriptive rule because, together with the sentence "do not eat food containing starch" one can get a prescriptive rules "do not eat potatoes"). Though Tupman's duty to obey the Assembly's prescriptions stem from the conjunction of art. 1 and 4, its imperative meaning depends only on art. 4.

It is far easier to concede that art. 1 is neither descriptive (of what exists independently from it) nor prescriptive (of what should be) but *immediately constitutive* of what art. 1 itself says. Legal thought has often come to the constitutive function intuitively.[2] It has been able to explain a remarkable number of rules of law.[3] Suppose that Pickwick has founded his PC on January 1st, 1820. It might be that the day before Smiggers had suggested: "Tupman should be a member of the PC". This would have been a prescriptive proposition *de jure condendo*. Having learned on January 2nd that such had been Pickwick's decision, he could have stated: "Tupman is a member of the PC". This was a descriptive

2 See the concept of *"Bestimmung"* in A Reinach and K. Larenz. One can see connections with the notions of *"constitutive rules"* of Searle and Ross.

3 For more on this and other similar norms attributing *status*, abrogative norms and the fundamental norm, see my essays *Le norme costitutive* (Milan: Giuffrè, 1974, temp. ed.), and *La forza costitutiva delle norme* (Rome: Bulzoni, 1972); I do not deal, there, with eidetic-constitutive norms and other norms the different character of which has been demonstrated by A.G. Conte.

proposition *de jure condito.* But the legislator can speak neither prescriptively de *jure condendo* nor descriptively *de jure condito*: when, on January 1st, Pickwick said "Tupman is a member of the PC", he must have used the proposition in a third sense, giving a constitutive meaning to what the previous day could only be prescribed and the day after, could only be described — he has used it *jus condens.*

Legal language designates perhaps more frequently the constituting act with terms such as *establish* (thus Pickwick established that Tupman should be a member of the PC). The difference between descriptive, prescriptive, etc. sentences has been represented, in the world of symbols, with special signs (for example "so" for assertions and "!" for prescriptions). In everyday language it is represented by the moods of verbs, typically with the indicative for the descriptive and with the imperative for the prescriptive function. The constitutive function cannot be represented either with the indicative, descriptive, or the imperative, prescriptive, but in practice hovers between one and the other. This is because it has immediate effects and is similar to a *fiat.*

Here, when I want to emphasise the constitutive character of a proposition, I shall use the indicative or the imperative tenses but followed by an asterisk. Thus "Tupman is* — should be* — a member of the PC" represents Pickwick's constitutive act. Such expedients *express* the particular acts of assertion, prescription and constitution or disposition.[4] An equivalent representation, which we shall not consider here, would consist in using terms which not only express but also *designate* those acts ("I assert, I prescribe, that Tupman shall be a member of the PC": in this case, we would deal with special classes of performatives or with those propositions which Russell considered true by definition because they indicated what they meant).

Articles 2, 3 and 5 can also be explained in constitutive terms. And the same can be said of art. 0. "The rules of the PC are* (shall be*) these" corresponds perfectly, in its function of constituting a set of rules, to the "the members of the PC are* (shall be*) these". Is however, possible to give an alternative explanation of art. 0 in prescriptive terms, as we shall see in a moment.

The fact, however, that the founder, or the legislator has laid down five or six sentences does not bind the legal theorist into thinking that the order has exactly five, or six, (basic) rules. They are only the material

4 For a discussion of modalities in a wider sense, see Prior's "*logical terms in a pragmatic capacity*" or Hare's neustic.

which he can reconstruct into complex, more basic structures even though in content the same. The two fundamental dimensions of the order are the code of conduct and the social structure (see §.1). Each of them can constitute a privileged point of reference. Two different reconstructions of the Statute are therefore possible. They can take, as the *definiens* of the legal reality either the code of conduct or the social structure. The first one corresponds to a strictly normativist conception, while the second one to a conception which can be called institutionalist. Though both will be treated here in a perspective which can be broadly said to be normativist. The normativity of the Statute and its interpretations will be maintained as presuppositions of both reconstructions.[5] It is interesting to note that the original statutory material can be remade into a normativist reconstruction or into an institutionalist reconstruction by using two principles of reduction.[6] They are respectively, the principle of elimination of fragments of norms, and the principle of elimination of the so called primary norms (secondary in Kelsen's terminology). Where can constitutive norms be situated in such reconstructions?

§3

Normativist reconstruction tends to put on the first level norms imposing certain conduct, determinate or to be determined, and to consider other norms not as self-standing but only as fragments or parts of the real norms. Schematically, one could present the principle of reduction of fragments of norms as follows: "As are Bs" + "Bs have a duty C" = "As have a duty C". For example, art. 1, "P, S and T are members of the PC", and art. 4, which, as we have seen in § 2 can be given the meaning of ""members of the PC must obey the prescriptions of the Assembly", can disappear and be reconstructed as a norm "P, S and T must obey the prescriptions of the Assembly". If we consider the third rule ("As have a duty C") as the recapitulating and essential norm, we notice how the original norm, which in itself did not imply any obligation ("As are Bs"), has no other function than that of spelling out the conditions of validity. In particular, the conditions of subjective validity, i.e. the

5 Such encounters between normativism and institutionalism are possible, as N. Bobbio, W. Burckhardt, M.S. Giannini and many other theoreticians have shown.

6 Used in particular by Kelsen and Ross.

recipients (As), of the obligations set by the real norm. By the systematic application of this reducing principle to articles 1-5, the whole Statute can be translated into a single, complex, rule of obligation. In substance, this is art. 4 and could be designated as art. 4-bis. It spells out the conditions of validity of the obligations and thus absorbs the criteria of articles 1-3 (recipients) and of art. 5 (absence of Assembly's abrogative decisions):

art. 4-bis: the members of the PC — i.e. P, S, T and those who have been declared members of the Assembly and have not been expelled for having refused on several occasions to adopt prescribed conduct — are obliged to obey the prescriptions which the Assembly has not abrogated.

Art. 0 is reduced to a means of establishing the validity of art. 4-bis within the order. Since one of the meanings of "valid norm" is that of "norm which must be observed", art. 0 can be worded as follows:

art. 0-bis: art. 4-bis must be observed.

Art. 4-bis, together with art. 0-bis, to which all the rules of the Statute have been reduced, can be considered as a typical normativist reconstruction of the given order. In it there are only norms directly spelling out obligations or conduct. They are therefore liable to be interpreted prescriptively, while all the norms of social structure or those implying in themselves no obligation — and therefore any constitutive norm — have disappeared. They have been absorbed and turned into particular clauses of the reconstructed prescriptive norm. Such a model requires, though, some touching up.

First of all of art. 4-bis. This article raises to a legal obligation any conduct prescribed by the Assembly. It therefore turns any prescription by the Assembly into a valid norm. However we need to introduce some distinctions. We know, for instance, through its records, that the Assembly used to address simple invitations to its members, for example that of sending, from time to time accounts, written accounts of their trips or researches. Such invitations equalled prescriptions but did not created real obligations and did not become, legally speaking, norms of the Pickwickian code and order. We shall therefore read art. 4-bis with this restriction. A member of the PC must obey those prescriptions which the Assembly lays down with the specific intention of introducing them into the normative code and order of the Club.

This is not particular to Pickwick's law. A parliament can approve a motion inviting the Government to do a certain thing which creates only a "political" commitment. It can instead approve a law legally binding the government to adopt the same conduct. Among private individuals also, two persons can reach a friendly agreement on certain reciprocal conduct, outside any legal bond. They could, if they chose, legally bind each other to follow that same conduct through a legal agreement. From the parliamentary motion and the friendly agreement, as well as from the invitation addressed by the Assembly of the PC, stem prescriptions and not rigorous legal obligations. Therefore there is in the legal obligation something more specific than the simple prescription. What that something is, is quite clear. The friendly agreement does not create legal bonds because while it does contain the intention to prescribe conduct, it does not include the *intention to create legal relations*, that is the will that behaviour should then become prescribed *within* the order. The characteristic element of the private or public normative act — contract, law and an obligation laid down by the assembly of the PC — is the intention that that prescription become valid or part of the normative order. It is not the wish that such a prescription exists as would be the case in those who lobby the legislature to introduce such a prescription in the code. Rather, it is the intention of the legislature itself, not *de jure condendo or de jure condito* but *jus condens*. Thus the intention of the legislature transforms the norm into something constitutive of the order of which it is part. The normative act which imposes a legal obligation has neither the sense of a mere and direct prescription ("one should adopt a certain behaviour") nor the sense of ethical-legal evaluation ("such prescription ought to be part of the normative order"). Rather it has the specific meaning of a dispositive act as to the consequences desired: "such a prescription belongs* (should belong*) to the normative order — is* (should be*) valid in the normative order". One can see this formula used in many cases by the legislature: "such an article is* added to the code". We are not talking of a simple prescription but of the disposition of validity of a prescription.

Thus, it is technically wrong to say that one has a legal obligation to observe, in general, the prescriptions of the assembly. Because by doing this one would make legally binding pure invitations, recommendations, motions, etc. Those prescriptions which are legally obligatory are the prescriptions which have the meaning of a disposition of validity in the sense we have defined. Thus art. 4-bis must be re-worded as follows:

art. 4-ter: members of the PC (more exactly those subjects indicated in 4-bis) are obliged to obey those rules that the Assembly has laid down as being part of (valid in) the normative order of the PC and has not abrogated.

But also art. 0-bis is largely inadequate to explain the principle of identity and unity of the valid norms. We need to look at another essential meaning of "valid norm", that is "norm which is part of a legal order". Secondly, if art. 0 ought to identify and give unity to norms valid in such a sense, we cannot just say that the norms are valid because derivable from art. 4-ter. We have to say that the norms derivable from art. 4-ter form the *totality* of valid norms, that is of the norms belonging to the order. More important than being a prescription, as art. 0-bis is, a principle of identification and unity —a basic norm— has to be a definition of the set of norms which compose the order. Thus art. 0-bis has to be split in two and reformulated as follows:

art. 0-ter (a) The normative order of the PC is the set of norms derivable from art. 4-ter.

(b) The norms ought to be observed.

Since the norms derivable from art. 4-ter are the prescriptions explicit and implicit approved by the Assembly, art. 4-ter and 0-ter together give us this normative definition (ND) of the order:

ND: (a) The normative order of the PC is the totality of prescriptions (implicit and explicit) that the Assembly has at any time laid down as being part of (or valid in) the order itself and has not abrogated;

(b) These prescriptions ought to be observed by the members of the PC (the subjects indicated in 4-bis).

We can see that ND defines either a (total) legal system or a momentary one,[7] more precisely the one by means of the other. It directly defines each moment of the normative order. Indirectly it determines the concept

7 Alchourron and Bulygin in *Normative Systems*, *supra* n.1, make a similar distinction.

of a total order, either as a succession of momentary orders or their union (that is as the class of all prescriptions, abrogated or not, valid at each moment).

Clause (b) in ND is prescriptive whereas clause a) is not. We have supposed that art. 0, with the entire Statute, was not an act of *jus condendo* nor production of an act *jus condito*. Rather it was an act by the founder himself as *jus condens*. NDa) and its logical equivalence have an equivocal constitutive function: the order is* this set, is* formed in such a way, only all those particular prescriptions, such as art. 1: "Tupman is* a member or belongs* to the PC" belong* to the order. The order of the club is such because Pickwick has defined it in such a way. We often encounter this sort of definition in literary or scientific work. The author of a scientific system can say: "the system is such and such". Kelsen says "the Pure Theory of Law *is* a theory of positive law". Here there is no prescription or taking something already created. Here we find constitutive definition (creation). In a complete and adequate normative reconstruction both of the content and basis (clause b of DN) of the order one can see prescriptions. But each act of normative production (the deliberations of the Assembly) and the fundamental and originating definitions ought to be thought of as constitutive in nature.

§4

One can also do an institutional reconstruction of the Statute. This is, in a sense, even more natural than a normativist one. A club can be seen straightforwardly as an institutional reality, defined as a particular set of people. We can say many thing about the club. For the most part we cannot do this without referring to norms, even prescriptive norms but the object to which all this is applied is a social group. The principle of "reduction", absorbing the primary norms into secondary of obligation and sanctions[8], can also benefit this institutional reconstruction. We can show this schematically: "As have an obligation to adopt behaviour C" + "Those who do not adopt behaviour C must (can) be punished with sanction S" = "Those who do not adopt behaviour C must (can) be punished with sanction S". Now, such a relation exists between art. 4 and art. 3. Therefore art. 4 can be absorbed by art. 3. We can go further. We have taken art. 4 into account by simply replacing "obligatory" by "declared as

8 See §2.

obligatory by the Assembly". We can also take art. 5 into account by making clear that no abrogation has taken place and art. 5 then becomes superfluous. We now have:

art. 3-bis: whoever has been declared by the Assembly as having ceased to belong to the Club for having repeatedly refused to follow the conduct made obligatory by the Assembly itself, and not abrogated by it, ceases to be a member of the PC.

The principle of the reduction of fragments of norms transforms the Statute into only one norm of conduct, art. 4-bis or 4-ter. In the same way, the principle of absorption into sanctioning norms transforms it entirely into norms of social structure, all of them constitutive (cf. §2). It simply transforms it into arts. 1 and 2 which lay down the conditions of PC membership and into art. 3-bis which lays down the conditions of the loss of such status. Previously the function of the norms of social structure was that of determining the conditions of applicability and in particular that of determining the addressees of the unified norm of conduct art. 4-bis or 4-ter (which made up the whole of the Statute). The roles are now exactly reversed. The norms of conduct help to determine what the conditions of expulsion are. To those conditions the structural norm art. 3-bis can then be applied.

After the absorption of the norms of conduct, the Statute is reduced to articles 1, 2 and 3-bis. These articles can, in their turn, be summed up in one and only one rule. This has, if we take art. 0 into account, a definitional and constitutive character parallel to ND. As we showed in §3, this article, because it expresses a principle of identification and unity, should be seen as defining all the norms to which it refers. Thus, within the institutional reconstruction with which we are dealing, art. 0 says that articles 1, 2 and 3-bis — laying down who is (becomes) and who is not (ceases to be) a member of the Club — form the totality of the norms regulating the Club itself. This then means that, on the basis of art. 0, articles 1, 2 and 3-bis determine all the conditions necessary and sufficient for a person to belong to the Club. By means of those conditions, they define the whole of the subjects which make the social order of the Club. Art. 0 and articles 1, 2 and 3-bis result in an institutionalist definition which can be worded as follows:

ID: The social order of the PC is, at any time, the set made of P, S, T and all those declared such by the Assembly, provided they have not been expelled for having repeatedly refused to follow the conduct declared obligatory by the Assembly and not abrogated by it.

We must repeat here what has already been said in relation to ND (§3). ID directly defines each moment of the social order. Indirectly it determines the concept of a (total) social order or, as the union of a succession of momentary orders (the set of those who, expelled and non-expelled, have been at any moment members of the Club). ID is not a persuasive definition *de jure condendo*, nor a descriptive one *de jure condito*, but expresses the act through which the *jus conditur* and the PC is laid down and structured in its social dimension. It is a constitutive definition.

Because the focus of this perspective is the social structure and because the norms of conduct are seen as determining the possibility of modification of that structure, the concept of obligation is itself influenced. In the logic of this perspective to say conduct is obligatory does mean it that it is thereby rendered an object of prescription. Rather it establishes constitutively that any contrary conduct involves the loss of membership status. Not only the ID but also the pronouncements of the assembly are constitutive norms. It follows furthermore that to be subject to an obligation doesn't mean that one is already an addressee of an imperative. Rather one finds oneself in a juridical position created by a norm. This fits with the model of institutional order of Santi Romano. According to him norms do not face an addressee (of an imperative) but a subject for whom the norms produce juridical consequences.

However, even here norms which establish obligations indirectly contain an ought. And this (as Santi Romano saw) does not come from the norms themselves but from their connection with the interest of those who are subjects to the norm, that is with the values shared by the actual and potential participants (§1). These values become the sources of the ought through a simple practical syllogism. Membership has worth, membership is lost if one doesn't follow certain conduct (that is the conditional situation created by the norm), therefore one ought to follow that conduct. The ought is present both in the normativist and institutionalist reconstruction. The difference being that in the first it is part of the content of the norm and in the second is derived from the values in which the norm is rooted. So, in the institutional reconstruction represented by ID, the elements of the social order are human subjects. The acts of norm production (the deliberations of the Assembly) and the definition ID itself are all constitutive in nature. They might then indirectly acquire a prescriptive or deontic sense in combination with the social values presupposed in the group.

§5

Through ND and ID, objective law can be reconstructed as a normative and social order respectively. In both cases the reconstruction takes the general form: this law is* (ought to be*), such and such order. A constitutive definition, therefore, and more specifically, a constitutive definition of the order. The constitutive definition here, should not be necessarily thought of as the single act of a particular person (we thought of art. 0 in this way only to make the point more vivid). Thus the definitions ND and ID are rational reconstructions of the theorist. ND and ID are always present, if sometimes implicitly, in the product of social processes. Indeed they express the creativity of those processes. And so, if humans make law, then ND and ID sum up the creativity required for an order to come into being. This might be the creation of one person or many; by a sudden inspiration or through mature deliberation. Pickwick and his acts can be considered as an incisive image (*à la* Quine) of the meaning of this process.

"This law is* (ought to be*) such and such an order" is furthermore a constitutive definition of an order. An order is social and normative and has the intimate structure of a system. This explains the possibility and function of definitions and constitutive norms.

Constitutive norms operate as a sort of *fiat* (§2). Those critics who wish to avoid magic or metaphysics think there is something mysterious and disquieting in the way in which these norms work. But the case of Pickwick gives us peace of mind. Because he has done nothing, as we have shown in ND and ID, than give life by definition to harmless creatures which are the elements of systems — just as in primary schools children play imaginative games. Pickwick has not said: "Let the PC be* a gold mountain" or "The PC is* absolute", but "the PC club is* (let it be*) such and such a system". And if we doubt that the PC exist as such and such an entity, this would be an excess of Cartesian doubt.

Obviously even the theory of systems has philosophical problems but we are not going to discuss them here. The way in which constitutive norms function and produce what we may call juridical consequences depends on the operations of the system and on the way in which stipulative definitions normally behave. This is independent of any philosophical problem about the systems. To see this better, we will compare the consequences of developing ND and ID with the a similar development in a simple definition of sets. In this *A1* and *B1* are definitions give by someone at a particular time (in the case of *B1* the future). *C1* and *D1* are the same as ND and ID with some temporal elements and simplification in the content. However we intend *C1*, as ND, to refer to the prescriptions, explicit or logically derivable, from the deliberations of the assembly.

A1: Let* I be the set of prime numbers between 0 and 100.	*B1*: Let* I' be the set of numbers that X will give.	*C1*: Let* the normative order of the CP at any moment be the set of prescriptions which, in that moment or before, the Assembly has made part of the order itself or valid in the order, and which up to now have not been derogated.	*D1*: Let* the social order of the PC at any moment be the set of persons who, at that moment or before, the Assembly has made part of the order itself (has made them members of the PC) and whom up to now it has not expelled.
A2: I is a set of prime numbers between 0 and 100.	*B2*: I' is a set of numbers which X will give	*C2*: The normative order of the CP at any moment is the set of prescriptions which, in that moment or before, the	*D2* The social order of the PC at any moment is the set of persons who, at that moment or before, the ssembly has made part of the

		Assembly has made part of the order itself, or valid in the order, and which up to now have not been derogated.	order itself (has made them members of the PC) and whom up to now it has not expelled.
A3: 41 is a prime number between 0 and 100	*B3*: 50 is a number that X has given	*C3*: The rule to pay a penny is a rule that at time T the Assembly has made part of (valid in) the normative order of the PC and has not derogated	*D3*: Winkle is a person who at time T the Assembly has made part of the social order (made him a member of the PC) and has not expelled.
A4: 41 belongs to I	*B4*: 50 belongs to I’	*C4*: the rule to pay a penny belongs to (is valid in) the normative order of the PC at time T.	*D4*: Winkle belongs to (is a member of) the social order of PC at time T.

A1, B1, C1, D1 are statements used as definitions while *A2, B2, C2, D2* are used *ex post* to talk of the set already defined. Thus *C1* and *D1* are constitutive definitions used by Pickwick *jus condens* while *C2* and *D2* are definitions used by an observer or legal official, *de jure condito*, to describe the set defined by Pickwick.

Further, *C3* and *D3* are the dispositive acts of the Assembly which can be explained in their turn by constitutive statements: “the rule to pay a penny is* valid in the order”, “Winkle is* a member of the PC”. And just as *C2* and *D2* describe the effect produced by the definition, *C4* and *D4* describe the effect produced by the Assembly. Thus we can explain the constitutive forceof both *C1* and *D1* and the acts of the Assembly. The move from *C1* to *C4* and from *D1* to *D4* has basically the same logic as the move from *A1* to *A4* and from *B1* to *B4*. The deduction in both cases is in two parts. The first from statement 1 to 2, the second from statement 2 to 4.

The move from the first to the second propositions in each column explains the constitutive nature of the definition. The statements in the second are, we might say, "true by definition". This means that they are true in virtue of the statements in row 1. One can consider the constitutive definitions of row 1 as the definitions of names and the statements in row 2 as tautologies. However, at least in C and D there are important pragmatic aspects to consider. These, again, are connected with the background of values. The Pickwickian world is interested in *D1* not because *D1* offers a shortened name but because it selects a set of people in whose selection are reflected Pickwick's own attitudes. It follows that the statement *D2*: "CP is the set of such persons" is not a tautology but gives us empirical information about Pickwickian values: "the set defined and selected by Pickwick is the set of such persons".

§6

The move from the second to the last statement in each column has the same logical base in the case of *A, B, C,D.* What is different is not the logic of the matter but the conditions for membership of an element to the set. It is these conditions which explain the particular aspects of sets such as *C* and *D* which are juridical orders. I will illustrate briefly four of these characteristics which are present in juridical phenomena: objectivity, temporality, causality and sociality. I will do this by contrasting them with *A* and *B.*

(a) Objectivity is the characteristic least defined. The consequences of juridical norms are objective in the sense that, even though laws are human voluntary acts, once made, their effects are independent of the people who make them. A similar phenomenon is evidenced in the relation between the constitutive definition of a set and its development, as can be seen in case *A*. The number 41 continues to be part of the set I independent of whether the person who made the definition thinks about it or not, whether he is alive or not. The objectivity is more marked in *B, C, D* because the element belonging to this set is dependent on uncertain events which happen after the definition of the set itself. But this does not mean that, should the facts foreseen in *C4* and *D4* take place, the consequences would not follow. The defining statements in the first line are human acts but as soon as they are made they become the objective reality described in *A2, B2, C2, D2*. From this point of view the consequences follow according to a logic which is independent of those who first made the definition.

(b) The set I defined by *A1* is a static set which has no history. A number belongs or does not belong to I once and for all. We are able, in a sense, to make sense of the a temporal dimension, of a history, in respect of the other sets. Already in case *B*: if X gives a number and later on another one, one can say that the set I' has been increased and has grown. I' can only grow, whereas in *C* and *D* all sorts of variations are possible. The normative and social order of the PC is able to make indefinite changes to the set by virtue of the Assembly's powers. In *C* and *D* the definition itself foresees this possibility of temporal change. Such definitions are characteristic of momentary sets. The PC as a total diachronic set (as we have already seen in § 3 and §4) is the set of the momentary sets, that is the set where the momentary sets are elements or subsets ($PC=\{PC_t\}_{teT}$ or $PC=U_{teT}PC^t$, where T is the temporal series). The concept of "a set at time T", necessary to explain the temporality of law, has differing interpretations which give different views of the standard concept of an atemporal set. The interpretation implicit in *C1* and *D1*, the most natural for this particular case, makes it a function of Assembly's decisions. Thanks to the temporalised concept of set used in *C1* and *D1* we can give a time to the juridical consequences (cf. *C4* and *D4*). It is possible to determine their changes and to describe life in the normative and social order of law temporally.

(c) *C3* and *D3* describe events which are the "juridical causes" of the "effects" described in *C4* and *D4*. If we consider this causality in the light of *A, B, C, D* its nature is clear. Certain facts taking place in the Assembly cause given conduct to be obligatory and give the quality of membership to a given person. That is that given rules and given individuals belong to the normative or social order of the circle. This is just the same as the fact that X has given a number make it belong to I' or the fact that a number is between 0 and 100 is a prime makes it part of I. We are not dealing here with a psychological, physical or deontic relation. Neither is it purely a logical relation. By themselves *A3, B3, C3, D3* do not entail *A4, B4, C4, D4*. This only happens because beyond the logic there are constitutive definitions *A1* to *D1*.

However, the causal facts pronounced by the Assembly are of a particular nature. They are a form of intentional causality and this distinguishes them from *A* and *B*. That 41 is a prime number between 0 and 100 (*A3*) is a "fact" caused by its belonging to the set I. That X has given the number 50 (*B3*) is an "act" which makes it belong to I'. It is the intention to produce the act and not the effect that is important — X could have picked a number randomly. But the fact that the Assembly makes Winkle a member of the PC (*D3*) is an act made with the knowledge and intention of giving Winkle the status of an element of the set. The same is the case when the Assembly makes a given rule a valid norm (*C3*). They are *ad hoc* intentional acts characterised by that knowledge and intention which is characteristic of the contractual mind (the intention to create legal relations in § 3). They are acts which represent the desired effect in their content itself ("Winkle is* a member of the PC") and which cause it legally. This is why every act of the Assembly can be reconstructed as a constitutive. Their constitutive capacity is nothing else but that intentional causality. But it would be a mistake to think of them as self-applying. They are acts whose causality comes from their content, but only, as we have seen, because of the fundamental definition which they presuppose. "Winkle is* a member of the PC" produces immediately the dispositive effect because such a disposition is a condition of membership of the PC by that Club's definition.

This causality is the basis of every other causal relation in the system. Causality works not only in the deliberations of the Assembly but in any fact which the Assembly in its turn decides as a condition for certain consequences. That is, any fact which we would commonly call the juridical cause of certain effects. In all cases where the Assembly makes valid conditional rules of the type: "if P then Q" (we can view structural norms in a similar way), then the immediate effect is that (i) the rule "if P then Q" belongs to the order and from this follows that (ii) *if* it is the case that P *then* the prescription "let Q be the case" belongs to the order. On the basis of that *if-then* its verification modifies the content of the system.

d) The constitutive nature and intentional causality of the acts of the Assembly are linked to the specific character of the social group which the Assembly embodies and with which the PC coincides. This is absent in cases *A* and *B*. We could imagine that in B, X is a collective name, like Assembly or PC and we could say that the Assembly has a function in C and D analogous to X's function in B. That would be the function of determining by its own acts whether some elements belong to their respective sets. But this analogy is limited. As we saw, the acts of X are causal, whereas the acts of the Assembly are intentional and *ad hoc*. This makes a profound difference to the nature of the class of persons involved in one or the other case. An aggregate is only a set of persons but a set of persons whose action is defined and guided by a common idea is more than that: it is a social group. The elements of X take part in the game involuntarily and unknowingly. The elements of X give a number but do not do it to further the purpose of I'. The definition of I looks to X but X has no idea of I'. Its action conforms to it but is not guided by it. Thus X is a mere aggregate. The position is different in C and D. The Assembly does not simply prescribe but intends that these prescriptions enter the normative order. It doesn't simply nominate someone but intends that that person enters into the social order of the club. But it is not only the definition of the normative and social order which take the Assembly into consideration. The Assembly itself keeps in mind this definition. It uses it as a criterion for the conditions according to which a rule or a person belong to the order, should the Assembly itself so rule. The actions of the Assembly do not merely conform to the order but are guided by it. In all its acts the Assembly implies the presence of law. That concept of law through which it acts is an essential part of the understanding of the law itself. It is this knowledge which is present in the set of subjects of the club which makes them a society or social group.

§7

Each model has limits and many interpretations. Some reconstructions of DN and ID are inadequate because they cannot understand some areas of juridical experience. Other models are inadequate because they do not exclude certain reconstructions. In fact an institutional reconstruction of the type ID is not universalisable. It is only possible for cases where there is a mechanism, as in art. 3, in which expulsion from the system represents, so to speak, the sanction of closure, the ultimate sanction of the system. Perhaps a similar model can deal with relations between individuals but certainly not with the law of the state. The normative reconstruction DN has general explanatory powers. However many other reconstructions are possible. For example one can define the order in terms of social structure, as a set of subjects to which certain norms of conduct refer. Or, in terms of more comprehensive structure, as a set formed in turn by a certain normative order and a certain social order linked by specific relations.

But in all these cases, what is constant is the constitutive definition of the order. To understand a law is to know what it *is*. To know what it *is* is to have a definition of it. But if law is what it is through a human activity, as a product of human knowledge and intention, then its definition is constitutive before it is descriptive. *C2* and *D2* presuppose *C1* and *D1*, the *verum* presupposes the *fieri*, the object presupposes the project which it constructs by definition. This is not an accidental part of the model. Certainly, as we saw in § 5, the definition translated in a sentence such as "law is* a set thus structured" is not merely a simple atemporal act, but summarises a creative journey. This has its own logic. If the constitutive definition of an order is the point from which that order takes its origin and develops, then in turn the definition is the conclusion of a more fundamental process. But this question I do not deal with here.

Eidetic-Constitutive Rules

by

Amedeo G. Conte

En totalitet ikke bestaar af ting men af sammenhænge.
A totality does not consist of things but of relationships.
Louis Hjelmslev

Not the bishop, or the knight, or the powerful castle is sacred in itself, but the game of chess is a noble game, and therein the knight is sanctified by the bishop, and the bishop by the queen.
Isak Dinesen [Karen Blixen]

0 *Introduction*

0.1 This paper *Eidetic-Constitutive Rules* is a contribution to philosophical deontics [*Deontik*, *déontique*, *deontica*]. It deals with the concept of eidetic-constitutive rules (the paradigm case of eidetic-constitutive rules is the rules of chess) and with two other concepts (anankastic-constitutive rules and anankastic rules).[1]

My typology is one of *concepts* and not of *phenomena*. But these concepts are fruitful ideal types (*Idealtypen*) for a theory of phenomena.

0.2. My paper is divided into three parts. The first part examines the relations between the three concepts of eidetic-constitutive rules, anankastic-constitutive rules and anankastic rules.

The second part evaluates John R. Searle's theory of constitutive rules.

The third part discusses the semiotic and epistemological relevance of the concept of eidetic-constitutive rules.

Law and Language, The Italian Analytical School, ed. A. Pintore and M. Jori (Liverpool: Deborah Charles Publications, 1997).

1 My essay *Eidetic-Constitutive Rules* is an abridged version of the paper *Regole eidetico-costitutive* presented at the Collegio Ghislieri in Pavia on 7th December, 1984.

1 *Eidetic-Constitutive Rules, Anankastic-Constitutive Rules, Anankastic Rules*

1.1 *Eidetic-Constitutive Rules*

1.1.1 *The Concept*

I will call eidetic-constitutive rules [*regole eidetico-costitutive*, *eidetisch-konstitutive Regeln*, *règles eidético-constitutives*] those rules which are a necessary condition of their object (of what they refer to). The paradigm case of eidetic-constitutive rules is the rules of the game of chess. The praxemes (i. e. the units) of the game of chess (the pieces, e.g. the bishop, the moves, e.g. castling, etc.) do not exist prior to the rules and are not independent of them. The rules constitute the game and (in the game) its praxemes (its units). Eidetic-constitutive rules are a transcendental condition (*ex ante*) of a praxis and a transcendental condition (*ex post*) of the cognizability of it.[2]

1.1.2 *History of the Concept*

That there are eidetic-constitutive rules can be seen prefigured in the writings of several authors.

1.1.2.1. Firstly, many authors argue that the eidetic-constitutive rules of a praxis are a transcendental condition (*ex ante*) of the logical possibility of that praxis and of its praxemes.

1.1.2.1.1. Thus the idea that in chess the identity of the pieces is determined by the rules (in other words, that a piece is the deontic place[3] of its own rules) is present in the writings of Johannes Thomae,[4] in Edmund Husserl[5], in Ernst Mally (the inventor of the adjective "*deontisch*'

2 The Italian, German and French counterparts of "praxeme" are "*praxema*", "*Praxem*", "*praxème*".

3 The Italian, German and French counterparts of "deontic place" are "*luogo deontico*", "*deontischer Ort*", "*lieu déontique*".

4 Cf. Johannes K. Thomae, *Elementare Theorie der analytischen Functionen einer complexen Veründlichen* (Halle an der Saale: L. Nebert, 1880, second edition 1898), 3.

5 Cf. Edmund Husserl, (1900-1901), *Logische Untersuchungen*, (Niemeyer, Halle an der Saale, 1900-1901; fifth edition: Tübingen: Niemeyer, 1968), II.I.69-70.

and of the substantive Deontik"),[6] and (last but not least) in Ludwig Wittgenstein.

In 1934 Wittgenstein even uses the English verb "to constitute" when talking of the rules of chess.

According to Wittgenstein, the squares [*Felder*] of the chessboard are not (contrary to what is suggested by their German name: "*Felder*") a neutral battlefield for the pieces, but are themselves pieces [*Figuren*] of the game: "auch das Feld ist eine Figur." In other words: the chessboard is not the neutral physical *place* of the *game*; it is the *deontic place* [*luogo deontico, deontischer Ort*, *lieu déontique*] of the rules.

Paradoxically enough, Wittgenstein's thesis has been anticipated by Gottlob Frege, an author who has denied elsewhere the constitutivity of eidetic-constitutive rules. According to Frege, the squares of the chessboard [*die Felder des Schachbretts*] are also pieces [*Figuren*]: "Die Felder des Schachbretts müssen hier eigentlich zu den Figuren gerechnet werden."[7]

1.1.2.1.2. The idea that the rules of chess constitute the *pragmèmes* (the *types* of moves, as opposed to the *tokens* of moves) can be seen in a book by Czeslaw Znamierowski (the Polish philosopher who put forward the concept of the *norma konstrukcyjna*).[8]

1.1.2.2. Secondly, many authors uphold the thesis that eidetic-constitutive rules constituting the praxemes of a praxis are a transcendental condition (*ex post*) of the cognizability of each instantiation (of each token) of the praxemes.

6 Cf. Ernst Mally, *Grundgesetze des Sollens. Elemente der Logik des Willens* (Graz.: Leuschner und Lubensky, 1926); *Logische Schriften*, (Dordrecht: Reidel, 1971), 189-191. The English, Italian, French and Polish counterparts of the German adjective "*deontisch*" are "*deontic*", "*deontico*", "*déontique*", "*deontyczny*"; the English, Italian, French and Polish counterparts of the German substantive "*Deontik*" are "*deontics*", "*deontica*", "*déontique*", "*deontyka*".

7 Cf Gottlob Frege, *Grundgesetze der Arithmetik* (Jena: Pohle, 1893-1903; phototyp. repr., Hildesheim: G. Olms, 1962), II.104.

8 Cf. Czeslaw Znamierowski, *Podstawowe pojecia teorji prawa. I. Uklad prawny i norma prawna* (Pozan: Fiszer i Majewski, 1924), 72-73; second edition: (Poznan: Górski i Tetzlaw, 1934), 107.

In eidetic-constitutive rules, the rheme [*rhema*, *Rhema*, *propos* (or *rhème*)] determines the theme [*thema*, *Thema*, *thème*]. On the concepts of rheme and theme, cf. Miorita Ulrich, *Thetisch und kategorisch* (Tübingen: Narr, 1985).

1.1.2.2.1. According to Max Weber, the rules of the German card-game called *Skat* are the presupposition for the empirical knowledge of this game.

1.1.2.2.1.1. Weber makes his thesis clear not by referring to the game of chess but to a German game of cards, *Skat*. It is only by referring to the constitutive rules of the game of *Skat* (rules that are *begriffskonstitutiv* for the delimitation of the object) that it is possible for an observer to select the relevant (the pertinent) phenomena.

For example, only by referring to the rules of *Skat* is it possible to decide that drinking beer [*Bierkonsum*] does not belong to the *ludus* (in my terminology: drinking beer is not a praxeme of the game of *Skat*).[9]

1.1.2.2.1.2. Weber's example of *Bierkonsum* provides an illuminating comparison. The act of a player drinking beer during a game of *Skat* is, seen from the outside, similar to the act of the priest drinking wine when he celebrates mass. But the similarity is illusory: drinking wine is a *praxeme* of the mass; drinking beer is not a *praxeme* of *Skat*.

1.1.2.2.2. That an eidetic-constitutive rule, and more precisely Hans Kelsen's basic norm (*Grundnorm*) is a transcendental condition of the cognizability of normative phenomena has been asserted by Felix Kaufmann in the course of his criticism of Hans Kelsen's theory of the *Grundnorm*.[10] There are no normative phenomena that exist before the *Grundnorm*. On the contrary, it is the *Grundnorm* that constitutes (*ex ante*) the normative phenomena and makes possible (*ex post*) the perception of them. (Friedrich Nietzsche wrote: "Es gibt gar keine moralischen Phänomene, sondern nur eine moralische Ausdeutung von Phänomenen": "There are no moral phenomena, but only a moral interpretation of phenomena.")

1.1.2.2.3. According to Alf Ross and John Rawls, the rules of a *game* (of a

9 Cf. Max Weber, "R. Stammlers 'Überwindung' der materialistischen Geschichtsauffassung", in *Archiv für Sozialwissenschaft und Sozialpolitik* XXIV (1907), 94-151; new edition in Max Weber, *Gesammelte Aufsätze zur Wissenschaftslehre* (Tübingen: Mohr, 1968), 291-359.

10 Cf. Felix Kaufmann, *Methodenlehre der Sozialwissenschaften* (Wien: Julius Springer, 1936), 297.

ludus) are a necessary condition for recognizing and interpreting the *play* (the *lusus*).[11]

This thesis can be formulated by using Charles Sanders Peirce's *type/token distinction*. A *token* of a rule-constituted praxeme is cognizable (and recognizable as a *token* of its *type*) only by reference to the eidetic-constitutive rules which constitute its *type*.

For instance, an act can be described as a *token* (as an instantiation) of the *type* of castling [*arroccamento*, *Rochade*, *roque*] only by reference to the eidetic-constitutive rules which constitute the type of castling.[12]

1.1.3 *Typology of Eidetic-Constitutive Rules*

1.1.3.1 *Deontic Rule* vs. *Ontic Rule*

In the set of eidetic-constitutive rules I distinguish two subsets: *deontic* rules, for example:

(1) The bishop ought to move diagonally

(2) The king ought to be moved from check

and ontic rules, for example:

(3) Check-mate occurs if and only if the king is in check and cannot escape from check by any move.

1.1.3.2 *Paradigmatic Rule* vs. *Syntagmatic Rule*

In the subset of deontic eidetic-constitutive rules I distinguish two subsets: *paradigmatic* rules, for example:

(1) The bishop ought to move diagonally

and *syntagmatic* rules, for instance:

(2) The king ought to be moved from check.

11 I call *ludus* the ludic system, the *game*, and *lusus* the ludic activity, the *play*.

12 Cf. A. Ross, *Om ret og retfærdighed* (København: Busck, 1953), 26, 201, and Rawls [1955], Alf Ross, *Om ret og retfærdighed* (København: Busck, 1953); John Rawls, "Two Concepts of Rules", *The Philosophical Review* LXIV (1955), 3-32.

1.1.3.2.1. Rules such as:

(1) The bishop ought to move diagonally

determine for each phase of the game the *paradigm* of possible alternative forms of proceeding with the game. Precisely because these rules determine the *paradigmatic axis* of the game, I have called them *paradigmatic rules* (using Louis Hjelmslev's opposition "syntagmatic" vs. "paradigmatic").

On the contrary, rules such as:

(2) The king ought to be moved from check

do not determine a paradigm of moves. Moving the king from check takes place through an instantiation of one of the praxemes of the game, but it is not a praxeme itself. Precisely because these rules determine the *syntagmatic* axis of the game, I have called them *syntagmatic rules* (using Louis Hjelmslev's opposition "syntagmatic" vs. "paradigmatic").

1.1.3.2.2. The difference between *paradigmatic rules* and *syntagmatic rules* explains a possibility which otherwise may look paradoxical: it is the possibility that *one* move can be made following *two* rules. *One* move is made according to *two* rules when, for example, a player whose king is under check moves it from check by moving it on to another square. In this case, this player uses *two* rules at the same time. He follows both the *syntagmatic* rule:

(2) The king ought to be moved from check

and the *paradigmatic* rule:

(4) The king ought to be moved one square at a time.

1.2 *Anankastic-Constitutive Rules*

1.2.1 *The Concept*

1.2.1.1. Let us consider the rule:

(5) Confirmation ought to be given (ought to be administered) by the bishop.

Clearly, rule (5) is not equivalent to:

(6) The bishop ought to give (ought to administer) confirmation,

though rule (6) appears to be its transformation from the passive to the active. Rule (6) is a *deontic* rule regulating the conduct of the bishop. Rule (5), on the contrary, is an *anankastic-constitutive* rule as to the validity [*validità*, *Gültigkeit*, *validité*] of confirmation.[13]

An anankastic-constitutive rule [*regola anankastico-costitutiva*, *anankastisch-konstitutive Regel*, *règle anankastico-constitutive*] is a rule which sets (lays down) a necessary condition of its object. The term "anankastic-constitutive rule" is derived from the Greek name of necessity: "*anánke*".

Another anankastic-constitutive rule is the rule on the validity of wills:

(7) Wills ought to be signed by the testator.

1.2.2 *Anankastic-Constitutive Rule* vs. *Eidetic-Constitutive Rule*

I have proposed two distinctions concerning the relations between anankastic-constitutive rules and eidetic-constitutive rules: an *ontological* and a *semantic* distinction.

1.2.2.1 *The Ontological Distinction between Anankastic-Constitutive Rules and Eidetic-Constitutive Rules*

(i) *Eidetic-constitutive* rules *are* a necessary condition of their object. For example, the rules of chess are a necessary conditions for the praxis of chess and for its praxemes.

(ii) *Anankastic-constitutive* rules, on the contrary, *set* (*lay down*) a necessary condition of their object. For example, the rule

(7) Wills ought to be signed by the testator

lays down a necessary validity-condition for wills.

13 I do not deny that it is possible for a normative system to include both the anakastic-constitutive rule (5) and the deontic rule (6). What I deny is that (5) is equivalent to (6) or that (5) entails (6).

1.2.2.2 *The Semantic Distinction between Anankastic-Constitutive Rules and Eidetic-Constitutive Rules*

(i) *Eidetic-constitutive* rules determine the connotation (I use "connotation" and "denotation" in the Millian sense) of the terms indicating their object. For example, the eidetic-constitutive rules of chess determine the connotation (the intension) of the terms indicating the praxemes of the game (i. e. of the terms "pawn", "castling", "check", etc.). In particular, the eidetic-constitutive rules of a praxis determine the connotation (the extension) of the praxeonyms (of the *nomina actionis*) which indicate the pragmemes of the praxis constituted by the rules. For example, the rules of chess determine the connotation (the intension) of the praxeonym "castling".[14]

(ii) *Anankastic-constitutive* rules, on the contrary, do not determine the connotation (the intension) of the terms indicating the entities which they refer to. They presuppose a connotation (an intension) of these terms and lay down necessary conditions to the entities these terms indicate. For example, the anankastic-constitutive rule

(7) Wills ought to be signed by the testator

presupposes a connotation (an intension) of the term ("will") indicating the act which it refers to and determines the *denotation* (the extension) of the term "will" by laying down a necessary validity-condition of wills.

1.3 *Anankastic Rules*

1.3.1 *The Concept*

An anankastic rule prescribes a behaviour not as such, but as a necessary condition [*condizione necessaria*, *notwendige Bedingung*, *condition nécessaire*, *condicio sine qua non*] to achieve an end pursued by its addressee.

Just as in the *definiens* of the term "eidetic-constitutive rule" and in the *definiens* of the term "anankastic-constitutive rule", so also in the *definiens* of the term "anankastic rule" there is the phrase "necessary

14 I have invented "praxeonym" (in the sense of "*nomen actionis*": its Italian, German, French counterparts are "*praxeonimo*", "*Praxeonym*", "*praxéonyme*") on the model of such words as "*toponimo*" ("place-name"). The Greek substantives "*ónyma*" and "*ónoma*" mean "name".

condition". The difference between *eidetic-constitutive* rules, *anankastic-constitutive* rules and *anankastic* rules can be summarized as follows:

(i) *Eidetic-constitutive* rules *are* a necessary condition of their object;

(ii) *Anankastic-constitutive* rules *set* a necessary condition of their object;

(iii) *Anankastic* rules *presuppose* a (relationship of) necessary condition.

1.3.2 *Anankastic Rule* vs. *Technical Rule*

1.3.2.1. The concept of anankastic rules is an *Idealtypus* (an ideal type) through which we can understand a very difficult deontic concept: the concept of technical rules.[15]

In the *definiens* of "technical rule" the concept of condition occurs not once but *twice*: The behaviour prescribed by a technical rule is prescribed both *on condition* [*sotto condizione, unter einer Bedingung, sous condition*] and *as a condition* [*come condizione, als Bedingung, en tant que condition*].

(i) In the first place, the behaviour is prescribed not as such (in itself), but *on the condition* that the agent (the addressee) is pursuing a certain end.

(ii) In the second place, the behaviour is prescribed *as a condition* for the aim of the agent to be achieved.

The first condition is subjective (*prohairetic* condition), the second condition is objective (*praxeological* condition).

1.3.2.2. As I have said, the concept of *anankastic* rules is an ideal type [*Idealtypus*] by which we can analyze the concept of *technical* rules. But the concept of anankastic rules does not cover all the senses of the term "technical rule". I have found *four sets* of technical rules:

(i) technical rules based on a necessary condition (*anankastic* rules),

(ii) technical rules based on a sufficient condition (*metathetic* rules),

(iii) technical rules based on a necessary and sufficient condition (*nomic* rules), and (last not least)

(iv) technical rules which are not based on a relationship of necessary and/or sufficient condition (*stochastic* rules).

15 The Italian, German and French counterparts of "technical rule" are "*regola tecnica*", "*technische Regel*", "*règle technique*".

1.3.3 *Anankastic Rule* vs. *Anankastic-Constitutive Rule*

The difference between anankastic and anankastic-constitutive rules is univocal. Anankastic-constitutive rules *set* (*lay down*) a necessary condition. Anankastic rules, on the contrary, *presuppose* a necessary condition.

But anankastic and anankastic-constitutive rules have not always been correctly distinguished. An example of this conceptual confusion can be seen in Agazzi. Agazzi calls some rules *constitutive* when they are in fact *technical*. For instance, according to Agazzi, "the rules for assembling and activating a machine" are constitutive rules "since they show in what way it is constituted".[16]

2 *Constitutive Rules in John R. Searle*

In Anglo-Saxon philosophy, the main contribution to the theory of constitutive rules has been made by John R. Searle.[17] But what does Searle mean by the phrase "constitutive rule"?

2.1 *X-Rules* vs. *Y-Rules*

Searle's "constitutive rules" are not homogeneous. The idea of a test to detect the heterogeneity of Searle's "constitutive rules" was suggested to me by a reading of Searle's own writings. As is well-known, for Searle, "constitutive rules" can be reduced to the standard form

(8) X counts as Y,

(9) X ha valore di Y,

(10) X gilt als Y.

Now, it is the very reduction to the standard form ("X counts as Y")

16 Cf. E. Agazzi, "Il problema della caratterizzazione conoscitiva della normalità e della devianza", in Orazio Siciliani, Piergiorgio Muzi and Mariano Bianca, eds., *Normalità e devianza* (Milan: Angeli, 1981), 19-38, at 21; *idem,* "The Presence of Values in the Social Sciences", *Epistemologia* V (1982), 5-26, at 14.

17 John Rogers Searle, "How to Derive 'Ought' from 'Is'", *The Philosophical Review* LXXIII (1964), 43-58; "What is a Speech Act?", in Max Black, ed., *Philosophy in America* (London: Allen and Unwin, 1964), 221-39; *Speech Acts. An Essay in the Philosophy of Language* (London: Cambridge University Press, 1969).

that shows that Searle's "constitutive rules" are not homogeneous:

(i) some (for instance, the "constitutive rule" of promise) are X-rules,

(ii) others (for instance, the "constitutive rule" of checkmate) are Y-rules.

2.1.1. Searle's alleged "constitutive rule" of promise:

(11) To make a promise is to undertake an obligation expresses the sense (the essence) of the act of promise.

Its paraphrase in the standard form ('X counts as Y') is:

(12) The promise counts as the undertaking of an obligation.

In this paraphrase, the term "promise" occupies the X-position. That is why I have proposed the term "X-rule".

2.1.2. On the other hand, Searle's "constitutive rule" of checkmate (3) determines not what checkmate is, but what counts as a checkmate. Its paraphrase in the standard form ("X counts as Y") is:

(13) Each check, from which the king cannot be removed through any move, counts as a checkmate.

In this paraphrase, the term "checkmate" occupies the Y-position. That is why I have proposed the term 'Y-rule'.

2.2. *Searle's Alleged "Constitutive Rule" of Promise*

Searle's "constitutive rule" of promise (like any "essential rule" of a speech-act) is not an eidetic-constitutive rule.

(i) Firstly, Searle's alleged "constitutive rule" of promise

(11) To make a promise is to undertake an obligation

is not eidetic-constitutive if 'eidetic-constitutive' is interpreted in the *ontological* sense. In fact, this rule is not a necessary condition of conceivability and/or possibility and/or perceptibility of (the act of) promise.

(ii) Secondly, Searle's alleged "constitutive rule" of promise:

(11) To make a promise is to undertake an obligation

is not eidetic-constitutive if "eidetic-constitutive" is interpreted in the *semantic* sense. In fact, this rule does not determine the connotation (the intension) of the term "promise". On the contrary, it just makes explicit what is implicit in the connotation of "promise".

3 *The Semiotic and Epistemological Relevance of Eidetic-Constitutive Rules*

3.1. *A Thought-Experiment with Eidetic-Constitutive Rules*

3.1.1. Suppose there were both rules (16) and (17):

(14) If the king is under check, castling is forbidden (is not allowed),
(15) If the king is under check, castling is obligatory.

Is there an antinomy (an inconsistency) here?

3.1.2. Paradoxically, if they are eidetic-constitutive rules, there is no antinomy (no inconsistency). If rules (14) and (15) are eidetic-constitutive rules, each determines *one* particular connotation of "castling", *one* particular connotation of "king", *one* particular connotation of "check". Therefore, "king", "castling", "check" have different connotations in these two rules.

3.2 *Eidetic-Constitutive Rules and Understanding (Verstehen)*

3.2.1. Do the eidetic-constitutive rules of a praxis enable one to understand [*verstehen*] action conforming to it?

An affirmative answer is suggested (though not explicitly asserted) by Georg Henrik von Wright. According to his book *Explanation and Understanding*, the constitutive rules of a praxis "play no characteristic or important role in the *explanation* of behaviour", but "are of fundamental importance to *understanding* behaviour".[18]

3.2.2. My answer is in the negative.[19] The eidetic-constitutive rules of a praxis make it possible to recognize tokens of the types constituted by

18 Cf. Georg Henrik von Wright, *Explanation and Understanding* (London: Routledge, London, 1971), 152.

19 Among the reasons for my negative answer is a reflection on Ludwig Wittgenstein's *The Blue and Brown Books* which I translated in the year1961: Ludwig Wittginstein, *The Blue and Brown Books* (Oxford: Blackwell, 1958), Ital. ed. by Amedeo G. Conte: *Libro Blu e Libro marrone* (Turin: Einaudi, 1983).

them. (For example, the eidetic-constitutive rules of chess make it possible to see the neutral movement of two pieces on a chessboard as a token of the type castling.)

But they do not enable the understanding of the individual (of the *ídion*) in its own individuality. Eidetic-constitutive rules does not make it possible to understand "*das Individuelle in seinem eigenen Individualsein.*"[20]

3.3 *Knowledge of Eidetic-Constitutive Rules*

3.3.1. Can eidetic-constitutive rules be inferred from the action which conform to them? Can the rules of a *ludus* (of a game) be discovered by observing the *lusus* (the play)? For example, can the rules of chess be read off by observing a sequence of moves?

3.3.2. My answer is in the negative. I think that they cannot. The eidetic-constitutive rules of a praxis cannot be inferred from the experience [*esperienza*, *Erfahrung*] of the *lusus* (of the play) because the eidetic-constitutive rules themselves are a necessary condition of that experience [*esperienza*, *Erfahrung*].

A token of a rule-constituted type (a token of castling, for example) is not recognizable as a token of its type unless one refers to the rules which constitute its type. It is only through the rules that a token of a rule-constituted type can be seen as a token, as an instantiation ("instantiation" was suggested to me by John Lyons) of its own type. One cannot see a neutral *movement* [*movimento*, *Versetzung*] in space as a *move* [*mossa*, *Zug*] in a game unless one already knows the eidetic-constitutive rules which constitute the type of that move.

20 The untranslatable play on words '*das Individuelle in seinem eigenen Individualsein*' was suggested to me by the German philosopher Hans-Georg Gadamer.

BIBLIOGRAPHY

Giampaolo M. Azzoni, *Il concetto di condizione nella tipologia delle regole* (Degree dissertation, Università di Pavia, 1985).

Norberto Bobbio, "Norma", in *Enciclopedia* (Torino: Einaudi, 1980), vol. IX, 876-907.

Amedeo Giovanni Conte, "Konstitutive Regeln und Deontik", in Edgar Morscher and Rudolf Stranzinger, eds., *Ethik. Akten des Fünften Internationalen Wittgenstein-Symposiums (Kirchberg 1980)* (Wein: Hölder-Pichler-Tempsky, 1981), 82-86.

Amedeo Giovanni Conte, "Paradigmi d'analisi della regola in Wittgenstein", in Rosaria Egidi, ed., *Wittgenstein. Momenti di una critica del sapere*, (Napoli: Guida, 1983), 37-82.

Amedeo Giovanni Conte, "Phénoménologie du langage déontique", in Georges Kalinowski and Filippo Selvaggi, eds., *Les fondements logiques de la pensée normative* (Roma: Editrice Pontificia Università Gregoriana, 1985), 179-195.

Tecla Mazzerese, "Metaregole", *Nuova civiltà delle macchine* III/3-4 (1985), 65-72.

Kenneth Lee Pike, *Language in Relation to a Unified Theory of the Structure of Human Behaviour* (Glendale: Summer Institute of Linguistics, 1954-1960, 3 vols.; second edition: The Hague: Mouton, 1967).

Piero Pollastro, *Regola costitutiva: Saggio d'analisi* (Università di Pavia: degree dissertation, 1982).

Wilhelm Windelband, *Naturwissenschaft und Geschichte* (Strassburg: Strassburger Rektoratsrede, 1894).

Ludwig Wittgenstein, *Philosophische Bemerkungen* (Oxford: Blackwell, 1964).

Wittgenstein's Lectures, Cambridge, 1932-1935, edited by Alice Ambrose (Oxford: Blackwell, 1979).

ACCEPTANCE IN THE THOUGHT OF H.L.A. HART

by

ALFONSO CATANIA

1 *The Internal and External Point of View*

I want to consider a part of Hart's thought which seems to me to be particularly interesting, that is the concept of acceptance. This has an important part in his thought, not only because it purports to be the best way of understanding the normative structure of law, but also, and this is the point that particularly interests me, because it constitutes the determining element in the formula "the effective acceptance of the ultimate rule of recognition". This purports to be the way we can find a solution to the problem of the existence of legal order without falling into Austinianism ("the general habit of obedience to the sovereign") or into Kelsenism the ("*Grundnorm* as a scientific hypothesis").

Our aim then is to explain the above quotation from Hart. Has Hart been able to find his own basis for legal order? Is acceptance, even though the limited acceptance of legal officials, the best way of solving this delicate problem?[1] Our first problem is that nowhere in his writings does

Law and Language, The Italian Analytical School, ed. A. Pintore and M. Jori (Liverpool: Deborah Charles Publications, 1997).

1 I shall make use of the following works by Hart: "Definition and Theory in Jurisprudence", *The Law Quarterly Review* 70 (1954), 37-60; "Legal and Moral Obligation", in *Essays on Moral Philosophy*, ed. A.I. Melden (Washington: University of Washington Press, 1958), 82-107; "Positivism and the Separation of Law and Morals", *Harvard Law Review* 71 (1958), 593-629; *The Concept of Law* (Oxford: Clarendon Press, 1961); "Il concetto di obbligo", *Rivista di filosofia* LVII (1966), 125-140, engl. transl.: "Legal Duty and Obligation", in *Essays on Bentham* (Oxford: Clarendon Press, 1982), 127-161; "Kelsen's Doctrine of the Unity of Law", in *Ethics and Social Justice,* ed. Howard E. Kiefer and Milton K. Munitz (New York: State University of New York Press, 1970), 171-199.

From the wide range of writings on Hart and from the work more directly linked with the problems dealt with in this essay, we might mention: N. Abbagnano, "Sul concetto del diritto", *Rivista di Filosofia* LIII (1962), 63-68; A.R. Blackshield, "Hart's Concept of Law," *Archiv für Rechts und*

Hart give an explicit definition of acceptance. He often talks about it and it appears that he gives it an important place in understanding some of the most pressing problems of legal theory, those of validity and legal obligation.[2] What is clear though, is what Hart thinks acceptance is not.

Sozialphilosophie XLVIII (1962), 329-341; L.J. Cohen, Review of H.L.A. Hart, *The Concept of Law*, *Mind* 71 (1962), 395-412; V. Frosini, "H.L.A. Hart, The Concept of Law", *Rivista internationale di filosofia del diritto* XXXIX (1962), 532-535; H. Morris, Review of H.L.A. Hart, *The Concept of Law*, , *Harvard Law Review* 75 (1962), 1452-61; G. Tarello, "Il concetto di diritto: una teoria generale 'analitica'", *Annali della Facoltà di Giurisprudenza dell' Università di Genova* I (1962), 141-155; B.E. King, "The Basic Concept of Professor Hart's Jurisprudence, the norm out of the bottle", *The Cambridge Law Journal* 22 (1963), 270-303; M.G. Singer, "Hart's Concept of Law", *The Journal of Philosophy* 60 (1963), 197-220; V. Frosini, "Introduzione", *H.L.A. Hart, Contributi all'analisi del diritto*, trld. V. Frosini (Milan: Giuffrè, 1964), vii-xvii; M.A. Cattaneo, "Introduzione a Hart, Il concetto di diritto", in Hart, *Il concetto di diritto*, trld. M.A. Cattaneo (Turin: Einaudi, 1965), IX-XVIII; D. Lloyd, *Introduction to Jurisprudence* (London: Stevens and Sons, 1965, 2nd ed.), 114ff.; W.L. McBride, "The Acceptance of a Legal System", *The Monist* 48 (1965), 377-396; U. Scarpelli, *Cos'è il positivismo giuridico* (Milan: Edizioni di Comunità, 1965); N. Bobbio, "Considerazioni in margine", *Rivista di Filosofia* LVIII (1966), 235-246; G.R. Carriò, "Sul concetto di obbligo giuridico", *Rivista di Filosofia* LVII (1966), 141-155; G. Gavazzi, "In difesa (parziale) di una concezione predittiva dell'obbligo giuridico", *Rivista di Filosofia* LVII (1966), 165-174 ; P.M. Hacker, "Sull'uso di 'dovere'", *Rivista di Filosofia* LVII (1966), 175-192; B. Leoni, "On a Recent Theory of the 'legal obligation'", *Il Politico* XXXI (1966), 535-539; A. Passerin D'Entrèves, "Intorno all'obbligo politico", *Rivista di Filosofia* LVII (1966), 156-164; R. Sartorius, "The Concept of Law", *Archiv für Rechts- und Sozialphilosophie* LII (1966), 161-193; G. Gavazzi, *Norme primarie e norme secondarie* (Turin: Giappichelli, 1967), 41ff.; L. Lombardi, *Saggio sul diritto giurisprudenziale* (Milan: Giuffrè, 1967, 2nd ed. 1975), 371ff.; N. Bobbio, "Ancora sulle norme primarie e secondarie", *Rivista di Filosofia* LIX (1968), 35-53, and now also in *Studi per una teoria generale del diritto* (Turin: Giappichelli, 1970), 175-197; K.K. Lee, "Hart's Primary and Secondary Rules", *Mind* LXXVII (1968), 561-64; H. Eckmann, *Rechts-positivismus and sprachanalystische Philosophie: der Begriff des Rechts in des Rechtstheorie H.L.A. Harts* (Berlin: Duncker & Humblot, 1969), esp. 80ff.; G.R. Carriò, "Principi di diritto e positivismo giuridico", *Rivista di Filosofia* LXI (1970), 127-148; A. Passerin D'Entrèves, *Obbedienza e resistenza in una società democratica* (Milan: Comunità, 1970), 67-86; J. Raz, *The Concept of a Legal System* (Oxford: Clarendon Press, 1970); G. Fassò, *Storia della filosofia del diritto* (Bologna: Il Mulino, 1970), III., 358f.

2 Chap. VI, "The Foundations of a Legal System", *The Concept of Law*, *supra* n.1, at 97-120, tells us how important Hart considers acceptance as a new way of

For him, it does not consist in (nor does he wish it so to do) in either mere observance of a norm, or its moral or political acceptance of it.[3]

Acceptance is not only a property of legal norms. Hart analyses the concept by looking at the character of habits and other social norms of which juridical norms are a part. Let us look at the following two cases which Hart refers to: (a) a group of people has the habit of going to the cinema on a Saturday evening; (b) in the group there is a rule according to which men *ought*[4] to take their hats off when entering a church.[5] These two statements have things in common. In both cases we can say that the majority of members do the behaviour in question. But in (a) the convergence of behaviour is sufficient evidence for the existence of the habit. In (b) we have to look for something more in order show the existence of a rule: there has to be an acceptance that is internal to the group "at least must look upon the behaviour of the group in question as a general standard to be followed by the group as a whole."[6]

To understand the norm, it is no enough to observe converging behaviour. It is necessary to show that deviation from the behaviour is considered wrong and cause for criticism and also constitutes good reason for that criticism. In other words, the norm's pattern of behaviour in so far as it is sustained by social pressure.[7] To understand this, we must

---

clarifying and solving the problem of legal validity. On the relation between acceptance and legal obligation, see *The Concept of Law*, 79-88; see also the two articles by Hart quoted above, *supra* n.1, "Legal and Moral Obligation", and "Il concetto di obbligo".

3 Hart, *The Concept of Law, supra* n.1, at 57 ff.; 86ff.; 111ff. We can recall here Bobbio's interpretation (*Considerazioni in margine, supra* n.1, at 244-245) of acceptance according to Hart:

> Seen in this way, acceptance is, on one hand, more than the pure obedience to the norm or to a normative system and, on the other hand, something less than the (moral) "approval" of a norm or of a system.

4 Italics have been added.

5 Hart, *The Concept of Law, supra* n.1, at 54.

6 *Ibid.*, at 55: "By contrast, if a social rule is to exist some at least must look upon the behaviour of the group in question as a general standard to be followed by the group as a whole." And Hart concludes: "A social rule has an internal aspect in addition to the external aspect which it shares with a social habit and which consists in the regular uniform behaviour which an observer could record."

7 "Social pressure" represents an important element in Hartian thought: not only does it act as a characteristic element of the concept of norm in contrast to the simple social habit, but also, on a quantitative level, it acts as an element

refer to what Hart calls "the internal point of view", that point of view of those who accept the norms and use them as criteria for conduct. This is not enough. Someone who, from the outside, records the internal point of view of the group, makes only an external statement. This is a particular type of the latter because he takes into account the internal point of view of the group. Only those who accept the rules and who use them as a model for behaviour can be said to make internal statements: "ought", "must" "right" "wrong".[8] This is particularly important for social norms. For juridical norms one has to look at other characteristics which cannot be ignored without incurring the risk of misrepresenting legal order. For Hart juridical norms are not only of one sort. He attacks the reductionism of Kelsen.

This is a formidable and interesting theory, purporting to disclose the true, uniform nature of law latent beneath a variety of common forms and

---

helping to determine which norms impose obligations: "Rules are conceived and spoken of as imposing obligations when the general demand for conformity is insistent and the social pressure brought to bear upon those who deviate or threaten to deviate is *great*" (italics have been added). If we carry on reading this test, we notice how social pressure, according to Hart, can lead us to detect differences between moral and legal obligations:

> Such rules [those imposing obligations] may be wholly customary in origin: there may be no centrally organised system of punishments for breach of the rules; the social pressure may take only the form of a general diffused hostile or critical reaction which may stop short of physical sanctions. It may be limited to verbal manifestations of disapproval or of appeals to the individuals' respect for the rule violated; it may depend heavily on the operation of feelings of shame, remorse, and guilt. When the pressure is of this last-mentioned kind we may be inclined to classify the rules as part of the morality of the social group and the obligation under the rules as moral obligation. Conversely when physical sanctions are prominent or usual among the forms of pressure, even though these are neither closely defined nor administered by officials but are left to the community at large, we shall be inclined to classify the rules as a primitive or rudimentary form of law.

(*The Concept of Law*, *supra* n.1, at 84). To identify the severity and the strength of the social pressure as the element which allows us to determine the norms imposing obligations seems to us to be a very vague solution indeed. In this sense, see Gavazzi, *Norme primarie e norme secondarie supra* n.1, at 59. See also on this subject R,J., Bernstein, "Professor Hart on Rules of Obligation", *Mind* 73 (1964), 563-566, and P. Mullock, "Professor Bernstein on Rules of Obligation", *Mind* Volume (1967), 435-436.

8 Hart, *The Concept of Law*, *supra* n.1, at 56.

expressions which obscure it.[9]

He puts forward a dualistic conception centred on obligation and power. Before we examine these two sorts of rules, the combination of which for Hart is the "key to the science of jurisprudence" and before we analyze the consequences of the relation between acceptance and these two different sorts of rules, we must first make some preliminary distinctions between the internal and external points of view. In particular there are two questions: (1) The significance of an "external statement" made by an observer who, without accepting the norms, indicates that others do. (2) Does the Hartian distinction derive in any way from Kelsen's distinction between normative and causal science?

The first question is particularly important for Hart because he uses it to show the two conditions which are necessary and sufficient for the existence of a legal system.[10] One of these is that "its rule of recognition specifying the criteria of legal validity and its rules of change and adjudication must be effectively accepted as common public standards of official behaviour by its officials".[11] This involves the observer assuming an external point of view and then referring to the acceptance in the group of certain rules (secondary rules) by some members of it (the legal officials). This can be done with an external statement of the sort we have looked at.

Since mere feelings are ruled out as the criteria of acceptance, we are led to look for something externally cognisable.[12] But what are these

9 *Ibid.*, at 36.

10 *Ibid.*, at 86ff.; see also 244.

11 *Ibid., at* 113. The other condition to be fulfilled for a legal order to exist, is that "those rules of behaviour which are valid according to the system's ultimate criteria of validity must be generally obeyed": the latter condition is the only one which must *necessarily* be fulfilled by private citizens. I would like to emphasise that the particular external point of view with which we are dealing is not, in Hart's mind, a theorised hypothesis which aims to perceive and explain the external point of view. In reality, the question of whether a legal system exists or not is solved with the help of external factual statements following the adoption of the external point of view. Since what must be clarified is whether legal officials accept secondary rules, what is needed is the internal point of view within the social group. But, says Hart, the acceptance of secondary rules must be *effective*: And thus we have the difficult problem of applying such a nebulous concept. We shall come back to these questions and to this part of the book. For this appears to me to be fundamental for the comprehension of Hart's thought.

12 Hart, *The Concept of Law*, *supra* n.1, at 56: "The internal aspect of rules is

externally cognisable characteristics? "Criticism", "self-criticism", "demand for conformity" appear too vague. They are not sufficient to dispel the fear that, contrary to Hart's intentions, something which denies the separation between law and morals has been introduced into positivist theory of law. These expressions seem to be more the manifestation of political and moral ideology than the simple expression of a "normative attitude".[13] Acceptance can be expressed through these elements but cannot be identified with them. They only constitute a sign which can help us to ascertain the "internal" and which sometimes cannot be expressed.

Thus our observer, who does not personally accept but wishes to show that others do, might be faced with a series of behaviour externally cognisable but not accompanied by these manifestations of "criticism" etc. Will he then have to deny the existence of acceptance? How will he be able

---

often misrepresented as a mere matter of 'feelings' in contrast to externally observable physical behaviour." See also 85-86. Here the argument is aimed at Ross: see 243.

13 If "criticism", "self-criticism", "demand for conformity" are elements leading us unequivocally to the acceptance of rules, what are the other elements that lead us to the evidence that rules are morally approved? (I have in mind here Bobbio's arguments, *Considerazioni in margine*, *supra* n.1, at 244ff.: see above note 3). In my view, the external elements are identical. Yet it would be possible to say that those who criticise because they *accept*, merely acknowledge the rule as being legally valid and hence use it as a model of behaviour for themselves and for others. Those who criticise because they *approve*, make a judgment on what the norm is about and consider it positively right. This makes the phenomenon of acceptance, i.e. "formal acceptance", separate from the *approval* of norms. This is not Hart's opinion. In his view, acceptance is an *inner* experience of the addressees, born out of an evaluation of the content of the norms. Hart's acceptance is not formal. To make this clear one must look to the clear, irreducible distinction between the point of view of those who accept and those who do not:

> At any given moment the life of any society which lives by rules, legal or not, is likely to consist in a tension between those who, on the one hand, accept and voluntarily co-operate in maintaining the rules, and so see their own and other persons' behaviour in terms of the rules, and those who, on the other hand, reject the rules and attend to them only from the external point of view as a sign of possible punishment.

(*The Concept of Law, supra* n.1, at 88). Were the acceptance merely formal, there would not be this distinction, since their acceptance as formally valid norms does not necessarily imply acceptance of their content. See further note 28.

to conclude that the members of the group accept the habit as a rule? Will it be by some sort or psychological enquiry? In both cases we run the risk of making mistakes because our only criteria are ambiguous and vague.

All that we can see from the outside is a series of behaviour which at the most is accompanien from the prescribed conduct. In the first case, all we ad, but not necessarily, by criticism in the case of deviatiore able to look at is the conformity or non conformity of the behaviour to the norm. We do not have enough external elements which are not merely conformity to the norm and this makes it impossible to decide whether or not the member or the group "obey" or "observe". There might be, behind the behaviour, something which is "unexpressed acceptance". In the second case, it is true that there are characteristics which can be distinguished from simple observance. But we cannot know how far they are the particular property of "acceptance". We are not able to distinguish those characteristics which are evidence of the behaviour and those which constitute acceptance. We can make at least one point about external statements which refer to internal points of view. Discovering acceptance externally is so difficult that we must ask how far can we base the existence of legal order on such a concept without running the risk of taking this "normative attitude" for the consent which truly comes from ideological considerations.

2. *Kelsen and Hart*

We now come to the second question. Can we derive the Hartian distinction between the internal and external point of view from the distinction Kelsen makes between normative and causal science?[14] In particular does the normative jurisprudence, which for Kelsen is part of normative sciences take the internal point of view, while sociological jurisprudence, which for him is causal science, takes the external point of view? We may recall that for Kelsen "normative jurisprudence deals with the validity of the law; sociological jurisprudence, with its efficacy".[15] One

14 See Scarpelli, *supra* n.1, at 57. One should note however that, though Scarpelli adopts Hart's distinction between internal and external point of views, he has his own version of it. When I ask whether that distinction corresponds to Kelsen's division between normative and causal sciences, I have in mind the Hart's view of it.

15 H. Kelsen, "The Pure Theory of Law and Analytical Jurisprudence", *Harvard Law Review* 55 (1941), 44-70.

only deals with juridical norms, the other with the behaviour of people in relation to these norms: "The sociology of law cannot draw a line between its subject — law — and the other social phenomena; it cannot define its special object as distinct from the object of general sociology — society — without in so doing presupposing the concept of law as defined by normative jurisprudence".[16]

Sociology, for Kelsen is the study of human behaviour assuming knowledge of the rules by which that behaviour is defined. We can thus see its complementary character with respect to legal science. For Kelsen the sociologist of law is able to ask questions about the efficacy of norms only if by norms he means those recognised as valid by legal science. Using Hart's distinction we can say, from the Kelsenian perspective, that the sociologist of law has an external point of view. But this is not a radically anti-normativist view, one which merely looks to regularity in behaviour without considering norms. Rather it is the point of view of the external observer who takes into account the internal point of view of the social group.

While it is quite easy to see the statements of the sociologist of law as Hartian external statements, or more accurately a type of external statements, it is not so easy to categorise the statements of the jurist as "internal statements".[17] If Hart, with the internal-external distinction, only wanted to say that judgment of the validity of a norm takes place from within the legal order by criteria which stem from that order, we would not hesitate to recognise this as Kelsenian distinction between normative and causal science. But, as we have said, the internal point of view for Hart is exclusively the point of view of those who accept the norms. And acceptance is extraneous to the pure theory of law. However we understand it, it constitutes a phenomenon which is a property of the addressee of the norms. Thus, for Hart, a judgment of validity is only an internal statement if made by an addressee who accepts the norms. Therefore, the jurist, unless we think that he accepts, however unconsciously, or ought to accept the norms which he judges valid, cannot make internal statements about them. He can only discuss validity assuming the acceptance of the norms by the addressees.[18] His judgments

16 *Ibid.*, at 53.

17 On various types of "external statements", see Hart, *The Concept of Law*, *supra* n.1, at 244.

18 This is how I interpret Scarpelli's opinion:

> In the positivistic school, a political choice is therefore inherent to legal

end up as being external statements based on someone else's internal point of view. Nor is it worth objecting that ultimately, all that is necessary for the existence of a legal order is the acceptance of the rule of recognition by the legal officials. And therefore the judgment of validity of all norms of the system is determined by their application independent of the attitude of the other members of the group. The jurist, within the Hartian system cannot get away from looking at the fact of acceptance of these norms. This is different for Kelsen. Kelsen starts at the bottom, raising the question of the validity of a legal decision. Climbing the levels to the top of the pyramid of the legal order, the jurist doesn't look for facts which explain the acceptance of the supreme norm. Rather, he finds a *Grundnorm* which, through its scientific-hypothetical character prevents the slide, inevitable in the Hartian system, from the world of the norms to that of the addressee.[19] On the Hartian model, the jurist has to look for

---

> practice and science. Since they consider a system of law from the internal point of view, the same criteria of validity is applied on the fundamental principles of the system as its operation. (*op. cit.*, at 88).

19 I do not, of course, deny the presence of empirical elements in the pure theory of law. Already in 1934 (before Kelsen's American experience) Treves noted that the basic norm "is not the generating principle of pure normativity, i.e. of pure legal duty, but rather the principle attributing normative validity to a mere fact. It changes a factual characteristic into a normative one thus establishing a permanent and unbreakable union between the 'is' and the 'ought'." He further says: "Kelsen declares that validity (*Geltung*) as pure duty is totally independent from effectiveness (*Wirksamkeit*), that is from operation in the realm of what is. However, even a superficial analysis reveals how often the pure theory of law itself forgets that and correlates the formal concept of validity to the empirical concept of effectiveness by stating that for any order to be valid some degree of effectiveness is needed. That is, the norms of the order must, up to a point, be followed" (*Il diritto come relazione* (Turin: Tip. Accame, 1934), 115-116).

In view of the importance which the pure theory of law attributed to the "fact" ("*sein*"), one could ask whether Hart, by refusing to consider the basic norm as a hypothesis, has revealed something which already, though confusedly, was in Kelsen's mind. This is also Blackshield's opinion, *supra* n.1, at 332: "The author's central concept of a rule of recognition is perhaps little more than a reinterpretation of Kelsen's basic norm, or at least little more than a clear articulation of what was confusedly implicit in Kelsen's theory." Or, more positively, that he has released Kelsen's normative theory from certain philosophical constraints which made it obscure and contradictory.

I see it in the following way. Kelsen's insistence in restating, even recently (see "Professor Stone and the "Pure Theory of Law"", *Stanford Law* the criteria of recognition, not by consideration of the dynamic aspects of the legal order, but through finding the rules of the recognition "effectively" accepted and used by legal officials. This refers to the real behaviour of human beings which Kelsen leaves to sociological jurisprudence. The object of the science of law is legal norms, but human behaviour only to the extent that it is determined by legal norms as condition or consequence, in other words, to the extent that human behaviour is the content of legal norms.[20]

The above remarks stem from comparing the internal-external distinction of Hart and the distinction Kelsen makes between normative and causal sciences. They draw our attention to an element in Hart's view of acceptance which partially limits the derivation of Hart's distinction from Kelsen's. On the other hand, this does not take away from the necessity of both points of view to understand the phenomenon which Lombardi calls the point of view of validity and the point of view of effectiveness.[21] For us then the Hartian internal point of view can only be the same as the normative point of view if we leave out acceptance. This is because the normative point of view is the point of view of the law and not of those who accept the norms.

Review 17 (1965), 1120-57), the basic norm's hypothetical character — even though the "*Sein*" in the form of the principle of effectiveness takes an increasing importance in his doctrine — stems from his awareness of the strength of the link between the concept of validity and the basic norm seen as a scientific hypothesis. If the *Grundnorm* were to become a fact, could legal validity still be a phenomenon separate from the empirical concept of effectiveness? Hart's criticism of the basic norm is found in *The Concept of Law*, *supra* n.1, at 105ff. and 245ff.; see also "Legal and Moral Obligation", *supra* n.1, and "Kelsen's Doctrine of the Unity of Law", *supra* n.1, in particular at 193ff. Literature on the basic norm is enormous. I mention only N. Bobbio, *Teoria dell'ordinamento giuridico* (Turin: Giappichelli, 1960), 51ff.; G. Gavazzi, *Elementi di teoria del diritto* (Turin: Giappichelli, 1970), 39ff. (and see bibliography at p. 52); R. Walter, "Der gegenwärtige Stand der reinen Rechtslehre", *Rechtstheorie* (1970), 69-95.

20 H. Kelsen, *The Pure Theory of Law* (Berkeley and Los Angeles: University of California Press, 1967), 70.

21 Lombardi, *supra* n.1, at 430ff.: "... dismissing one point of view in favour of the other is difficult and even pointless"; and further: "... both points of view, that of validity and that of effectiveness, seem profitable. They can provide explanations and complement each other. Thus we cannot accept the one view only since in doing so we risk endangering our comprehension of law" (at 439).

3. *Acceptance and Primary Rules*

As we have said above, Hart never gives an explicit definition of acceptance. We can however say with some confidence that the idea of acceptance originates and develops in the context of Hart's account of primary rules, as if it were the route to a complete elucidation of the rules. It is also applied to secondary rules. All the more so because ultimately the existence of the legal order rests not only on the mere observance of rules of conduct on the part of the citizens, but also on the acceptance of the rule of recognition by the legal officials. Thus acceptance become an indispensable element only in the context of secondary rules. The question arises as to whether acceptance is the same in respect of primary and secondary rules. Whether the distinctions between them so clearly put by Hart makes it impossible to apply the same concept of acceptance to each. Thus we have to consider the distinction between primary and secondary rules more closely.

Hart, through the examination of the defects of a "simple society", one which is defined as consisting exclusively of rules which prescribe conduct, succeeds in defining what is indisputably a legal order. A "simple society" which is the primitive form of social structure, is characterised by uncertainty, its static nature and inefficiency. The society is static because it doesn't have ways of creating new rules. It is inefficient because it lacks means of resolving disputes, ascertaining facts and applying sanctions. It is uncertain because there are no ways of resolving disputes as to the existence of rules.[22] The society gradually realises and produces remedies for these defects, by having rules whose function is to "facilitate" other norms. A modern state, a complex order, is characterised by something more than norms which prescribe duties, but by rules which are parasitic on other rules, on those which prescribe duties.[23] However, secondary rules are not only defined as rules relative to other rules. Hart, in contrast to primary rules which impose obligations, defines secondary rules as norms which confer power.[24] Though it is true that secondary

22 Hart, *The Concept of Law*, *supra* n.1, at 89ff.

23 *Ibid.*, at 92: "While primary rules are concerned with the actions that individuals must or must not do, these secondary rules are all concerned with the primary rules themselves. They specify the ways in which the primary rules may be conclusively ascertained, introduced, eliminated, varied, and the fact of their violation conclusively determined."

24 *Ibid.*, at 79: "Rules of the first type concern actions involving physical movement or changes: rules of the second type provide for operations which

rules are always directed towards primary rules, one cannot say that the conferring of power is essential to their definition. As has been shown, secondary rules do not always confer power.[25]

Notwithstanding these criticisms,[26] Hart's secondary rules are extremely important for understanding law and for adding a more dynamic dimension to the complexity of the legal order.[27]

---

lead not merely to physical movement or change, but to the creation of variation of duties or obligations."

25 See Bobbio, *Ancora sulle norme primarie e secondarie*, *supra* n.1, at 43, 185, where he asks: "Why does Hart, having successfully highlighted that which is specific to the relation between primary and secondary rules, develop this in a more questionable direction for the rest of the book by stating that primary rules are those establishing duties and secondary rules those conferring powers?" Other comments put the accent on the rules of recognition which only indicate criteria of validity and cannot therefore confer powers: Cohen, *supra* n.1, at 408; Gavazzi, *Norme primarie e norme secondarie*, *supra* n.1, at 71: "How can a norm be said to confer powers when all it does is to point out one or more requirements to make primary norms more certain?"; Lloyd, *supra* n.1, at 117ff.; Sartorius, *supra* n.1, at 166: "The rules of recognition which specify the authoritative sources of law, unlike the rules of change and adjudication, are not 'necessarily' power conferring rules at all."

26 A distinction between primary and secondary rules is of course antithetic to Kelsen's "*reductio ad unum*". One should note that while Hart's primary rules go back to pre-Kelsenian positions, his doctrine of secondary rules in a sense develops the pure theory of law. Kalinowski is of this opinion ("Théorie, métathéorie ou philosophie du droit. Réflexions sur "The Concept of Law" de H.L.A. Hart et "On Law and Justice" d'Alf Ross", in *Archives de philosophie du droit* XV (1970), 179-195): "Le maître autrichien fait en réalité ressortir la dualité des règles juridiques dont les unes déterminent le comportement des autorités publiques quant à l'application des sanctions alors que les autres établissent des compétences législatives. Ceci amène M. Hart à distinguer entre les règles juridiques primaires et les règles juridiques secondaires" (at 190). On the problem of distinguishing between primary and secondary rules, see Gavazzi, *Norme primarie e norme secondarie*, *supra* n.1, at 75-127; at 94-95 we find a comparison between Hart's and Kelsen's positions: "... power conferring rules are in both authors' opinion law creating 'means', i.e. instruments enabling primary rules formation and modification. There is in substance some analogy between Hart and Kelsen as far as power conferring secondary rules are concerned."

27 See Lombardi's and Bobbio's observations on the relation between secondary norms (for Bobbio second level norms) and the concept of organisation. Lombardi, *supra* n.1, at 388ff., says: "Hart's ignorance of the institutional theory of law, and in particular of Santi Romano's work is regrettable: it would have allowed him to produce a more acceptable explanation as to why

There is something particularly convincing, therefore, in the relationship of instrumentality that Hart treats as interconnecting primary and secondary rules; but he pays too little attention to the necessity (in our view an ineluctable necessity) of analyzing the concept of acceptance in the light of that relationship. This concept was introduced in explaining primary rules and then taken up again in the context of explaining secondary rules, but taken up without sufficient regard to the instrumental character that the author had highlighted as the essential element, the fulcrum of the distinction between primary and secondary rules. Acceptance was introduced together with primary rules and was used in respect of secondary rules without sufficient consideration of the relation between primary and secondary rules.

Above, we have tried to show the difficulties arising when we try to discover in the addressee of norms that normative attitude which Hart calls "acceptance". We have expressed reservation about the possibility of distinguishing that from outright "approval". Notwithstanding these remarks, it is possible in the case of primary rules, to speak of acceptance as the attitude of those who use the norms as models of conduct and criticise themselves and others for deviation from that pattern of conduct.

---

secondary norms are indispensable to law" (at 390). Bobbio, *Ancora sulle norme primarie e secondarie*, *supra* n.1, at 52, says: "My feeling is that, in spite of its fundamental importance within the institutional theory, the concept of organisation has been left undefined, the reason being that there was no way of defining it other than that of using the notion of second level rules, from which the organisation stems." I fully agree but wish to add (recalling at the same time some remarks in an article by Bobbio himself, "Law and force", *The Monist* XLIX (1965), 321-341) that Kelsen already defines organisation by way of rules of structure. Even more, his theory of law as organised coercion is an extreme and somehow natural consequence of the fact that, following Jhering's steps, he views law from the point of view of secondary rather than primary rules. See H. Kelsen, *General Theory of Law and State* (Cambridge Mass.: Harvard University Press, 1945); *idem*, *Reine Rechtslehre, Einleitung in die rechtswissenschaftliche Problematik* (Leipzig and Vienna: Deuticke, 1934); *idem*, *Reine Rechtslehre,* IInd ed. (1960), 215ff. Hart does not share in Kelsen's idea of law as organised coercion, an idea adopted and developed instead by K. Olivecrona, *Law as Fact* (London: Oxford University Press, 1939; 2nd ed. London: Stevens & Sons 1971), 123ff., and A. Ross, *On Law and Justice* (London: Stevens & Sons, 1958; Berkeley: California University Press, 1959), 29ff. See also Bobbio (in addition to his article quoted above), *Teoria della norma giuridica* (Turin: Giappichelli, 1958), 209-210 and 220-221; *idem, Teoria dell'ordinamento giuridico* (Turin: Giappichelli, 1960), 61ff.

We mean that there is no logical barrier to going beyond the externally observable conduct of norm addressees, and without regard to issues of conformity or non-conformity, but through analysing other elements, affirming the presence of acceptance. However we have then carefully to distinguish what is evidence of authentic consensus. As far as rules of conduct are concerned, the "normative attitude" does not need to be accompanied by a behaviour which is expressed by following the norms. Neither does the observance of the norms imply its acceptance by the observer. For example, we can accept the rule which says that a car has to stop at a red traffic light and, at the same time, on certain occasions and for various reasons, break that rule.[28] Non-observance of the rule is logically independent from the question of acceptance. We can on the other hand refuse to accept the above norm and at the same time, through fear of sanctions, observe it. We can, again, take the position of someone, who, without accepting or refusing the norms, wishes to explain the relations between the addressees and the law. This is not a purely hypothetical observer. We can see such a point of view in the activity of those who, not being addressees of the legal order (they are not of the same nationality), study the behaviour of members of the group in relation to the rules.

Here we come across our observer who seeks externally to express the internal point of view of the group.

For him both observance and acceptance appear distinguishable and not necessarily connected. It is easy for our observer to see if the norm is observed but not so easy to find out whether it is accepted. This is because the first operation is based simply on correlating the behaviour prescribed by the norms to the actual behaviour (leaving aside the problem of interpretation). The second demands a difficult and delicate analysis as to the motives which have prompted the behaviour of the addressee. Thus we can say with Hart that Tim, if for example he acts exclusively through fear of sanctions, has merely followed the rule. If he

28 On the views of those who do not accept the rules, see Gavazzi, *Norme primarie e norme secondarie*, *supra* n.1, at 55; on the same question, see Hacker's remarks, *supra* n.1; see also Morris, *supra* n.1, at 1460, who asks: if acceptance of a legal order can be based on such diverse considerations such as "calculation of long term interest", "disinterested concern for others", "traditional attitude" etc. why cannot it be induced by the sheer fear of sanction? Why should the fact of considering norms as a sign of a possible sanction be viewed as a "refusal to accept" norms? "I see no reason to single out fear as the single motive precluding acceptance."

has acted because he thinks that the norm is a model to follow for himself and other group members, he has accepted and accepts the norm.

Notwithstanding the difficulties inherent in the meaning of acceptance and above all in distinguishing it from an ideological and moral response to the norm, we are clearly concerned with the attitude of the addressee when he confronts primary norms. Because they impose obligations, prescribe and constitute models of conduct.

4. *Acceptance and the Rules of Recognition*

We now turn to secondary rules. As we have seen, they are introduced to remedy the defects of the hypothetical "simple society" in which there are only rules of conduct. To remedy these defects rules of change, recognition and adjudication are introduced.

In looking at acceptance in relation to secondary rules, we shall only look at rules of recognition. They are the most important of the secondary rules, since not even a "simple society" can do without them.[29] They also get rid of uncertainty, give us criteria for recognising primary rules and tell us the conditions of validity of rules. Our interest is specially in the problem of validity.

Now what sense can we make of the expression "acceptance of the rule of recognition" and how can we, as in primary rules, keep the question of acceptance separate from that of observance?

We have seen how the relation between acceptance and primary rules is a relation between a model of behaviour and a critically reflective attitude in respect of that model. But if the rule of recognition only consists of criteria which ought to be followed, conditions which have to be accepted in order to identify a valid norm of the system, it is problematic to speak of acceptance, at least in the sense used in respect of primary rules. Rules of recognition, according to Hart, are not able to provide a model of behaviour because, by definition, only primary rules do that.[30]

29 See Hart, *The Concept of Law, supra* n.1, at 89ff. and Bobbio, *Ancora sulle norme primarie e secondarie, supra* n.1, at 46, 188: "I call simple systems those which only comprise of primary rules in addition to the rule(s) to be used to identify the system (which somehow pre-exist(s) the formation of the system and without which there would not even be a normative system)."

30 See Gavazzi, *Norme primarie e norme secondarie*, *supra* n.1, at 57; see also Morris, *supra* n.1, at 1459: "I am here not entirely sure about the status of permissive and power-conferring rules. Do such rules provide standards from

The rule of recognition, as a secondary rule, is enabling. It is the way we find out the other rules of the system. According to Hart, it doesn't prescribe, it points out. How can this be subject to critically reflective attitude?

We can understand this expression used when talking of norms of conduct. In this context, we can understand a statement of the following kind: Tim accepts the rule according to which he has to stop at a red traffic light but on certain occasions he deviates from that prescribed conduct. In this case, one can say that Tim's conduct doesn't deny his acceptance of the rule. In fact we can say it is precisely on the occasions when he doesn't observe the rules that he will criticise himself for not doing so. But in what sense can one say that Tim accepts a rule according to which a law is what parliament says but on certain occasions he doesn't?

We use rules of recognition only when we want to know what the valid rules of the legal order are. Use and acceptance here are very strictly connected. So much so that it is not possible to accept some criteria of validity but in some instances use other criteria. When we use other criteria, it means that we no longer accept the earlier ones. In fact acceptance does not mean adherence to a model of behaviour but only that the rule which we are using is recognised as "correct" for the identification of valid rules within the system.

Hart does not appear to be conscious of the way in which acceptance means something different in respect of primary and secondary rules. And yet when he speaks of acceptance of the rule of recognition by the legal officials he sees the need to qualify the word. The expression he uses is "effective acceptance". But "effective acceptance" does not mean anything other than that the acceptance of the rule necessarily follows from its use, or inversely the use of the rule necessarily implies its acceptance.

The most important consequence of this is that, when Hart gives the two necessary and sufficient conditions for the existence of a legal order, he finishes with a solution not dissimilar from the Austinian one which he had set out to deny. Austin bases the existence of legal order on the habit of obedience by the members of the group to the sovereign. Hart bases the

---

which people may deviate?" The situation is even more particular for the rules of recognition which can only be defined as rules relative to rules: neither do they impose duties nor do they confer powers.

existence of a legal order on the two conditions which respect the dualistic character of a theory of legal norms. Both these conditions are cognisable externally by observing the norms of conduct by the citizens and the use of the norms of recognition by the legal officials. In the first condition, acceptance is not necessary, it is sufficient that the members of the group observe the rules for whatever reason. In the second, acceptance is evidenced by the use of the norms but means something else. Thus, in both cases, what is important is the objective behaviour of human beings and not their attitude to the rules.

IN (PARTIAL) DEFENCE OF A PREDICTIVE CONCEPTION OF LEGAL OBLIGATION

by

GIACOMO GAVAZZI

1. *The Predictive Conception and the Normative Conception of Obligation*

Hart's analysis of the concept of obligation represents yet another convincing critique of predictive theory.[1] Moving on from Bentham, Austin and Holmes, Hart puts forward a notion of legal obligation which hinges upon the concept of norm. A normative theory of obligation, therefore.

The two opposing conceptions may be summed up as follows: the predictive concept attempts to define obligation in terms of sanction, whereas the normative attempts to define it in terms of norms. We are certainly dealing with two very different, indeed opposing conceptions here. The first looks at obligation from the point of view of what happens *later*, from the point of view of its consequences, and in particular the consequences of its violation. The second looks at it from the point of view of what happens first, it is primarily concerned with what brought about the obligation in the first place. And since predictive theory is primarily concerned with sanctions, it could be said that the moment of violation, actual or potential, represents the ideal point from which to examine the phenomenon of obligation. The normative conception requires a more distanced viewpoint, from which it is possible to observe both the violation and observance of obligations.

In speaking of the normative conception, I refer to Hart's conception. This is to be distinguished from other conceptions of obligation which,

Law and Language, The Italian Analytical School, ed. A. Pintore and M. Jori (Liverpool: Deborah Charles Publications, 1997).

1 For critiques of predictive conceptions see, for example, *Definition and Theory in Jurisprudence* (Oxford: Clarendon Press, 1954); "Legal and Moral Obligation", in *Essays on Moral Philosophy*, ed. A.I. Melden (Washington: University of Washington Press, 1958), 82-107; and, for a more extended critique, *The Concept of Law* (Oxford: The Clarendon Press, 1961).

despite their apparent normativism, display some of the same defects as predictive theories. Like the latter, they tend to view things exclusively from the point of view of the sanction and thus from the violation of the obligation. These theories define obligation as conduct which runs counter to what is prohibited.[2] Hart does not present a detailed critique of these theories. However, it would not be difficult to adapt some of the criticisms levelled at the predictive conception in *The Concept of Law* to the present case.

The predictive conception has never aroused much interest among jurists. However, this is not enough to discredit it completely. This is amply demonstrated by the very fact that Hart returns to this theme again and again. Indeed one almost has the feeling that its critique is something of a hobby horse for him.

Some of Hart's criticisms of predictive theory seem unfounded. I will attempt to refute them, without, however, embarking upon a whole hearted defence of the predictive conception. I do not wish to argue that the predictive conception is an appropriate framework through which to understand and describe the phenomenon of law in all its complexity. In other words, I am not at all convinced that the predictive thesis escapes all of Hart's criticisms. I am, however, convinced that some of the criticisms levelled against it do not hold water under close scrutiny.

I propose to discuss the following two points. Firstly, according to Hart the predictive conception cannot give a necessary condition for establishing the truth of propositions that assert that X has an obligation *a*.

Secondly, Hart applies J.L. Austin's distinction between the meaning and the force of linguistic expressions[3] and accuses the predictive conception of confounding the force of propositions which assert an obligation with their meaning. To put it more precisely: according to Hart, the probability of a sanction, which for predictive theory constitutes the meaning of propositions which affirm obligations, does not form part of the meaning of these propositions. Rather, it forms part of their force. I remain unconvinced by Hart's arguments on both counts.

2 I am referring in particular to Kelsen's theory. See, for example, *General Theory of Law and State* (Cambridge Mass.: Harvard University Press, 1946).

3 J.L Austin, "Truth", in *Philosophical Papers*, ed. J.O. Urmson and G.J. Warnock (Oxford: Clarendon Press, 1961), 85-101; "Performative Utterances", in *Philosophical Papers*, *ibid.*, 237-239; and in particular *How to do things with Words*, ed. J.O. Urmson (Oxford: Clarendon Press, 1962), ch. VIII.

2. *Obligation and the Prediction of Sanctions*

According to Bentham[4] statements relating to obligations have a factual content and assert the existence, real or probable, of a sanction in the case of the commission or omission of certain behaviour. The statement "X has the legal obligation *a*" means, according to Bentham and according to predictive theories in general, that "if X does not do *a*, then he will in all probability be subject to (the sanction) Z carried out by A (a public authority)".

It is obvious that the credibility of any concept of obligation is a measure of the extent to which consideration is given to the types of situations in which X did not do *a* , or in which if he did the opposite of *a* (which means he violated the obligation) he was not subjected to a sanction. A theory which refuses to acknowledge that obligation, however it is defined, is something that regards the future would attract little interest. Neither would one which restricted itself to considering obligation as relating to actions carried out in the past. A simple account of actions carried out in a past which has no relation to the world of our present and future actions has no room for the concept of obligation.

The predictive theory of obligation is aware of this need. And, in my view, it is precisely for this reason that it puts more emphasis on the probability of a sanction than on its actual imposition. The "predictions of sanctions" into which statements of obligation ought to be translated according to predictive theory are guaranteed to the extent to which the probability of sanction exists in the specific case. "X has an obligation to do *a*" is true to the extent that the assertion that Z will probably happen in the case of non *a* is guaranteed.

Hart has another, more straightforward objection[5] to the interpretation of the concept of obligation based on the element of prediction. According to Hart, the probability of a sanction is not sufficient justification to say that X has an obligation. In Hart's view, the (guaranteed) probability of a sanction is not a necessary reason because:

(1) X has an obligation to do *a*

is not contradicted by

4 See note 15 in Hart's article, "Il concetto di obbligo", in *Rivista di filosofia* LVII (1966), 125-140 (engl. transl. of "Legal Duty and Obligation", in *Essays on Bentham* (Oxford: Clarendon Press: 1982), 127-161).

5 Hart, *The Concept of Law* , *supra* n.1, at ch.5 section 2.

(2) if X does not do *a*, X will not be subject to sanctions.

According to Hart, the two propositions can be affirmed simultaneously *without contradiction*. If this were true, the probability or non-probability of sanctions being imposed on X for not doing *a* would not constitute sufficient reason for saying that X has, or does not have, an obligation to do *a*.

On the other hand

(3) X has an obligation to do *a*

can be affirmed simultaneously *without redundancy* with

(4) If X does not do *a*, he will probably be subjected to Z by A.

If this were true, (3) and (4) would each mean something different and the probability of a sanction affirmed by (4) would therefore not be sufficient to establish whether the proposition "X has an obligation to do *a*" were true or not.

Everything now depends upon whether or not there is a contradiction between (1) and (2) and upon whether or not there is redundancy between (3) and (4).

It is clear that according to Bentham's definition of obligation there is a contradiction in the first case and a redundancy in the second. Bentham defines the concept of obligation in a certain way, namely as the probability of incurring a sanction for behaving in a particular way. It is obvious that once a term has been defined in a certain way, it cannot then be used to denote something else without creating misunderstanding and confusion. If we accept Bentham's definition, then "X has an obligation to do *a*" means, and should always mean, "if X does not do *a*, X will probably incur the sanction Z". If the contradiction between (1) and (2) and the redundancy between (3) and (4) are not always clear, this is because in one of the two propositions which make up the pairs (1) and (2) and (3) and (4) respectively, the term obligation is used to denote something other than the "probability of incurring a sanction". Such a shift in meaning would be nothing out of the ordinary in everyday language and would not be called into question. What is a matter of some dispute, however, is whether it is possible to use the terms contradiction and redundancy to highlight the similarities and differences between a proposition in a technical discourse (or one which claims to be such) and a proposition in ordinary language. It is clear, and it seems to me that not even the Oxford philosophers would have disputed it, that two propositions can only be said to contradict each other if they both share the particular logical syntax of a particular language. It does not make sense to speak of contradiction outwith the context of a particular logical syntax. It would be like saying that there is a contradiction between the astronomical statement that the earth rotates on its own axis for a period of 23 hours and 56 minutes and the ordinary language statement that the sun rises in the morning and sets in the evening.

The fact that it is impossible to establish a relationship of contradiction between heterogeneous statements does not mean that it is impossible to compare them in some way. The very act of comparing them will show up the difference in meaning between the two statements and the fact that they belong to different linguistic universes. The truth or falsity of each is established within the discourse to which each belongs.

In my view the two ordinary language statements "X has an obligation to do *a*" and "X will not incur any sanction if he does not do *a*" are in no way contradictory. This is because they are saying two different things. There is no contradiction because there cannot be one. The same can be said of the presumed redundancy between the statement "X has an obligation to do *a*" and the statement "if X does not do *a*, then he will probably incur sanction Z".

We may sum up as follows: either propositions (1), (2), (3) and (4) belong to ordinary language and there is thus no contradiction or redundancy between them because they are "talking" about different things; or propositions (1) and (3) belong to everyday language and propositions (2) and (4) belong to technical language (the one established with Bentham's definition of obligation). In the latter case, it is not possible to talk of contradiction or redundancy because the propositions are of a different order. Finally, one could argue that all four propositions belong to the same technical discourse and if the definition of obligation is adhered to there is a contradiction between (1) and (2) and redundancy between (3) and (4).

It seems to me that Hart did not make it sufficiently clear to which of these three possibilities he was referring. To judge from the tenor of his previous observations, it would seem that Hart was thinking of an opposition between a concept belonging to a technical language (defined and definable on the basis of Bentham's presuppositions) and "the current ideas that show themselves in the habitual and effective uses of the words 'obligation' and 'duty'".[6] What he was thus alluding too was an opposition

6 Hart, "Il concetto di obbligo", *supra* n.4, at 133.

between technical language and everyday language. But if this is the case, then he cannot pose the question in terms of the relationship between contradiction and redundancy. All he can do is point out that the expressions have different meanings and indicate the reasons (not only the formal ones, like those relating to the presumed non-contradiction and non-redundancy) that might lead us to reject the Benthamite notion in favour of the broader one deriving from ordinary language. I am not saying that this is not Hart's preferred route. Indeed his criticisms of predictive theory, namely that it fails even to "establish a sufficient condition for the truth" of assertions of obligation seem to point in this direction.[7] According to Hart, the "fundamental objection is that the predictive interpretation obscures the fact that, where rules exist, deviations from them are not merely grounds for a prediction that hostile reactions will follow ... but are also a reason or justification for such reaction and for applying the sanctions".[8] It is difficult to disagree with Hart on this point.

Up until now I have maintained, contrary to Hart, that the propositions "X has an obligation to do *a*" and "if X does not do *a*, he will probably not incur sanction Z" do not contradict each other. Similarly, there is no redundancy between the statement "X has an obligation to do *a*" and "if X does not do *a*, he will probably incur sanction Z" because both sets of statements belong to different universes of discourse. It would appear that if the latter condition is not met, that is if the statements belong to the same universe of discourse and the definition of obligation is respected, the first two statements stand in a relation of contradiction and the second two in one of redundancy.

Let us consider the following hypothesis: "If it were true that the statement that a person had an obligation meant that *he* was likely to suffer in the event of disobedience, it would be a contradiction to say that he had an obligation, e.g. to report for military service but that, owing to the fact that he had escaped from the jurisdiction, or had successfully bribed the police or the court, there was not the slightest chance of his being caught or made to suffer".[9] If there really were a contradiction between the two statements, the conception of obligation which led us to such conclusions would be completely useless and absurd. We would have

7 Hart, "Il concetto di obbligo", *supra* n.4, at 134.

8 Hart *The Concept of Law, supra* n.1, at 82.

9 Hart, *The Concept of Law, supra* n.1, at 82; for analagous examples, but in the present tense, see "Il concetto di obbligo", *supra* n.4, at 134.

two absurdities. On the one hand, every time we knew for certain that a particular person would not incur sanctions whatever he did, we would have to say that that person had no obligations (even if other people who find themselves in the same situation incur sanctions). On the other hand, in order to establish if a person really has an obligation we would have to suspend judgement, exhort the person whom we suspect of having an obligation to violate it, and wait (for how long?) to see whether or not the sanction will be applied.

In fact, objections such as Hart's misrepresent the predictive and probabilistic nature of assertions concerning obligations. Although the theory of probability is far from clear, one thing seems certain. Assertions of probability do not relate to the individual case, or, even when they appear to do so, they are in fact founded upon a series of cases and are valid for the generality of cases of a certain type. There is no more of a contradiction between the affirmation "Joe Bloggs has obligation a" and the assertion that Joe Bloggs will not incur any sanction because he enjoys special privileges or because he has taken refuge in Venezuela than there is between saying that Nearco is tipped to win the Derby and that on the contrary Ringo will win because he has been doped.

What this boils down to is the fact that something turns out against expectations, or simply differently from what was considered probable, does not in the least contradict the assertion regarding the probability of an event. Otherwise it would not be a question of probability but of certainty.

In my view, Hart's mistake was to emphasise the predictive character of the conception without taking into account the probabilistic aspect of the predictions themselves. It must be said that predictive conceptions have not made much of an attempt to refine their concepts in this respect. The following distinction might help to make this more clear. Among the various propositions which assert the existence of an obligation, it is worth distinguishing between those which have an individual subject (Joe Bloggs, Caius, Sempronius) and those which have a collective subject (the head of the family, the owner of a country estate etc). Both types of proposition can state whether or not a sanction is likely to be applied. But is it probability in respect of a class or in respect of the individual which should become the criterion to assert the existence of an obligation? There seems to me no doubt that we have to opt for the first of these if we are to avoid the absurdities pointed out by Hart. It would thus be possible to say that a particular person has an obligation if the class of persons to whom that particular individual belongs is likely to incur sanctions when it behaves in a certain way.

But then, one might ask, how is it possible to determine the class of people to whom Joe Bloggs, Caius and Sempronius belong if not through the very norms which are so alien to the predictive conception with its insistence on empiricism and behaviourism? To this I would reply that it is not my intention to defend legal realism as such, but merely the aspects of probability emphasised by predictive theory. These, if I am not mistaken, are not irreconcilable with a normative conception of law.

3. *The Force and Meaning of Predictions of Sanctions*

According to Hart, it is also a mistake "to have put forward as the meaning of obligation an aspect which is not in fact part of its meaning but is characteristic of the force which assertions of obligation frequently assume".[10]

It seems to me, however, that predictive theories do not fall into this trap. It is important to note, however, that this differs somewhat from the usual, generally well-founded criticism according to which the predictive conception fails to make clear the reason for, or the justification of, the application of sanctions when confronted with someone who has broken an obligation.[11] Nor is it a question of "having presented in the form of a predictive connection a consequence that was merely subordinate and secondary to the normative phenomenon".[12] Hart's accusation is, in my view, much more serious.

According to Hart, the meaning of a proposition is a constant element regulated by general linguistic conventions. These conventions, and hence the meaning of a proposition determined on the basis of these conventions, remain unchanged however the proposition is used. The force of the proposition, on the other hand, has nothing to do with its meaning, but the specific use which is made of it. It therefore varies according to the uses to which it is put and according to the speaker's intentions. The meaning of the proposition, however, remains constant. The example provided by Hart makes this clear: the proposition "there is a bull in the field" has the same meaning whether it is used as information, as a

10 Hart, "Il concetto di obbligo", *supra* n.4, at 134.

11 Hart, *The Concept of Law*, *supra* n.1, at 82.

12 Hart, "Il concetto di obbligo", *supra* n.4, at 140.

prescription ("don't go into the field") or as a warning ("watch out or you could get gored!"). The use and the force may vary, but the meaning remains constant.

In what sense then does the predictive conception put forward something as meaning which, according to Hart, is in fact part of the force of the proposition of obligation? I suspect that Hart's misgivings stem from having put to much emphasis on Bentham's reformist intentions. It may be that for Bentham, who was an implacable critic of law from a utilitarian point of view, assertions of obligation functioned as a warning, as alarm bells signalling the danger of a sanction. But whatever for Bentham was *the force* or the function of assertions of obligation, for him too they primarily had the meaning of predictions of sanctions. The assertion that something is likely to happen has nothing to do with the force of the proposition that states this probability. It is, however, true that the proposition that predicts a certain event can be used for different purposes and thus have a different force. To return to Hart's example, the meaning of the proposition "there is a bull in the field" remains constant, but its force varies according to the circumstances in which it is used. However, the proposition "if you go into this field you're likely to be gored by a bull" is not a "force" of the first, but a different proposition altogether. Its meaning is completely unrelated to that of the first, and its force varies according to how it is used. It can give someone who doesn't know anything about bulls some useful information. It can act as a warning, or as an incitement to someone to commit a daredevil act. The same can be said of propositions which assert obligations interpreted as predictions of sanctions. The prediction of sanctions is not part of the force of the propositions which state it on the contrary, it is constitutive of their meaning. This is true even if predictions of sanctions can, more readily than mere assertions of obligation, assume the force of warnings. However, this depends on their having a more specific conventional meaning. The proposition "whoever goes into the field will probably be gored by the bull" can more readily be used as a warning than the proposition "there is a bull in the field", since in the latter case it would have to be understood that the bull was alive and that it was not tied up, etc.

LAW AND ORDINARY LANGUAGE

by

GIORGIO LAZZARO

1. *Judicial Arguments*

Among judicial arguments, there is one that can be seen as an *appeal to ordinary language*. The *occasional* reference to ordinary language as justification for an interpretative choice, betrays a deep judicial conviction. The law (or more precisely the legislator) uses, *in general*, a technical language.

This seems to go against the Enlightenment doctrine that the legislator must express himself in the clearest and simplest way. This the legislator must do in order to be understood by every citizen. The best way to achieve this, would be to make legal language like the language which citizens use in their everyday communications. Technical language, it is claimed however, is necessitated by modern law. The subject matter of the regulation of modern legal orders is so complex that the use of a technical language is the only way to deal with the requirements of synthesis and conciseness.

I want here to discuss the basis of such requirements. It is clear that judges often assume that there is a discrepancy between legislative and ordinary language. Looking at court decisions, we get a picture of the two languages running in parallel. In the absence of any indication of the contrary, they do not connect. Even here, reference to the dictionary is only *an additional reason* for the attribution of a particular meaning to a legislative expression.

We can see an example in the controversy as to the meaning of the expression "transfer of houses". This appeared in the famous tax law, n.408 of 1949. The purpose of this law was to ease housing reconstruction. It was said:

The appeal against the decision is based firstly on a mere lexical argument. It is argued that the law uses the term *transfer* and that the

Law and Language, The Italian Analytical School, ed. A. Pintore and M. Jori (Liverpool: Deborah Charles Publications, 1997).

meaning of such a term is wide to the point of including the transfer of any right. It would thus be wrong to limit its scope to the transfer of property only.

This argument is easily countered. "Transfer of houses" here has the same meaning in juridical language as it has in ordinary language. It always means the transfer of property.[1]

On the basis of this the Court of Cassation concluded that the tax benefits granted to the sales of residential houses (the reduction of the registry tax) should not be extended to the creation of a usufruct.

I want to use this reasoning to illustrate, when necessary, this particular approach. I will only add that the solution chosen by the court is backed by further arguments. Among these, is the argument that the expression "transfer" is not well suited to the description of a juridical situation where a non pre-existing right comes into being. The transfer of a quid which does not yet exist is not possible. We can call this argument "the argument from the efficacy of the statute as formulated" and it will be worth coming back to.

Our general theme needs to be expanded if we are better to understand the value of the reference to ordinary language in the practice of the judges and other legal functionaries. It is also important to face the problem of the complex relation which exists not only between juridical and ordinary language but also, as we shall see, between law and ordinary language.

2. *Ordinary Language as the Object of Rules*

We must not forget one aspect of the relationship between law and ordinary language. The way in which "ordinary" people communicate and express themselves can itself become the object of legislation. So the law suppresses certain verbal behaviour, considering it as liable to affect some individual or general interest. Defamation can be considered an example of the former and laws against blasphemy and obscene language as examples of the latter.

But the law does not always limit itself to prohibiting the use in public of certain words. Sometimes it attempts to *correct* the current, and sometimes widespread, use of certain terms. It thus displays a tendency to perform a *therapeutic* function with respect to ordinary language. The

1 Cass., 2nd March 1964, n. 475, in *Giurisprudenza italiana*, 1964, I, 1, c.402.

law, for example, limits the way in which certain commercial products can be described. Certain description will only be allowed if the product meets specific requirements. The aim here is clear. It is both to promote quality and to protect the consumer from misdescription. To ensure that the names of certain goods, having a high reputation are not taken by others. An example is the law of 10th April, 1954, n.125. Art. 2 regulates the names of cheeses in Italy and lays down the conditions under which cheeses can be given certain names. In a regulation under this law (the presidential decree of 30th October 1955, n.1269) the conditions of applicability of inter alia, "Fontina" cheese is laid down. Here we are clearly dealing with a definition. More precisely, with legislative definition.

It seems to me that those who have dealt with "legislative definitions" have not sufficiently underlined the fact that such definitions are of a very particular kind. If anything, they are *normative* in two different ways. Not only do they represent a directive for the interpreter, but above all, they represent a directive for the citizen. They do not merely clarify a term used in the law. In fact, were it not for the definition, there would be no reason for the legal disposition. A law which imposed the name "fontina" on fontina cheese would not do anything. One can see the definition of "fontina" in our example as a species of redefinition. A practice is acknowledged and taken into account. Some amendments are made but these are for reasons that we have seen above (to protect the consumer etc.). We are not concerned here with a finer and more precise definition of "fontina".

Furthermore, laws which guarantee typical products are undoubtedly an interference by the legislator in ordinary language. It is not just a case of legally sanctioning a prevailing linguistic practice in order to protect it. The legislator tries to modify the practice. This can be seen in the fact that in the first instance the concerning the definition of "Fontina" did not require it to be produced in the Val d'Aosta. It later did so and thus modified linguistic practice.

It might be said that prescriptions as to the names of products concern mainly the language of traders. They therefore concern themselves with a technical language, that is commercial language. But this cannot be true unless we specify what a technical language is. For these norms are intended to interfere in the communications between traders and public. They try to induce the latter into using their own language more rigorously. An attempt is made to convince consumers, in their own interest, to make their language more technical.

Are these laws effective? That is a different problem. It is a fact that often consumers do not even know these norms and proceed imperturbably to using characteristic trade-marks in their wider and traditional meaning. This is exactly what happens with the word "fontina". Italian consumers, even the Piedmontese, keep calling cheeses produced outside the territory of Val d'Aosta "fontina" as well. This, even though the characteristics of such cheeses are only vaguely similar to those of the genuine ones.

This happens also with the word "cognac" which an Italo-French convention attributes exclusively to brandy distilled in certain specific areas of France. The unaware Italian consumer keeps asking for "cognac", sometimes mispronouncing it, when asking for brandies distilled in Italy or Spain. Ordinary people therefore, sometimes rebel against linguistic impositions, even though they are laid down in their own interest. But the legislature continues to suggest models of practice where everybody, producers and traders, retailers and individual buyers, would use certain words with different meaning than before. These meanings always being more restricted. Furthermore, because these sort of trade marks are selected following a careful analysis of the product and of the methods of production; because the definitions consist in large part of quantitative values (percentages of substances, measurements in degrees of temperature, acidity, alcoholic content, etc.); these terms, as adopted by law, appear to have a technical as opposed to ordinary meaning.

3. *Ordinary Language as a Source of Law.*

Law therefore, has some influence — or at least a tentative influence — on ordinary language. But is there a reciprocal influence? I would say that, in some cases at least, there is. We can, firstly see ordinary language, or more precisely, the change in the ordinary language, influencing the law in "popularisation" of factory trade marks. The royal decree of 21st June 1942, n.929, says at art. 41:

> A factory trade mark will expire in the following cases:
> (1) if the trade mark has become a general term for a product or merchandise.

Thus, the right to the exclusive use of a trade mark will be lost if the habit of calling certain types of goods by the actual trade mark has become strongly rooted among the public. “Nylon” is a good example. Sometimes transcribed as “nailon” in Italian, it is a synthetic fibre in widespread use. Originally, it was the name of one manufacturer’s product. But it soon came to mean a generic fibre such as wool and cotton. And it remained thus in ordinary language. In a more local context, something similar happened with “*cuneesi al rum*”, a small sweet covered with chocolate. This was, for a long time, the object of controversy between the original manufacturer and his imitators.

With this “popularisation” of the trade mark, there follows an adjustment of law to fact. That fact however, being a linguistic fact. It is a change in ordinary language which creates a new juridical situation, in this case the extinction of a right. It must be said however, that some maintain that the advent of a new linguistic practice on the part of consumers is not enough. To that should be added lack of action by the title holder against the use of the trade mark by other manufacturers. Even so, the driving element within the complex state of affairs that leads to the loss of title is a linguistic fact, the force of which is irresistible.

Up to now we have been dealing with instances of the direct influence which ordinary language has on juridical situations. Such influence is foreseen and established in legislative dispositions.

But the indirect influence which ordinary language and its evolution has is much more relevant. It is this influence which affects the interpretation of legislation. For this indirect influence, some conditions are necessary. First of all, the particular law must have been in force for some time, so as to allow a partial change in the meaning of some expressions. Secondly it has to deal with to matters to which citizen refer to in their lives.

This latter condition enables us to see the phenomenon of the “projection” of the juridical norm in a new light. This term was introduced, at the beginning of this century, by K.G. Wurzel.[2] The following examples were used by him to illustrate it. A law of 1700 introduced a tax on mills powered by “mechanical force”. This law could equally have been applied to steam and electrical mills, even though water and wind were the only mechanical forces known in 1700. We cannot understand what happens here as “subsumption” in the narrow meaning; It is not even an analogy because nothing is added to the

2 In his essay *Das juristische Denken* (Wien: Perles), the first edition of which dates to 1904.

concept of "mechanical force". The concept is applied directly to steam mills since this is allowed by the linguistic use of the adjective "mechanical".

Another example given by Wurzel is that of a law which made the forgery of money illegal. This was promulgated at a time when only coins existed. Later on, when bank-notes were introduced, it was held without controversy (on the basis of the same law) that the forgery of bank-notes was also illegal. Jhering though this to be applying the law by analogy. According to Wurzel however, it was not an analogy. Had it been so, one would have spoken of analogy when gold coins were added to silver ones, or when a different type of banknote was printed. The term "money" is simply projected on to new kinds of money, without thinking that a lacuna in the law has been filled. What allows the projection is a contingent event, a particular turn in ordinary language. The direct application of an old law will be possible if an old word is used in order to designate a new kind of thing. If a new word has been devised, such application will not be possible. Resort to analogical extension, if allowed, will be necessary. For strictly speaking, it would have been possible to apply the tax on mills powered by mechanical force to the new steam mills without controversy. It would have been different in respect of the new electrical mills. For in ordinary language one distinguishes electrical energy from mechanical energy. If electrical energy had commonly been called electro-mechanical, then the situation would have been different. Then electrical energy could have been subsumed under mechanical energy as a sub-species of the latter.

Projection is an acute problem in those areas where analogical application is forbidden. The original field of a law is widened or narrowed by wholly contingent events, in this case the vagaries of ordinary language. It may appear shocking that it happens this way and not through more reasoned arguments. But it is not as simple as that. One should not think that a quirk of ordinary language is capable of determining, in a quasi mechanical way, the subterranean evolving interpretation which takes place when there is projection. Often, behind the narrower or wider interpretation of a legislative term, behind the application or non-application of a law, lie wide conflicts of interests.

We are not thinking here of some technical novelty, some new instrument, product or method of production. Here the effects of the so-called projection can be all but disregarded. Rather, I am thinking of when a new product, which can be dangerous or harmful, comes on the scene. The rules regulating or limiting its use will depend upon the contingency of what it is called.

Novelty can consist in human behaviour that is socially relevant or liable to be singled out juridically. In respect of the former, one can mention mass nudism. For the latter, the new forms of organised strike. It is likely that when norms relating to strikes were first promulgated in modern juridical orders, some forms of workforce unrest were not practised and perhaps not even imagined. Later on came wild cat strikes, work to rules and other more sophisticated forms of strikes. Whether such forms of union pressure were included in the juridical notion of "strike", and so in the laws concerning strikes, depended no doubt on many complex political factors. However, the fact that in ordinary language such behaviour was also called "strike", and that no other word was used, may also have been a contributing factor.

4. *Technical Language*

In what has gone before, the notion of "technical language" has often been used. But how, and in response to what, does a technical language grow up alongside an ordinary one? Here it would be useful to consider Preti's contribution to the subject.[3] There we find confirmation of the fact that, inevitably, when the same term passes from ordinary language to technical language, it undergoes a change of meaning. To put it more precisely, a parallel transfer of meaning.

Let us try to understand, says Preti, what a technical language or constructed theory is. They are the same:

> The essential elements are axioms and a calculus or syntax, whichever you prefer ... A set of axioms is a set of propositions conventionally accepted as primitive; among them, there are terms, which are also primitive and are defined through the axiom system itself. The axioms of elementary geometry (Euclidean) give a definition of the "straight line": Within that elementary geometry, "straight line" *has no other meaning* than that given to it by the set of axioms. It would be better not to use the expression "straight line" outside Euclidean elementary geometry. But since the codes and the constitution do not include norms on the subject, it is possible to use the same expression. In this case, however, *its meaning is different.*[4]

3 "Linguaggio comune e linguaggi scientifici", now in *Saggi filosofici* (Firenze: La nuova Italia 1976), 127-220.

4 *Ibid.*, at 161.

The axioms in a well constructed axiom system, adds Preti, must have certain characteristics. They must not be contradictory, they must be independent and the system must be complete. All this eliminates indeterminacy. There is no room for vague notions in a language constructed in such a way.

The following is the main way in which technical language acts to eliminate the many indeterminacies found in ordinary language: with a suitable axiomatisation, determining the field of application of a symbol; dividing a sentence into a group of linked sentences, each of which includes no indeterminacy; or introducing criteria and rules for use.

But what relation is left between notions constructed in this way and notions of ordinary language? Preti clarifies:

> In general, the analysis of ordinary language expressions in a technical language does not involve simple clarification or an elucidation or discovery of the meaning which the expressions have in ordinary language. In reality, the analysis itself *creates* their meaning by introducing semantic rules specifying it.

From a different point of view, in so far as they are wholly defined within that language, the terms of a technical language are no longer those of the ordinary language — even though there is still a verbal resemblance. Neither are they equivalent. On the contrary, the terms of the technical language and of the ordinary language become incommensurable.

A theory so constructed could, at the very most, establish a connection between some of its expressions and certain expressions of the ordinary language. Never an equivalence.

Such requirement, Preti concludes, was called by Broad the *principle of Pickwickian meanings.*[5] According to Broad, whenever mathematicians define certain series of rational numbers all having the same formal properties as the irrationals ÷2 and ÷3 and call such a series "irrational numbers", they use such expression in a Pickwickian meaning. When theologians say that the second person of the Trinity is the "Son" of the first one, they use the word "son" in a Pickwickian meaning. To use an expression in a Pickwickian meaning, means therefore that it is used to indicate something different than that which the term properly designates. It does this in such a way, however, that the term and the corresponding Pickwickian word have in common certain formal

5 "Filosofia critica e speculativa", in *Filosofi inglesi contemporanei,* ed. J.H. Muirhead (Milan: Bompiani, 1939), 274ff. The term, however, was coined by Moore.

properties.

Preti goes on:

> when Newton refers to colours as "waves with a certain degree of refrangibility", he clearly uses *colour* in a Pickwickian meaning. For example, the colour *yellow*, when we see it through a spectrum is dependent upon the presence of waves having a certain degree of refrangibility. Because of this, we use the expression "yellow colours" or "yellow light" to designate any light with the same degree of refrangibility, independent of the way in which we see it. In certain circumstances, for example, we can *perceive* a "yellow light" as having a different colour.

We can see in Preti's example that behind the notion of *ordinary language* there is an idea of *ordinary meaning* and also that of *sense experience* which is in some way linked to the former. Ordinary meaning and sense experience can lead to knowledge, which while not scientifically exact, might nevertheless be useful for practical ends.

Preti makes this point more clearly later. He shows how it is the introduction of mathematical rigour into a discipline which had historically been one of the ways, if not the principal way, of eliminating indetermination and ambiguities in ordinary language. Physics, for example, is based on *measurement*. But what is more interesting for Preti is to see how, through measurement, terms which in ordinary language are vague, become determinate.

Some examples have become classic because they can already be found in Galileo. Take the concepts of "far" and "near" (*Saggiatore*) and of "heavy" and "light" (*Discorso sulle cose che stanno sull'acqua*). Paraphrasing we can illustrate Galileo's concept as follows. The terms "far" and "near" are vague. The same thing can be both far and near; a carrier says that Naples is near to Rome, a lady complains that the church is too far way from her house. It becomes precise by establishing how far point A is from point B. The same is the case with "heavy" and "light"; here also they acquire precision with measurement.[6]

Measurements which compare several distances are rougher. A from B is twice the distance of B from C. This still remains unsatisfactory. Rome is far more distant from Naples than the house from the church. But the expression "far more distant" is still a very vague expression. In practice this leads to the use of standard measures such as the metre, the kilometre, the light-year etc.

Several vague terms in ordinary language become determined

6 *Ibid.*, at 176.

analogously. Complex mathematical procedures help to substitute the concept of "curve" for the vague idea of "round" and the concept of "with a larger curve" for "rounder". This can result in a noticeable difference between sensory perception and scientific concepts. An ellipse in, certain circumstances, can appear as a circle to the human eye. Therefore some shapes, which are ellipses in geometry, are called round in ordinary language, reflecting sensory perception.

Preti continues his analysis of the "correspondence" between scientific concepts and notions of ordinary meaning by examining the relation between theoretical propositions and *protocols* i.e. statements of observable facts. For our purpose, however, we can stop here. What is most important for us is the case the *same* word appears in both ordinary language and technical language.[7]

5. *Can a Normative Language be Technical?*

Preti's considerations are still very useful when we examine the nature of a technical language. But they raise many problems. Firstly, he speaks of technical language as the equivalent of scientific and theoretical language. But from the fact that it is clearly distinguishable from ordinary language, does not follow that a technical language is always constructed in the rigorous manner that Preti claims. It is not only scientists who have a language of their own, made out of terms which do not appear in ordinary language. Craftsman also do. Mechanical engineers, for example use terms such as "boring-machine" and "boring" the meaning of which might escape a person not knowledgeable in mechanics, however learned he may be.

It also appears, from all the examples that he gives, that Preti considers language in its *descriptive* function only. Whether a language with a *normative* function can be technical, in his sense, remains to be seen. Put another way, is it possible to achieve rigour and precision in system of messages which has a prescriptive function? Is an axiomatics possible in such a field? At first glance, something of the kind appears to take place with certain systems of rules. These are the so-called

7 A different problem is that of the relation between the technical terms used by empirical sciences and ordinary experience vocabulary, when dealing with terms different one from the other: see C.G. Hempel, *Fundamentals of Concept Formation in Empirical Science*, Ital. transl. by A. Pasquinelli, *La formazione dei concetti e delle teorie nella scienza empirica* (Milan: Feltrinelli, 1961), 27ff.

constitutive rules like those of the game of chess — to give an often used example. Carnap says:

> But system of rules of chess is also a calculus. The chessmen are the symbols (here, as opposed to those of the word-languages, they have no meaning), the rules of formation determine the position of the chessmen (especially the initial positions in the game), and the rules of transformation determine the moves which are permitted — that is to say, the permissible transformations of one position into the other.[8]

Is there therefore, in normative systems, rigour but meaningless symbols? Ernst Mally thinks not. He believes that the rules of chess give the pieces a *functional meaning*:

> It is because of these rules that one piece is characterised as "king", another one as "bishop", a third one as "pawn". Within the game, the name of a piece is nothing else but the expression of its "function", a stenographic indication of its *funktionale Bedeutung*. It is through its rules that the essence of the piece is determined. In the same way, in the system of axioms formulated for Euclidean geometry by David Hilbert, "point", "straight line", "plane" are determined only through the postulates of the system.[9]

There is therefore a parallel and analogy between certain theoretical-descriptive systems and certain systems of rules. For the chess game, however, there is less of an analogy in respect of the relation between the *names* as symbols of the system and the same *names* as words of the ordinary language. Obviously, the "knight" in the chess game is a different thing from the "knight" we know of. It does not even appear to be a "knight" in a Pickwickian meaning. The very formal properties which made the theologians call "son" the second person of the trinity, are missing. Why have chess pieces been given the fantasy names which we all know? Probably the answer lies in the fact that the game had, or acquired, the symbolic meaning of a battle. Whether this is true I cannot tell. But they could have been identified in other ways, with numbers, letters, colours, etc. Moreover, it is true that the notion of "constitutive rule" is also used when referring to systems of rules more complex than the game of chess. For instance, John R. Searle says:

8 *The Logical Syntax of Language*, trld. Amathe Smeaton (London: Routledge and Kegan Paul, Trench: Trubner & Co. Ltd., 1937), 5.

9 "Formalismus", in *Logische Schriften* (Dordrecht: Reidel, 1971), 189, quoted by A.G. Conte, "Parerga leibnitiana", in A. Martino, E. Maretti and C. Ciampi, eds., *Logica, informatica e diritto* (Florence: Le Monnier, 1978), 217-255, at 240.

> I want to clarify a distinction between two different sorts of rules, which I shall call *regulative* and *constitutive* rules. I am fairly confident about the distinction, but do not find it easy to clarify. As a start, we might say that regulative rules regulate antecedently or independently existing forms of behaviour; for example, many rules of etiquette regulate interpersonal relations which exist independently of the rules. But constitutive rules do not merely regulate, they create or define new forms of behaviour. The rules of football and chess, for example, do not merely regulating playing football or chess, but as it were create the very possibility of playing such games.[10]

The reference to (American) football is interesting. For it is a game where the regulated behaviour are not "moves", able to be reproduced on something like an electronic chess board. Neither can they be transmitted in the same way as chess moves by means of a simple notation which locate the moves on the board. They are bodily movements, which exist, in their materiality, as running, jumping, etc., even apart from the rules of the game.

From another point of view, the purposes of the game, including scoring, can be achieved through a practically infinite variety of behaviour. Therefore such behaviour may not only be invalid, it can also be illegal within the game and as such punished. A "foul", on the other hand, would have no meaning in the game of chess. I use this example because the rules of these sporting games where the teams share the same field of play are very similar to legal rules. In both cases we find invalidity and sanction; void acts which must, at the very least be repeated, and illegal acts which are repressed.

Even actions in the game of football do not have the meaning they would have without a system of rules. Legal orders can be seen as games from another point of view as well. For rules institute formality and ascribe effects to behaviour that would appear totally senseless and arbitrary without the rules.

At this point, the question of whether a rigorous normative, and as such technical, language is at all possible, becomes complicated. The number of questions increases. Is an axiomatics of a system of *constitutive* rules possible? Is an axiomatics of a system of *regulatory* rules possible? Finally, is an axiomatics of a complex system, made up of both constitutive and regulatory rules possible? What kind of a system of rules do the games we have been talking about games? How does that strange game foreseen by the juridical order, look among them?

10 *Speech Acts* (Cambridge: Cambridge University Press 1969), 33.

6. *The Rigour of a System of Rules*

For a language to be rigorous, it must contain in it a form of *syntax*. "Contain in it" is not a satisfactory way of putting it. For the fact that a language can be made rigorous and be purified by some meta-language is of no interest here. On the contrary, the very fact that such an operation is necessary would imply that in the beginning the object language was anything but rigorous. I have in mind here the conception of juridical science as a rationalisation of legislative language, put forward by Bobbio around 1950. His hypothesis, as is well known was that legislative language was no less equivocal, incomplete, and incoherent than so called ordinary language.

Furthermore, for normative language to contain its own syntax, it should be possible to express the syntax in the language which is the object of the syntax. This problem, posited by Carnap, has generally been resolved in the affirmative.[11] But can we do so for a system of rules? If so, then I would tentatively suggest that the syntax should also be expressed by way of rules or, better, by statements capable of being used prescriptively. This is the only way in which the language could be fully uniform.

Let us recall how, according to Preti, an axiom system is constructed. (i) By determining the field of application of a symbol; (ii) by dividing a proposition into a group of propositions, each of which should not contain indeterminacy; (iii) by introducing criteria and rules for operation. Are such operations possible and useful in respect of a system of rules?

Let us first look at (ii). It is certainly possible to do this with rules. But whoever does this will only have succeeded in producing a larger number of ordinary rules or first order rules. He will not have formulated syntactical rules, second order rules or rules about rules.

We are left with (i) and (iii). Since we are dealing with a system of rules, it seems to me that it all comes down to prescriptions as to how to interpret the symbols which the rules themselves contain. A given normative language — one made up of a determinate, however large, number of statements — is rigorous on condition that all terms and expressions used have previously been defined. I do not consider it essential that there should be *transformation* rules because the system is (or can be) made of a limited number of precepts. If this were to be the case however, then the alleged syntax of the normative language would

11 *The Logical Syntax of Language*, *supra* n.8.

concern itself only with the semantics of the language itself. But this is not so. In fact some of the rules concerning the interpretation of a statement (whether in its descriptive or prescriptive function) also concern the so called syntactic dimension of the language. That is, they concern the relation of symbols to each other, forgetting their meaning. Here I have in mind equivocal expressions such as, "[of] containers and wrappings of products made abroad". One could easily find such an expression in a law. It is equivocal because the adjective phrase "made abroad" could refer either to "products" or to "containers and wrappings" or even, in the absence of punctuation, to "wrappings" only. The ambiguity, however, can be eliminated with the formulation of an interpretative rule such as: "In a set of genitives followed by an adjective, the adjective will refer to the last of the nouns".

According to Carnap, to consider two terms as synonyms, as having the same meaning, without making clear what that meaning is, appears — to Carnap at least — a syntactic consideration. But this is usually the case for whoever externally describes a normative system, pointing to its lack of rigour. By contrast, it is, to say the least, bizarre for someone engaged in making rules to use two different terms for the same thing and then assert their synonymy. But it happens.

For all that, the principal means by which a normative language can be turned into a rigorous language is through the explicit definition of the terms used. Given what we have said above, that might not be sufficient. Suppose that, in a law, the terms "container", "wrapping", "product" and "made abroad" were explicitly and exhaustively defined. In the absence of an interpretation rule like the one mentioned above, we would still have something equivocal.

To sum up, the conditions for a system of rules to be rigorous and for the language expressing it to be technical are the following:

(a) all the terms used should be expressly defined

(b) all the possible syntactic relations among the terms used should be made clear.

Condition (b) is usually not explicit. This is because the interpreter of a system of rules applies the syntactic rules of his own language subconsciously. In the same way, as we have already seen, Euclidian geometry used to take in, as its own syntax the syntax of Greek language and Aristotelian logic. But, as we have already seen, the syntax of the language is not sufficient when dealing with some rather complicated expressions. And, to eliminate any indeterminacy, a further rule is necessary to provide a limit to the discretionary power of the interpreter.

In conclusion, it might be possible to express rigorously a very simple system of rules. A system with a small number of rules (like a decalogue) is conceivable. It would be accompanied by, say, a hundred statements aimed at specifying the meaning of all the terms used and all the possible relations between them. It will not be wholly perfect. But it will be perfectible by the addition of new interpretive decisions each time a question of doubt arises. What is not practically possible is the rigorous formulation of a complex system of rules of the size of one of our codes. The number of terms would be too large and the odds would be on the results being unsatisfactory.

But for me, it is not the character of the component rules, constitutive and regulating (or, if you like, regulatory) that is of decisive importance. It is perhaps easier for a simple system of constitutive rules to be unambiguous. The game of chess does not lead, in general to controversies of an interpretative character between the players. But the rigorous formulation of the regulations of a teetotallers' club is not difficult, if constructed with a few well devised rules. And this is still true if the club's rules refer to behaviour, such as drinking, which exists irrespective of any rule.

It is more difficult to formulate with rigour the rules of the game "football", even though its rules can appear to be all constitutive. For the variety of behaviour hypothesised by the game necessarily lead to vagueness in the terms used. One need only look to such terms as "push" "protest" etc. Here also the number of rules necessary to "make clear" both the meaning of the terms used and their relation one to another would outweigh the "clarity" gained.

7. *Legislative Language*

The legislative language cannot, therefore, be rigorous in the same way that a scientific language is. It cannot even be rigorous in an analogous manner. Analogous, because in the one case we are dealing with a language which has a descriptive function and, in the other, with a language which has a prescriptive function.

How then, do jurists see legislative language as a technical language? Francesco Messineo says:

> There might be several elements at play in producing an interpretation. Among them might be the dictionary or literal. In this respect laws should

> have the meaning which comes from the meaning of the words from which they are composed, considered together (12 prel.). One should note however that, as a rule, a norm makes uses of juridical terms in their technical meaning (an exception, in art. 1851, deposit). This often, if not always, moves away from the ordinary meaning. If in doubt, one should lean towards the technical meaning (art. 1369). "Cancellation of mortgage, unworthyness, ingratitude, absence, consumable things, alluvion, merger" are some examples of terms with a technical meaning remote from the ordinary meaning (there are many others). [12]

Messineo thus shows that legislative terms should be understood in their technical meaning and gives us examples. When in doubt, he says, one should lean towards the technical meaning, relying on art. 1369 c.c.:

> In case of doubt expressions which can have more than one meaning shall be understood in the sense most suitable to the nature and object of the contract.

"Relying on", is a typical formula which lawyers make use of, when showing that they are applying some analogy. He thus takes for granted that the rules for interpreting contracts can be extended to the interpretation of statutes. Something which will have to be discussed. What are, then, those expressions "most suitable to the nature and the object of the contract"?

It does not appear to mean "technical" in the sense of the conventional language of the parties. For it is true that those who make use of contracts, traders, farmers etc. have their own jargon which is expressed in the contract. But if this was to be the meaning of "technical" then art. 1369 should have made this clear. Art. 1369 seems however, to refer to the *aim* and *causa* of the contract. Thus what art. 1369 can tell us about statutory interpretation is that we should look to the purpose and point of the statute. It cannot tell us more than that and therefore provides no solution to the whether technical or ordinary meaning should be preferred.

8. *Factual Terms and Normative Terms*

Lawyers maintain that, in most cases, legislative terms have a technical meaning. This leads us to further questions.

As soon as a word enters a theoretical system or a system of measurement, it assumes a Pickwickian meaning. Water for the chemist is a compound of hydrogen and oxygen, which can also exist as a gas; it

12 *Manuale di diritto civile e commerciale* (Milan: Giuffrè, 1957), 97.

ceases to be the liquid of our ordinary knowledge. For the physicist yellow refers to the refraction of luminous waves; it is not the yellow of our visual perception.

Does then a word assume a new meaning merely by being part of a rule? No. The word "mushroom" on a sign saying, "It is forbidden to pick up mushrooms", does not differ in meaning from the word used in a statement such as, "mushrooms grow near trees".

However, it is easy for a word to assume a Pickwickian meaning, if it is used in a constitutive rule or in a system of constitutive rules. Juridical norms create the meaning of some terms (whether or not we can consider them constitutive rules). The term "president of the Republic" draws its meaning from the "constitution" no less than "goalkeeper" draws its meaning from the rules of football.

From this point of view, *some* legislative terms are, undoubtedly, technical. "Some" is used advisedly. For one should distinguish terminology (using the now current terminology). Put simply, *factual terms* are those describing fragments of reality, leaving aside the rules. *Normative terms* are those describing facts or situations qualified by rules or systems of rules. Factual terms are indispensable: it would not be possible for rules, even juridical rules, to do without them. Normative (or systematising) are not. They are used, for convenience, by complex systems of rules.

If such a distinction were to be accepted, the conclusion should be that factual terms are not necessarily technical. And in fact they rarely are. Under what conditions do factual terms assume a technical meaning? At a first glance, only when given an express definition in law. Alf Ross points out:

> The definitions found in law are not, usually, of this kind, but are technical definitions, i.e. definitions through which a term in common use is given a specific meaning. This, in order to ensure a greater precision of application, is conveyed through quantitative criteria. This is how "wood" is defined as *an area of at least one acre covered with trees at least 2 yards tall.* [13]

In such cases everything that enables a term to be considered technical is there; the conventional character of its meaning; the fact that it takes a past linguistic practice as a model; the transition from quality to measurement. Such cases, however, do not give rise to problems of interpretation for the very reason that the laws themselves provide

13 "La definizione nel linguaggio giuridico", in *Diritto e analisi del linguaggio*, ed. U. Scarpelli (Milan: Comunità, 1976), 212.

additional explanations.

Normative terms, on the other hand, seem technical even when they have not been an express definition in the particular law. Keeping in mind Messineo's examples, let us look at the term (superficie). The term "superficie" is implicitly defined in the civil code. Art. 952 says:

> *Constitution of the right of superficie*. The owner can constitute the right to erect and maintain a structure above the soil in favour of others, who acquire ownership of it. He can likewise transfer ownership of an existing structure, separately from ownership of the soil.

The permission granted to the owner of the ground gives precision to the term "superficie". The articles which follow and which specify the length and conditions for extinguishing this right, give further precision to the term. We are left in no doubt that the term "superficie" has acquired a new meaning. The "superficie" in the civil code is a concise summary of a large number of linked rules. Without these rules it would not have the meaning it has. It has very little to do with what it means in ordinary language. This is, it must be said, is the limiting case. The difference in meaning is much less pronounced in other terms.

9. *Doctrinal Terms*

Going back to Messineo's examples, one at least of the terms given technical meaning is, without doubt, *factual*. Thus, "consumable things". Furthermore, no express definition can be found in the civil code nor — I think — in any other part of the law. How then, can we justify the assertion that its meaning is technical?

An observation is necessary here. One does not only find legislative language alongside ordinary language. There is also a *group* language. This is juridical in the sense that it uses the traditional terminology of lawyers. Thus when it is argued that legislative terms should be interpreted according to their technical meaning, this might refer to this special juridical language. This is technical in the same way as medical or the engineering languages are technical. This is quite a different matter from arguing that legislative language is technical because rigorously constructed by the legislature itself.

Nearly all legislative terms go back to legal works produced much earlier than the present codifications. So much so that it is possible to go to those works for help in establishing meanings. Moreover, that lawyers' language is a rigorous language is widely held to be doubtful. In his attempt to construct an "axiomatic" theory of law, Luigi Ferrajoli puts it bluntly:

> It is not difficult to show that current juridical doctrine does not satisfy any of the requirements commonly called for in a scientific discipline ... Its terminology lacks the rigour and univocity which are the first preconditions for the consistency of the concepts employed.

And further:

> When perusing the monumental legal encyclopaedias or when looking at the analytical indexes, even in the most comprehensive treatises, one faces thousands of terms. All these are, or have been, used in the most equivocal and different meanings. Many of them are synonyms, still holding good out of sheer habit. When dealing with law, there is the feeling of moving in a tower of Babel. Each lawyer has his own personal terminology, and a large part of his work consists in finding the difference between his and others.[14]

Even leaving aside such a pessimistic vision, the ambiguities of the so-called juridical language are often obvious. We could think of the term "plagio" which covers two very different things: the unacknowledged copying of a literary or artistic work and the total subjection of a person to one's will.

Consulting a juridical lexicon or an encyclopaedia can help the lawyer in understanding what certain laws prescribe. We can now say that some terms of technical appearance — such as, merger, alluvion — are clearly of doctrinal origin. Some of these terms, however, do not rise problems of interpretation because they are not in fact the object of interpretation. They do not appear in the actual legislation but in the rubrics which precede the articles of the code, particularly the civil code. We can see this in the term *alluvion* which appears exclusively in the rubric (title) of art. 941. That article itself gives an implicit definition:

> The increments of land that are formed successively and imperceptibly on lands along the banks of rivers and streams belong to the owner of the land.

Such explanation aims at establishing that they belong to the "owner of the ground". *Alluvion* itself is superfluous in helping to understand the article. It is there perhaps for completeness and to make it easier to locate the law.

Whatever the reason, the technical meaning is made clear by looking at the rubric and the text of art. 941 together. This meaning is not at all like its ordinary language meaning, flooding. *Alluvion*, in the ordinary

14 *Teoria assiomatizzata del diritto. Parte generale* (Milan: Giuffrè, 1970), 2.

meaning of flooding could well figure in some special law. One which for example dealt with the measures to be taken in the event of natural disasters. It could also however, be included in legislative enactments such; *Alluvion* belong to the owner of the estate'. In this case, the meaning would have been totally obscure if traditional legal vocabulary had not been taken into consideration.

It is the same for "consumable things" to which Messineo gives a technical meaning. All handbooks present more or less the same argument. One should not be allowed to be deceived by the ordinary meaning of the expression "consumable". There is nothing in the natural word which does not change or deteriorate and could there be seen as "consumed" by use. We much search for the meaning of the term *consumable* in economics. Thus "consumable things" are those things which cannot be used by people without losing their individuality (food) or without having to be alienated (money), etc.

Art. 995 which (besides having the rubric consumable things) establishes:

> If the usufruct includes consumable things, the usufructuary has the right to make use of them and has the obligation to pay their value at the termination of the usufruct according to the agreed valuation.

This means that an immediate question of interpretation rises as to the meaning of the legislative term "consumable things". In this case however, the meaning could be selected in relation to the *ratio* of the disposition alone. Although the knowledge of the legal vocabulary undoubtedly helps the interpreter.

One can say therefore that *factual* terms also are liable to appear *technical* if they are of doctrinal origin. Even though no rule as to their usage figures in the legislative enactments. It is for terms of this kind that the question, "technical or ordinary meaning?" is the most important.

10. *The Terminology of Special Laws*

There are — it is true — some cases when the interpreter must chose between the ordinary meaning of a word and the technical meaning which it acquires because of the definition in a code.

Such is the case presented by Messineo as an exception to the rule that the technical meaning should prevail. It refers to art. 1851 civil code which says:

> *Advance secured by irregular pledge*. If one or more claims are secured by deposits in money, goods, or securities which have not been identified or for which the bank has been given a power of disposal, the bank shall return only that sum or that share of goods or securities which is in excess of the amount of the secured claims.

The term "deposit" must be understood in the ordinary meaning of the word, disregarding the definition in art. 1766:

> Deposit is a contract by which one of the parties receives a movable thing from the other under a duty to keep custody of it and return it unchanged,

which turns it into a technical and conventional term. Art. 1851 however does not appear to refer to a formal "contract of deposit".

This example is rather exceptional and interpretive doubts more likely arise with terms used not in codes but in special laws. These doubts are also more likely to arise, as has been said, with factual terms. Here it can happen that the judge alludes to the technical meaning of a term in a not wholly accurate way. He does not refer to rules for the use of the term which can be deduced, explicitly or implicitly, from the legislative enactments themselves. Neither does he refer to the linguistic habit, consolidated by generations of legal functionaries. Rather he refers to a particular meaning which can be given to the term by reference to the aim which seems to have been the motive of the enactment.

A technical meaning then, would be any meaning whatsoever as long as it diverges from the common meaning. If, for some reason, a judge does not consider it satisfactory to give a term its ordinary language meaning, he then maintains that that word has, in law, a technical meaning. Judges sometimes do this by invoking the "*ratio*'" of the enactment they interpret. If so, there is no problem. But when they do not refer to the "*ratio*," then the invocation of the technical meaning is nothing more than rhetorical expedient.

This way of going about is frequent. So much so that an explicit reference to the ordinary meaning of a term stands out as a rarity.

I remember an old decision which went:

> Indeed, it is wrong to claim, as the decision did, that the term "apartment", used in the second paragraph of art. 12 (fixing a 100% increase for apartments with luxury features) is to be restricted to inhabited property.
>
> The ordinary meaning of the word "apartment" should not necessarily be seen as inhabited property. Rather it should be seen, more generically, as an aggregate of several rooms with service areas annexed. This aggregate, whatever its use may in fact be, is to be seen as a self-standing unit separated

> from the rest of the house or building [15]

It is more than likely that the judge used this interpretation to arrive at the solution that he wanted. For one cannot see why the rents of luxury premises used as offices should be excluded from the provisions of art. 12. One can see however that a dictionary has been consulted. The expression "aggregate of rooms" is used by many Italian dictionaries when defining "apartment". The judge indicates his wish to consider the etymology of the word. Here there is no doubt that the term "apartment" is interpreted according to its literary meaning. Doubts may arise as to whether by ordinary language here one means the language spoken in everyday life. If this were the case then it appears to me that "apartment" would be used — like "accommodation" — as an equivalent for house. This judgement, however, is of great interest as it prefers to refer directly to the dictionary, in the context of a dispute between citizens, which went as far as the Court of Cassation.

It might be the case that, in some instances, two alternatives interpretations of a legislative enactment might be offered; one by reference to common parlance and the other by reference to the learned terminology of lawyers.

Here I have in mind the Piedmont Regional law, 12th August 1976, No.42 in which art. 16 states:

> Acts which simply aim at confirming, repeating or executing provisions which have already been adopted and perfected according to the law, and in general all non dispositive deliberations, are not subject to control. In any event, a list of such acts must be transmitted to the competent organ of control which is entitled to ask for a copy of the provisions adopted.

Right from the start, the question of identifying those acts aiming at confirming, repeating and executing, and thus exempt from the compulsory control, was a hard one. In particular, the question raised as to whether "notarial acts [deeds]" which expressed the rulings of the public administration were included within this article. The question is all but irrelevant when they stipulate loans with large banks for the financing of public works. In this context, any delay or complication in an already complex procedure, is pernicious. The beginning and the completion of public works is delayed. Inflation leads to increased costs and so on. The attempt to ease the procedure by avoiding a double control here looks commendable. This would be possible if the legislative

15 Cass., 11 June 1953, N. 1702, in *Giurisprudenza italiana*, 1954, I, 1, c. 190.

expression "Acts aiming at carrying out measures previously adopted" was to be understood by reference to a usage which is common not only among ordinary people but also among civil servants in public administration. "Act" is typically the notarial act [deed]. Rulings in public administration are generally called "deliberations", not "acts". The language uses in administrative law handbooks and treatises is different. The reason being that, there, "act" has a wider meaning which includes any declaration of will of the public administration.

According to common parlance, there is no reason why the stipulation of loans should be excluded from art. 16. It is an act, one which carries out a previous "measure" i.e. a "deliberation" of a public body. What more should one wish?

There are arguments of substance for this. The most unprejudiced civil servants point out that here there is no "dispositive content" which is not included in a previous decision. If for instance, the conditions of the loan were different (different interest or security), then a new decision would be necessary. But if that is not the case, all that is done by the act is to carry out the intention, already expressed, of contracting a debt. The "*ratio*" of art. 16 would be fully obeyed.

However, the interpreter's inclination to understand the legislative language through ordinary language has a role to play. It does appear that there are two types of interpreters, not only among judges but also among civil servants. Those who have a good ear for the spoken language and if necessary consult the dictionary; and those who are conditioned, instead, by their memories of study and rush to read once again the treatises. I don't wish to vilify the latter. But I feel that their way of proceeding is more apt to lead towards formalistic interpretations. By formalistic interpretations I mean those that do not sufficiently take into consideration the point of the enactment.

11. *The Confidence of the Citizenry*

Sometimes judges (and civil servants) show a tendency to assume that (within reasonable limits) legislative and ordinary language are similar. But how can one justify that? What principle is involved? It seems to me that it could be the same principle as that which governs the interpretation of private legal acts, the so called "trust" principle. It is astonishing how little (if at all) this principle is referred to in matter of legal interpretation. The addressees of legislative enactments, or at least of some of them, are the citizens. Their reading of these enactments raises in them expectations which deserve protection. It is not unlikely for the citizen to have adopted a certain behaviour out of his faith in a particular meaning of these enactments. What meaning? It is quite natural for the citizen to trust that such meaning is the same as that which those words possess in the language in which he expresses himself, not the meaning they would have in some esoteric language unknown to him. Lawyers, however, are of a different opinion. Again Messineo says:

> Taking into consideration the *intention of the law* can sometimes lead to a change in the result of the interpretation from that given by the literal meaning of the norm (arts. 1362, 1364, 1365).

And further:

> From the fact that restrictive and extensive interpretation are admissible ... it is possible to argue that the *real intention of the law* prevails over the meaning which can be deduced from its context. The opposite principle applies, as a rule, to the statements of one single individual.[16]

But a certain lack of coherence emerges from these two passages. On one hand there is the analogical extension the interpretation of contracts to laws. But the fact that the same could happen for the principle of trust is excluded.

Let us now turn to where Messineo "argues" the predominance of the *intention* of the law over the *text*.

> *Intent of contracting parties*. That which was the common intent of the parties, not limited to the literal meaning of the words, shall be sought in interpreting the contract (art. 1362).
> *General expressions*. No matter how general the expression used in contract, they only include the objects as to which the parties intended to contract (art. 1364).
> *Illustrative examples*. When a case is mentioned in a contract in order to explain a clause, unmentioned cases to which the same clause could reasonably be extended are not presumed to be excluded (art. 1365).

These three quotations refer to an anti-literal, restrictive and extensive interpretation of contract clauses. One must bear in mind the following difference: while the first two specifically envisage the parties' "ordinary intention" and "projects", the third outlines parties' objective interest which can be taken into account, "reasonably". It must be remembered though, that in the case of an agreement, each party is both author and addressee of the agreed declarations. The same is not true for legislative

16 *Manuale di diritto civile e commerciale*, I, pp. 98 and 104.

enactments where the addressees are different from the addressors (if it is at all realistic to think of the term legislator anthropomorphically). Furthermore, contract clauses affect the restricted number of subjects who formulate them and, possibly, a few others. Laws affect the interests and the behaviour of millions of people. So what then justifies an analogical extension? Finally, the idea of *the intention of the legislator* itself has been the object of so many reservations (it has even been ridiculed) that is no more possible to speak seriously of it. Or at least, any reference to it should be qualified.

This is not, therefore, the right way to deny legitimacy to the principle of trust in the interpretation of legislative enactments. To the contrary, there are other good reasons for interpreting legislative words through ordinary language in order to protect the citizen's expectations. There has been strong objection to this. It has been argued for example, that in modern states the citizen does not know the formulations of the law, even though he abides by them. This happens because often the law does nothing more than reproduce models of behaviour already widespread. Thus, on this way of looking at it, law would consist more of *declaratory* norms rather than *proclamatory* norms, following a terminology which goes back to Geiger. If this were true, there would be no sense in a criterion of interpretation which presumes a *reading* by the citizen.

But is the ignorance of the citizenry as wide as that? To the contrary, there are laws which are directed specifically at people and which they consult personally. Think of the *equo canone* law (a rent-control statute, which is the object of common disputes between landlords and tenants). This kind of law aims at establishing new relations among subjects and proposes unusual models of behaviour. It therefore is essentially proclamatory. Further, we can think of laws fixing the juridical and economical status of hosts of civil servants. These laws also are consulted by a large number of people. In fact, here the analogy with the contract appears to be even stronger. These laws have a strong contractual background stemming, as they do, from the complex and detailed agreement between the unions and the competent ministries.

All this should induce those who compile laws to make greater use of the *ordinary language*. Besides, such requirement is not exclusive to the field of law. A recent bill has been presented to the Italian Parliament concerning the relation between doctor and patient. This establishes the obligation of the doctor always fully to inform the patient of his condition without hiding anything for whatever reason. In addition however, it lays down a duty to do so in terms the patient can understand, avoiding as far as possible, technical terms. Thus to use ordinary language.

Had I been in charge of the constitution I would have imposed on the legislator a similar duty. The duty to avoid at all costs technical terms and to express things in ordinary language. What the effectiveness of that would have been, is not clear. But that is not to say that it would have no effect at all. Similarly, one could conceive an "obligation" imposed on the judge to interpret law according to ordinary language. The idea is not as absurd as it looks. When we look at some the rules on the interpretation of statutes in force in Great Britain (contained for the most part in the Interpretation Act 1889), we see a rule according to which words should be given their meaning in the ordinary language broadly used at the time when the law was enacted.[17] Strictly speaking, the principle of trust would rather require to resort the ordinary language used at the time when the law is applied. This temporal specification might have been of some importance in Great Britain, where some laws have remained in force for a long time. For us it is not so important since the life span of our special laws is so short.

Since the obligation to interpret according to ordinary language codes does not exist, I can only suggest it to the judges humbly, but with good reason.

12. *The Impropriety of Ordinary Language*

According to some, the very characteristics of ordinary language prevent it from being used by the interpreter. First, because of its lack of precision; secondly, and in some cases, because of its lack of propriety. Lack of propriety in what sense? Ordinary language does not only include factual terms in the narrow sense. There are also terms which have a meaning only in relation to a rule. For example, "right of way", which supposes the existence of a rule establishing whose right it is to go first and whose duty it is to wait. In ordinary language, there are also terms referring to juridical norms. Sometimes, there are terms which are not directly borrowed from legislative terminology or from the lawyers' language.

"Registration of a transfer deed" (*voltura*), for example, cannot be

17 See W. Twining and D. Miers, *How to do Things with Rules* (London: Weidenfeld & Nicolson, 1976), 209ff.

found in legislative language. When applied to something other than the registration of real property, *voltura* betrays an embryonic knowledge of a set of rules. Thus, the use of this term whenever a commercial undertaking or a vehicle is transferred, shows that the user is aware that, apart from the private agreement, an administrative authority must intervene to authorise or certify it.

Finally, there are terms and expressions which *distort* the technical meaning. For instance, "agreement to sell" (*compromesso*) is a popular and widely used word. This is ordinarily used to indicate the preliminary contract of sale/purchase of property. People in general do not know that *compromesso* in the code of civil procedure, is an agreement preliminary to an arbitration (see the rubric of art. 806).

A similar expression is "legitimate (succession)" (*legittima*). Such an expression indicates, in popular use, that portion of the inherited estate, which is reserved for some determinate relative, in particular for the children and the surviving spouse. The civil code calls this the "reserved portion" and lawyers call it "the share of the reserved portion". In legislative language, on the other hand "legitimate succession" means the succession in cases of intestacy. The difference, or even conflict, between ordinary language and juridical language is, in this case, so intense that it might turn into a source of misunderstanding in the interpretation of wills. For example when (as often happens) one encounters the clause: "I leave to my wife the *legittima* ....." *Legittima* indicates different things in the two languages, worst still, two separate sets of rules.

It should be pointed out that these examples are drawn from the linguistic usage of Nothern Italy. I am not sure whether they apply to other areas. In any case, it seems to me that such solecisms do not prevent ordinary language from serving as a point of reference for the interpreter. We should rather disperse a prejudice: that whenever the same word figures both in ordinary and in the technical-juridical language, the ordinary meaning is wider and less certain while the technical meaning, narrower and more precise. Such is not the case for the term *alimenti*. In ordinary language it corresponds to "foodstuff" and its meaning is relatively unambiguous, even if in time of famine, "foodstuff" turns out to mean berries and roots. In juridical language *alimenti* (alimony) is definitely wider. It includes, besides food, first necessities of human existence such as lodging, clothes, schooling, etc. But it is also extremely vague because it is a relative concept. It depends upon specific circumstances such as the state of need, position in society, economic condition. These are circumstances which are liable to be considered largely from a subjective point of view. This confirms, if anything, how unwise it is to use *alimenti* in a technical meaning. This is all the more the case since the word clearly appears in its ordinary meaning in laws relating to hygiene and fair trading.

We must counter one final prejudice: that using the technical meaning results in a wider consensus among interpreters than if ordinary language were to be used. This is not true. Consider art. 2043 of the civil code:

> *Compensation for unlawful acts*. Any fraudulent, malicious or negligent act that causes an unjustified injury to another obliges the person who has committed the act to pay damages.

How should one interpret the unjustified nature of the damage? According to ordinary language, which considers it as being what is against prevailing values? Or should one attribute a technical meaning to it, and read anti-juridical for unjustified? "Unjustified" is essentially vague. Ordinary language therefore, offers the interpreter a very weak reference point. It would however be disingenuous to believe that an agreement among interpreters on the particular meaning of the word unjustified in art. 2043 can easily be reached. There are many ways to understand "anti-juridical". One could require that the damage inducing behaviour be expressly forbidden by law; or for the prohibition to be accompanied by a specific sanction; or for the behaviour not to be specifically authorised. Any of these solution is reasonable. Though none can easily be seen in the law itself. The specificity of the meaning of "unjustified" in art. 2043 is therefore a mirage.

13. *Beccaria's Advice*

One could see Beccaria's advice against the background of the possibility of understanding legislative terms according to ordinary language: the judge should limit himself to the scrupulous observance of the letter of the law. This is considered by many to be absurd, especially when read with another statement by the same author: the judge must not interpret the law. As we all know, the famous, passionate yet non too rigorous passages of the famous booklet, *On Crimes and Punishments*, have drawn much criticism.

Some of these criticisms are rather scholastic. How can the judge, it has been asked, exclude himself from interpreting the law when legislative enactments are but vehicles, black signs on white paper, which the legislator uses to express his precepts? And how is it possible to retrace the genuine "thought" of the legislator by sticking to the letter without looking to the spirit? The letter mortifies, the spirit vivifies, and so on.

However, Beccaria's message gets through if we bear in mind that the meaning he gives to interpretation is an oscillating one. At one time he translates the Latin word "*interpretatio*" which had till then a very wide meaning to the point of including doctrinal elaboration and analogical extension. At another he means, more simply, the operation of preferring one meaning to all the possible meanings the law might have. Therefore the prohibition in respect of interpretation is twofold. Firstly, he forbids analogical extension of the law. This is because the judge must not produce a further syllogism one of the premise of which is (and could not be otherwise) the similarity of the cases. Secondly, the judge is forbidden to make obscurity in the law clear on his own, without turning to the sovereign legislator's authority.

One should never also forget that Beccaria deals, first and above all, with penal laws. It must be remembered that the first prohibition, in respect of analogy in criminal matters, is shared by nearly all modern codes. The second meaning we considered, against the interpretation or explanation of texts by the judges, lead to less lasting institutions, such as the "*Référé Législatif*" or the "*opportune rapresentanze*'" to the king, which the Albertian civil code referred to. Such institutions acted, as far as they did act, in civil and administrative matters as well.

But besides those two prohibitions, one can point to a positive prescription: the advice to the judges to observe scrupulously the letter of the law. Is such prescription really absurd? Has it become obsolete? Does it stem from the fact that one fails to distinguish between legislative enactment and normative proposition? Or does it still retain some weight today?

One can, it seems to me, read it in a modern way. We can see Beccaria's insistence on the letter of the law as saying that ordinary language should be respected. We thus have a view, that though contestable, is not clearly unacceptable. We must then understand Beccaria's cryptic statements in this way.

He says:

> The disorder that arises from rigorous observance of the letter of a penal law is hardly comparable to the disorders that arise from interpretations. The temporary inconvenience of the former prompts one to make the rather easy and needed correction in the words of the law which are the source of

> uncertainty, but it curbs that fatal license of discussion which gives rise to arbitrary and venal controversies.[18]

As usual, it is not easy to understand what Beccaria means by interpretation. Should he mean analogical extension, the above passage would be easy to understand. The judge must not *add* anything to what the law says expressly. Should socially damaging and dangerous behaviour remain unpunished as a consequence of that, it could be then easily remedied through a change or a widening of the law.

But here Beccaria reveals a naive belief: that as long as there is no gross widening of the law, the meaning is unequivocal. This is also repeated by some exponents of the free law movement. They argue that a law can mean only that which it contrives to express clearly. Beyond that, the judge has a free choice, he should always explain his doings openly and clearly. This supposes the existence of an area, however limited, where the attribution of a meaning to some words is an essentially objective fact.

If, on the other hand, interpretation means the recourse to the "spirit" of the law, the above passage tells us something more subtle. This is only the case, as I have said, if we mean by "literal interpretation", "lexical interpretation" and that latter refers to ordinary language. This is not to say that the meaning of words in ordinary language is unequivocal. Obviously that would be silly. What is true however, is that on occasion, the reference to ordinary language *reduces* rather than widens the range of meanings. It very often happens, for example, that one party puts to the judge a meaning which deviates from ordinary language and which therefore widens the range of meaning. Thus once in the Court of Cassation, the appellant proposed to the judge a different (wider) meaning of *transfer* than used in the ordinary language of those in the property trade.

One might say therefore, that the reference to ordinary language represents a move toward (greater) objectivity and less arbitrariness on the part of the interpreter. This means that Beccaria's advice still has some value. The judge should stand by the ordinary meaning of the words, even beyond penal matters. The result might not be satisfactory. In this case it is the job of the legislator to intervene and modify the law to compel future judges to modify their decisions. The temporary drawback of decisions not wholly satisfactory is a minor ill. The existence of several

18 C. Beccaria, *On Crimes and Punishments,* chap. IV, "Interpretations of the Laws" (Indianapolis: Bobbs-Merrill, 1963), 16.

incoherent decisions is a much greater evil. For this represents uncertainty over a long period of time.

But Beccaria says further:

> If the interpretation of laws is an evil, another evil, evidently, is the obscurity which makes interpretation necessary. And this evil would be very great indeed where the laws are written in a language that is foreign to a people, forcing it to rely on a handful of men because it is unable to judge for itself how its liberty or its members may fare.[19]

The foreign language which Beccaria attacked was first of all Latin. But it is true of any esoteric language which the legislator delights in using, claiming it is necessary to have a "technical" language for the elegant formulation of a norm.

So the invitation is for the legislator to use, as far as possible, a simple and clear language on the model of the spoken language. But there is also an invitation for the judge: give the words of the law the meaning which they have in the ordinary language, unless the consequences are aberrant. Better still, by so doing, the judges would have a chance to punish the legislator for not having accepted the first invitation. Through the use of literal interpretation they can frustrate the legislator's intention (in so far as it can be retraced). This can lead the legislator to adopt a different behaviour. To avoid indulging in the use of technical terms and conventional formulae hard to understand.

14. *Forked Precepts*

There are therefore good reasons in favour of the trust principle even in the interpretation of the law. Some conformity of legislative language with ordinary language should be presumed so that, as far as possible, citizens can more easily *read* the law. Consistency with ordinary language, however, does not consist only in respect of the meaning of individual words. Ordinary language can also serve as a model in respect of its structures and cadences.

Let me explain. For the legislator to be clear and comprehensible the language of the law must not (forgive the expression) be forked. That is to say, the same word, the same sentence, must not indicate, at the same time, two different things. Consider art. 21 of the Italian constitution:

> Everyone shall have the right freely to express his own thoughts, orally or in

19 *Op. cit.,* chap. V, "Obscurity of the Laws", at 17.

> writing or by any other means of dissemination.
>
> No previous authorization shall be required of the press and it shall not be subject to censorship.
>
> Sequestration may be resorted to only by an argued decision of the judicial authorities for offences for which sequestration is expressly authorized by the laws governing the press, or for breach of the rules that these laws prescribe in order to identify the persons responsible for such publication.

And further, at the last paragraph:

> Printed publications, spectacles, and all other displays that offend public decency are forbidden. The law will make adequate provision to prevent and suppress such violations.

In the light of this article it is possible (and has been done) to argue the legitimacy of a law establishing, at the administrative level, advance censorship, over the theatres and cinemas. Those favouring censorship as a defence of public morality point to the word "prevent". This seems to them to allude to advance censorship. This can be countered. "Prevent" does not refer to cinema and theatre shows only but jointly with printed publications. The second para. of Art. 21, however, expressly forbids any form of authorization or administrative censorship for printed publications. This means that "prevent" should assume a twofold meaning. As far as printed publications are concerned, it should allude only to forms of sequestration, ordered by the judiciary and taking place after distribution to the public. As far as theatre and cinema shows are concerned, it should allude both to forms of sequestration or prohibition following contact with the public, and to forms of control and prohibition before that contact has taken place. This would be, to say the least, a bad example of legislative technique, liable to create doubts into the minds of the addressees of the law. It is much better to interpret "prevent" in such a way that it has the same (narrow) meaning for both printed publications and for theatre and cinema shows. Conclusion, the Italian Constitution does not allow advance censorship for theatre and cinema.

I would call this the *argument from the linearity of the legislative dictate*. For most cases, such argument allows as a result a full compatibility between normative propositions drawn from two different legislative enactments. By full compatibility I mean the absence of a relation of rule/exception to the rule between the two normative propositions. Such a relation does not represent an antinomy in the proper sense. There are innumerable laws which are interpreted as being an exception to others without any problem thereby arising. Sometimes however, (particularly in constitutional matters) it is preferable that no exceptions are set to the rule, in order to avoid a conflict, or even the hint of a conflict, between two principles both present in the text. I also have the feeling, and it is rather more than a feeling, that the less sophisticated reader of a text of law is more inclined to assume that each disposition regulates all by itself a separate subject matter. Thus one might say that the principle of the trust of the citizen also supports this arguments.

Art. 21 could be interpreted in a totally different way. It could be argued that the last para. contains a derogation to the prohibition to impose censorship when it is a matter of *preventing* offences to public morality. But this would be an implicit derogation which would not help the clarity of the text. Furthermore, the assumption that there is full compatibility between legal dispositions could be an arguments in itself. This is confirmed by a commentary note in the Constitutional Court's decision of 12 July 1965, no. 70, on the subject of judicial declaration of natural paternity.[20]

Central to the question was the interpretation of art. 30, last paragraph:

> The law shall state rules and limitations regarding investigation of paternity.

How should the *limitations* be understood? Is it in the sense that the legislator can in many ways set conditions, through norms of *substantial* law, to the attribution of the status of natural child (in the same way as it used to bar any action to the children of incestuous and adulterous unions)? Or is it also in the sense that the legislator can lay down procedural rules for the purpose of obstructing any action taken by whoever claims to be a natural child? Which interpretation one chooses makes it more or less possible to justify enactments as those in art. 274 of the civil code. There it was established that a judicial declaration of natural paternity and maternity is admissible only when there is consistent evidence and when the court rules as to admissibility, having heard the parties and gathered any information relating to the case.

Now, if one were to conclude that art. 30, last para. can limit the trial itself, then it would appear as an exception to art. 24 of the constitution which says:

> Everyone may proceed at law for the protection of his rights and legitimate interests.

20 S. Chiarloni, "Diritto di azione e diritto di difesa nel procedimento preliminare per la dichiarazione giudiziale di paternità e maternità naturale", *Giurisprudenza costituzionale* X (1965), 865-881.

> Everyone shall have the inviolable right of defence in every phase and stage of any legal proceedings.

However the commentary says that such interpretation should be excluded. Its author expresses "the conviction that when faced with two possible interpretations of a norm, one leading to its identification as being an exception to the rule, the other leading to seeing it as fully compatibility with the rule, one should stand by the second one, in particular when dealing with constitutional norms. Requirements of simplicity and clarity of law in the constitutional field are extremely important. So much so that in this case any conclusion that one rule is an exception to another should, because of all the problems involved, be explicit and unquestionable."

Simplicity and clarity. These are values which do not have their own justification. They find their justification when referred, once more, to the trust of the addressees — of whoever can be addressee of constitutional norms.

This type of argument is also true as far as ordinary norms are concerned. In some cases, however, judges reject this argument. In a case concerned with interpreting art. 78 of the act which imposed exceptional property taxes (approved by presidential decree of 9th May 1950, nr. 203): The following are exempt from the exceptional tax of the previous article:

> (a) companies whose activities, in the last five years, have been solely limited to the ownership and the management of urban property ..

The question was raised whether the exemption could be granted to a company which, during the length of time foreseen by the tax, had owned only areas stemming from the demolition of building destroyed during the war. The financial administration argued for the negative, because the combined expression "ownership and management" could refer to buildings but not to areas without standing buildings on them. The Court of Cassation held differently:

> It is possible to answer that the two terms in the combined expression can be separated and that management can refer to buildings only, while the expression ownership can concern any kind of property. One should not also exclude the possibility that a building area can be exploited autonomously, other than by the erection of buildings. In such a case it would turn into a management activity, such as in the case of an urban area used for car parking or similar.[21]

21 Cass., 14 January 1965, nr. 70, in *Giurisprudenza italiana*, 1966, I, 1, c. 490.

The Court of Cassation acknowledges therefore that a legislative expression can be forked, i.e. providing a different area of reference for every subspecies of "urban property". The fact that the judges considered the argument, even though they did not gave it decisive weight, is significant.

ON MORAL AND LEGAL JUSTIFICATION

by

LETIZIA GIANFORMAGGIO

I

This paper deals with justification. My primary aim, therefore, is to make clear what I mean by "justification". In so doing, I shall distinguish justification from other objects of inquiry that it should not be confused with. This confusion occurs because we have several objects that refer to the same phenomena. I realise that it is impossible to offer a linguistic description of these phenomena without its being theory-laden. Unfortunately, however, it is impossible to point to something and say that this is precisely what I had in mind. Accordingly, I shall be content to characterize as precisely as possible the scope of the phenomena I am interested in, avoiding words like "foundation", "justification", "logic", "reason", "discourse" etc. At least, in so doing, I shall not beg the question.

II

The area to which I intend to refer contains:

(a) The assumption of criteria for judgement and action in the area of interpersonal relations; the assumption being neither accidental nor predetermined.

(b) The judgements that follow from those criteria.

(c) The actions that follow from those criteria (they can in their turn produce criteria for judgement and action).

From the above, my analysis will concern a linguistic object, namely, the string of sentences expressed by the judging or acting agent, the conclusion of which is a judgement or an ought-judgement of what is to be done. It is worth stressing that this string of sentences does not aim at ascertaining the value of the conclusion. Rather, it aims at making the

Law and Language, The Italian Analytical School, ed. A. Pintore and M. Jori (Liverpool: Deborah Charles Publications, 1997).

conclusion be accepted by giving it the value of supposedly accepted premises, or criteria.[1] It is important to keep this object of inquiry distinct from another one, that is from the judgements and the actions themselves, and from the decision to express certain judgements and perform certain actions. Social scientists (in particular economists) and philosophers of science often deal with the rationality of human behaviour, with the logic of choice. This is not my object of inquiry. Rather, my object is the rationality, or the logic, of the string of sentences that I referred to above.[2]

There is a third object of inquiry that is not easily distinguishable from my own, though I believe the distinction is also very important. Like the first one, it is linguistic in character. Unlike the first, however, it is not a discourse. It does not belong to the enterprise of communication. Rather, this object belongs to a speculative enterprise. An enterprise concerned with knowledge, the aim of which is the identification of criteria

1 I am inclined to believe that law and morals, as objects of inquiry, are essentially linguistic phenomena. I am not able to argue for such a strong thesis here. Accordingly, I will simply assume that my object of inquiry (i.e., moral and legal justification) is a linguistic one.

2 There is such a sharp distinction between the first and the third object because I focus more on legal than on moral issues. Indeed, within the field of morals, such a distinction is by no means so sharp. However, I believe it is there, too. Let us consider, for example, the free rider principle, a puzzle for social action theorists. No doubt, from the standpoint of legal methodology, the problem of whether tax-evasion is rational never arises. Rather, the following problems may often arise: (a) whether or not the arguments made in support of tax-evasion are rational, or reasonable; (b) whether or not the particular "explanations" the court provides for deciding a particular tax-evasion case in a certain way are rational, or reasonable; (c) whether or not the "explanations" one provides in general to claim that deciding tax-evasion cases in a certain way is good are rational, or reasonable. The last problem is clearly a moral problem too. It is clear to me that moral theory does not (and cannot) deal with the problem, whether or not the behaviour of free rider is rational. I see moral theory as dealing, rather, with the problem of whether ought-judgements about behaviour is (or can be) rational or reasonable. Social scientists, economists particularly, do not deal with such a problem. To sum up: the theory of social action concerns the rationality (appropriateness, efficiency) of human actions. Morality and law, on the contrary, focus on whether an action is (morally or legally) right. Finally, moral and legal theory, if conceived as theories of moral and legal reasoning, focus on whether judgements about an action being (morally or legally) right are rational or reasonable (may, or may not, be rationally or reasonably justified).

for judging and acting. Obviously, such an identification of criteria presupposes using other criteria. These criteria, however, are *meta-criteria*. They do not direct the activities upon which judgements are given. Rather, they direct the activity of making judgements.

Sometimes the linguistic expressions of the speculative enterprise may coincide with the string of sentences that constitute my object of inquiry. However, two people going the same way are not necessarily doing the same thing. Though in a village the same road leads both to the church and to the pub, going to mass is nevertheless different from going to have a drink.

The argument above should have made clear that speaking about morals and/or law and logic, or about reason in morals and/or law, is *never* speaking about the second object of inquiry. Rather it is about either the first, or the third, or both. In the latter case reducing these two objects of inquiry to one is an ambitious thesis. Or rather, it is two different and incompatible ambitious theses. One would reduce the first object to the third and the other would do the contrary.

III

In moral and legal theory, we usually call "rules" the above criteria, and "decisions", the actions and judgements grounded thereupon. I propose to refer to the first object of inquiry as the "justification of moral and legal rules and decisions"; to the third as the "foundation of moral and legal rules and decisions". There are moral and legal theories that only deal with issues of "foundation", and theories dealing only with issues of "justification". A classical example of a foundation-theory is the that of Kelsen, according to which every problem of justification is utterly beyond the scope and interests of the "Pure" Theory of Law. A clear example of justification-theory is that of Perelman which is meant to be a theory about legal and moral justification, not about law and morals. However, Perelman's theory cannot help also being a theory of law, suggesting that the justification of legal rules also embraces the issues of foundation. As we shall see below, however, this never holds so far as legal rules and decisions are at stake. It does hold whenever moral rules and decisions are at stake, provided we do not hold that one of the basic features of morals is its positive character.

IV

Those acquainted with legal theory will realize that the meta-criteria above amount to the secondary rules legal theorists usually refer to. Regarding the combination of primary and secondary rules as the distinctive feature of a legal system is almost a commonplace among legal positivists (or, better, normativists). H.L.A. Hart, for instance, distinguishes simple normative systems (e.g. moral systems), that only consist of primary rules, from complex systems, that is legal systems consisting of both primary rules (or rules of conduct) and secondary rules (or meta-rules).

Yet, it would be wrong to infer the following from the combination of such a thesis with my distinction between foundation and justification: (a) in simply normative systems rules are obtained by means of justification; (b) that in complex normative systems (e.g., legal systems) rules are obtained by means of foundation. In my view, simple normative systems, which are already a distinct whole, present one (and only one) problem of foundation. No problem of justification arises. On the contrary, complex normative systems present many meaningful problems of justification. Indeed, it only makes sense to ask an agent who is competent (authorized) to produce rules for the reasons why one rule rather than another. Kelsen clearly understood this point (though he did not always make it lucidly). His distinction between static and dynamic normative systems is not to be mistaken for the distinction between simple and complex normative systems.[3] Kelsen's static systems as well as his dynamic systems are

3 Cf. H. Kelsen, *Reine Rechtslehre* (Leipzig and Vienna: Deuticke, 1934), 62: *idem*, *General Theory of Law and State* (Cambridge Mass.: Harvard University Press, 1946), 110-115. In these two essays, two of his best known works, Kelsen offers a clear-cut distinction between static and dynamic normative systems. In his 1928 essay, *Die philosophischen Grundlagen der Naturrechtslehre und des Rechtspositivismus* (Charlottenburg: Pan Verlag Rolf Heise), however, Kelsen clearly claims that such a distinction is valid from a purely analytical perspective only. From a phenomenological perspective, on the contrary, he believes the distinction to be utterly invalid. Neither a pure static system nor a pure dynamic system could actually exist. Again, in his 1960 *Reine Rechtslehre* Kelsen questions the soundness of the distinction between static and dynamic orders, though on opposite grounds. In his 1928 *Grundlagen*, Kelsen maintains that no purely dynamic system can exist, since provided its Grundnorm cannot be valid according to some dynamic criterion, it must be valid according to some static criterion. In his 1960 *Reine Rechtslehre*, Kelsen solves the problem by saying that the basic norm of a

complex. The difference between static and dynamic systems consists in their criteria for identifying valid rules. That is to say, their secondary rules have different contents. We should therefore distinguish between three kinds of normative systems. The so-called simple systems (Hart); complex static systems (Kelsen); and complex dynamic systems. As a matter of fact, simple systems should not be called "systems" at all, because they are constructed in such a way that there is no need for decision-making in particular situations. They are made up of just one rule. The concept of a simple normative system worked out by Hart is not a good one. Indeed, one cannot conceive of a simple normative system, since "order" or "system" usually conveys the idea of a whole, and a whole cannot be defined but in terms of some criterion for identifying the elements of which it is constituted.

Perhaps, the only instance of *simple* moral system, in the technical sense employed here, is the Kantian moral system. It is founded by a pure act of reason and has a purely formal content. It does not need to be

---

dynamic system can never be laid down, but can only be presupposed. As to static systems, Kelsen claims that the basic norm can be neither presupposed, nor grounded on some static criteria. It must therefore be grounded on some dynamic criteria. In 1928, Kelsen provides a very clear reason why no purely static system can exist: "Eine eingehende Untersuchung dieser Frage zeigt, daß die natürliche Rechtsordnung — ihre Existenz vorausgestzt — in ihrer Anwendung auf die konkreten Tatbestände des sozialen Lebens notwendig *positiviert*, das heißt zu positiven Rechts weden muß, weil die generellen abstrakten Normen des natürlichen Rechtes nicht anders als durch menschliche Tat konkretisiert, zu individuellen Normen werden können" (at 15). Obviously we can consider "die natürliche Rechtsordnung" as a synonym of "static normative system", and "positiviert werden" as a synonym of "to be turned into a dynamic system": see *Die philosophischen Grundlagen,* at 17-19. Some thirty years after, Kelsen addresses the same problem: "Aus dem Liebs-Gebot Christi können eine Fülle besonderer Moralnormen logische abgeleiten werden" (*Reine Rechtslehre* 1960, at 200); yet he does not make clear that it is one thing to "deduce" and another to "apply". In his posthumous work, Kelsen seems to go back to his former, 1928 ideas about logic and norms, and puts completely aside the distinction between static and dynamic normative systems: "Insofern als eine Moral-oder Rechtsnorm auf ein Individuun angewendet werden kann — das Individuum gelobt oder getadelt, gegen das Individuum eine Zivilexution oder Strafe gerichet werden kann — auch wenn dieses Individuum die auf es angewedtete Norm nicht anerkennt, kann die Moral- oder Rechtswordnung in bezug auf dieses Indiviuum nicht nur als heteronom, sondern auch als objectiv gültig bezeichnet werden": H. Kelsen, *Allgemeine Theorie der Normen* (Wien: Mainz, 1979), 66.

"adapted" to particular, empirical situations.[4]

V

In the light of the argument above, one may claim the following. Every normative system, "system" because it is also constituted by secondary rules, presents both a problem of justification and a problem of the foundation of the elements of the system.

An element that is founded within the system is said to be "valid". If the rule "John ought to do X" is founded, it follows that the normative statement "John ought to do X" is true. We may distinguish between voluntaristic and rationalistic theories of the foundation of rules (substantive, and not formal *à la* Kant since that those are not theories of the foundation of rules *within a system*). In other words, "John ought to do X" can be a true statement either because reason proves it, or because somebody wants it so. The first kind of foundation is peculiar to Kelsen's static systems; the second to Kelsen's dynamic systems. What I wish to stress is that in both cases the procedure of foundation is the procedure by means of which we can know what we (or John) ought to do.

An element that is justified within a system is said to be "right". I shall not specify whether I use "right" as a synonym of "just" or "correct". In ordinary language we never specify it, and such an ambiguity of the term "right" is one of its peculiar features. In any case, I claim that what I shall say about the process of justification does hold both when we use "to justify" to mean "establishing that a rule is just" and when we use it to mean "establishing that a rule is correct". This claim is very important for my purpose. If this were to be proved wrong it would refute my thesis.

To begin with, it is worth noticing that we can never find out whether some rule or decision is right. The question: "Is it true that smoking is not allowed here?" demands a simple yes or no. The question: "Is it right that

4 Cr. E. Tugendhat, "Zur Entwicklung von moralischen Begründungsstrukturen im modernen Recht", in *Archiv für Rechts und Sozialphilosophie, Beiheft N.F.* 14 (1980), 1-20, at 13:

> Für Kant gilt nämlich nicht nur wie für jede rationale Ethik das Moralprinzip apriori, vielmehr sollen auch die konkreten Normen, die sich aus dem katgorischem Imperativ ergeben, apriori gelten ... Kant wird nicht müde, drauf hinzuwisen, daß, im Unterschied zu den Regeln der Lebensklugheit, das moralisch Gebotene ohne weiteres von jedem erekennbar ist, daB keine Rücksift auf die empirischen Umstände und also auch keine Überlegung erfordet. (p. 13).

smoking should not be allowed here?" is usually understood as: "What do you think of this prohibition?", "What is your opinion about it?", and demands neither a yes or no answer nor something like: "In my opinion, it is right". Rather, it demands something like: "In my opinion it is right because ...". This is to say that one cannot discover whether some rule or decision is right. Neither can one decide for it to be right. One does not decide that a rule is right. One decides to lay down or follow a rule because one thinks it is right. This is quite a different thing. Here it is useful to remember the distinction I made between the three different objects of inquiry.

One can establish that a rule, or an ought-judgement, is right only by means of arguments. On the one hand, the sentence "It is forbidden to smoke in this room, but I do now know why" and the sentence "It is forbidden to smoke in this room, but there is no reason" are meaningful. On the other hand, "The prohibition to smoke in this room is right, but I do not know why" and "The prohibition to smoke in this room is right, but there is no reason" are performances of infelicitous linguistic acts, like the famous sentence: "The cat is on the mat, but I do not believe it."

My thesis here is at once very strong and very trivial indeed. It is that every statement that something is right amounts to an invitation to reasoning, discussion, and confrontation or, at least, presupposes (and makes us to presuppose) them. My thesis then, is the opposite of Ross' s

To invoke justice is the same thing as banging on the table:

> ... It is impossible to have a rational discussion with a man who mobilises "justice", because he says nothing that can be argued for or against.[5]

VI

Some remarks as to my terminological choices are in order. The word "justification" somehow conveys the same meaning as "excuse". As a matter of fact, a really important part of the meaning of "justification", as I understand it, is an "answer to actual or potential criticism and objections". For instance, our laws impose a duty of justification as a means for controlling the working of certain political and legal agencies (in fact, such a control is exercised either by other agencies, higher in the legal hierarchy, or by public opinion, or both). Though the law does not impose the duty of justifying its normative choices to every agency it

5 A. Ross, *On Law and Justice* (London: Stevens, 1958), 274.

wishes to control, nonetheless the fact that some agencies do have such a duty clearly shows that the law regards their decision-making as worthy of being subject to control.[6]

Every justificatory enterprise is meaningful only within communicative interaction, within actual or hypothetical dialogic contexts. Justification requires confrontation, scrutiny of different positions and perspectives, analysis of arguments and counter-arguments in order to take a decision. No room for justification is left when no objection arises. Obviously, there is no need for a flesh and blood opponent. The opponent may even be what is called the inner voice of conscience. If I have decided to go out and visit friends, or to go to a concert, it makes no sense saying that I decided on the right thing to do, unless I think my decision might be criticized. In other words, judgements about the rightness or wrongness of an action are nonsense unless other interests are at stake besides my interest in visiting friends or going to a concert, for example the interest of somebody at home who might need me, or my own interest in surviving, if to visit friends I have to take a dangerous road. If I say that going out was the right thing to do (instead of saying that I am happy to have done it, or that going out was good for me, I mean to say the following: I have thought about the whole issue, about the different interests at stake, and I am able to provide criteria for my choice. Indeed, I wish to make my criteria known; I wish people to participate in a discussion about what I regard as a "matter of principle", not as a matter concerning a single event.

Maybe my ought-judgement and the arguments I make for it are just *a posteriori* rationalizations of an impulsive decision of mine A decision I took long before having reflected upon, and balanced, the different interests at stake. This does not matter at all for the purpose of my argument. The reason this is so can be seen if we recall the distinction I made between the three different objects of inquiry. Is there somebody who would claim that a certain decision of a judge is inadequately or incoherently justified *because*, as a matter of fact, the judge had already decided to acquit the defendant as soon as he saw her in the courtroom (she really reminded him of his late wife)? Is there somebody who would claim that, in such a situation, the fact that the judge spent days and nights studying the case and, accordingly, laid down an elaborate decision is irrelevant? Clearly, in the argument above there is no connection

6 Cf. T. Sauvel, "Histoire du jugement motivé", *Revue du Droit Public et de la Science Politique en France et à l'Etranger* 71 (1955), 5-53.

between the premise and the conclusion. That "because" is utterly misleading.

VII

Since I have given the reasons why I use "justification" in the way I do, I have to argue why I do not use "foundation" here. Using that term in the sense that I clarified above. I believe that it is misleading to use "foundation" (*Begründung*) to mean reasoning in support of some rule or practical decision. "Foundation" always refers to issues of validity; but "validity" in moral and legal theory does not have the same meaning as in logic. In logic, we predicate the validity of strings of propositions and of structures or arguments. On the contrary, in moral and legal theory, we predicate the validity of rules. We should therefore avoid such terminological choices that may lead us to disregard this basic difference. Disregarding this difference badly affects the realization of one of the central theses of non-cognitivism in ethics and jurisprudence. This is the thesis that the (logical) validity of an argument is not enough to establish the (legal or moral) validity of a rule. This thesis would be meaningless if there were no actual difference between the validity of an argument and the validity of a rule. It is worth stressing that from this thesis one cannot infer (unless one plays with words) the conclusion that provided no argument can establish the validity of a rule, no "practical reasoning" can really be valid. We can, therefore, correctly call "foundation" the whole set of arguments supporting the correctness, and/or the justice, of a rule or practical judgement. We can do this if, but only if we are able, on the one hand, to keep the issue of the foundation of a rule separate from the issue of its validity. And, on the other hand, we do connect the foundation of a rule with its reasonableness. Unfortunately, this runs contrary to linguistic habits too deeply rooted to be eradicated.

By saying so, I do not wish to suggest that an unhappy terminological choice is responsible for what I believe to be a theoretical mistake. Rather, it is disregarding the three objects of inquiry above that is responsible for that mistake. As a matter of fact, terminological choices reveal whether somebody is, or is not, aware of an issue and its importance. I think we should avoid using "foundation" (*Begründung*) to refer to the activity of providing arguments for rules, if we want to be safe from the mistake I pointed out.

VIII

As I said above, both static and dynamic normative systems present problems of foundation and problems of justification of rules and practical decisions. However, it is worth emphasizing that the relation between laying down, justifying, and founding a rule within the two kinds of systems is utterly different. In what follows I shall analyze this issue.

Static system are essentially open, flexible ones. Dynamic systems, on the contrary, are closed and rigid. In static systems, rules are created by means of *derivation*. In dynamic systems, on the contrary, rules are created by means of *production*. The elements of a static system are like precious stones, they have to be excavated, extracted and brought to light. Everything is already there, waiting to be discovered. However, we have to know where to look for it, how to bring it out to light and, above all, how to recognize it. Is it really a gem or a piece of glass? Is it the masterpiece of a great sculptor or a shapeless stone? In a static system competent agents decide these issues. Here "competent" means "expert"; it does not mean "authorized". Accordingly, in a static system everybody can argue that the so-called competent are a fraud, that their decisions are not justified at all. Everybody can say the king is naked. In a dynamic system this is impossible. If the highest dignitaries of the kingdom say that the king is the commander-in-chief of the armed forces, regulating the life and the death of his subjects, one cannot just say: "It is not true". One needs the support of many brave and well-armed fellows.

Such a sharp difference between static and dynamic systems exists only in theory. In practice, the difference tends to become vague. Indeed, in every kind of system there is a tendency towards making its dynamic elements predominate over its static ones. On the one hand, being an expert means being authorized to be an expert. On the other hand, one becomes an authorised expert not because of one's knowledge and experience, but because of the logic of power . In every society, one of the most effective unwritten rules, though its effectiveness may vary greatly, states that whoever says "The king is naked!" is a fool. Even in a pure static system it is one thing to know what the elements of the system are. It is another to be able to derive them. Even in geometry, I can both acquire information about what theorems are valid, and discover new theories. On the one hand, unlike Kantian morality, geometry is a fact; it is not the private business of every geometer. On the other hand, however, geometry is not a natural fact. Rather, it is a social, i.e. cultural fact. Geometry is the outcome of the acquisition, storing-up, and transmission of knowledge over the centuries. It is the outcome of continuous developments and criticisms. If this were not the case, studying geometry would require only studying a set of postulates. One would come to know at once everything about it. Geometry would not be a science; it would be outside of history.

From the fact that everybody is authorized to construct a theorem, it does not follow that everybody is able to do so. Conversely, anyone who is not able to test the validity of some theorem may nonetheless know that it is valid, and use it in his everyday work.

I believe the argument above does hold not only for geometry, but also for systems of rules of behaviour consisting of both general rules and decisions on particular issues. What should we do here and now? How should I have to judge a certain action? Unless by "morality" we mean something altogether different from a modifiable cultural object (or a system of effective social rules subject to be changed), we cannot deny that *deriving* a rule also implies *producing* that rule. Provided one has taken into account, and weighed up, the set of circumstances affecting the derivation of the rule. These are precisely the circumstances Kant believed not to be worth considering.[7]

I claim that any derivation of a rule always requires some decision-making. Deciding whether a specific event does, or does not, fall under a general rule.

In the light of the argument above, one may conclude that, appearances notwithstanding, *static* normative systems (i.e. those systems where a rule is valid because its content has been logically derived from the content of other valid rules) are also *dynamic* systems. As a matter of fact, static systems too regulate their own production, though in a different way from those systems that Kelsen calls "dynamic". Above, I argued that no existing social order can be a pure simple system

7 Cf. I. Kant, *Grundlagen zur Metaphysik der Sitten* (Leipzig: Modes and Baumann 1938), 22-23: "Was ich also zu thun habe, damit mein Wollen gut sei, dazu brauche ich gar keine ausholende Scharsinnigket ... Es wär hier leicht zu zeigen, wie sie, mit diesem Compasse in der Hand, in allen vorkommenden Fällen sehr gut Bescheid wisse, zu unterscheiden, was gut, was böse, pflichtmäßig order pflichwidrig sie, wenn man, ohnse sie in Mindesten etwas Neues zu lehren, sie nur, wie Socrates that, aufihre eigenes Princip aufmerksam macht, und daBeralso keiner Wissenstaft und Philosopie bedürfe, um zu wissen, was man zu thun habe, um ehrlich und tut, ja sogar um weise und tugendhaft zu sein."

à la Hart. Now we see that no existing social order can be a pure static system *à la* Kelsen either.

Between law and morals there is a difference of degree, not of kind. Morals are a system of rules that are mainly the spontaneous products of a society, the natural function of which is social control. Law, especially in Civil law systems, is mainly the product of the decisions of specific political bodies. These decisions are meant to affect the moral rules upon which a given society rests. In particular, the law effects a (risky) trade-off between the values of justice and rightness, on the one hand, and the values of certainty and efficiency, on the other.[8]

The difference between legal and moral systems, therefore, is neither the one made by Hart, nor the one made by Kelsen (at least at one, well known, stage of his thinking). Of course there is a difference, and a very important one, between law and morals. The difference concerns my specific object of inquiry, justification. Particularly with respect to its relationship with the act of laying down a rule. I argued above that both legal and moral systems regulate their own production (in a more or less explicit, more or less detailed, more or less rigorous way). Every moral or legal decision produces moral or legal norms. Moral systems, as rational systems (static in Kelsenian terminology) produce individual moral decisions only. General moral rules are derived from other more general rules. Legal systems (as systems constituted by a framework of delegations of normative powers) produce general rules too. Moral and legal decisions alike are possible objects of justification. Both in moral and legal systems, whoever makes a decision claims implicitly to be justified in so doing, even though he is not eager to face somebody else's objections and calls for explanation. Both in moral and legal systems, however, it is one thing to justify a decision and another to make it. Accordingly, it is not inconsistent (though, perhaps, immoral) not to make the decision one regards as the morally or, legally best justified, because of weakness, love, money, aesthetics, politics, or power.

In any event, there is quite an important difference between legal and moral justification. In moral systems, the linguistic act by means of which, at the end of the process of justification, a moral choice is said to be right, always lays down a moral rule. In legal systems the linguistic act by means of which, at the end of the process of justification, a legal choice is said to be right, lays down a legal rule only in given cases, specified by

8 Cf. S. Stoljar, *Moral and Legal Reasoning* (London: Macmillan, 1980), 133: "Law adds a further stabilising element to moral practices."

other legal rules. Such a difference, however, vanishes a soon as we look at what happens in practice. As a matter of fact, a specific moral decision may be so unimportant within a moral system as a whole, that it can be utterly neglected while giving an account of the system. A moral decision will be worth considering only when it occurs so often as to become a sociologically perceptible phenomenon. In legal systems, above all Civil Law systems, a similar situation occurs with regard to giving accounts of the doctrinal opinions of jurists and courts. No doubt, courts do produce law for particular cases. However, from the viewpoint of the legal system as a whole, this is regarded a something very similar to the doctrinal opinions of jurists. Its acceptability by other courts, or jurists or both, does not rest upon the formal competence of the court which produced it. Rather, it rests upon the rule being rationally justified. This is another proof that the law has a moral, and therefore a rational, basis.

IX

Justifying a decision is something different from making it. However, within a rational-material system (I do not call it "static" for the reasons I gave above) the competence to decide is attributed to whoever is able to justify his decisions. Within a rational-formal system (I do not call it "dynamic" for the reasons I gave above) the ability to justify one's decisions is only one among several, varied, requirements for being competent to decide. The value of preserving the certainty of the law, even when justice is at stake, requires that.

What I have just said concerns the distinction between the first and the second object of inquiry. We are by now used to hearing that rules are reasons for decisions. Yet, this should not be understood as if there were no causes behind decision-making, but only reasons. Rather, "rules are reasons for decisions" should be understood as an elliptical assertion. In my view, the explicit version of this assertion states: "rules are reasons on the basis of which decisions are justified". Indeed, decisions can be made without any reason to support them. This, however, does not imply that they could not be justified on the basis of some rule. Deciding and justifying are, therefore, two quite different things. What about the relationship between the first and the third object of my inquiry? What is the difference between justifying and founding something, within legal and moral systems? For my claim is that there is a difference between these two activities, both in legal and in moral systems.

Founding a rule means recognizing that it is valid, ascertaining its validity, and ascribing validity to it. From a logical point of view, rules are *posterius* within the process of justification, and *prius* within the process of foundation. Logically, rules pass through the stages of justification, promulgation and foundation, in that order. We can found a rule if, but only if, it has already been laid down. But we do not need a rule to be there in order to justify it. Indeed, this is obvious: the conclusion of an argument comes after, not before, the premises and the development of the argument. But if I want to test whether a piece of metal is gold or brass, there must be the piece of metal first!

It is worth noticing that Kelsen, in showing the difference between static and dynamic systems, does not start with (an imaginary) dialogue which starts with a question like: "What should I do?". Rather, Kelsen makes it start as follows: "Why should I do *this*?", provided we already know what *this* is.[9] Kelsen's entire argument would be meaningless if the starting question really were the first one above. Let us see (A and B being our *dramatis personae)*

A: "What should I do?"

B: "What you are required to do".

A: "What am I required to do, then?"

B: "What X is authorised to require you to do, in virtue of the authorization that Y and W gave to make requirements of you". (And so on).

Surrealistic shadows haunt situations like this. Were such a procedure meant to inform somebody about what he should do, rather than informing somebody that he really should do what he has been requested to do, nobody would ever do anything. Or rather, everybody would do everything. Indeed, provided nothing precisely is being requested, everything is being permitted.

What about static systems? The same situations would occur. Indeed, if to the question: "What should I do?" the answer were: "Whatever you can derive from the rule 'Thou shalt love they neighbour as thyself'", somebody would throw his neighbour into the fire in order to make it easier for him to enter Heaven (or use atomic bombs to stop Japanese imperialism, or squat down on a pillar amidst the desert praying for the salvation of mankind). Almost everything could be derived from such a rule. Kelsen does not make the dialogue start with the question: "What should I do?" (and rightly so). Rather, Kelsen's starting

9 Kelsen, *Reine Rechslehre, supra* n.3, at 197-200.

point is the following: "Why should I go to school?". Here the difference is crucial. Kelsen has always kept to this formulation of the problem, even in his later and his posthumous works. The problem has always been one of the validity of rules and decisions, rather than of their justice and correctness. Besides, one cannot quote Kelsen in support of the thesis that the processes by means of which rules and decisions are justified are not "logical", and, therefore, one cannot really say either that they are correct or incorrect. This is so because Kelsen never mistook "validity" for "correctness". In fact, in his posthumous work Kelsen deals with the issue of correctness while dealing with the relationship of "Entsprechung" between rules. This relationship Kelsen rightly regards as a "Subsumptionsbeziehung".

X

In the light of the distinction I draw between justification and foundation, I now turn to Kelsen's views on law and logic. When distinguishing between justification and foundation, I argued that justification should always be understood as an answer, even when nobody is actually asking for it. I argued that justification always makes sense within (actual or hypothetical) dialogical contexts. Indeed, by "dialogue" I mean any situation where many different interests and views can be legitimately respected and expressed.

This is not the case with foundation. I argued that foundation has not necessarily the shape of a discourse. It is not reasoning in contexts of communicative cooperation. It is not a social enterprise at all. Rather, foundation is an intellectual effort, a lonely undertaking, a game where partners and opponents alike are not needed. It might be objected that Kelsen offers a dialogical representation of the foundation of rules both in static and dynamic systems? This is not a strong objection but I deal with it so as to clear up a widespread misunderstanding in the interpretation of Kelsen on law and logic.

As I have said, from the fact that foundation is not a discourse (it does not need an interlocutor), it does not follow that it could not have a linguistic shape. As a matter of fact, a sequence of questions and answers is the simplest way one can find to exhibit the logical structure of foundation; to identify the premises; the intermediate stages; and the conclusion of the reasoning by which it is constituted; and to keep those three elements distinct. Formulating it in terms of mathematical reasoning does not imply that it is a problem where it is impossible to find any solution without facing somebody else's views and interests. A situation where one should wait for somebody else's arguments and answers in order to solve the problem, since one cannot see or guess what these arguments and answers could be. Like in a "mathematical drama", where there are no real characters, in real life one cannot find a father and a son acting as Kelsen makes them act. They would be automata. Real sons, asking why they should go to school, do not want to know who is authorized to give them orders. Rather, they want to know why they are obliged to go to school. Real fathers will often answer: "Because I say so"! Then, if the sons retorts: "But why should we do what you tell us to do?", the fathers will not certainly answer as follows: "Because this is so according to the civil code (or: to he Holy Bible)". Rather, they will laugh at their sons, or express anger at them. Sons are well aware that they should obey their fathers, at least so far as they are stronger than them. Only in philosophy books can this question asked by sons to their fathers be understood as requests for information. In real dialogues, these questions have to be understood either as challenges (or provocation), or as attempts to make father discuss on a par with them.

Kelsen does not care about real dialogues. Indeed, the problem Kelsen has in mind is different from the problem flesh and blood sons have. Kelsen entertains a problem of foundation. Sons want to know how to identify what their real duties are. In theory, in order to know, the subject and the object of knowledge are enough; you need to ask anybody. You do not even need to ask those who imposed the duties. They would always try to suggest that those duties are real ones, even though it is not the case (I use "real duties", referring to Kelsen's theory, and not out of my personal views about the objectivity of duties). Indeed, the only thing worth asking whoever imposed a duty upon us is the following: "Why did you impose that duty upon us?" That is to say, we should ask him to give us the reasons why he decided in a certain way. A real dialogue will follow thereafter. This is the right time for justification.

XI

Kelsen makes use of a further (pseudo-) dialogue situation in order to show the basis of the validity of rules in static systems. Also to keep that distinct from the basis of validity of dynamic systems (or systems that regulate their own production). Here, for Kelsen, the matter becomes very complex. In my view, on the contrary, the matter is utterly clear.

The question says: "Why should I refrain from cheating?" The answer says: "Because men should tell the truth". Clearly, this answer always presupposes some interpretation of the rule that is the premise of the argument. Consider the following case: doctors know that the only way to make a seriously ill patient better is telling him tenderly, "Everything is all right! You are really recovering fast". What does it mean "to tell the truth" in a case like this? There is only need of a rule when there is a real issue is a stake, a concrete case. In this event, there is no set of rules. Rather, there is just one rule.

As I said above, every system is, by definition, dynamic. Let us consider again the case above. In a room, a doctor is discussing with a relative of the patient the way to treat him. They hold different opinions about this issue, yet an opinion has to prevail. Not because somebody is authorized to decide instead of somebody else, nor because they ought to follow a procedure designed for cases like that. Rather, they need to agree on a specific view only because the patient would certainly be worse off if different persons (the doctor and the relative) gave him different pictures of his health. Accordingly, it is likely that they will make their own proposals, argue for them, defend them against the opponent's arguments, and, finally, make a common decision. For they should, finally, decide. Indeed, the patient is waiting for information, he does want to know how he is. It is not sure that both the doctor and the relative are strongly committed to the decision they made. It is not necessary either, provided everybody abides by the common decision. Were a friend to ask why he should also abide by that decision, the doctor and the relative could quite correctly answer: "Because we have decided so". It is worth asking whether there is a difference between the situation above and what normally happens in a jury-room? And what is the difference between the situation above and the relation between what happens in the jury-room and the judgement proclaimed in the court-room? In theory, I claim, there is no difference. In real life, there are nether static nor dynamic normative systems. Indeed, if what I just said is right, they cannot be conceived as two models either. They are just two metaphors. The static system is the metaphor of the process (or function) of justification of rules. The dynamic system is the metaphor of the process (or function) of the foundation of rules.

RULES, VALIDITY AND STATUTORY CONSTRUCTION

by

RICCARDO GUASTINI

1. *Weak and Strong Sense of "Validity"*

Contemporary legal-philosophical literature is crowded with a lot of competing theories of validity.[1] In this paper, however, I am not going to

Law and Language, The Italian Analytical School, ed. A. Pintore and M. Jori (Liverpool: Deborah Charles Publications, 1997).

1 Any mention of Kelsen's well known works is unnecessary in this connection. Some outstanding contributions in recent literature are the following: C.E. Alchourrón and E. Bulygin, *Normative Systems* (Wien: Springer, 1971), ch. 5; E. Bulygin, "Sobre la regla de reconocimiento", in *Derecho, filosofía, y lenguaje. Homenaje a Ambrosio L. Gioja* (Buenos Aires: Astrea, 1976), 31-39; *idem*, "Enunciados jurídicos y positivismo: respuesta a Raz", *Análisis filosófico* 1/2 (1981), 49-59; *idem*, "Time and Validity", in A.A. Martino, ed., *Deontic Logic, Computational Linguistics, and Legal Information Systems* (Amsterdam: North-Holland, 1982), II.65-81; *idem* , "Validez y positivismo", in *Segundo Congreso Internacional de Filosofía del derecho. Comunicaciones* (La Plata: Asociación Argentina de Filosofía del derecho, 1987), I.241-55; *idem*, "An Antinomy in Kelsen's Pure Theory of Law", *Ratio Juris* 3 (1990), 29-45; N. Bobbio, "Per un lessico di teoria generale del diritto" (1975), 125-146, reprinted in R. Guastini, ed., *Problemi di teoria del diritto* (Bologna: Il Mulino, 1980), 47-55; "Sul ragionamento dei giuristi" (1955), reprinted in P. Comanducci and R. Guastini, eds., *L'analisi del ragionamento giuridico. Materiali ad uso degli studenti* (Turin: Giappichelli, 1989), II.161-179; A.G. Conte, *Nove studi sul linguaggio normativo (1967-1978)* (Turin: Giappichelli, 1985), chs.3 and 5); *idem*, "Minima deontica", *Rivista internazionale di filosofia del diritto* 65 (1988), 425-475; M.D. Farrell, *Hacia un criterio empírico de validez* (Buenos Aires: Astrea, 1972); H.L.A. Hart, *The Concept of Law* (Oxford: Clarendon, 1961), ch. 6; Marín Hernández, *Teoría general del derecho y de la ciencia jurídica*, (Barcelona: PPU, 1989), ch. 10; C.S. Nino, *La validez del derecho* (Buenos Aires: Astrea, 1985); E. Pattaro, *Lineamenti per una teoria del diritto* (Bologna: Clueb, 1985); J. Raz, *The Concept of a Legal System* (2nd ed., 1973), Italian translation *Il concetto di sistema giuridico*, ed. P. Comanducci (Bologna: Il Mulino, 1977), chs.4 and 5; *idem,* "Legal Validity", in J. Raz, *The Authority of Law. Essays on Law and Morality* (Oxford: Clarendon, 1979), 146-159; A. Ross, "Validity and the Conflict between Legal Positivism and Natural Law", *Revista*

discuss anyone of these theories. My purpose is to propose a — perhaps less worn-out — analysis of the actual uses of the term "validity" in the common language of Italian lawyers, viz. jurists and judges.[2] Italian law is a civil (statutory) law system, the essential features of which are: (a) a rigid constitution, i. e. a constitution which cannot be either repealed or derogated by ordinary legislation; and (b) the judicial review of legislation, which falls under the competence of a Constitutional Court entitled to declare null and void any statutory rule inconsistent with the constitution. Anyway, I flatter myself with the hope that my analysis could also hold for the linguistic usage of civil lawyers at large.

I shall begin by noticing that the term "validity" is subject to changeable uses. In my opinion, in dogmatic literature one could find at least two concepts of "validity", and distinguishing between them seems to be convenient. For the present moment I assume validity to be a property

---

Juridica de Buenos Aires (1961), 46-93; Italian translation "Il concetto di validità e il conflitto tra positivismo giuridico e giusnaturalismo", in A. Ross, *Critica del diritto e analisi del linguaggio*, ed. A. Febbrajo and R. Guastini (Bologna: Il Mulino, 1982), 137-158.; U. Scarpelli, *Cos'è il positivismo giuridico* (Milan: Comunità, 1965). ch.7; R.S. Summers, "Toward a Better General Theory of Legal Validity", *Rechtstheorie* 16 (1985), 65-83; J. Wróblewski, "Tre concetti di validità", *Rivista trimestrale di diritto e procedura civile* 36 (1982), 584-595.

2 Cf. V. Crisafulli, "Gerarchia e competenza nel sistema costituzionale delle fonti", *Rivista trimestrale di diritto pubblico* 10 (1960), 775-809; *idem*, *Lezioni di diritto costituzionale* (Padova: Cedam, 1984, 5th ed.), vol. 2, 178ff.; C. Esposito, *La validità delle leggi* (1934, reprinted Milan: Giuffrè, 1964); L. Ferrajoli, *Diritto e ragione. Teoria del garantismo penale* (Bari: Laterza, 1989), 348ff., 90 ff.; M.S. Giannini, "L'illegittimità degli atti normativi e delle norme", *Rivista italiana per le scienze giuridiche* 7 (1954), 39-71; R. Guastini, *Dalle fonti alle norme* (Turin: Giappichelli, 1990), chs.13, 14, 15; F. Modugno, *L'invalidità della legge* (Milan: Giuffrè, 1970, 2 vols.); *idem, Lezioni sul linguaggio giuridico* (Turin: Giappichelli, 1985); *idem, Appunti per una teoria generale del diritto. La teoria del diritto oggettivo* (Turin: Giappichelli, 1988), 102ff.; A. Pizzorusso, *Delle fonti del diritto* (Bologna: Zanichelli, 1977) 236ff.; A. Ruggeri, *Gerarchia, competenza, e qualità nel sistema costituzionale delle fonti normative* (Milan: Giuffrè, 1977); A.M. Sandulli, "Legge (diritto costituzionale)", *Novissimo digesto italiano* (Turin: Utet, 1963), 9, 630-651; *idem, Il giudizio sulle leggi* (Milan: Giuffrè, 1967); F. Sorrentino, *Le fonti del diritto* (Genova: ECIG, 1985, 2nd ed.), 10ff.; G. Volpe, *L'ingiustizia delle leggi. Studi sui modelli di giustizia costituzionale* (Milan: Giuffrè, 1977); G. Zagrebelsky, *Il sistema costituzionale delle fonti del diritto* (Turin: Utet, 1984), 36ff.

of rules (or norms).

(a) In a strong sense, "validity" means "membership": a rule is valid (or invalid) within a certain legal system, as a member of it. Within a given legal system, a valid rule is a rule which meets the criteria of identification which are peculiar to that legal system. In each legal system the criteria of identification of rules lie in the meta-rules concerning the so-called sources of law, as well as in the meta-rules concerning the solution of inconsistencies (e. g. "lex superior derogat legi inferiori", "lex posterior derogat legi priori", etc.), and so on.[3]

(b) In a weak sense, "validity" means — *à la* Kelsen — "existence".[4] Unfortunately, the concept of existence, in its turn, is not entirely clear. In the present context, however, an "existing rule", quite simply, is a rule which was actually created, laid down, i.e. formulated and enacted by a rule-creating authority (a *prima facie* competent authority).

My paper is devoted to the analysis of the first concept of validity, hence of the strong sense of the term.

Perhaps, it is timely to remark that there is no coincidence between the two concepts. For example, where the weak sense is chosen, in Italian legal system a rule voted by Parliament and enacted by the President of the Republic counts as a "valid" rule, notwithstanding its inconsistency with the constitution. On the contrary, if the strong concept of validity is chosen, such a rule is obviously "invalid" because of the rigid character of the Italian constitution (consistency with the constitution being a necessary condition of validity in the strong sense).[5]

Besides, validity in the weak sense, mere "existence", is not devoid of

3 In the present context, the normative concept of "validity" as "binding force", stipulated by Kelsen, is disregarded.

4 However, in Kelsen there is no clear cut distinction between membership and mere existence. Cf. H. Kelsen, *Reine Rechtslehre* (1960), Italian translation *Dottrina pura del diritto*, ed. M.G. Losano (Turin: Einaudi, 1966), ch.5; *idem,* "Recht und Logik" (1965), Italian Translation "Diritto e logica", in Comanducci and Guastini, *supra* n.1, at vol. 2, 65-98. On this subject see M. Barberis, "La norma senza qualità. Appunti su 'validità' in Hans Kelsen", *Materiali per una storia della cultura giuridica* 11 (1981), 405-438; R. Guastini, "Introduzione", in H. Kelsen, *La teoria politica del bolscevismo e altri saggi*, ed. R. Guastini (Milan: Il Saggiatore, 1981), 7-32; Bulygin, "An Antinomy in Kelsen's Pure Theory of Law", *supra* n.1.

5 That is the meaning of the principle "lex superior derogat legi inferiori": properly speaking, the lower rule is not "derogated" (i.e. repealed) by the higher one; rather, it is invalid.

any legal effects. On the contrary, "existence" is a sufficient condition for rules to be applied. In other words, invalid rules too are susceptible of judicial application: at least, until their invalidity (in the strong sense) is not "declared" (in a constitutive way) by a competent organ (the Constitutional Court, as far as statutory rules are concerned).[6]

2. *Validity Statements and their Subject-Matters*

What do validity statements deal with? According to a widely accepted view, statements on the validity of rules are sentences provided with the standard form: "The rule *R* is valid/ invalid".[7] Such sentences are usually investigated by wondering about the problematic meaning of the word which works as the syntactic predicate of the sentence, i.e. "valid", while the meaning of the word which works as the syntactic subject, i.e. "rule", is neglected as unproblematic. This is the way I proceeded too in the foregoing section.

Such a proceeding, however, is grounded upon a couple of implicit assumptions, which are highly problematic: first, that validity is a property of "rules" and nothing else; second, that the concept of "rule" is unambiguous and does not require any philosophical analysis. Indeed, both assumptions, although widespread in dogmatic and legal-

6 Kelsen, *Dottrina pura, supra* n.4, at 298-310.

7 Indeed some authors maintain that validity judgments can be expressed by deontic sentences as well, viz. by sentences which iterate statutory provisions. Cf., e.g., E. Bulygin, "Norms, Normative Propositions, and Legal Statements" (1982), Italian translation "Norme, proposizioni normative, e asserti giuridici", in P. Comanducci and R. Guastini, eds., *L'analisi del ragionamento giuridico. Materiali ad uso degli studenti*, (Turin: Giappichelli, 1987), vol. 1, 7-37; Kelsen, *Dottrina pura, supra* n.4, at ch.3; G.H. von Wright, *Norm and Action. A Logical Enquiry* (London: Routledge & Kegan Paul, 1963); *idem, Practical Reason* (London: Routledge & Kegan Paul, 1983), 130ff. Such a tenet, however, is not sound. Juristic deontic sentences cannot be construed as validity statements. For some criticism cf. H. Kelsen, "Derogation" (1962), Italian translation "La derogazione", in H. Kelsen, *La teoria politica del bolscevismo e altri saggi*, ed. R. Guastini (Milan: Il Saggiatore, 1981), 189-206; *idem, Allgemeine Theorie der Normen* (1979), Italian translation *Teoria generale delle norme*, ed. M.G. Losano (Turin: Einaudi, 1985); *idem,* "Zur Theorie der Interpretation" (1934), Italian translation "Sulla teoria dell'interpretazione", in Comanducci and Guastini, *supra* n.1, at vol. 2, 107-120; T. Mazzarese, *Logica deontica e linguaggio giuridico* (Padova: Cedam, 1989); Guastini, *Dalle fonti alle norme*, *supra* n.2, at ch.3.

philosophical literature, just seem to be fallacious.

In the first place, according to the common language of lawyers, validity is a property not only of rules, but of normative or rule-creating acts too. The phrase "normative act", however, is actually used in two different senses. In the first sense, "normative act" denotes a human action which amounts to the production of rules (e.g. the act of legislating). In the second one, the same phrase denotes the result, the product, of a normative action, i.e. a normative text or document: a set of provisions (e.g. a statute). In the following, I shall use this phrase in the first sense only: accordingly, by "normative act" I mean the act of producing a legal source, while I name "normative text" the source itself.

In the second place, in the common language of lawyers, the word "rule" (as well as "norm") is not used in a fixed and uniform way .[8] On the one hand, lawyers usually talk of "rules" as to refer both to statutory provisions and to their meaning contents. On the other hand, they also use "rule" as to refer to prescriptions which are not expressly enacted by law-givers, but are construed by lawyers themselves, e.g. in view of filling gaps in the legal system. As a consequence, one could distinguish three senses of "rule".

(a) In the first sense, rules are but statutory provisions, i. e. the sentences embodied in legal sources.

(b) In the second sense, rules are the meaning contents of such sentences as determined by means of statutory interpretation (expressed or explicit rules).

(c) Finally, in the third sense, rules are prescriptions which were not actually formulated by the law-giving authorities, hence prescriptions which are not drawn from statutory texts by means of statutory construction, but are formulated *ex novo* by lawyers themselves (unexpressed or implicit rules).[9]

8 R. Guastini, *Lezioni sul linguaggio giuridico* (Turin: Giappichelli, 1985), ch. 1; *idem,* "Redazione e interpretazione dei documenti normativi", in S. Bartole, ed., *Lezioni di tecnica legislativa* (Padova: Cedam, 1988); *idem, Dalle fonti alle norme*, *supra* n.2, at ch.1.

9 Cf. A. Peczenik, "Non-Equivalent Transformations and the Law", in W. Krawietz, K. Opelak, A. Peczenik and A. Schramm, eds., *Argumentation und Hermeneutik in der Jurisprudenz* (Berlin Duncker & Humblot, 1979), 163-176 (*Rechtstheorie*, Beiheft 1): "There are some cases whose solution is not explicitly given in the sources of the law, like statutes, precedents, legislative drafts etc. A lawyer, *inter alia* a judge, can still solve such cases, *via* legal reasoning whose conclusion is a proposition about a valid rule of law applicable

My suggestion is that a refined theory of validity ought to distinguish among the following: (1) validity of normative acts; (2) validity of expressed rules; (3) validity of unexpressed rules; (4) validity of statutory provisions. The reason for distinguishing is a matter of course: different criteria of validity hold for acts, for expressed rules, for unexpressed rules, and for statutory provisions, respectively.

However, this chain of distinctions — especially the distinction between statutory provisions and rules — is no matter of course: it just asks for some preliminary elucidations.

3. *Statutory Construction*

In order to clarify the distinction between statutory provisions and rules, it is convenient to start by a stipulative definition of "statutory construction". By "construction" or "interpretation" (within legal experience) I mean the ascription of meaning to any normative text, i.e. any text produced by some rule-creating authority, hence any text, e.g. a statute, which can be *prima facie* identified as a legal source within a given legal system.[10]

Accordingly, legal interpretation amounts to a decision concerning the meaning of a normative text. Such a definition is aimed at stressing that

---

to the case. But from where is this rule "taken"? Not from any other written source. In fact, the rule is *constructed*; the sources of the law constitute mere arguments used in the process of construction. Still lawyers speak *about* such non-written but valid legal rules, not equivalent with the statutes, precedents, legislative drafts etc. Since such rules come to existence only when the judges etc. mention them, and have not existed one second before, the judges etc. in fact do not speak *about* legal rules but they speak *in* legal rules, they create them." Cf. Bobbio, "Sul ragionamento dei giuristi" (1989), *supra* n.1; R. Guastini, "Production of Rules by Means of Rules", *Rechtstheorie* 17 (1986), 295-309; *idem* , "A Framework for the Analysis of Judicial Discourse", in C. Faralli and E. Pattaro eds., *Reason in Law* (Milan: Giuffrè, 1987), vol. 1, 281-300; A. Peczenik, *The Basis of Legal Justification* (Lund: Lund University Press, 1983).

10 G. Tarello, *Diritto, enunciati, usi. Studi di teoria e metateoria del diritto* (Bologna: Il Mulino, 1974), 389ff., 403ff.; *idem, L'interpretazione della legge* (Milan, Giuffrè, 1980), ch.1. Several senses of "interpretation" are listed in R. Guastini, "Some Remarks on the Conceptual Framework of 'Law's Empire'", *Ratio Juris* 1 (1988), 176-180.

statutory construction is no merely cognitive activity.[11] Interpreting asks for the evaluation of competing meanings and the choice of just one meaning among them.[12].

Properly speaking, statutory construction is a mental activity: something which happens inside the mind.[13] However, mind activities are only subject to psychological analysis. Treating statutory construction as a mind activity would make it impossible to work out any logical analysis of it. For the present purposes, it is convenient to treat statutory construction not as a mental operation but rather as a discourse. In other words, it is convenient to investigate not statutory construction as such but its "literary" result, viz. dogmatic works, judicial decisions, and the like. In view of a logical analysis, interpretation is but the discourse of interpreters.

Now, interpreters' discourse amounts to a set of interpretive sentences (plus a set of arguments aimed at justifying the chosen interpretation). By "interpretive sentence" I mean any sentence to the effect that a certain text expresses a given meaning, hence any sentence provided with the standard (although sometimes perhaps concealed) form: "'*T* means *M*", where *T* stands for a normative text and *M* stands for the meaning ascribed to such a text by an interpreter whatsoever (a jurist, a judge, etc.). In such a formula, *T* is placed in inverted commas since, within interpreters' discourse, it is but a quotation from the discourse of the law-giving authority. A normative text, in its turn, is but a set of normative sentences (i.e. sentences provided with a prescriptive sense). Well,

(a) I name "statutory sentence" or "statutory provision" any sentence which is a part of a normative text;

11 Statutory construction is usually pictured as an activity aimed at "ascertaining" the meaning contents of statutes and/or the "will" of the legislators. Cf., e.g., G.R. Carriò, "Sobre la interpretación en el derecho" (1965), Italian translation "Sull'interpretazione giuridica", in P. Comanducci and R. Guastini, eds., *L'analisi del ragionamento giuridico. Materiali ad uso degli studenti* (Turin Giappichelli, 1989), vol. 2, 127-151; M. Jori and A. Pintore, *Manuale di teoria generale del diritto* (Turin: Giappichelli, 1988).

12 Kelsen, *Dottrina pura, supra* n.4, at ch.8; H. Kelsen, "Zur Theorie der Interpretation" (1934), Italian translation "Sulla teoria dell'interpretazione", in Comanducci and Guastini, *supra* n.11, at II. 107-120. Cf. M. Troper, "Kelsen, la théorie de l'interprétation et la structure de l'ordre juridique", *Revue internationale de philosophie* 138 (1981), 518-529 (issue on *Kelsen et le positivisme juridique*).

13 Kelsen, "Sulla teoria dell'interpretazione", *supra* n.7.

(b) I name "rule" or "norm" any sentence which is the meaning ascribed (by anyone) to a statutory sentence (or to a fragment of a statutory sentence, or to a combination of statutory sentences, or to a combination of fragments of statutory sentences).

In other words, a statutory sentence is a rule-formulation, a part of a text not yet interpreted, whereas a rule is a part of an interpreted text. In the standard formula of interpretive sentences, "'*T* means *M*", *T* stands for a statutory sentence, while *M* stands for a rule. Interpreting is analysing a statutory sentence (a rule-formulation) and producing a rule. In this sense, legal rules do not pre-exist to statutory construction: on the contrary, they are just the result of interpretive decisions.

Perhaps, I should remark that, according to my chain of definitions, there is no ontological difference between statutory sentences and rules. Rules, as well as statutory sentences, are but sentences. A statutory sentence is a sentence formulated in the language of a law-giving authority, whereas a rule is a sentence formulated in the language of the interpreter: a sentence which the interpreter assumes to be synonymous with the statutory one. Rules amount to re-formulations of statutory provisions.

Therefore, statutory construction is a sort of "translation" from the language of a legal source to the language of a lawyer. In a sense, my distinction simply reproduces the (quite obvious) distinction between the statutory language and the juristic (and/or judicial) one.

Now, it is important to stress that, in a sense, the proposed distinction is often ignored by lawyers. I mean that lawyers, in their common language, usually name "rule" or "norm" both the sentences formulated (enacted) by the legislators and the sentences which are formulated by lawyers themselves while interpreting normative texts.

Such a usage is strictly connected with the fallacious belief that there is a "proper" meaning of words, as well as with the "formalistic" (i. e. non-sceptical) theory of statutory construction: I mean the theory according to which statutory construction is but knowledge, viz. knowledge of pre-existing rules (since rules are deemed to be already existing in legal sources, before and independently on any interpretive decision).

4. *Statutory Sentences and Rules*

My point is that lawyers' common usage is misleading since, in my view, there is no correspondence one-to-one between statutory sentences and rules. In this section I shall try to give a number of reasons for such a statement.[14]

(1) In the first place, any rule-formulation whatsoever is vague and/or ambiguous. That amounts to saying that the meaning of any statutory sentence is controversial, and therefore that each statutory sentence can be interpreted in several ways. From this point of view, one could say that no statutory sentence expresses just one rule. On the contrary, any statutory sentence expresses two or more disjointed rules. Facing any statutory sentence, one can always ask: "Does *T* mean M_1, M_2, or M_3?". A

14 T. Ascarelli, "Giurisprudenza costituzionale e teoria dell'interpretazione", *Rivista di diritto processuale* 12 (1957), 351-64; V. Crisafulli, "Questioni in tema di interpretazione della Corte costituzionale nei rapporti con l'interpretazione giudiziaria", *Giurisprudenza costituzionale* 1 (1956), 929-49; *idem*, "Disposizione (e norma)", in *Enciclopedia del diritto* (Milan: Giuffrè, 1964), vol. 13, 195-200; *idem*, "Le sentenze "interpretative" della Corte costituzionale", in *Studi in memoria di Tullio Ascarelli* (Milan: Giuffrè, 1969), vol. 5, 2871-2894; *idem*, *Stato, popolo, governo. Illusioni e delusioni costituzionali* (Milan: Giuffrè, 1985), 39ff.; Giannini, *supra* n.2; *idem*, "Alcuni caratteri della giurisdizione di legittimità delle norme", *Giurisprudenza costituzionale* 1 (1956), 902-28; R. Guastini, *Lezioni*, *supra* n.2, at ch.1; *idem*, "Redazione e interpretazione", *supra* n.8; *idem*, *Dalle fonti alle norme*, *supra* n.2, at ch.1; C. Lavagna, "Sulle sentenze additive della Corte costituzionale", in *Scritti in onore di Gaspare Ambrosini* (Milan: Giuffrè, 1979), vol. 2, 1131-1144; *idem*, *Istituzioni di diritto pubblico* (Turin: Utet, 1985, 6th ed.), 23ff., 31f., 971ff.; E.T. Liebman, "Contenuto ed efficacia delle decisioni della Corte costituzionale", *Rivista di diritto processuale* 12 (1957), 507-25; L. Montesano, "Norma e formula legislativa nel giudizio costituzionale", *Rivista di diritto processuale* 13 (1958), 324-39; *idem*, "Le sentenze costituzionali e l'individuazione delle norme", *Rivista di diritto processuale* 18 (1963) 20-54; A. Pace, "Identità o differenza tra la questione di costituzionalità della norma e la questione di costituzionalità della interpretazione?", *Giurisprudenza costituzionale* 10 (1965), 1650-1656; P. Perlingieri, *Il diritto civile nella legalità costituzionale* (Napoli: Esi, 1984), ch.8; *idem*, *Scuole tendenze metodi. Problemi di diritto civile* (Napoli: Esi, 1989), 283; A. Pizzorusso, "La motivazione delle decisioni della Corte costituzionale: comandi o consigli?", *Rivista trimestrale di diritto pubblico* 13 (1963), 345-407; *idem*, *Delle fonti del diritto* (Bologna: Zanichelli, 1977), 22ff.; A. Pizzorusso, G. Volpe, F. Sorrentino and R. Moretti, *Garanzie costituzionali*, *Commentario della Costituzione* a cura di G. Branca (Bologna: Zanichelli and Roma: Foro Italiano, 1981), 113ff.; G. Zagrebelsky, *La giustizia costituzionale* (Bologna: II Mulino, 1988, 2nd ed.), 279ff. Cf. P. Amselek, "Le droit dans les esprits", in P. Amselek and C. Grzegorczyk, eds., *Controverses autour de l'ontologie du droit* (Paris: PUF, 1989), 27-49; C. Grzegorczyk and T. Studnicki, "Les rapports entre la norme et la disposition légale", *Archives de philosophie du droit* 19 (1974), 243-256.

lot of rules (one or another one) can be drawn from just one and the same rule-formulation, depending on the different interpretive attitudes, evaluations, and choices of jurists and/or judges.

(2) In the second place, leaving aside interpretive controversies, many statutory sentences (perhaps all of them) are provided with a compound meaning, i.e. they express not just one single rule, but more joined rules: "T means M_1, M_2, and M_3". In other words, every single lawyer usually draws a lot of rules from one and the same rule-formulation. This case is different from the previous one. In the previous case, one had to decide the meaning of a rule-formulation, and that asks for the choice among plenty of possible meanings. Whereas, in the present case, one has already decided the meaning of a given statutory sentence, but one did discover that such a meaning just amounts to a number of independent rules.

(3) In the third place, it could happen that two different statutory sentences are perfectly synonymous. In such a case, one and the same rule is expressed by two rule-formulations: "Both T_1 and T_2 mean M". In many cases, one meets a first sentence which expresses — say — two rules, M_1 and M_2, and a second sentence which expresses two other rules, M_1 and M_3, one of which is identical with one of the rules expressed by the first sentence: the meanings of the two sentences just overlap.

Till now I have adopted a very large concept of "rule", since, according to my stipulation, any statutory sentence expresses a rule or a set of rules, notwithstanding its character (e.g. deontic or not). However, in legal theory, one can find some narrower concepts of "rule". In some views, for example, rules are but commands (or a sort of commands); as a consequence, only deontic sentences, i.e. ought-sentences, do express "rules", while non-deontic sentences (e.g. derogatory provisions, statutory definitions, and so on) do not express any "rule" at all since they are not commands directed at human behaviour. In other views, a "complete" or "accomplished" rule can be expressed only by a sentence which determines who ought to (or may, or may not) do what in what circumstances; as a consequence many statutory sentences do not express "complete" rules, but only "parts" of (complete) rules.

(4) Well, if a narrow concept of rule is accepted, one must conclude that there also are some statutory sentences which do not express any rule at all. However, in this connection, we should better distinguish between two different senses of the statement that a given statutory sentence does not express any rule:

(4.1) In a sense, some statutory sentences do not express any rules because they just express something else: e.g. a principle (provided that legal principles are something different from rules),[15] a political programme, an evaluation, etc.

(4.2) In another sense, some statutory sentences do not express any rules because they express no "accomplished" or "complete" rule: in other words, there are sentences which express but a "part", a "fragment", of a rule. Such sentences are actually used by lawyers for construing "complete" rules, but such "complete" rules are the result of the juristic combination of a set of independent statutory sentences.[16].

Furthermore, one can use the phrase "fragment of rule" in two slightly different senses:

(4.2.1) In the first sense, a sentence expresses a fragment of rule because it does not refer to human behaviour (hence it does not express any rule of behaviour), but it refers to another statutory sentence or rule (e. g. determining its scope). This is the case, e.g., of statutory definitions, of derogatory rules, of status-conferring rules, etc.

(4.2.2) In the second sense, a sentence expresses a fragment of rule since it includes a term which presupposes the previous construction of other statutory sentences: e.g. the sentences which expressly define such a term. (In the first sense of "fragment of rule", statutory definitions are fragments of every other statutory sentence in which the defined term is used. In the second sense of "fragment of rule", all the statutory sentences which include a term defined elsewhere in legislators' language are fragments as well, since they can be used in judicial application only in association with the sentences which define such a term.)

(5) Finally, according to a view which is widespread among lawyers,

15 Such a tenet is held, e.g., by R. Dworkin, *Taking Rights Seriously* (London: Duckworth, 1978, 2nd ed.).

16 Some suggestions in K. Olivecrona, "Legal Language and Reality", in *Essays in Jurisprudence in Honor of Roscoe Pound,* ed. Ralph A. Newman (Indianapolis-New York: The Bobbs-Merrill Co., 1962), 151-91; Italian translation: "Linguaggio giuridico e realtà", in U. Scarpelli, ed., *Diritto e analisi del linguaggio* (Milan: Comunità, 1976), 239-283; A. Ross, *Directives and Norms* (London: Routledge & Kegan Paul, 1968), §26; *idem* , "Definition in Legal Language", in *Logique et Analyse* 3-4 (1958), 139-49; Italian translation "La definizione nel linguaggio giuridico", in U. Scarpelli, ed., *Diritto e analisi del linguaggio* (Milan: Comunità, 1976), 199-214; "Tû-Tû", *Harvard Law Review* 70 (1957), 812-825, Italian translation "Tû-Tû" in U. Scarpelli, ed., *Diritto e analisi del linguaggio* (Milan: Comunità, 1976), 165-181.

any legal system does not include only the rules which can be drawn from the existing rule-formulations by means of plain interpretation: every legal system also includes a lot of rules which do not correspond to any statutory sentence whatsoever. In other words, legal systems include statutory sentences without rules, as well as rules without statutory sentences. Usually, principles of law fall within this class.

(5.1) In a weak sense, a rule does not correspond to any rule-formulation since it is drawn not just from one isolated sentence, but from a set of combined sentences.

(5.2) In a strong sense, a rule does not correspond to any rule-formulation since it is a merely implicit or unexpressed rule: i.e. a rule which was not expressly enacted by the legislature, but is construed by lawyers (jurists or judges) by means, e.g., of analogy.

As a matter of course, the concept of unexpressed rule does not fit with the proposed definition of rule (*supra*, § 3: any sentence which is the meaning ascribed to a statutory sentence). Such a definition suggests that there are no rules without statutory provisions which formulate and express them, no rules without corresponding speech acts of law-giving authorities.[17] Furthermore, such a definition makes rules dependent on interpretation. However, it is timely to stress that unexpressed rules are not the result of interpretive activities, since statutory construction, understood as ascription of meaning to texts, obviously asks for statutory texts to be interpreted. Unexpressed rules are the result of the so-called "interstitial legislation" by jurists and judges.[18]

At any rate, the expected conclusion of this section is that there is no correspondence one-to-one between statutory sentences and rules. The clear-cut separation of the two is of great importance in the analysis of a number of topics: e.g., validity (since different criteria of validity hold for

17 C.E. Alchourrón and E. Bulygin, *Sobre la existencia de las normas jurídicas* (Valencia: Oficina Latino-americana de investigaciones jurídicas y sociales, 1979); *idem,* "The Expressive Conception of Norms", in R. Hilpinen, ed., *New Studies in Deontic Logic* (Dordrecht: Reidel, 1981), 95-124; E. Bulygin, "Norms and Logic: Kelsen and Weinberger on the Ontology of Norms", *Law and Philosophy* 4 (1985), 145-163; M. Troper, "Les théories volontaristes du droit: ontologie et théorie de la science du droit", in P. Amselek and C. Grzegorczyk, eds., *Controverses autour de l'ontologie du droit* (Paris: PUF, 1989), 53-68; Wright, *Norm and Action*, *supra* n.7.

18 Peczenik, "Non-Equivalent Transformations and the Law", *supra* n.9; Guastini, "Production of Rules by Means of Rules", *supra* n.9; *idem,* "A Framework for the Analysis of Judicial Discourse", *supra* n.9.

rules and for statutory sentences) as well as derogation (since explicit derogation acts upon statutory sentences, whereas merely implicit derogation acts upon rules. [19] I now turn back to the analysis of validity statements.

5. *Validity of Normative Acts*

A normative (rule-creating) act, such as commanding, forbidding, derogating, and so forth, is but a speech act. Normative acts, however, are speech acts which are governed not only by linguistic rules, but also by legal rules, viz. by second-order rules (meta-rules) concerning the production of law. In this connection, at least two kinds of meta-rules should be mentioned:

(a) Competence-conferring rules, i.e. rules which entitle a given subject (a state organ) with the "function", "power", or "authority" to enact legal rules (usually within certain borderlines as to the subject matter of regulation);

(b) Procedural rules, viz. rules which provide procedures as to the exercise of the ascribed competence.

Well, a given normative act is valid if, and only if, it has been performed in accordance with the meta-rules by which it is governed. Thus, the validity of a normative act depends both on the performing subject and the adopted procedures. The act is valid if, and only if, it has been performed both by the entitled subject and in accordance with the required procedure.

Hence the validity criterion of normative acts is compliance with meta-rules of competence and procedure [20].

6. *Validity of Rules, Expressed and Unexpressed*

As far as validity of rules is concerned, one has to distinguish between the expressed and the unexpressed rules.

(a) Two conditions are required for the validity of expressed rules. On

19 R. Guastini, "A Theory of Derogation", in A.A. Martino and F. Socci Natali, eds., *Automated Analysis of Legal Texts. Logic, Informatics, Law* (Amsterdam: North Holland, 1986), 495-514.

20 R Guastini, "Problemi di analisi logica delle decisioni costituzionali", in P. Comanducci and R. Guastini, eds., *Analisi e diritto* (Turin: Giappichelli, 1990), 77-97.

the one hand, an expressed rule should be the meaning (one of the possible meanings) of a statutory provision enacted by a normative act being, in its turn, valid. On the other hand, an expressed rule should not be inconsistent with any other "superior" rule (i.e. any rule which is higher-ranked in the hierarchy of legal sources). E.g., in Italian legal system, a rule is valid if, and only if, it can be drawn (by means of arguable construction) from a rule-formulation belonging to a validly enacted statute and, furthermore, it is not inconsistent with constitutional provisions.

(b) Two conditions are required for the validity of unexpressed rules as well. On the one hand, an unexpressed rule should be drawn — by means of appropriate arguments — from a valid expressed rule (or from a set of valid expressed rules). On the other hand, an unexpressed rule should not be inconsistent with any other superior rule. E.g., an implicit principle is valid, if and only if, its existence can be argued on the basis of a set of expressed rules and, furthermore, it is not inconsistent with constitutional provisions.

Therefore, in both cases, the validity of rules is a quite different thing from the validity of normative acts. It is no matter of compliance; rather, it is a matter of consistency. The validity of a given rule is conditioned by its consistency with higher or superior rules in the hierarchy of legal sources. E.g., the validity of rules embodied in statutes depends on their consistency with constitutional rules, the validity of rules embodied in governmental regulations depends on their consistency with both statutory and constitutional rules, and so forth.

7. *Formal and Material Validity*

The foregoing analysis allows for a clarification of two phrases which often occur in dogmatic literature, namely "formal validity" and "material validity". The distinction runs like this [21]:

(a) Formal validity amounts to the lack of so-called "formal vices". In this context, "vice" means a reason for invalidity. A "formal" vice is a ground for invalidity which depends on non-compliance with competence-

21 Bobbio, "Sul ragionamento dei giuristi", *supra* n.1; Crisafulli, "Gerarchia e competenza", *supra* n.2; *idem, Lezioni*, *supra* n.2, at 180ff., 362ff.; *idem* , *Stato, popolo, governo, supra* n.14, at ch.6; Guastini, *Dalle fonti alle norme*, *supra* n.2; A. Pizzorusso et al., *Garanzie costituzionali*, *supra* n.14, at 99ff.; G. Zagrebelsky, *supra* n.2, at ch.2; *idem*, *supra* n.14, at ch.5.

conferring and procedural rules. As a matter of course, the subject matter of such meta-rules are normative acts.

Hence, strictly speaking, formal validity is a property of normative acts: it is but the validity of normative acts, as discussed above (§ 5). However, metaphorically speaking, formal validity can be ascribed to both statutory provisions and rules as well. A statutory provision is formally valid when enacted by a formally valid act. A rule, in its turn, is formally valid if, and only if, it can be drawn *via* construction from a formally valid statutory provision.

It is timely to stress that, as a matter of course, unexpressed rules cannot be formally valid, since such rules are not formulated by any normative authority, hence they are not produced by any (formally) valid normative act. From the "formal" point of view, unexpressed rules are, in this sense, necessarily invalid.[22]

(b) Material validity, in its turn, amounts to the lack of so-called "material vices". A material vice is a ground for invalidity which depends on inconsistency of a given rule with higher rules in the hierarchy of legal sources.

Hence, material validity is a property of rules, both expressed and unexpressed. However, metaphorically speaking, one could ascribe material validity to statutory provisions too. A statutory provision is materially valid when it is the source of materially valid rules (i.e. valid rules can be drawn from it by means of construction).

8. *Validity of Statutory Provisions*

Finally, the validity criteria of statutory provisions too can be clarified. Such a topic, usually ignored in legal-philosophical literature, is of great significance, since valid statutes alone may be used and interpreted as sources of rules in the judicial decision-making process. In other words, only valid statutory texts may be used in the justification of judicial decisions, whereas invalid statutory provisions are not even a proper subject matter of judicial construction.

As a starting point, it has to be remarked that, properly speaking, statutory provisions are neither valid nor invalid, since formal validity is a property of normative acts while material validity is a property of rules. There is no such thing as a peculiar validity of statutory texts as such.

22 Peczenik, "Non-Equivalent Transformations", *supra* n.8.

This amounts to saying that the validity of a statutory provision entirely depends: first, on the validity of the normative act by which it was enacted; second, on the validity of the (expressed) rules which can be drawn from it *via* construction.

Namely, on the one hand, a statutory provision, being the product of a normative act, can be said to be "formally" valid when produced by a formally valid normative act. Therefore, the criteria of formal validity of statutory texts just amount to the validity criteria of normative acts (*supra*, § 5). As a matter of course, the formal invalidity of a normative act entails the invalidity of the whole normative text produced, no matter what the meaning contents of its single provisions could be.

On the other hand, a statutory provision is deemed to be "materially" valid if, and only if, the rules which can be drawn from it are materially valid on their turn.

According to the rulings of the Italian Constitutional Court, a statutory provision is valid, provided that it expresses at least one materially valid rule. However, a statutory provision is invalid if all the rules which it expresses are materially invalid. Usually, the Italian Constitutional Court declares null and void any statutory provision which is not susceptible to any construction consistent with the constitution, in such a way that all the rules expressed by such a provision are inconsistent with higher-ranked rules. Sometimes, however, one and the same statutory provision is liable to several constructions (*supra* , § 4): it can express both rules consistent with the constitution and rules inconsistent with it. In such cases, the Court usually refrains from declaring null and void the provision (hence the text) as such. Nullity and voidness holds only for one (or more) of the rules which can be drawn from such a text *via* construction. As a consequence, the provision preserves its validity. Hence it is still susceptible to use and construction in judicial decision-making. However, it may not be interpreted in such a way as to give rise to inconsistency with the constitution.[23]

Hence, the criterion of material validity of a statutory provision amounts to its capability of expressing (at least) one rule consistent with the higher-ranked rules of the legal system.

23 Crisafulli, "Le sentenze "interpretative"", *supra* n.14; *idem, Lezioni*, *supra* n.2, at 396ff.; Guastini, *supra* n.20; Pizzorusso, "La motivazione ...", *supra* n.14; Zagrebelsky, *supra* n.14, at ch.7.

9. *Relationship Between Formal and Material Validity*

What is the legal status of a rule which is, say, formally valid but materially invalid? What is the status of a materially valid rule which is nevertheless formally invalid? In order to answer such questions, it seems quite important to understand the relationship between the criteria of formal and material validity as applied to rules as well as to statutory provisions. Indeed, formal and material validity are wholly independent criteria. Formal validity is a condition neither necessary nor sufficient of material validity. Furthermore, material validity is, so to say, higher-ranked than formal validity.

In the first place, formal validity is no sufficient condition for material validity. In other words, a formally valid expressed rule may, nevertheless, be invalid from the material standpoint. However, its material invalidity is deemed to be more important than its formal validity. Hence, that rule is held to be invalid *tout court*.

For example, suppose that, in the Italian legal system, the Parliament, which is entitled to legislative authority, produces a set of statutory provisions according to the procedural rules laid down in the constitution. Such provisions, as well as the rules which they express, are formally valid. Suppose however that the rules embodied in one of these provisions are inconsistent with the constitution (e.g. because they amount to infringement of a constitutional liberty-right). As a consequence, given the rigid character of the constitution, such rules, as well as the corresponding provisions, will be deemed to be invalid (materially invalid, notwithstanding their formal validity).

In the second place, formal validity is no necessary condition for material validity. In other words, an unexpressed — hence formally invalid — rule may, nevertheless, be quite valid from the material viewpoint. However, its material validity is deemed to be more important than its formal invalidity. Hence, that rule is held to be valid *tout court*. Lawyers, indeed, accept as valid (from the material viewpoint) a lot of rules which were not expressly formulated and enacted by any law-giving authority whatsoever, provided that such rules can be inferred from some expressed rule or combination of expressed rules.

Thus, there is a sort of hierarchical relationship between the two validity criteria: in case of conflict between them, the material criterion prevails over the formal one. Material validity is "stronger" than formal validity. As a consequence, if a certain rule is both formally and materially valid, fine. However:

(a) an expressed rule, being formally valid, is deemed to be nevertheless invalid if inconsistent with higher rules;

(b) an unexpressed rule, being formally invalid, is held to be nevertheless valid provided that it can be persuasively drawn from some (formally valid) expressed rules.

10. *Lawgivers' Language Transformed by Lawyers*

Finally, on the grounds of the foregoing analysis, I shall try to highlight the nature of two proceedings which are quite common in juristic work, both in legal dogmatics and judicial reasoning: I mean the filling of legal gaps and the solution of normative inconsistencies.[24]

(a) Legal gaps are usually filled up by the construction of unexpressed rules which, although devoid of formal validity, are regarded as valid from the material viewpoint. Hence, such a proceeding turns into the addition of (unexpressed) rules to the legal system.

(b) A normative inconsistency between two rules is usually cleared up by withdrawing one of the conflicting rules: this way an expressed rule, although formally valid, is regarded as invalid from the material standpoint. Hence, such a proceeding amounts to the subtraction of an expressed rule from the legal system.

Indeed, while filling gaps, lawyers add to the legal system certain rules, which are, however, only materially valid. While clearing inconsistencies, they withdraw from the legal system certain rules, although they are formally valid. In this sense, notwithstanding the widespread legal-positivistic view, the legal system is not produced by legislation alone. Rather, it is produced by both legislation and juristic work.[25] Indeed, the legal system is the set of formally valid expressed rules enacted by the legislature, minus the expressed rules which are materially invalid, plus the materially valid unexpressed rules.

These remarks suggest so-called legal "science" (i.e. actual legal dogmatics) to be a quite peculiar "science": a science which does not confine itself to take knowledge of its subject-matter, but transforms it by and large.

According to a view which is widely accepted among legal

24 Guastini, *Lezioni*, *supra* n.2.

25 Bobbio, "Sul ragionamento dei giuristi", *supra* n.1.

philosophers, legal dogmatics amounts to a descriptive meta-language the object of which is the prescriptive language of legal sources.[26] Such a view is not sound. On the one hand, the language of legal dogmatics is not entirely descriptive, since jurists often do not describe pre-existing rules, but formulate new (till then unexpressed) rules. On the other hand, the language of legal dogmatics is no meta-language, since jurists do not confine themselves to "talk about" legal sources; on the contrary, jurists usually transform such sources.

As a matter of course, such a work of transformation is made possible by the peculiar nature of the subject-matter of legal dogmatics. Legal dogmatics is a discourse the object of which is but another discourse (the discourse of legal sources). Therefore, legal dogmatics and legal sources are provided with the same "ontological" nature: both amount to discourses. That allows for a continuous osmosis between them.

26 Kelsen, *Dottrina pura*, *supra* n.4, at ch.3; N. Bobbio, "Essere e dover essere nella scienza giuridica", *Rivista di filosofia* LVIII (1967), 235-62, reprinted in his *Studi sulla teoria generale del diritto* (Turin: Giappichelli, 1970), 139-73; *idem*, "Scienza del diritto e analisi del linguaggio", *Rivista Trimestrale di Diritto e Procedura civile* IV (1950), 342-367, reprinted in U. Scarpelli, ed., *Diritto e analisi del linguaggio* (Milan: Edizioni di Comunità, 1976), 287-324.

THE SEMANTICS OF THE THEORY OF LAW

by

LUIGI FERRAJOLI

1. *The Extension of the Theory of Law*

When speaking of the theory of law (or of a particular theory of law), we talk of its "object", "universe of discourse" or of a "semantic model". By this I mean the totality of things and/or experiences the theory speaks of. The only meta-theoretical presupposition of this very generic notion is that the theory of law is conceived of as an empirical rather than analytical or philosophical theory: a theory whose terms and propositions have a semantic relation to a particular sphere of experience or reality. The term which is conventionally used to describe this sphere of experience or reality is "law". More precisely, if we do not consider "natural law" to correspond to any realm of experience or empirical reality, "positive law". That later term is used to describe law (or laws) that can be observed in time and space.[1]

The semantics (which is itself a meta-theory) of a theory of law is concerned with identifying that set of things and/or experiences which form the object of the theory of law and by reference to which the propositions formulated in the theory are interpreted and verified. I will

Law and Language, The Italian Analytical School, ed. A. Pintore and M. Jori (Liverpool: Deborah Charles Publications, 1997).

1 This essay is a first reflection on the semantics of the theory of law from the point of view of a theory of law which I am in the process of developing. It does not include an examination of the pragmatic and syntactic dimensions of legal-theoretical language. They must be dealt with separately.

There is a clear link between "legal empiricism" or the conception of law as an empirical rather than philosophical theory, and "legal positivism" or the identification of the object of the theory and of the legal science with "positive" law. In Norberto Bobbio's words, "law as fact" rather than "law as value", "real law" rather than "ideal law", "law that is" rather than "law that must be", N. Bobbio, *Il positivismo giuridico* (Turin: Giappichelli, 1961), 190 and 196; *idem*, *Giusnaturalismo e positivismo giuridico* (Milan: Edizioni di Comunità, 1965), 105; *idem*, *Intervento* alla *Tavola rotonda sul positivismo giuridico* (Milan: Giuffrè, 1967), 70.

distinguish the problem of the "object" or universe" of the theory of law, that is, its "semantic interpretation" into two questions or issues. This distinction roughly corresponds to the two meanings of "meaning" in logical theory. The first issue which will concern us is what might be called the "extension" of the theory of law, that is the field of inquiry denoted by it. The second is what we might describe as its "intension", that is the conceptual contents expressed or connoted by it.

The question of the extension of the theory of law can be identified with questions as to the field of experience to which the theory can be applied and by reference to which its propositions are true. The (highly discussible) term "general" in phrases like the general theory of law, certainly refers to the "extension". All that needs to be said about the extension here is that it is left to the discretion of the theorist. In each case it varies, according to a well known logical principle, inversely to the intension of the theory.[2] We can hypothesize two limiting cases. On the one hand it is possible to conceive of a theory of law which assumes as its empirical referent all the conceivable legal orders which exist or have ever existed, ranging from the legal orders of primitive societies to the highly developed ones of modern states, culminating in international law. On the other hand, it is possible to imagine a theory of law whose universe of discourse is restricted to a single legal system: for example, the Italian law of December 31, 1982, or Roman law at the time of the XII tables. The first example represents a more philosophical approach to legal theory. Here the prime concern is the working out of legal concepts which are universal in that they can be applied or interpreted in all possible realms of legal experience. This means that in addition to being an extremely general theory of law it will also be extremely generic and elementary, with maximum extension and minimum intension. Its capacity to analyze and explain the structural differences between various positive law systems will for this reason also be rather limited. In the second case, on the contrary, we have a theory of law which draws from the legal dogmatics of a particular form of positive law and whose propositions will be verified by exclusive reference to this particular form of positive law. This particular theory of law is thus neither general nor generalizable: its explanatory powers are restricted to the particular field within which it operates. It thus displays maximum intension and

2 E. Nagel, *The Structure of Science: Problems in the Logic of Scientific Explanations* (Indianapolis: Hackett Publishing Co., 1961).

minimum extension or empirical range.[3]

The most important theories of law developed in this century represent a middle way between these two alternatives. However much the exponents of such theories may argue to the contrary, they are not "general" theories in the true sense of the word. They cannot be interpreted or verified in all realms of legal experience (in saying "all" one embraces those which exist now, those which have existed or those which are possible). They apply solely to historically determined legal systems: modern state laws. Neither are they theories which apply to one legal system alone. They can be applied to a variety of positive law systems, provided they are relatively homogeneous. It is important to establish that every theory of law, in as far as it can be said to be *empirical*, is spatially and temporally restricted. Its extensionality is inversely proportionate to its intensionality. The epithet "general" applied to "the theory of law" is both ambiguous and redundant. It merely alludes to the fact that all legal *theory* is by definition fairly wide-ranging in scope compared to the specific dogmatics of individual systems of positive law.

2. *Normativism and Legal Realism*

The question as to what constitutes the object and universe of the theory of law is considerably more complex. Here we are not concerned with the extension of the word "law", or the realms of experience to which the theory of law is applicable, but the intensional connotations of the terms and theses which refer to them. But first of all we must elucidate the specific nature of the empirical experience in respect of which it is possible to ascertain the truth of propositions of the theory.

Just what do we mean by "empirical experience"? In the present context it is taken to refer to what are commonly called "observed facts", irrespective of the instruments, methods and procedures of observing them. The semantic problem with which we are then faced is as follows:

3 It is doubtful whether, in these two limiting cases, we can talk of the theory of law in the sense of "empirical theory". In the first case, the "empirical" character of the theory might be lost. It aims at fixing normatively the abstract or ideal conditions for "law". It does this by producing *a-priori* concepts which have connection with a determinate field of observation. In the second case, we risk losing "theory". Since here we only refer to one specific sphere of positive legal experience, it cannot be much different from legal dogmatics.

what are the "observed facts" of the theory of law and, more generally, of legal science?[4]

There are two possible and rather different answers to this question. The first answer is that the "observed facts" of the theory are *juridical norms*, that is to say the group of more or less codified rules which make up the positive law of the legal system. These facts are linguistic phenomena which, even if not expressly codified, can in each case be seen as meaningful propositions with prescriptive function. In modern systems of positive law, which are characterized by state control of the sources of law, these propositions are also formulated and systematized in normative documents which taken together form a complex linguistic universe. This legislative discourse is expressed in a legal language, more or less technical and characterized by internal unity, relative coherence and completeness.

However, it is also possible to argue that the facts in question are *juridical phenomena* in general, understood as human actions in respect of a particular system of positive law and as the way in which the latter functions. These phenomena are not merely linguistic facts, nor indeed are they merely normative propositions. As well as being norms they are also activities, events, people, relations between people, procedures, interpretations, legal or illegal practices on the part of public bodies, particularly those in charge of jurisdictional decisions. In short, everything that is connected with legislative discourse and that is legally qualifiable on its basis.

Philosophy of law has provided us with these two diverse ways of looking at the issue. The first can be characterized as a *normative* theory; legal science as both normative and descriptive (of norms). The second can be described as a *realistic* theory; legal science as a purely descriptive sociology of juridical phenomena. These two approaches obviously belong to different semantic universes and correspond to two different models of legal theory. The first model is represented by *legal dogmatics,* which focuses upon the actual norms made by the legislature and ascertains their meaning and their validity in legal terms. The second model is represented by *sociology of law*, which focuses upon human behaviour by which it ascertains the causes and the degree of effectiveness of norms.[5]

4 R.B. Braithwaite, *Scientific Explanation* (Cambridge: Cambridge University Press, 1953).

5 "Sociology of law" is used here in Ross's wide sense and refers not only to sociological studies but also to "political, psychological and historical" studies

We can use here a distinction of Herbert Hart's: the first model looks at law with the internal point of view; the second model deals with the external point of view.[6]

It is clear that these two semantic models have their own specific methodological instruments. The object of legal dogmatics is the *analysis of legal language*, that is juridical interpretation of those empirical data which consist of the normative propositions of legislative discourse.[7] The object of sociology of law and realistic legal theory is in large measure extra-linguistic and depends on *sociological observation* and investigation.

3. *Juridical Truth and Factual Truth*

The difference between the two semantic models illustrated above implies a difference in the truth conditions for propositions of legal dogmatics and sociology of law. The truth of propositions of sociology of law is a *factual truth* in the strict sense. It depends on the correspondence

---

"on law in action", or on law as a phenomenon of social life: A. Ross *On Law and Justice* (Berkeley: California University Press, 1959), ch. I, §4, note 1.

Concepts such as "legal dogmatics" and "sociological jurisprudence" as well as "theory of law" are studied separately here for methodological reasons in order to differentiate them semantically. In practice, of course, they come together in various ways. They also combine with purely factual discourses, judgments of value, ideas of critical interpretation of law, legal policies, views as to the methodology of science and legal interpretation.

6 H.L.A. Hart, *The Concept of Law* (Oxford: Clarendon Press, 1961). U. Scarpelli suggests that the distinction between the external and internal point of view should be used to explain the different approach to the study of law adopted by sociology of law and positivistic legal science (called here "dogmatics"): see *Cos'è il positivismo giuridico* (Milan: Edizioni di Comunità, 1965), 53-58.

7 N. Bobbio, "Scienza del diritto e analisi del linguaggio", *Rivista trimestriale di diritto e procedura civile* IV/2 (1950), 342-67, repr. in U. Scarpelli, ed., *Diritto a analisi del linguaggio* (Milan: Edizioni di Comunità, 1976), 287-324 [see pp.21-50, in this volume]. It is scarcely worth mentioning the two meanings of "interpretation" that are used here. In the expression "semantic" or "empirical interpretation" of a theory, it designates (see section 5) the attribution of meaning to concepts and statements within the theory by way of propositions which can be linked or reduced to the empirical data gathered. In the expression "legal interpretation" it designates, instead, the observational activity of the lawyer. Since the object of observation here is linguistic, it consists of analysing the meaning of concepts and statements in the legislative language.

of the proposition with observable reality. In this it resembles all other empirical sciences. The empirical truth of the propositions of legal dogmatics, on the other hand, is very different and is determined by their correspondence with normative legislative discourse. We can call the second type of truth *juridical truth*. Here we do not look at events but at norms, or taking into account a possible distinction between "normative sentences" and "norms", at normative sentences or documents alone.[8] In legal dogmatics, norms both furnish the criterion of empirical verification and form the observable data.[9] The meaning of "normativism" derives not so much from the central place assigned to norms, rather, it lies in the meta-theoretical assumption that norms are the sole semantic reference for the discourse of legal science. One can see this reference when one looks at the meta-normative fragment "norm n says that" (or "in the sense of" or "on the basis of norm n"). These can always be prefixed to a dogmatic description of juridical phenomena. These perform the same function as the expression "it is the case (at place p and time t) that" performs in relation to other descriptions of empirical phenomena. It thus asserts the descriptive proposition by stating its semantic correspondence with the reality which is the object of inquiry. In the case of propositions of legal dogmatics, this reality is constituted by reference to what positive

8 On the distinction between "normative sentences" and "norms" (the latter seen as the result or end product of the interpretation of the former), see G. Tarello, "Studi sulla teoria generale dei precetti, I, Introduzione al linguaggio precettivo", in *Annali della Facoltà di giurisprudenza di Genova* (Milan: Giuffrè, 1968), reprinted in *Diritto, enunciati, usi* (Bologna: Mulino, 1974), 135-269; *idem*, *L'interpretazione della legge* (Milan: Giuffrè, 1980), 63-67. The distinction is a useful one, provided it is made clear that the result of the interpretative activity on the normative text is not itself a norm but a statement of the norm. The norm is the normative text seen as the object of the interpretative statement. (The interpretation can be the result or the end product of a decision or of a proposal beside being the result of an investigation. But such a possibility does not prevent it from remaining a statement; the same can be said of postulates and definitions within theory. At the level of pragmatics they are grounded in a similar manner.)

9 Of course, legal truth is also factual truth, where "factual" is given a wide meaning — in the sense of "empirical" or "non analytical". It too is an empirical truth relating to the linguistic facts specifically studied by the lawyer, i.e. legal norms, or more precisely legal texts or documents or sources. Having said this, expressions such as "factual truth in a narrow meaning" (or simply "factual") and "legal truth" are not confusing if the former is understood as referring to factual events and the latter to what norms say about those events.

legal norms say. We will return later to the different question concerning the semantics and pragmatics of normative language. This concerns degrees of decidability, or, inversely, contestability of juridical truth asserted on the basis of the observation or interpretation of what the norms say.

Our contrasting the legal and the factual truth suggests that they tend to be divergent. The legal dogmatician will answer the question "how is theft punished in Italian law?" by quoting articles 624 and 625 of the Italian penal code. Thus "theft is punished (all thefts are punished) with up to three years imprisonment and a fine of between 12,000 and 200,000 lire or higher or lower penalties, depending upon aggravating or mitigating circumstances". The sociologist of law, however, looks to the crime statistics on the relation between thefts reported to the police and convictions for theft during, for example, the last ten years. He is then in a position to say that approximately ninety-six per cent of all thefts are not cleared up. Therefore not all thefts, but only a small proportion are punished. These two answers appear contradictory, but are both true. The "statistical" answer is factually true, and the "penal code" answer is juridically true. If one considers that the first reply does not rule out the proposition "*it is the case that* not all thefts are punished" and the second reply does not rule out the proposition "*norm n says that* all thefts are punished", then it appears that the two statements are perfectly compatible.

We can explain more precisely this divergence and compatibility. To do so one has to analyze the meaning of "true as to the facts" and "juridically true" and the differing conditions in which they can be asserted of a proposition. In particular it is necessary to develop an adequate semantic notion of the concept of "juridical truth". It useful here to recall the classical correspondence theory of truth. This says that a proposition is true if and only if it refers to an existing state of affairs. Moving on from this intuitive notion, Alfred Tarski formulated his own semantic conception of truth and constructed the following rigorous definition materially adequate to the term truth:

X is true if and only if p

where "X" is the meta-linguistic name of "p" and "p" is any sentence (for example: the sentence *"snow is white" is true if and only if snow is white*).[10]

10 A. Tarski, "The Semantic Conception of Truth and the Foundations of

According to Tarski, this equivalence determines "the conditions under which we will consider the usage and the definition of the term 'true' as adequate from the material point of view". The consequence of this is that "every equivalence obtained by replacing 'p' by a particular sentence, and 'X' by a name of this sentence, may be considered a partial definition of truth, which explains wherein the truth of this one individual sentence consists".[11] In order to understand what facts determine the truth of the two sentences outlined above, and particularly the one based on a norm, we only have to substitute for the variables "p" and "X" in Tarski's definition:

(a) It is true that "it is the case that not all thefts are punished" if and only if it is the case that not all thefts are punished.

(b) It is true that "a norm n says that all thefts are punished" if and only if a norm n says that all thefts are punished.

In legal discourse the meta-linguistic fragment "a norm n says that", which appears in the *definiendum* of (b), is generally understood. This fragment is precisely the meaning of the term "juridically" in the expression "juridically true". In the same way the fragment "it is the case that" in the *definiendum* of (a) can be seen as synonymous with the expression "factually" in "factually true". If we accept this and thus the equivalence between "'factually' true that" and "true that 'it is the case that'" and "'juridically' true that" and "true that 'there is a norm n that says that'", we can transform (a) and (b) as follows:

(a') It is "factually" true that "not all thefts are punished" if and only if it is the case that not all thefts are punished.

(b') It is "juridically" true that "all thefts are punished" if and only if a norm n says that all thefts are punished.

We can thus formulate the two following definitions of "factual truth" and "juridical truth":

(a") F is "factually" true if and only if f

(b") J is "juridically" true if and only if j

in which "F" stands for the name of the factual proposition "f" about what

---

Semantics" (1944), reprinted in H. Feigl and W. Sellars, eds., *Readings in Philosophical Analysis* (New York: Appleton-Century-Crofts, Inc., 1949), 52-84.

11 *Ibidem*, at 55.

actually is the case, and "J" stands for the name of the juridical proposition "j" about what a norm says ought to be the case. Both "F" and "J" are meta-linguistic propositions; "f" and "j" are propositions of the object language of which "F" and "J" speak. We will call one a "factual language" and the other a "juridical language". Finally, the norms, or "normative propositions" to which juridical propositions pertain belong to what we call "normative language" (or sometimes "legal" or "legislative" or "of the legislator"). This in turn is the object language of the juridical language.

It is important to emphasise that the proposed definitions of "factual truth" and "juridical truth" do not duplicate Tarski's concept of "truth". They are the partial definitions of the term "true" referring specifically to the sentences analyzed here, both of which are derived from Tarski's general definition of truth. The term "juridically" means the same thing as the proposition "a norm n says that" which is part of the proposition upon which truth is predicated in the semantic meta-language. The expression "factually" is totally redundant, and was introduced (as was its synonym "it is the case that") only as a counterpart to the expression "juridically". Both "juridically" and "factually" do not connote the term "true" but form part of the content of the propositions upon which truth is predicated. It is for this reason that these expressions are in quotes.[12] Their function is solely to indicate that the propositions refer to (or, if one prefers, are "interpreted" or "satisfied" or "realised" by) two distinct semantic models or universes of discourse. In (a), (a') and (a") the *definiens* is the description of an extra-normative fact, or, as Kelsen would

12 This warning should be enough to counter a possible objection of "a critical realism" which could be raised against our partial definitions of "factual truth" and "juridical truth". Answering a similar objection, Tarski himself specifies that the words "in fact" (or "factually" or "it so happens" or similar) — and similarly the word "juridically" — could induce error (and should therefore be avoided) but do not affect the semantic notion of truth. The function of this notion is not to state the conditions in which an empirical proposition can be said to be true, but only the conditions in which the word "true" should be used. When we pronounce, in a certain language, an empirical proposition (for example: "norm *n* mentions all punishable thefts"), we must at the same time state in a proper meta-language that it is true. In other words, the fact of saying that a proposition is true if and only if it states what the norm says leaves unanswered the question of the meaning or of the prescriptive content of the norm in question. To say that the proposition "snow is white" is true if and only if snow is white leaves unanswered the question of whether snow is indeed white.

say, an "is" (or an "is not"). In (b), (b') and (b") it is a description of a norm, that is of a linguistic fact which states the "ough" of such a phenomenon. More precisely, the definiens in (b), (b') and (b") asserts two things: the existence of a norm ("a norm n says that") and what it prescribes ("that all thefts are punished"). The first thing is the "existence" of the norm.[13] The second thing is the "sense" or the

13 The "existence" of the norm designated by the proposition which is called true and which we have named as "in force", has nothing to do either with norm's "validity" or with "effectiveness". "Validity", "invalidity", "effectiveness" and "non-effectiveness" are predicated of norms in existence or in force and indicate respectively their conformity (or non conformity) to the norms that produce them and their conformity (non conformity) to the facts of which they speak. The existence of, or the fact of being in force, for a norm is the specific situation described by legal propositions which can be called true by reference to that situation.

Having made a distinction between prescriptions and statements relative to prescriptions, Tarello then criticises the thesis according to which "the attribution of duties and prohibitions" (for instance "marriage imposes on the spouses the mutual obligation of cohabitation, fidelity and support") would sometimes entail "a strange counterpart in reality, which would be the existence of a norm assigning duties and prohibitions" (Tarello, *Diritto, enunciati, usi*, *supra* n.8, at 248). One could agree with this and also with the thesis that prescriptive sentences are not dependent on reality (*ibidem*, at 251), or do not have a denotation or an extensional reference (though it is doubtful whether prescriptions of impossible or, on the contrary, unavoidable behaviour could be given any meaning). It is difficult to understand what difference there is between (a) the fact of saying that the reference of "the better expressed proposition" in the sentence "art. 143 c.c. says that marriage imposes on the spouses the mutual obligation of cohabitation, fidelity and support" — that is not in a norm (neither true or false) but in its interpretation expressed by a true or false assertion — that that reference is in fact "the existence" of the norm of art. 143 c.c., and (b) the fact of saying that such reference is "something much less extravagant and more concrete: the fact that at the time of the civil code publication, that which was published was a document consisting of articles numbered progressively, where art. 143 was made of graphemes each corresponding to certain words of the Italian language, set in a certain way" *ibidem*, p. 248). This fact — the promulgation — is what Tarello would call an "utterance" of the normative sentence (*ibid*, pp. 144-46). It is not any utterance but a performing utterance, i.e. the empirical positively normative fact which has given life or force or existence to the norm (or if one prefers, to the "normative" document, which consists still now, "of those graphemes ..."). A fact which, in any case, allows us to speak, in relation to legal norms — and unlike moral norms — of "positive", "in force" norms or norms "given" or "produced" by the legislator, in "prescriptive content" of the norm.[14] We can thus say that *a proposition is juridically true if and only if it expresses the meaning of a valid legal norm in force*.

However much juridical language is not a formal language, it appears to me to satisfy all Tarski's requirements. This is because the use of the term "true" referring to the propositions expressed in it does not give rise to antinomies such as the so called "liar's paradox".[15] In the first place, in juridical language there are no semantic terms such as "true" or "false", even if these terms do occasionally appear in it, when, for example, one talks of the norms which define false witness. They appear in the norms themselves and do not refer to other norms in other propositions of the juridical language, but to the facts of which the norms speak. In other words, norms never say (nor prescribe) that a proposition is true, but at most that it is obligatory or not obligatory to tell the truth.[16] In the

---

other words, of empirical data which legal dogmatics has specifically investigated.

14 Whether that which a proposition says "about what a norm says" corresponds or not to what the norm says is a question concerning the interpretative procedure adopted for that norm. In the same way, whether the proposition "snow is white" corresponds or not to the fact that snow is white is a question which concerns procedures for the observation of snow (see *supra* n.12).

15 Briefly, these requirements are: (a) for the language of the propositions called true not to be "semantically closed", i.e. it should not include terms such as "true", or "designates" or "defines" or similar references to terms in this same language; (b) the language which applies truth as a predicate should be a language, such as "meta-language", distinct from the "object-language" in question; (c) as a consequence, the meta-language should be a richer language than the object-language as it should contain one word for each enunciation and thus comprise it all as if it were part of it (Tarski, *supra* n.10, at 56-62).

16 Other terms which according to Tarski cannot be part of the object-language are those expressing relations between sentences, such as "designates" or "defines". Such terms figure in fact both in the normative language and the legal language whenever there are legislative or dogmatic definitions. However any danger of antinomy in these cases is in my opinion excluded because of the constraining quality of dogmatic definitions. As we will say later, these are lexical definitions, aiming at clarifying the meaning of the words defined or used by the legislator in a normative way (this is absent when the word in question is not normatively defined or is not designated in a normative function. We then have a theoretical word of the theory of law.) On the "constraining" character of legislative definitions, see U. Scarpelli, *La definizione nel diritto*, in *idem*, ed., *Diritto e analisi del linguaggio*, *supra* n.7, at 194 (his thesis is based on a duty of adherence to the law); A. Belvedere, *Il*

second place, the codified nature of the normative language, the fact that it is formulated according to specific rules of norm-production and the fact that propositions in it are all identified or identifiable, enables us to distinguish rigorously three types of language. Firstly, the normative language in which norms are formulated; secondly, juridical language, which, in respect of normative language, is meta-linguistic and in which it is possible to reformulate all that is said in the norms; and, thirdly, the semantic meta-language, (meta-meta-linguistic in respect of normative language) which asserts the truth or falsity of what is said in the object or juridical language in which the norms are reformulated or interpreted. Finally, this codified structure of normative language allows us to give a name in the semantic meta-language to all statements in the juridical object language, that is, to mention its content by citing the source in which the normative statements to which they refer appear.

The uniqueness of the concept of "juridical truth" thus resides in the fact that it is ascribed to propositions in a juridical object language which in turn deals with another language, normative language, the language which (as we shall see later) determines the formation rules of juridical language). Norms (or normative propositions) are thus the specific linguistic facts or linguistic states of affairs to which juridical propositions refer. The latter are thus juridically true or false according to their

---

problema delle definizioni nel codice civile (Milan: Giuffrè, 1977), 161ff. He links the constraining character of legislative definitions with the fact that they are norms like all others. For a wide historical survey see Tarello, *L'interpretazione della legge, supra* n.8, at 157ff. The problem is a fundamental one. Were we to deny the constraining character of legislative definitions and designations, and more generally of "what the norms say", not only would the lawyer's "adherence to law" be compromised, but above all we would lose all objective and inter-subjective criteria enabling us to control legal dogmatics. We would then be unable to define the legal truth of propositions without the risk of antinomies. We would be unable to argue for their legal truth or falsity. If, on the other hand, it is true that norms represent those facts which the dogmatic lawyer specifically investigates, "faithfulness" (or adherence or correspondence) to norms as a principle is to him as valuable as "faithfulness" (or adherence or correspondence) to facts as a principle, is to any scientist. This is true even when, as it might happen, the same normative proposition allows for various interpretations. It might be difficult to decide upon their truth. In each case though there are legal arguments as to their being closer to what the law says (to the letter of the law, or to its *ratio*, etc.).

empirical correspondence or non-correspondence to that of which they speak.[17] It is difficult to say whether this particular characteristic of legal dogmatics — its semantic status as comprising assertions that are true or false on the basis of norms — justifies or precludes calling legal dogmatics a normative science (a question which has been the subject of lengthy debate).[18] Without doubt the adjective "normative" is inappropriate in this context, given that strictly speaking only norms are normative while the juridical propositions of the dogmaticians are assertions about norms. If, however, one wants to use this expression in relation to legal dogmatics, the only plausible meaning is the semantic notion of juridical truth as empirical truth, having as a specific reference or observational basis, norms. That is to say, their meaning or content, their existence or force. We can thus describe legal dogmatics as a *normative* discipline, not so much because it focuses on the content, value or source of norms, but because it is exclusively interpreted and verified by norms. In this it is different from sociology of law which is exclusively interpreted and verified by facts and thus is a purely *descriptive* discipline.

By defining "factual truth" and "juridical truth" in this way we have developed a rigorous criterion for distinguishing on the semantic level "factual propositions" from "juridical propositions". The former are all those things for which factual truth or falsity can be predicated. The latter are all those things for which juridical truth or falsity can be predicated. Among the former are not only sociological propositions or

17 This is also why norms (i.e. propositions pertaining to normative language which is the object of legal propositions), though they might have the same literal form as the latter, are neither true or untrue. To say that a norm is true (or false) is a non-sense similar to saying that an object, for example a fact, is true or untrue. In this light, the difference between our definition of "legal truth" and Georges Kalinowski's "truth of norms" definition is easier to understand (G. Kalinowski, *Il significato della deontica per la filosofia morale e giuridica*, in G. Di Bernardo, ed., *Logica deontica e semantica* (Bologna: il Mulino, 1977), 262). The former refers to legal propositions about norms and sees them as object-propositions neither true nor untrue and the latter reproduces in normative cognitivism Tarski's definition of truth.

18 See in particular N. Bobbio, "Essere e dover essere nella scienza giuridica", *Rivista di filosofia* LVIII (1967), 235-62, repr. in *idem*, *Studi per una teoria generale del diritto* (Turin: Giappichelli, 1970), 139-73; J. Wróblewski, *La normatività della scienza giuridica*, Ital. transl. by G. Lombardi, in U. Scarpelli, ed., *Diritto e analisi del linguaggio, supra* n.7, at 325-44; G. Kalinowski, *Disputa sulla scienza normativa*, Ital. transl. by G. Ferrari (Padova: CEDAM, 1982).

abstract factual propositions, but also *particular factual propositions* which refer to a single concrete fact. For example, "Tim has given Charles a thousand pounds", "Sandy is in Saughton Gaol at the moment", etc. Among the latter we find both the propositions of legal dogmatics formulated by jurists, and also propositions which might be called *operative juridical propositions.*[19] These are formulated by judges during the application of norms, for example "this (particular activity) is theft", "such a contract is invalid", etc.

Like particular factual propositions, these propositions do not speak directly of norms as do the propositions of legal dogmatics, but of particular concrete facts, upon which a legal judgement is based. But like dogmatic propositions, they too are open to judgements of juridical truth or falsity based on their reference to norms. They can thus be clearly distinguished from particular factual propositions, both of which appear in the discourse of norm-appliers. For example, of the four reasons for acquittal in the Italian penal code, Tim is acquitted because "the fact did not occur", "he did not commit it", "there is insufficient evidence" or "the fact did not constitute a crime". The first three are concrete factual propositions because they are true or false on the basis of the truth or falsity of the facts. The fourth, however, is a juridical operative proposition because it is juridically true or false on the basis of what the norms say:

> (a''') The proposition "the fact ascribed to Tim did not happen" is "factually" true if and only if the fact ascribed to Tim did not happen.
>
> (b''') The proposition "the fact ascribed to Tim does not constitute a crime" is "juridically" true if and only if the fact ascribed to Tim does not constitute a crime (or there does not exist any a norm according to which it constitutes a crime).

The distinction between operative juridical propositions and particular factual propositions is essential for the purposes of a semantic metatheory of empirical verification of "law-applying" discourses and therefore of the control (also law applying) over these discourses in matters of fact and/or law. Moreover, it allows for the analysis and control of that specific juridical operation which consists in the "subsumption" of fact into norm, an operation based on factual as well as juridical arguments. The distinction is also a useful analytical tool when we come to theoretical

19 The meaning I give to "operative" is that which I suggested in "Interpretazione dottrinale e interpretazione operativa", *Rivista internazionale di filosofia del diritto* XLIII (1966), 290-304.

problems which have a meta-theoretical dimension, e.g. the problems of validity and effectiveness and the relations between them.

4. *Juridical Refutation and Factual Refutation*

The different semantic references of propositions of sociology of law and legal dogmatics result in different conceptions of empirical falsifiability. Factual truth is a truth which is factually refutable, in the sense that it is always possible by further empirical investigation to find contradictory facts. It is also juridically irrefutable in the sense that it is independent of what the norms say of the facts. Juridical truth, on the contrary, cannot be refuted factually. It is independent of what is the case. It is only refutable juridically either on the basis of a different interpretation of the norm or of other valid norms which conflict with it.

What marks legal dogmatics out is precisely that its propositions are factually irrefutable. Unlike the observational propositions of other empirical sciences, and of sociology of law in particular, the propositions of legal dogmatics cannot be contradicted by factual enquiries or possible future events. Dogmatic legal propositions can thus be differentiated from operative legal propositions, which, as we have seen before, resemble concrete factual propositions in that they are about facts or concrete events, even if it is only to qualify them legally by subsumption. On the strength of our definitions of "juridical truth" and "factual truth", we can say that the dogmatic legal are propositions of which *only* juridical truth or falsity can be predicated. Factual truth is irrelevant, since these propositions can only be refuted juridically and not factually. The operative legal propositions, on the contrary, are ambivalent, given that both juridical and factual truth (or falsity) can be predicated of them. Thus it is possible to verify or falsify them juridically and factually. For example, the proposition "the act ascribed to Tim does not constitute a crime" can be corroborated or falsified both juridically and factually. In the former case by showing that a norm which says it is a crime either exists or it does not. In the latter case, by proving that the act in question does not exhibit the characteristics of what the norm defines as the crime. The same can be said of the proposition "this contract is invalid because it is not in writing". This can be refuted juridically, by denying the existence of a norm which gives this ground of invalidity; or factually, by proving that the contract was made in writing. A further example is "Tomorrow, November the 5th is the closing date for university applications". This is refutable both juridically (the 5th of November is not the legal date), and factually (today is not the 4th of November).

Every time then, a proposition speaks of a concrete fact and refers it to norms, the proposition can be understood and treated both as a concrete factual proposition and as an operative juridical proposition. It is precisely because of this ambivalence that any proposition of a legal judgement need to be both warranted as to the facts (*motivazione fattuale*) and warranted as to the law (*motivazione giuridica*) The two semantic models of truth thus assume procedural relevance. One need only consider the jurisdictions involved in controlling a judgement. Factual refutation is possible only on appeal before the regular courts; for this reason the judges of these courts are called "judges on the merits" ("*giudici di merito*"). Juridical refutation, on the other hand, is possible also before the Court of Cassation, which only judges the legality of the decision under review, precisely because it is competent to enquire into and control juridical and not factual truth. Moreover, this ambivalence is a feature of all concrete propositions which also carry a semantic reference to rules. For example, the phrase "this shot is a goal" spoken by a spectator during a football match can be contradicted both factually (the ball did not really go into the net) and on the basis of the rules of the game (it was offside). In particular, the so-called judicial truth — like rival "truths" which confront each other in any adversarial process — is almost always a mixture of juridical and factual truth. We are not concerned with an equivocation here. Rather, any operative juridical propositions is semantically ambiguous in that it refers to two distinct universes of discourse, that of facts and that of norms. It is the task of the analysis of juridical language to decide in each case whether the proposition is used in a juridical or factual sense, and thus whether checking its truth is a "question of fact" or a "question of law".

Legal dogmatics, on the other hand, is only interested in questions of law. This being the case, its propositions only admit of verification or falsification that is juridical and not factual.[20] It is precisely this factual irrefutability that justifies the use of the word "dogmatic" in respect of

20 Referring to past decisions might be seen as an exception to the principle of the factual irrefutability of legal truth, both at the dogmatic and operative levels. This reference to what in reality are facts, might appear as the intrusion of realistic or factual argumentation. A precedent however is only relevant in respect of its authority or persuasive nature. It is not therefor a "fact" from which one can induce a decision but a norm of legal interpretation.

these propositions. It is not only the case that the jurists accept norms as if they were dogmas, but it is also the case that for these propositions the analysis of the normative language in which they are formulated represents the sole method of their empirical verification or falsification. This is, incidentally, what Kelsen meant by the "inviolability of the norm", according to which juridical norms, as opposed to natural laws, cannot be contradicted by any actual fact as no actual fact can compromise their validity.[21] The apparent paradox depends upon an equivocation: Kelsen confuses the object language of the norms with the juridical meta-language of dogmatics.[22] This forces him to attach the judgement of "inviolability" (which properly speaking is a meta-dogmatic judgement of irrefutability) to norms, which are in their nature "violable", instead of attaching it to juridical propositions about norms. The judgement of inviolability applies not to the validity of norms, but to the juridical truth of the propositions asserting the validity of the norms. The validity of the norms constitutes jointly with the meaning of the norms, the object (or referent) of judicial propositions. The judgement of inviolability, therefore, applies only to the truth of other propositions which are metalinguistic as to the juridical propositions and which properly assert the norms' validity and normative meaning in the dogmatics. And because this truth is purely juridical, it is not factually refutable.

We shall distinguish three classes of propositions which deal with law, depending upon the method of verification adopted: (a) factual propositions, general (or sociological) and concrete, which are true if and only if they are factually true; (b) juridical operative propositions, which are true if and only if they are true either factually or juridically; (c) propositions of legal dogmatics which are true if and only if true juridically. Other specific epistemological characteristics of dogmatics as contrasted with sociology of law and other empirical sciences follow from this definition of juridical truth.

Firstly, since the empirical universe of legislative discourse consists in a finite though large number of norms, legal dogmatics is one of the few cases of what logicians call "perfect induction", that is the induction of hypotheses on the basis of a finite number of cases.[23] This brings us to another related characteristic. Contrary to appearances, the theses of

21 H. Kelsen, *The General Theory of Law and State*, translated by Anders Wedberg (Cambridge, Mass.: Harvard University Press, 1945).

22 This criticism is broadly voiced by Kalinowski, *Disputa*, *supra* n.18, at 103 ff.

23 Braithwaite, *supra* n.4, at 19 note 8.

legal dogmatics are often existential statements (referring to particulars). They display the form of general or universal propositions simply because they reproduce the form of the juridical norm they analyze. These have usually the form of a universal proposition. Thus in the example already given, the dogmatic proposition "all thefts are punished by imprisonment" is not a generalization induced from an infinity of norms. It is but simply a short form for the existential observative proposition "in the Italian penal code there is a norm n which says that 'all thefts are punished by imprisonment'". In dogmatics we do not usually seek scientific laws in universal form but by and large singular or existential assertions of the existence (*vigore*) and meaning of the positive norm which is the object of enquiry.[24] And even the few universal propositions that one finds always have a determinate or at least a determinable number of norms as a semantic reference. This means that legal dogmatics is no different from, for example, geography. It is an empirical discipline which does not have the capacity to predict the order of future events. One does not find here the type of probabilistic hypotheses found in the sociology of law.

The factual irrefutability of juridical truth and its "perfect induction" undoubtedly represents an advantage for legal dogmatics in respect of other empirical sciences, and in particular the sociology of law. This might lead us to believe that legal dogmatics is more rigorous and more certain than these other empirical sciences. But of course this is not the case. Dogmatic propositions are very unlikely to have the same form as normative propositions and thus to satisfy rigorously our definition of "juridical truth". If this were the case, legal dogmatics would have no explanatory function. Even if factually irrefutable, the truth of juridical propositions is still an empirical truth which can be refuted juridically. This is done on the basis of a different interpretation of the norm applied

24 The reading of norms and their metalinguistic reformulation (which is not all that legal interpretation is about but represents the first step of any interpretative procedure) relate to what early neopositivism used to call "protocol propositions" or "protocols" or "basic assertions" (see O. Neurath, "Protocol Propositions", in *Philosohical Papers 1913-1946*, ed. R. S. Cohen and M. Neurath (Dordrecht and Boston: D. Reidel, 1983), 91-99; R. Carnap, "Überwindung der Metaphysik durch logische Analyse der Sprache", in *Erkenntnis* II (1932), 219-241; K.R. Popper, *The Logic of Scientific Discovery* (London: Hutchinson, 1959). Even when legal propositions interpreting individual norms result in questionable manipulations of the norms' meaning, their existential and metalinguistic form is nevertheless maintained. This allows them to be verified through observation.

or of another norm which it is assumed should apply. Jurists have many different opinions and the juridical truth of their hypotheses is often conflicting and undecidable. This is so for the following reasons: (a) the legal language in which norms are formulated is ordinary language, which is inevitably polysemic and lacking in rigour; (b) legislative discourse is always inconsistent "gappy" and contradictory; (c) juridical interpretation is often the result of value choice.

Let us take two rather more complex examples than the example of theft used above. The first concerns the first of the two conditions of juridical truth suggested by our definition, that is the validity or existence of the norm designated by the hypothesis the truth of which is in question. Let us take the following hypothesis:

> The Minister of the Interior, with the consent of the Prime Minister or the prefects to whom this power has been delegated, can by decree declare a state of emergency in the case of danger of disorder or a state of martial law for so long as it is necessary to entrust public safety to the military authorities, with the suspension in both cases of some constitutional guarantees.

One can say that this is juridically true if one considers that articles 214-19 of the law of Public Safety (18 June, 1931), although possibly constitutionally invalid, remain nevertheless in force until the Constitutional Court has occasion to decide upon their validity or otherwise. One can also consider them juridically false if one considers that those norms have been directly abrogated by the constitution since they so obviously contradict articles 1, para 2, 13, 70, 76, 77, 78, 102 and 103, para 3.[25] The second example concerns the other condition of the juridical truth of dogmatic propositions, that is their correspondence with the meaning or prescriptive content of the norms which they designate. The same facts can be used to answer the question as to whether a person who appropriates something entrusted to his care is committing theft or embezzlement. In a particular case, and supposing that we are in possession of all the evidence, one can attach greater importance to fact that the offender has taken away something from somebody or, rather,

25 The first of these two these has been upheld, among others, by F. Modugno and D. Nocilla, "Stato d'assedio", in *Novissimo Digesto Italiano* XVIII (Turin: Utet, 1971), 281 and 289. The second one has been upheld by F. Cuocolo, "Gli atti dello Stato aventi 'forza di legge'", *Rivista trimestriale di diritto pubblico* XI (1961), 158. Some also support the first thesis arguing that the T.U.L.P.S.' articles, 1931, mentioned above, are not only in force but also valid and in conformity with the Constitution: for example, A.M. Sandulli, *Manuale di diritto amministrativo* (Napoli: Jovene, 1964), 47.

that the offender possesses something that does not belong to him/her.[26]

These controversial cases abound in doctrine and jurisprudence. Controversies of the second type are particularly frequent. They originate in what we might call "semantic antinomies". The following are examples of these: is stealing electricity by fiddling the meter aggravated theft, fraud or misappropriation, or all or some of these? Is a false certification of a signature a public ("falso in atto pubblico") or administrative fraud ("falso in certificazione amministrativa")? Is the contract I might make with a joiner to build a bookcase to my specifications one for the hire of his labour or for sale of an item yet to be built? I think that these controversies are insuperable, precisely because the outcome does not rest on observation of facts because in these examples we have considered abstract "kinds of crime" (*"fattispecie astratte"*). Rather, they rest on interpretative argument, which is, as we know, often contestable. In these cases, the only rigorous control of juridical truth is the logical consistency of the dogmatic and/or theoretical propositions with each other. Though these propositions may be accepted as premises by any particular jurist, they are essentially contestable. Thus it is to lack of contradiction within the discourse that we look for proof. Unfortunately, as we shall see later, in legislative discourse there are often antinomies which are more serious than the incongruencies and semantic antinomies. They make the consistency criterion impossible to apply. Even the possibility of what we have shown above makes it clear that the factual irrefutability of legal dogmatics goes with an almost unlimited juridical refutability. This makes the hypotheses of legal dogmatics permanently uncertain and changeable and its content just as uncertain and contestable.

5. *Observation and Theorization. Analysis of Language and the Axiomatic Method in Legal Science*

As we have already said, "normativism" and "legal realism" represent two different semantic models or models of empirical interpretation of the theory of law. They correspond to two possible universes of legal science:

26 In favour of the first thesis, see Cass. Sec. III, 15.1.1962, "Giustizia penale", 1962, II, p. 957, m. 842; Cass. Sect. III, 3.2.1965, *ibi*, 1965, II, p. 385. In favour of the second thesis, see Cass. Sect. II, 8.2.1965, "Cassazione Penale, Mass. Ann.", 1965, p. 759, m. 1337; Cass. Sect. II, 19.11.1968, *ibi*, 1970, p. 219, m. 251.

the linguistic universe of norms looked at from the internal point of view and the extra-linguistic universe of events looked at from the external point of view. So legal dogmatics and sociology of law, the analysis of legal language and sociological observations, juridical truth and factual truth, juridical refutation and factual refutation can be seen as disciplines, methods of enquiry, criteria of verification and empirical control at two distinct levels: the level of observation and interpretation of norms and the level of observation and discovery of facts. Together these constitute the level of observation of legal science.

The distinction between normativist theories and realist theories is thus a much more fundamental distinction and one which does not match the usual distinction between normativist, institutionalist and relativist theories of law. The latter distinction is solely concerned with the content of the theory and looks to the different presupposed theoretical concepts which make up the definition of law or which are assumed as fundamental for the theoretical discourse (namely: "legal norm", "institution" or "legal relation"). The distinction between normative and realistic theories of law, however, concerns the different empirical referents and semantic interpretations which the theory admits.

In order to understand the nature of the semantic relation which joins the theory of law to dogmatics (normativist interpretation) and the sociology of law (realist interpretation), we have to look first to the relation between the discourse and observation language and discourse and theoretical language of the science of law. It is well known that the distinction between observation language and theoretical language was, in the theory of science, a useful instrument with which to analyze the scientific language of all empirical sciences which had reached a certain level of development. According to this distinction, the observation language, is the language in which the descriptive or extra-logical terms "designate objects or observable processes, or observable properties or relations of such objects (for example, 'Zurich', 'cold', 'heavier')". Theoretical language, on the other hand, is a language which includes, in addition to logical terms, only "terms which cannot be explicitly defined on the basis of observational terms (for example, 'mass', 'temperature')".[27]

27 R. Carnap, "Linguaggio osservativo e linguaggio teorico", in *Analiticità, significanza, induzione*, ed. A. Meotti and M. Mondadori (Bologna: il Mulino, 1971), 49-62, at 50. On the distinction between observation language and theoretical language, see also R. Carnap, "Il carattere metodologico dei concetti teorici", in *Analiticità, significanza, induzione*, 263-313; C.G. Hempel,

The former of these two languages is common or natural language. This is assumed to have an immediate semantic relation with the entity observed in reality, so that it is possible to "decide [for each of its terms] by direct observation whether it can be applied to the given situation".[28]

The latter language is an artificial language, without direct semantic reference to observable entities. It can thus be used to formulate concepts and assertions which, although they can be confirmed to the extent to which they can explain and systematize the results of observable experience, are not, however, directly connected with this experience. These concepts and assertions are developed deductively according to an explicit and rigorous syntax. The two languages correspond to two distinct levels of discourse and scientific development. The observational level, that is the direct description of empirical data, which allows only elementary generalizations (for example "wood floats on water, whereas iron sinks"). The theoretical level, however, allows the formulation of scientific laws in terms of abstract and hypothetical entities (for example, Archimedes principle, which uses the theoretical concept of "specific gravity"). The connection between the two levels, which is necessary for a theoretical system to be able to count as an empirical theory, is assured by "empirical" or "semantic" interpretation of the theory. This is achieved by a consistent process of the introduction of "interpretative propositions" which connect any such theoretical terms with any such observable terms. This performs the dual function of conferring empirical meaning on theoretical constructs and making them susceptible to verification on the basis of empirical phenomena.[29]

This model can also be used in the science of law. Here one can also

---

Fundamentals of Concept Formation in Empirical Science, Ital. transl. by A. Pasquinelli (Milan: Feltrinelli, 1961), 27ff. and 104ff.; *idem* , *Riflessi dell'opera di Carnap sulla filosofia della scienza*, in P.A. Schllip, ed., *La filosofia di Rudolf Carnap*, Ital. transl. by M.G. de Cristofaro Sandrini (Milan: Il Saggiatore, 1974), vol. II, 659-84, and Carnap's reply: "Carl G. Hempel sulle teorie scientifiche", at II, 938-45; W.V.O. Quine, "La teoria e l'osservazione", *Rivista di filosofia* I (1975), 1-19.

28 Hempel, *Fundamentals, supra* n.27, at 106.

29 *Ibid.*, at 113ff. On the empirical interpretation of theories see also R. Carnap, *Foundations of Logic and Mathematics,* in *International Encyclopedia of Unified Science* Vol. I, n.3 (Chicago: University of Chicago Press, 1939), Ital. trans. by G. Preti (Turin: Paravia, 1956), 91ff.; *Idem,* "Il carattere metodologico dei concetti teorici", *supra* n.27, where interpretative propositions are called "rules of correspondence".

use the same general distinction between observation and theorization, and between the relative levels of language and discourse. The only difference is that there are two observation languages. In the first, observations of facts are formulated. In this respect it is not unlike the observation language of every other social science (for example, "Tim is at present in prison", "the majority of prisoners in Italy are on remand", etc.). In the second, observations or interpretations of norms are formulated. This is the language of juridical science (and, more generally, of "normative" sciences in the sense described above). These are always particular assertions of the existence and meaning of a single norm, or of correlations and generalizations referring to several norms, individuated or able to be individuated. We shall return later to the difficult problem of the relation between these two discourses and observation languages and between their different criteria of meaning and empirical verification in a possible model of a unified legal science. First of all one has further to clarify in what sense the language of dogmatics can be seen as an "observation language", indeed as the most important and most elaborate of the two observation languages of legal science. Very different because it belongs to a level which is different from the "theoretical language" of the theory of law. Propositions of legal dogmatics are, according to our model, propositions which are true or false on the basis of norms. They do not designate things or events or properties or relations between things or events, but the meaning of that linguistic entity which is the "norm". Their observational character thus resides not in their semantic reference to things or events, but in their reference to norms. This depends on the fact that the legal dogmatician, as we shall see later, observes neither things nor events but only norms. He is only able to perceive what the norms themselves tell him — hypothetically and normatively — about things or events. This may puzzle those who are not prepared to consider norms, and linguistic phenomena in general, as "observable facts",[30] not even in the restricted and technical sense given to this term by linguistic analysis, which assigns them meaning as propositions of a normative kind. On the contrary, that the legal dogmatician's task is to observe norms will be taken as a matter of course in an empirical conception of positive law which equates the existence of juridical norms simply with their "being promulagated" ("*vigore*") (instead of identifying it, as we shall see later, with their "validity" or their "effectiveness"). The empirical conception thus conceives of the force or existence of a norm not as

30 In the very broad sense of B.R. Braithwaite (see above note 4).

something mysterious, but as an observable fact just like others, even though it does so using different instruments. Despite this both juridical dogmatic and juridical theoretic languages do have a problem in defining their own technical terms. What this amounts to is the "reduction of the term" for which a definition has been offered into "terms designating properties which can be determined by direct observation"[31] (of things and of events). But this is a problem which concerns the specific techniques of observation or juridical interpretation of norms (and which goes back to the semantics of normative language). It also concerns the procedures which join empirical interpretation to theoretical concepts and constructs. This is different from the problem of the levels of language, that is, the object language of norms, the language of dogmatics which is an observation language in respect to the language of the first level, and the theoretical language of legal theory. In these we find the various languages and levels used by law.

The language of legal dogmatics, then, can be straightforwardly characterized as an observation language (of norms, not of things or extra-linguistic events). In this it differs from the language of legal theory which is precisely a theoretical language. These two languages, because of the different ways in which they are constructed, can be distinguished in a clearer and more precise way than in other empirical sciences. In fact, the concepts and statements of dogmatics are constructed through the analysis or interpretation of legal language. Through a means which, bearing in mind the linguistic nature of the normative universe, plays the same role in legal science as experimental observation does in natural science. The concepts and statements of legal theory, on the other hand, are constructed by hypotheses and abstractions which can be formalized and axiomatized in the same way as all other empirical theories. More precisely, the juridical concepts of legal dogmatics are elaborated by *lexical definitions* in the broad sense which includes so-called "redefinitions". That is to say by propositions which are meant to elucidate the meaning of corresponding words used by the legislator and

31 U. Scarpelli, "La definizione nel diritto", in U. Scarpelli ed., *Diritto e analisi del linguaggio, supra* n.7, at 184. On this question see also A. Ross, "Definition in Legal Language", in *Logique et Analyse* 3-4 (1958), 139-49, Ital. trans. "La definizione nel linguaggio giuridico", in U. Scarpelli, ed., *Diritto e analisi del linguaggio* (Milan: Comunità, 1976), 199-214; H.L.A. Hart, "Definition and Theory in Jurisprudence", *Law Quarterly Review* 70 (1954), 37-60; U. Scarpelli, *Contributo alla semantica del linguaggio normativo* (1959) (Milan: Giuffrè, 1985).

normatively established by the legislator itself. The assertions of dogmatics are formed in the same way. These are merely meta-linguistic reformulations of legal propositions which clarify their sense and identify their normative content. The juridical concepts of legal theory are, on the other hand, introduced by *stipulative or conventional definitions* established by the theorist and assumed by him for the explanatory purposes of the theory.[32] All the other theses or theorems of the theory are derived from postulates which are assumed in the same way as the definitions and which represent the premises of the theory, if that theory is developed in axiomatic form.

There are then two different methods, one exegetical and the other logico-deductive. They are used in the formation of concepts and dogmatic and theoretical propositions and give rise to two different languages. These in turn correspond to two different levels of discourse according to the scheme shown in respect of empirical science in general. In as far as it is concerned with the analysis of the meaning of normative propositions in laws, the observation language of dogmatics is merely the judicial meta-language in which the legal language which is the object of analysis is reformulated. It is the same ordinary or natural language used by the legislator and suitably reconstructed by the interpreter. The theoretical language of legal theory, not having a direct reference or connection to normative discourse, is a conventional or artificial language. That is to say, it is entirely constructed by the theorist and can as such be formulated according to an agreed and rigorous logical syntax.

We make this clear with some examples. The terms "contract", "contract of sale", "mortgage", "possession", "commercial trader", "small business man", "theft", "fraud", "vagrant" etc, are observation terms which designate dogmatic concepts, the use of which is established by the norms in which they are found (in the examples given, articles 1321, 1470, 1813, 1140, 2082 and 2083 of the Italian Civil Code and articles 624, 640 and 203 of the Penal Code) and in which they fulfil a direct normative function. In many of these cases, the rules governing the use of such terms are given expressly by the legislature through norms (or fragments of norms) that have the effectively the form of proper legal definitions. In others, this is only indirectly or implicitly determined by the normative contexts in which the terms appear. In all cases, these terms are meta-linguistic names for norms and their meaning is directly expressed by a

32 On the distinction between "lexical definitions", "stipulative definitions" and "re-definitions" see Scarpelli, *Contributo, supra* n.31, at 27-33.

norm. It follows that definitions given by the legal dogmatician effectively reconstruct the normative content assigned to the terms by the legislator. The only freedom the jurist has is that of interpreting the linguistic text. Thus one can see the definitions as propositions which can be true or false, more precisely as juridically true or false according to the notion of juridical truth defined above.[33]

Completely different is the semantic status of terms such as "norm", "system", "validity", "effectiveness", "juridical act", "illicit", "sanction". "transaction", "subjective right", "power", "obligation", "person", etc. These terms do not designate entities which are observable or directly identifiable through the analysis of legal language. It would be a waste of time to attempt a definition on the basis of the legislative vocabulary, or to search for the meaning through the reconstruction of the possible uses to which they are put in the norms. We do not find terms such as "regulation", "transaction", "effectiveness" used in legal language; and when such terms, for example, "subjective right", "obligation", "illegal act", "validity", "personality", etc are used, they are not binding for the jurist because their meaning is drawn from their current use in the scientific language. What we are dealing with here are theoretical terms which designate concepts which have no immediate relation to observable legal reality[34] — whether by reality we mean the normative or the factual universe. These terms are introduced through propositions which are not meta-linguistic reformulations of the norms, but conventions or stipulations designed to systematize and explain the observable phenomena in the field of dogmatics or sociology of law. It follows that while lexical definitions of dogmatic concepts can be juridically true or false by reference to their semantic correspondence with the norms, an analogous judgement is not possible for the (stipulative) definitions of

33 Hempel, *Fundamentals, supra* n.27, at 11-12. On the subject of (lexical) definitions which analyse the meaning of words already used and can therefore be called as true or untrue in relation by reference to linguistic use, Hempel speaks of "real definitions" or "analysis of meaning". He calls "nominal definitions" those conventions or (stipulative) definitions "used to introduce or to define a new expression" (*ibid.*, at 5-25).

34 See Hart, "Definition and Theory", *supra* n.31, at 38: "There is nothing which simply 'corresponds' to these legal words and when we try to define them we find that the expressions we tender in our definition specifying kinds of persons, things, qualities, events, and processes, material or psychological, are never precisely the equivalent of these legal words though often connected with them in some way".

theoretical concepts. The theoretical range and explanatory capacity of these stipulative definitions of theoretical concepts can only be tested against the corresponding concepts and observational propositions of dogmatics and sociology of law. Naturally, as in other scientific languages, the distinction within "juridical language" as a whole between "juridical observation language", used either "dogmatically" or "operatively", and "juridical theoretical language" is not a rigid and absolute one. Many dogmatic terms can, with due care, usefully be redefined in theoretical terms. Conversely, many of the theoretical terms, if employed with a normative function in legal language, will also require dogmatic definitions i.e.definitions strictly bound to the specific way the legislator used these terms.

The distinction between the observational level of legal dogmatics and the theoretical level of legal theory is one which pertains: (1) to the way in which the respective discourses are formulated, (2) to the criteria by which they are controlled, (3) to the syntax and semantics of the languages. Bearing all this in mind, legal dogmatics can be defined as the ensemble of concepts and propositions which aim to clarify and explain the meaning of norms. These concepts and propositions are elaborated and at the same time judicially verified or refuted by means of legal language analysis. They are formulated in a language which is meta-linguistic with respect to the language of statute law and case law, from which it also derives the rules governing its use. This ought to be enough to exclude the possibility, put forward, for example, by Norberto Bobbio, of establishing at the level of dogmatics a rigorous juridical language according to an agreed-upon logical syntax.[35] This would be achieved by the analysis of normative discourse. Although legal language makes itself out to be a specific technical language, it is in fact a "natural" language as opposed to an "artificial" one. A natural language cannot be formalized in any way, but only analyzed in a meta-language which is itself natural, even if of greater clarity and precision.[36]

The theory of law can be conceived of as an organised — or organisable — system of concepts and propositions according to a rigorous logical structure determined beforehand. It is based on the empirical data provided by dogmatics and/or the sociology of law. These concepts and

35 N. Bobbio, *Teoria della scienza giuridica* (Turin: Giappichelli, 1950), 217ff.

36 This is a case where "object-language and meta-language coincide, as when, for example one speaks of Italian in Italian": Carnap, *Foundations, supra* n.29, at 2.

propositions are, can, or ought to be, constructed by the "axiomatic method", which consists in the following three types of operations: (a) by the stipulation according to agreed formulation rules, of "primitive concepts", that is a small number of concepts not defined from the other concepts, as well as "postulates" or "axioms", that is those propositions not derived from other propositions of the theory; (b) by the definition, according to the same rules, of the remaining concepts of the theory, which are defined by means of the primitive concepts and/or other concepts which are in turn derived from the primitive concepts; (c) by the derivation, from agreed transformation rules, of the remaining propositions of the theory which are derived from postulates and/or from definitions and/or from other propositions previously derived from the postulates and/or definitions.[37] The language of this type of theory is clearly an "artificial" or "conventional" or "formalized" language. It is constructed by the theorist on the basis of formation rules which he himself has established. The theoretical discourse produced in such a way only allows for one mode of truth: we look to the consistency of the postulates and the definitions of the propositions derived from them by agreed-upon transformation rules.

The theory of law thus constructed is no more "normative" than any other theory. It is a system which is independent of specific semantic reference, since none of the three operations described above establishes a direct link between empirical data, concepts and theoretical propositions. It is clear, however, that if such a system is to count as a theory *of* law and if its statements, as well as logically consistent, are to be verifiable or refutable by empirical observations on the level of dogmatics and sociology, there has to be some connection between the two levels of language and discourse. What this means is that the concepts and statements at the theoretical level must serve as explanatory models of juridical experience as it is understood at the observational level of dogmatics and/or the sociology of law. This connection is assured no

37 For a clear description of the axiomatic method, see A. Tarski, *Introduction to Logic and to the Methodology of Deductive Sciences* (New York: Oxford University Press, 1941), 117-119; see also R. Carnap, *Introduction to Symbolic Logic and its Applications* (New York: Dover Publications, 1958); R. Blanché, *L'axiomatique* (Paris, PUF, 1955); Hempel, *Fundamentals, supra* n.27, at 11f.; Braithwaite, *supra* n.4, at 26 ff. For an initial provisional use of the axiomatic method in legal theory and only in relation to a few general concepts (in particular, "norm", "act" "effect", "juridical situation") see my *Teoria assiomatizzata del diritto. Parte generale* (Milan: Giuffrè, 1970).

differently than in other empirical theories, by "semantic" or "empirical" interpretation of the theory, that is, by a process of reducing the theoretical-artificial language to the observation language of legal dogmatics (in the case of normativist interpretation), or sociology of law (in the case of realist interpretation). For example, in the theory of law, the theoretical concept of "juridical norm", can be considered either as a primitive or as a concept defined by other equally abstract theoretical concepts (one thinks of the Kelsenian definition of the norm as a "scheme of interpretation" or as an "expression of an ought"). It can thus be interpreted in normativist terms by means of a reductive or connotative proposition in dogmatic terms of the type "when one speaks of a 'norm', one is referring to whatever prescription is contained in a law in force or in other sources which are in force because based upon a law in force". It can, however, also be interpreted in sociological terms, as in "Rules are conceived and spoken of as imposing obligations when the general demand for conformity is insistent and the social pressure and the social pressure brought to bear upon those who deviate or threaten to deviate great".[38]

As far as the syntactical dimension is concerned, there is no difference between the theory of law and other empirical theories. They all use the same method. This consists of the stipulation of postulates, conventional definitions based on a restricted number of primitive terms and the deduction of all other terms from them by logical rules. The difference concerns the semantic dimension of the theory, that is its interpretation at the observation level. This is linked to the particular nature and complexity of the empirical universe of legal science, which, as we know, can be observed both internally as a linguistic normative universe and externally as merely a factual one. These alternative points of view represent the specific connotation of the semantics of the theory of law and at the same time the central problem of juridical epistemology. The problem is that the two points of view which we have identified with "normativism" and "realism" are different not only in respect of their models of experience (the interpretation or analysis of the language of norms and sociological observation of factual events) but also in their respective models of truth (juridical truth and factual truth).

We may now ask ourselves the following question. Do these two semantic models represent true alternatives, as the usual opposition between normative and realistic theories of law would have us suppose, or

38 This second characteristic of "norm" figures in H.L.A. Hart, *The Concept of Law* (Oxford: Clarendon Press, 1961), 84.

are they compatible? What problems arise if we assume they are incompatible, and what difficulties do we encounter is we assume that they are compatible? Is an integrated model of legal theory possible? In other words, can we have a model which refers to both universes of discourse simultaneously, the empirico-normative and the empirico-factual?

6. *"Level" of Norms, "Level" of Observation and "Level" of Truth*

Legal science is generally taken to comprise the ensemble of dogmatics which results from the so-called "particular legal disciplines" ("civil law", "penal law", "constitutional law", etc). It also comprises the whole of the theory of law interpreted normatively by dogmatic enquiry in a particular area of positive law. Sociology of law is the study of the way concrete legal systems function. It does not go about this by analyzing the meaning of legal norms. It is generally considered to be a science in its own right, completely independent of juridical science which is primarily conceived of as "legal doctrine" and/or case law.

This disjunction between the observation levels of legal science is the source of many grave difficulties. We have seen the difference between juridical truth and factual truth in the answers to the banal question "how is theft punished in Italy?" In this case, as we said before, there only appears to be a contradiction. The juridical truth of the answer "all thefts are punished by up to three years' imprisonment" relates to the enactment of the norm about theft, and thus about what "ought" to be the punishment for theft. However the factual truth of the answer "only a small number of thefts are punished" relates to the description of facts, and thus concerns the effective punishment of theft, the "is" or "is not".

Let us take two other examples. To the question whether there is freedom of expression against public authorities in Italy, the dogmatic jurist will reply in the affirmative. He will quote article 21 of the constitution, which states that "everyone shall have the right freely to express his own thoughts, orally or in writing or by any other means of circulation". But the same jurist, and not only the sociologist of law, will also have to reply negatively. Here he will quote articles 278, 279 and 290 of the Penal Code, which punish an "affront" or an "insult" to the President of the Republic, Parliament, the Constitutional Court, the Police and the Armed Forces. The second example: to the question whether a subjective right is always actionable in court, the jurist will answer in the affirmative. He will quote article 24 of the constitution, which states that "everyone may proceed at law for the protection of his rights and legitimate interests". The same jurist will also have to give a negative response if he looks to the subjective rights given by the Constitution — such as the right to work, the right to health, the right to equal pay and in many cases the same rights of liberty — he will see that the subjects of these rights will only have locus in the courts if there are procedural norms providing for that.

We have, therefore, two pairs of responses which are true but which also contradict each other. Unlike the contradiction between legal truth and factual truth, which we saw when we looked at the answer to the question "how is theft punished in Italy?", in the two examples above the two answers seem to assume the same observational base. For both of them this is the legislative discourse, the system of norms which is the object of the legal dogmatician's enquiry. More precisely, the first pair of answers show a case of "antinomy", that is inconsistency between norms; the second show a case of "lacuna", that is the incompleteness or absence of norms. In both these cases, one would be able to conclude that observable reality is contradictory.

Such a conclusion would obviously be inconceivable if the "reality" to which it referred was the universe of actual events. It is, however, perfectly conceivable, if paradoxical, in the case of the reality involved in legal dogmatics, which, as we know, is a universe of discourse that consists in turn in a discourse — that of the legislator — formulated in ordinary language with all the logical and semantic imperfections inevitably involved in a discourse without special formalization, especially one as complex and highly articulated as any discourse using normative propositions. It is a well known fact that developed systems of positive law include norms about production of norms which govern both antinomies and lacunae. They provide criteria for determining which norm is to prevail in cases of conflict and, in cases of gaps, how they are to be extended by analogy. However, these criteria are not always sufficient to remedy the contradictions found in dogmatic discourse. They are not able to do so in our two examples. In general, they are not able to solve the contradictions — in a system such as the Italian one, which is based on several normative levels — each time an inferior norm comes into conflict with another norm. As the first example showed, solving the antinomy by applying the criteria of hierarchy, and this is where it differs from the *lex posteriori and the lex specialis* criteria, is not simply a theoretical matter. It needs an operative interpretation without which the inferior norm remains in force, even if supposed invalid. Again, in the second example. If the lacuna complained of exists because the legislation provided for by the constitutional norm does not exist, then no analogical reasoning can supply it.

There is a fundamental difference between antinomies and lacunae in respect of levels of norms and those which we described above as "semantic antinomies". These latter are always juridically refutable, since they are generated by the ambiguities of legal language and of the propositions of legal dogmatics. These semantic antinomies are no different from lacunae and antinomies between norms of the same level in that they can always be resolved theoretically. This is so even if the differences of opinions stemming from them cannot always be decided with certainty. One can, for example, have very different opinions as to whether a particular action is to be called a theft, an embezzlement or neither of the two. The opinions would nevertheless all be based upon law. Whatever solution the jurist adopts, it will be justified by its consistency with other legal propositions and opinions, which he holds as correct, concerning related or implied matters. For example, someone who holds that a particular action is a theft rather than an embezzlement does so on the basis of certain views of "detention" and "possession" which will be different from those of someone who considers the action embezzlement.

On the other hand, when confronted with an antinomy or a lacuna concerning norms of different levels, the same jurist will have to admit contradictory hypotheses into his discourse. He could, in theory, say that a particular norm can be annulled or declared invalid. But until such a norm has been declared invalid he cannot say that it does not exist or that its meaning is different. The jurist is faced with a conflict between norms which generate a contradiction between hypotheses which are both juridically true in as much as they can be verified by norms. When confronted by an antinomy, the most he can do is complain that a particular norm "should not" exist normatively or logically. And when confronted by a lacuna he can say that a particular norm "ought to" exist normatively or logically. And yet nothing will change the true state of affairs: in the first case the norm exists whereas in the second it does not exist.

How are we to resolve this paradox? This is a deontological as well as a logical problem. It calls into question the intellectual and scientific role of the jurist. On the one hand, simply accepting the contradictions would compromise the internal consistency and thus the logical truth of the dogmatic discourse. As well as being contestable in the sense described above, it would become inconsistent and thus have no meaning content. On the other hand, to negate the contradictions would compromise the semantic correspondence with the normative universe. Thus the empirical truth of the dogmatic discourse would be falsified by juridical experience. This latter solution is the one normally preferred by jurists. They see systematizing legislative discourse as one of their principal tasks. They set out to remove all traces of antinomies and lacunae, almost as if consistency and completeness were an internal imperative of the system rather than merely a practical or theoretical requirement. Naturally, as we have already seen, this work is doomed to failure. The jurists' attempts to systematize often end up concealing rather than solving the antinomies occurring in the legislative discourse. Many antinomies merely reflect deep divisions which are rooted in the very structure of the legal order and the historical conditions which produced it. They cannot be denied or minimized. Take the principles — constitutional and not — of strict legality, of the presumption of innocence, of the burden of proof, of individual responsibility, and parity between the accuser and defender. Compare them with the penal system in its institutions and norms, the power of the police, objective responsibility, preventive detention, of the various procedural methods of our penal system. We can see that they visibly contradict each other.[39] In these cases, the jurist is not able, as in the case of semantic antinomies, to accommodate all these contradictory principles within the same universe of discourse. Moreover, the fact that such contradictions exist is shown by each jurisdictional pronouncement of invalidity.

There is only one way to explain the unresolved juridical difficulties present in the legislative discourse without inconsistency. This is to recognise, at the level of meta-theory of law, that in systems of positive law structured on more than one normative level, each normative observation level is at the same time a factual observation level in respect of norms at a higher normative level. Consequently it is to recognise that

39 I have underlined the wide conflict existing between different normative levels in our penal system, under the entries "Reato (profili teorici)", "Reato (profili reali)", "Pena (principi teorici)", "Pena (profili reali"), "Processo penale (principi teorici)", "Processo penale (profili reali)", in C. Donati, ed., *Dizionario critico del diritto* (Milan: Savelli, 1980).

judgements of legal truth always relate exclusively to the normative level to which the norm in question belongs, whereas they are judgements of factual truth in respect to norms at the higher level. This ambivalence of norms can in turn be explained by the fact that within the normative universe, which we have generally identified as the universe of dogmatic discourse, the lower level norms can be see as facts or behaviour (of the legislature or, more generally, of judicial officials) in respect to norms at the higher level. The qualification of lower level norms as valid or invalid by normativist-dogmatic judgement corresponds to the qualification of norms of the higher level as effective or ineffective according to a realist-sociological judgement. It thus follows that the statement:

1) "there is no freedom of expression against public authorities in Italy"

is juridically true only in respect of the Penal Code on the basis of which it is formulated. On the other hand it is juridically false even if factually true in respect of article 21 of the constitution. On the basis of article 21 of the constitution, on the other hand, the opposite statement :

2) "there is freedom of expression against public authorities in Italy"

is juridically true. The juridical truth of the first statement is, in respect of the juridical truth of the second, a factual truth. In fact, the level in which the juridical truth of the first statement is asserted (the level of the penal code) is a norm-observation level and it will become, in its turn, a fact observation level in respect of the higher normative level in which the second proposition is asserted. Hence the contrast between the two truths is not a contradiction between two juridical truths at the same level. Rather it is a difference between a factual truth and a juridical truth. This is determined by the fact that the higher norm is broken or ineffective and the lower norm is consequently invalid even if it still in force. In the same way as the difference between the factual truth of the hypothesis "not all thefts are punished" and the juridical truth of the hypothesis "all thefts are punished with up to three years' imprisonment" is determined by the fact that the norm on the basis of which it is asserted is broken in a certain number of cases and thus rendered ineffective.

As we have seen, except for those at the highest level, all norms can be regarded both as norms (from the internal point of view, or in respect of the inferior factual or regulated level) or as facts (from the external point of view, or in respect of the higher normative or regulating level). It is clear that recognising that norms are ambiguous in this way amounts to recognising that an exclusively normativist or an exclusively realist approach to the universe of "law" is insufficient. It also means recognising that it is necessary to integrate the two approaches and the semantic models which go along with them. Not only are these not incompatible, but they cannot be thought of as alternatives or treated as mutually exclusive without running the risk of a significant number of the propositions of juridical science being inconsistent or empirically false. The coherence of every scientific discourse on law, and the drive for a unified legal science, does not mean that the normative system itself is consistent or complete. Indeed it can only be achieved by recognising that inconsistency and incompleteness are intrinsic to each normative domain articulated on more than one normative level. These structural characteristics can in turn be understood and explained without running into difficulties, provided that on the theoretical plane one recognises the dual nature of "norm" and "fact" in every normative phenomenon. On the level of semantic meta-theory, it is important to recognise that every normative observation level can be "normative" and "factual" at one and the same time. The difficulties outlined above can only be overcome by a theory of law which includes: (a) a theory of juridical norms in general as propositions which express deontic modalities, that is juridical situations of "can be" (powers) or of "ought to be" (duties) and which hence always admit both the "is" (in the case of factual compliance), and the "is not" (in the case of factual defiance) of the state of affairs which the propositions deontically require; (b) a theory of juridical norms in the modern *Rechtsstaat* which allows us to distinguish in every normative phenomenon the norm from the fact (or act) by which it is produced. The fact ought to be seen as being regulated in its turn by norms and thus as either conforming to or deviating from them according to whether it represents their application or breach; (c) a theory of the effectiveness or ineffectiveness of norms as quantitative concepts relating to the realisation or non-realisation of normatively established juridical situations. This should make it always possible to determine the "degree of effectiveness", and in particular the "inverse degree of ineffectiveness" of a norm in relation to the number of times it is carried into effect. An example of the ineffectiveness of norms from the field of criminal law would be the so-called "black figure" of crimes which have gone unpunished. For constitutional norms the analogous figure would be the number of unconstitutional laws in force because they have not been annulled or perhaps a record of the gaps or occasions upon which they have not been applied, etc; (d) a theory of the degrees or levels of norms which conforms to the meta-theory described here. Each level of norms is norm–observational in respect of the lower factual level and fact observational in respect of the higher normative level. This theory sees the consistency or inconsistency between norms of different levels as being related to the conformity or otherwise of the lower level normative fact (or act) to that of the higher level; (e) a theory of the validity or invalidity of norms. This runs parallel to the theory of the effectiveness or ineffectiveness of norms. The validity/invalidity theory is related to the effectiveness/ineffectiveness theory by the reciprocal relationship of implication between the effectiveness of the higher-level norm and the validity of the lower-level norm and the ineffectiveness of the former and invalidity of the latter.

A theory of law of the type briefly outlined above is neither normativist nor realist but both at the same time. This is because it assumes as its observation level the normative as well as the factual level and sees them as two sides of the same domain. In this way the consistency and inconsistency between norms of different levels come to be identified on the one hand with the validity and invalidity of the lower-level norm in respect of the "ought" of the validity (and consistency) given by the higher-level norm. On the other hand, consistency and inconsistency between norms on different levels can be identified with the effectiveness or ineffectiveness of the higher-level norm in respect of the actual "is" or "is not" of validity (and the consistency) of the lower-level norm. The different normative levels correspond to different observation levels and thus to different levels of truth.

We can thus recognise and resolve the two conceptual confusions which normative and realistic theories of law more or less explicitly run up against. These exist not only on the theoretical plane, but first and foremost on the meta-theoretical semantic plane. The normative theories identify "validity" (*validità*) with the "existence" (*esistenza*) of norms and the realistic theories identify "effectiveness" (*effettività*) with the "existence" of norms. For the purpose of this essay the "existence" of norms has been referred to by saying that they are "in force" (*vigore* or *vigenza*). These identities are the result of an equivocation. There are such things as invalid juridical norms, as can be seen by each pronouncement of constitutional illegitimacy and more generally by each judicial act of annulment. And there are also ineffective juridical norms, as is demonstrated every time their breach is evidenced by facts which constitute breach. The mistake, common to both normative and realistic theories, is to confuse theoretical questions, like those of validity and effectiveness, with meta-theoretical questions, like those concerning the existence of norms, which is no more than the empirical referent of the semantic notion of "juridical truth". In the same way, the "existence" of facts is the empirical referent of the semantic notion of "factual truth". It is possible to claim, in the light of the ambivalence of juridical norms and of the distinction between operative juridical propositions and factual propositions, that judgements of validity and invalidity of a norm are *operative juridical propositions*. These propositions can be verified or refuted on the basis of another norm and precisely of the higher level norm which regulates the production of the first one.

Judgements of effectiveness and ineffectiveness, on the other hand, are *factual propositions*, which can be verified by facts, more precisely, by those lower-level facts (or acts) which constitute observance or lack of observance of norms. It is clear that when the norm whose effectiveness is in question, is a norm regulating the production of other norms, the facts by which we judge whether or not it is effective are whether it produces valid or invalid norms. These facts are themselves detectable by means of juridically verifiable judgements resting on the same norm which is deemed effective in the first case and ineffective in the second.

"Validity" and "invalidity", "effectiveness" and "ineffectiveness" rather than "existence" or "non existence" designate contingent properties of norms which do exist. These can be seen as two sides of the same coin. These two perspectives correspond to two different universes or observation levels. Validity and invalidity designate the "legal" conformity or non-conformity of the normative fact, shown juridically by reference to the higher-level norm. Effectiveness and ineffectiveness, on the other hand, designate the "factual" observance and non-observance of the norm, shown by reference to lower-level facts. Both sets of predicates denote a strictly dyadic relationship. The first is a relation of conformity between the normative fact (or act) and the norm which governs it; the second is the converse relation of the observance or non-observance between the norm and the fact (or act) governed by it.

Alf Ross was justified in his critique of the Kelsenian thesis that the validity of a norm depends upon the validity of the higher-level norm until one reaches a basic norm, the validity of which rests on its effectiveness.[40] But one cannot conclude, as Ross and the realists did, that the validity of each norm, and not only that of the basic norm, is dependent upon its

40 Ross, *On Law and Justice*, *supra* n.5.

effectiveness. In reality, the validity of a norm relates not to the validity but to the meaning or prescriptive content of the higher-level norm, no matter whether the latter is valid or invalid. In the same way, if this is not an absurd analogy, the consistency or logical truth of a proposition depends on the proposition from which it is derived and not on the latter's truth or falsity. Thus in order to say that a norm n^1 is valid in respect of a norm n^2 it is not necessary to look to the validity of n^2 in respect of norm n^3 right up to a hypothetically basic norm. It is sufficient to look exclusively at norm n^2 in relation to which one makes a judgement of validity. On the other hand, the effectiveness of a norm relates to the observable facts at the factual level below it. We thus have to talk about "degrees" of effectiveness or ineffectiveness in relation to the quantity of facts which constitute its observance or non-observance. Naturally, effectiveness or ineffectiveness can also be predicated of the norms which do not have as their object facts in their turn normative and in general of all juridical modalities. It is for this reason that the opposition "effectiveness"/"ineffectiveness" — usually considered by jurists to be of merely sociological interest — can be seen as the central dichotomy of legal theory on the basis of which all other oppositions can be explained: not only observance and non-observance of norms, but also their validity, invalidity, the legitimacy or illegitimacy of states of affairs, the missing or vitiated exercise of power, and the legal or illegal nature of behaviours.

7. *Semantic Models and the Explanatory Scope of Legal Theory*

As we have seen, the incoherence or partial empirical falsity of scientific discourse can be attributed to a purely normative approach to legal theory. This is the principal argument against the attempts to dissociate the two observational levels — the normative and the factual — of legal science. There is a second line of argument which looks to the implications of such theories. This claims that they do not have the explanatory capacity one would expect of empirical theories.

Looking solely at the norm from the internal point of view, an exclusively normative approach only allows us to check what the norm says, and, more precisely, to ascertain and to interpret its meaning. And since norms are only deontic modalities of the behaviour they refer to, a legal science which is the product of this type of approach can only represent the "ought" of juridical phenomena as they are deontically hypothesized by the norm. If it is indeed true that the juridical truth of dogmatic propositions which interpret norms is a truth which is irrefutable because it is totally independent of what happens, then it is also true that the analysis of the meaning of the norm cannot tell us anything about the effectiveness of juridical phenomena or the effective functioning of legal systems. In other words, the analysis of normative language does not tell us anything about the reality of facts, but only, one might say, about the reality of laws. More precisely, it gives us a picture of how the normative system sees itself through its own norms. As we have shown, this picture is full of contradictions. This is because that gap between norms and facts, systematically ignored by the identification of validity with existence, is intrinsic to the normative universe itself. It is within this same universe that each norm is viewed as a fact in respect of a higher-level norm. It follows that a theory of law to which we assign a purely normativist interpretation is, as it were, a picture of law (including both facts and norms), as it "ought to be" at each of its normative levels but not what it effectively "is" in respect of the corresponding factual levels.[41]

On the other hand, a rigidly realist theory of law only allows us to describe the effective functioning of a legal system, based on direct factual observation. But it does not look to whether the phenomena it observes conform to the norms which govern them since these are specifically legal in nature. If a Martian from the external point of view were to observe everything, and even interview the recipients of norms to see what feelings of obligation accompanied their behaviour, he would not be able to understand very well what a no parking sign in the centre of Rome, so cavalierly disregarded by everybody while the authorities turn a blind eye, means. Another example might be the illegality of a large number of the measures adopted by the police, which are in each case based on unconstitutional norms or ones of dubious constitutionality. If he were to identify the existence of legal norms with their effectiveness, he would not be able to understand the conditions of the validity of norms which, although ineffective, continue to be in force. Nor would he be able to understand the conditions of invalidity of effective norms in force. Still less would he be able to understand the profound differences between

41 This outlook — which contradicts the empiricist assumptions of legal positivism which contrasts the "law that is" and not with "the law which ought to be" (see above note 2) — justifies Alf Ross's accusation of "legal idealism" against Kelsen's normativism, and Ross's identification of it with natural law theorising (Ross, *ibid.*).

jurists and legal officials in respect of the same legal problem and the same concrete case. If norms do not tell us anything about facts, we are not able to learn anything about norms by observing facts. Thus the determined realist is only able to grasp the factual picture of a legal system and not how the legal representation diverges from this.

Thus a legal science which is exclusively normativist or realist is not only limited but also marred by its one-dimensional approach. Neither of these can explain the real difference between the normative representations and the real functioning of the legal system. This difference, innate since norms can always be broken, is all the more marked in modern legal systems. This is both because of their increasing complexity, multiplication of normative levels and inter-normative conflict, and also because higher-level norms are more "advanced" than lower-level norms. The former usually establish the civic and political values upon which the entire political system is legitimated. The latter reflect the interests, contingent normative strategies, conflicts of power and competence, and perhaps the illegal functioning of institutions.

Thus a phenomenon such as the present-day crisis of the *Rechtsstaat* which political scientists see as central, remains largely misunderstood, and in many cases even ignored by jurists. This crisis is characterized by the following: the obsolescence of the principles of legality; the multiplication of state services which operate in non-legal forms; the inadequacy of the normative structures of the old liberal state to guarantee new rights and control the new functions of the welfare state; the growing illegality of state apparatuses and the elusive and hidden nature of the centres of real power. On the one hand, the dogmatic-normativist approach proves unable to provide sound knowledge of the legal system, precisely because it has gone beyond its own complex and inconsistent normative self-representation and in many areas has developed outwith legal forms. On the other hand, the purely sociological-realist approach cannot take account of the growing division between the normative and the factual universe and always risks, if pursued to its logical conclusion, the reduction of law to facts.

The danger is that these two conceptions, the first more widespread in juridical culture than the second, favour dangerously ideological models of legal science. The one based on uncritical contemplation of a normative system; the other on an uncritical and more or less resigned acceptance of its own mechanisms and functions. More precisely, an exclusively normativist legal theory, in so far as it precludes enquiries into the ineffectiveness of norms, and thus of the invalidity and illegitimacy of an important part of the normative system and of the organisation of power, risks making the ideological mistake of confusing norms with reality. It defines and analyses the normative principles of the penal process such as publicity, the rights of the defence, the burden of proof and the presumption of innocence, but neglects the fact that they are contradicted not only at the operative level but at the legal level. It also formalizes and systematizes principles of legality, of typicality, publicity and of judicial review of all administrative acts. It ignores, however, illegal and hidden practices, the huge shift in competences and the mechanisms of immunity that characterize vast areas of public administration and government action. It defines the theoretical concept of "punishment" as a sanction following on a crime and applied through the trial and rids it of extra-normative connotations. But it does not consider the broad range of preventive and coercive measures and of the administrative operations of the police. And this is without speaking of the concrete and different mechanisms of punishment that operate in jails, contradicting the theoretical principles of strict legality.

Conversely, an exclusively realist legal theory obliterates the normative and in so doing risks replacing law with reality. Likewise, this precludes the identification of the levels of validity and illegitimacy present in the legal system. This is even more dangerous than a purely normativist approach. A crude form of legal realism can be wedded with an even cruder pragmatic politics. This can lead to the devaluation of the normative value of law, and the identification of law with the power and the identification of law with decisionistic and anti-*Rechtsstaat* models of legal organisation. Alf Ross's use of the rules of chess as "a model for the concept of valid law" and "a scheme of interpretation" of the corresponding social acts has, unfortunately, a defect.[42] Chess players hardly ever break the rules (and if they do they are immediately corrected), whereas the public organs which produce norms do. And to call their actual behaviour "valid law" has as great a legitimatory function as that of normativists who only think of valid laws as "existing".

A legal theory which has an adequate explanatory capacity, and at the same time is free from logical and semantic difficulties, ought to be able to represent both its normative and factual universes and the interactions between the two. It should be able to explain both what actually happens and what legally ought to happen. The difference between the two

42 Ross, *ibid.*

universes is not only the principal problem, but also the most important object of enquiry for legal theory. As we have already indicated, the integration of the two semantic models can be achieved by a legal theory of effectiveness and ineffectiveness, and connected with that, of validity and invalidity. We are thus able to explain and predict the possible differences between the normative level, and more generally between the normative and factual universes. The first task of legal theory is to analyze the relations between observable phenomena at different levels — the normative and the factual — of the legal universe. To show why they are different and also to show how the first effectively serves to legitimate the second and the second to thwart the first. There is not just a scientific purpose here, but also a civil one. It can serve as an important instrument for the analysis of laws in force. It must be noted, however, that this is not a critical theory from the point of view of natural law. We are not here saying what laws "ought" to be, but how the positive law fails to measure up to its own standards. This involves further work on the "pragmatics" of legal theory.

THE OBJECT AND METHOD OF LEGAL SCIENCE

by

MARIO JORI

1. *The Problem of Legal Knowledge*

Contemporary theory of law owes much to the work of Norberto Bobbio. In my view, one of Bobbio's most important contributions to legal culture is his work on legal science, sometimes described as (cognitive) jurisprudence or, as the knowledge or description of law. In fact, as we shall see, all of these areas form part of the study of legal theory as a whole.

Bobbio's contribution is important not only because of its intrinsic value, but also because it stimulated debate on these and related issues in Italy. The Italian debate is particularly interesting for two reasons. Firstly, because it provided a way of linking and developing two lines of enquiry which had up till then remained separate. The Anglo-Saxon tradition of common law and the continental one of civil law. As we shall see, this is what made it possible to bring together the "objectivist" and the "methodological" approach to the problem of legal knowledge. Secondly, by drawing on some of Bobbio's key concepts, the Italian debate on legal science has transcended the limitations of positivist theory. It has thus avoided the danger of this type of legal theory. That is the danger of becoming an ideological reflection and justification of legal systems in the west today, masked as a detached (or pure) analysis of such systems. Even although Bobbio did not pursue these arguments all the way, his contribution to the debate is crucial to our understanding of the issues involved and our assessment of any conclusions reached.

Recent work in this area often make use of the following illustration of the difference between law and description of law. A good example would the passenger who says to the driver: "You can't park here". Despite apparent similarities, this sentence takes on a very different meaning when uttered by a policeman. In the first case the passenger is merely

Law and Language, The Italian Analytical School, ed. A. Pintore and M. Jori (Liverpool: Deborah Charles Publications, 1997).

describing what is the law; in the second, the policeman is accepting and using the law. In the first example then, we are dealing with cognitive discourse; in the second with prescriptive discourse which is in itself a (repetition of) a legal norm.[1]

This apparently straightforward example should help us to understand an important problem in legal theory or philosophy. Is it possible, and if so, how, to describe law independently of purely subjective opinions and the values it describes? If such a description were not possible, concepts and expressions such as "the law states that ..."; "in this country it is legally permitted to ..."; "in Italy it is forbidden by law to ..." would cease to have any meaning. Indeed if one cannot have inter-subjective knowledge of what constitutes law at a particular time and in a particular place, then it is no longer possible to make statements of the kind illustrated above. Or, to put it another way, they must be considered illusory.

There is no doubt that the problem of legal knowledge is not a simple one. It has ramifications in many, perhaps all, of the most important questions debated in modern legal thought. This is another reason why the car-driving example cited above cannot make a great contribution to the theoretical debate. I think, however, that it is worth pausing to take a closer look at one aspect of the example which legal theorists have more or less ignored. They have been more concerned with tackling the immediate theoretical and methodological problems and determining what should be the true focus of legal science. They have not dwelt on the type of legal ambience and psychological attitude which highlight the existence of the problem and the urgency of a solution.

It is worth reflecting on the car passenger's attitude and on the situation in which he finds himself. By trying to describe existing law (whatever that means) he risks putting himself in a somewhat difficult and embarrassing situation. He may be faced with a somewhat irritated response. His friend may take his well-meaning comment to be an injunction to obey the law, albeit couched in extremely diplomatic terms. To the car-driver there would not be much to distinguish it from the type of remark made by a policeman. The passenger might feel tempted to come out with a comment such as "you could get fined, you know, as you are not allowed to park here" in an attempt to soften the blow and to suggest that he has only the driver's best interests at heart.

1 For example, the anecdote is told by A. Ross, *Directives and Norms* (London: Routledge and Kegan Paul, 1968), 36-37.

This is a general as well as a legal problem. What we have here is the difficulty of referring to norms without wanting to be seen to be commending them or imposing them as models of behaviour. As we shall see, there is nothing magical about any of this. After all, norms are primarily models of behaviour.[2]

It is extremely important to remember that it is possible, although difficult, to adopt this psychologically neutral attitude towards norms which have a wide social currency. In ordinary as well as theoretical language there are ways of expressing this with relative ease. This is a comparatively recent phenomenon. Albeit people have been critical of elements of their social environment for a long time, it is only relatively recently, however, that it has become accepted practice to express such views. Only recently for individuals to have not only the right but the duty to subject existing norms to critical scrutiny. This has resulted in a radical reversal of the burden of proof as compared to pre-modern social criticism. Even norms which have been in existence for a long time and have gained widespread social acceptance must be seen to be better than all the possible alternatives.

Returning to law, we may contrast the emotional quandary of the man in the street faced with norms towards which he wants to remain neutral with the comparative ease with which the professional lawyer confronts the same problems. To an outsider the way lawyers tackle such issues appears cynical and legalistic.

At this point it is necessary to distinguish between two distinct types of jurists. On the one hand there are solicitors and barristers who are paid to help their own clients arrive at a legal solution which is most advantageous for them. These members of the legal profession are certainly able to distinguish between the two types of legal discourse illustrated by our example. On the other hand there are the public legal officials, primarily judges. They are certainly less ready to make the distinction, given that they are professionally obliged to "take the part of the law", even if it is not logically and psychologically essential for them to give this their full ethical and political backing (judges can be cynical too).

This cynicism on the part of the legal profession can be viewed as no more than one aspect (albeit a somewhat disagreeable one) of a cultural attitude which is a fundamental part of our culture as a whole, and not just of our legal culture. It is possible to talk of law without expressing

2 On the question of norms as models of behaviour, and on that of normative meaning, see Ross, *supra* n.1, whose solutions, on the whole, I share.

any moral commitment to it, either in order to criticise it or merely to describe it. Despite the apparent contradiction, it is possible to say: "one must do *x* (legally speaking), but one must not do *x* (morally speaking)". The words in brackets make it clear that different normative systems are being referred to. This seems to eliminate the contradiction. If, however, we want to insist on the claim that there is no real distinction between norms and descriptions of norms, this would have consequences even in law itself. These consequences would extend well beyond criticisms of the immorality of a category of jurists.

In any case there are few radical critiques of contemporary law which have denied the possibility of any objective and scientific description of law.[3] Indeed many have limited themselves to denying that the description usually provided by legal positivistic jurisprudence as practised in the west today is scientific at all. Others have accepted jurisprudence as a (possible) science. They have made this the central tenet of their theories of law, even if they clearly lack some of the conceptual instruments necessary in order to analyze the phenomenon in a satisfactory manner. The most striking example of this is Hans Kelsen, who made the scientificity and neutrality of legal knowledge the corner stone of his theory and battled over the distinction between *Rechtssatz* and *Rechtsnorm* for decades. Kelsen even went as far as to put forward the thought-provoking but essentially confused thesis of the "double ought" which was present in the acceptance of rules or norms. According to this view the ought contained within the mere description of a rule, and thus devoid of power, would be complemented by the addition of an other one which would be "activated" by the act of fully accepting the norm.[4]

Kelsen's thesis provoked a lively debate. The consensus was that the best way of tackling the problem of the relations between law and legal description was to consider both as discourses, a legal discourse and discourse describing legal discourse. At this point modern linguistic philosophy seemed to have the most suitable conceptual instrument to

3 For a typical example of this sort of legal realism see K. Olivecrona, *Law as Fact* (London: Stevens and Sons, 1971); radical critiques can be found in those few marxist scholars who have dealt in sufficient depth with the problem: for example, U. Cerroni, *Marx e il diritto moderno* (Roma: Editori Riuniti, 1972), in particular chap. III.

4 See on the subject M.G. Losano's excellent illustration, "Per un'analisi del "Sollen", in Hans Kelsen", *Rivista internazionale di filosofia del diritto* XLIV (1967), 546ff.

hand. The theory of levels of discourse, which would allow one to take account of the fact that a (meta) discourse could have another discourse as its object.[5] This has opened up new approaches, or reopened old ones which seemed closed off, to contemporary analytic or linguistic philosophy. Examples can be seen in epistemology or in linguistics.[6] It has effectively meant that linguistic philosophy has made the problem of cognitive jurisprudence its own. It is this area to which we shall now turn. Problems of the type emerging from Kelsen's thesis have undoubtedly been resolved. For example, the question of whether the "ought" has the same meaning in norms and in propositions about norms[7].

However, despite the fact most people accept that norms (both legal and non-legal) have a semantic-prescriptive component which can be treated as a linguistic object, two highly problematic aspects of the description of law remain. (1) it is by no means certain (even for linguists) what is the correct analysis of the linguistic description, what is the type or specific method of descriptive meta-linguistic relation, or what fact is the object of such description;[8] (2) it is extremely doubtful, indeed it is one of the most hotly debated issues, as we shall see later, that legal descriptions can be reduced to mere linguistic descriptions. That law can be reduced solely to linguistic-semiotic entities.

Thus our example of the driver who was ready to flout the law does not lead us to any easy solutions. Nevertheless, it allows us to express the

5 See G. Kalinowski, *Querelle de la science normative* (Paris: R. Pichon et R. Durand-Ausiaz, 1990), 91ff. It also includes a comment on Amselek's criticism of Kelsen.

6 The first difficulty which the theory of levels of discourse has helped to solve is that of finding a place for philosophy itself. This became the methodology of science. For an important analysis of these developments at the beginning of linguistic philosophy, see J.O. Urmson, *Philosophical Analysis* (Oxford: Clarendon Press, 1956).

7 Thus Bobbio is right in saying that what changes is not the meaning of the *Sollen* "but the context in which the *Sollen* is used": N. Bobbio, "Essere e dover essere nella scienza giuridica", now in *Studi per una teoria generale del diritto* (Turin: Giappichelli, 1970), 162.

8 A good analysis of the issues and an attempted solution can be found in Ross, *supra* n.1. My feeling is that investigations in legal theory have gone further than those in linguistic philosophy or linguists.

The linguistic standpoint has lead to the almost complete neglect of the positivistic thesis of norms as expression of will; such thesis has been criticised, for example, by K. Olivecrona, *Law as Fact* (London: Faber, 1971), chap. II. Olivecrona is wrong when he identifies that thesis with positivism.

meaning of the problem of legal knowledge in the theory of law. It shows the different ways in which it can present itself in different cultures and legal realities.

In the first place there are many situations in which the man in the street finds it psychologically difficult to distinguish between the description and use of norms. However, as we have seen, such a distinction comes naturally to lawyers today. According to some positivist theories of law (Kelsen, for example), this could mean that positive lawyers have discovered a way of describing law, that is legal norms and perhaps rules in general, which is scientific and value neutral. On the other hand, the critics of legal positivism have maintained that the legal positive distinction between description and use of law is illusory and misleading, that is to say ideological. If this were true, then a considerable part of legal culture and discourse today (in the west at least) would turn out to be self-deceptive or misleading. Perhaps, for precisely that reason, socially functional.

According to the radical critics of legal positivism, in order to make law truly scientific it would be necessary to bring cognitive jurisprudence into line with models of the description of norms or rules already applied by other social and historical sciences. Despite appearances and declarations to the contrary, say these critics, such models have not through legal positivism already penetrated the law. The positivistic conception of law, which is the one which currently holds sway in western legal circles, would in fact result in a false representation, the hidden defence of ideological submission to the existing legal norms. However "cynical" the lawyer might appear, he would turn out to be a conformist who accepts the norms because they are followed by the majority. Far from being in the vanguard of those who are critical of the normative, he would be the exponent of an old and superseded mentality. Even although he might not appear so at first.[9]

Secondly, there is an issue which is worth looking at in more detail. The distinction between description and acceptance of legal norms is the raison d'etre of a whole category of jurists, those who defend particular interests, especially those of the individual, in western legal systems. It is professionally less clear-cut and necessary in the public functionary,

9 This state of mind is characteristic of communitarian social organisation. The distinction can first be found in a classical study, that of F. Tönnies, *Community and Society,* trans. C P Loomis (Michigan: Michigan State University Press, 1957).

especially the judge. The judge, according to the legal positivists certainly has to know the law and be able to distinguish it from his own personal preferences. But he must do this in the act of applying it, committing himself on the level of values in favour of the law itself. As far as academic lawyers are concerned, they occupy a position somewhere between the first two roles. Their influence is usually greatest where the influence of judicial jurisprudence is minimal. This has important consequences, as we shall see, for the way in which the problem of legal description tends to be dealt with in different western legal cultures today. In general we can say that we might expect differences in the way in which the problem is dealt with, depending upon the extent to which the legal environment is dominated by the figure of the judge.

When we describe law, just what is it that we are describing and how are we going about it? These are the two fundamental questions in the theory of legal science, or, to put it another way, two ways of asking oneself the same fundamental question. In fact we soon realise that we are dealing with a whole group of related problems. These encompass not only the problem of the nature and existence of legal norms, but also questions of the validity, interpretation, effectiveness, definition (of the concept) of law, of the fundamental norm, etc.[10]

There are obviously a great number of issues at stake here, among the most serious and difficult in legal theory. These can be approached from different starting points and analyzed in different ways. Indeed it is almost impossible even to formulate the questions themselves in a neutral manner without pre-judging the outcome.

There is one approach to our problem which seems the most simple and natural. It consists in looking at what constitutes the object of legal description. According to the Kelsenian analytical approach we are dealing for the most part with something called a legal norm or a legal rule. In fact these expressions describe little more than the existence of a problem. What does it mean to say that a legal norm exists, and thus that it can as such be known and described? A more pompous way of putting it is to say that we have a problem concerning the "ontic structure of the norm"[11] or that we are dealing with the ontological problem of the norm.

It is true that this approach is potentially the most direct, if not the

10 The link between these problems emerges in several papers presented at the Turin meeting (19 March 1967) on "*Essere* e *dover essere* nella scienza giuridica", in *Rivista internazionale di filosofia del diritto* XLIV (1967).

11 See for example Kalinowski, *supra* n.5, at 111.

simplest. But it is also potentially the most limiting, and may make the problem appear less complex than it is. Above all it risks hiding the fact that the analysis extends to include an investigation of the problem of method in legal knowledge (Hart is a good example of the merits and defects of this approach).

The problem of method is in effect the same problem viewed from a different angle, namely that of the method with which it is possible to produce acceptable legal knowledge. Clearly there is no way in which the methodological approach can avoid engaging with the object of cognitive jurisprudence. However there is clearly a need to tackle a whole range of rather complex and general philosophical questions, primarily those concerned with scientific method.[12]

These two approaches to the problem of legal description are not imaginary models. They in fact correspond to the two different ways in which the problem has been tackled by Anglo-Saxon legal theory and by continental European legal theory. Legal theorists in Britain and the United States were primarily concerned with explaining the object of legal discourse, to the point of occasionally forgetting to ask themselves whether they were dealing with descriptive or scientific discourse. Legal theory in the rest of Europe was primarily interested in comparing the so-called descriptive arguments of jurists with the scientific models put forward by contemporary epistemology.

In modern continental legal culture nowadays, the issue of legal science is certainly a vexed question and one which continues to exercise legal theorists and philosophers to no avail. Given that the problem of legal knowledge is an issue which is of great concern to legal philosophers on both sides of the Atlantic, it is impossible to give a convincing theoretical justification for the prevalence on the continent of the methodological approach. It is however possible to explain it sociologically, by highlighting the differences in legal reality which have made continental legal philosophers focus on the abstract methodological aspect of the problem. This can largely be explained by the considerable importance accorded to legal doctrine/dogmatics by law professors in

12 The two problems of object and method can be clearly separated if by object one means a raw fact, independent and pre-existing the application of the method. In any other view, an object becomes an internal object, produced or at least selected by science. Of course, many of the classical problems relative to the classical theory of knowledge and perception resurface in the philosophy of analytic science.

continental Europe. Jurists in continental Europe have always laid more emphasis on the purely intellectual dimension of legal knowledge. As compared to judges and barristers, law professors enjoy considerable prestige. The fact that judges are public employees rather than lawyers nominated after a distinguished legal career somehow diminishes their prestige in the eyes of legal academics. Precisely because they do not constitute a homogeneous group, barristers and judges, who represent the practical side of the legal profession, have less prestige. As we shall see, the situation is different in Britain and the United States. This fact might help to explain why the approach to the problem of legal knowledge is somehow different in these countries. As I am primarily concerned with theoretical rather than historical or sociological issues, I shall limit myself to some general observations. I refer those who are interested in the historical and theoretical aspects to Bobbio's *Teoria della scienza giuridica.*.[13] This, as well as providing a lucid account of the historical evolution of legal science, is also an important contribution to the theoretical debate.

Kelsen's classic contribution should be kept in mind as a background. It constitutes the background to nearly all the themes of recent legal philosophy. His propositions are a starting point and crossroads to the most important contemporary discussions.[14] I have previously mentioned, the reasons why analytic legal philosophers, who have been able to use the theory of levels of discourse, have made extensive use of Kelsen's ideas. Other authors, though moving in opposite directions, share a similar debt. Olivecrona, Ross, Wróblewski, Kalinowski (to mention some of the most important non-Italian Continental European scholars) have all dealt in depth with the problem of the method of legal science, producing remarkable monographs.[15]

When dealing with legal description, continental theoreticians keep in mind the method used in their countries, i.e. that of the positivistic legal

13 Turin: Giappichelli, 1950. Moreover, it is not Bobbio's first contribution on the subject, as he himself underlines in his essay, *supra* n.7, at 140.

14 On this particular point, see Amselek's criticism of Kelsen. P. Amselek, *Méthode phénoménologique et théorie du droit* (Paris: R. Pichon et R. Durand-Ausiaz, 1964), is enlightening.

15 Among K. Olivecrona's works, see *supra* n.3; among A. Ross's works, see *On Law and Justice* (London: Stevens, 1958); among J. Wróblewski's works, see *La normatività della scienza giuridica,* now in U. Scarpelli, ed., *Diritto e analisi del linguaggio* (Milan: Edizioni di Comunità, 1976), 325ff.; among Kalinowski's works see *supra* n.5.

science. They are fast at reaching the core of the question, the specific feature of legal positivistic descriptions which can be less easily reconciled with a method of scientific description. We are dealing here with the method by which they pre-select the matter to be described, the individuation of *legal* norms.

The crucial importance of this is evident in Kelsen's writings. Here is how Kalinowski sums up Amselek's criticism of Kelsen: "If legal science is to be positive [...] or, in other words, descriptive [...] it cannot deal with the problem of the validity of norms. Where would legal science find the distinguishing criterion between valid and invalid norms and remain a *descriptive* science without turning at the same time into a one which *values* and *regulates?*" [16]

Alf Ross in particular, and the Scandinavian realists in general, have given a clear and coherent answer, though critical of positivistic practice. Ross is also critical of Kelsen and maintains that for legal knowledge to be scientific, it must have a sociological knowledge of the effectiveness of norms. The Kelsenian thesis that legal norms exist (and can be described) if they are valid by reference to the criteria laid down by the basic norm (which in its turn must be effective) appears to Ross, at best, an indirect and difficult way of asserting the principle of effectiveness. The only principle able to ensure that legal knowledge takes social facts into account.[17]

Obviously, like any answer to the problems of science, Ross's answer looks both to the identification of the method and the object of the science. For Ross, the method which enables us to gain legal knowledge is the same empirical one as used for social sciences; its object is particular social phenomena, namely legal norms. He tackles the methodological question in *Law and Justice*, where legal science is defined as an empirical and predictive social science. He looks at the object of such a science mainly in *Directives and Norms*, where norms are defined as being social facts connected in unique ways by mean of effective prescriptions).[18] Ross is thus among the very few who have provided systematic contributions to the theory of legal description using both approaches.

While providing an answer to the problem of legal *knowledge*, Ross

16 Kalinowski refers to Amselek's writing quoted above, *supra* n.14 (Kalinowski, *supra* n.5, at 96).

17 Ross, *supra* n.15.

18 See in particular Ross, *supra* n.15, at 8, 9 and 10; *Directives and Norms* (London: Routledge and Kegan Paul, 1968), ch. IV.

and the others must also solve the problem of *legal* knowledge. That is the specific characteristics of legality. Within the framework of an empirical social science, such as Ross's cognitive jurisprudence would then become, the classical problem of the definition of the concept of law would be a much less crucial issue. It would then turn into problem of identifying a field of research, sufficiently homogeneous and useful for a unified explanation. Such field is easily identified by Ross, who uses an idea now firmly established within legal theory. Legal facts are the facts of *organised physical coercion* and of the norms which regulate them.[19]

The methodological solution given by Scandinavian realists like Ross is very attractive. It make use of an undoubtedly respectable scientific model and it seeks clarity and coherence for the principles which should inspire the description of law. To some however, the sociological model has a major drawback. Given legal science is, or should be, empirical, how then should the "description" presently produced by positivists be classified? One suspects that they should be set in the same category as astrologers and similar dubious characters who, though producing pseudo non-empirical science, still enjoy undeserved social consideration.[20] At the worst, therefore, positivist lawyers would produce ideological pseudo-description; at the best, they would produce — intermittently and unknowingly — empirical and sociological science.

So we encounter a feature at the root of many theories relating to the methodology of legal knowledge: the accusation brought against legal dogmatics and judicial jurisprudence that it produces ideology under the cover of a descriptive activity; of secretly prescribing (modifying the law) instead of scientifically limiting itself to a mere reproduction of the existing law.[21]

There are two objections against such a critical attitude. One is rather an attitude and the other is more of an objection proper. The first could be summed up in the blunt words of an Arabic saying: "Dogs bark and the caravan proceeds". In Bruno Leoni's more measured words:

19 Ross can therefore claim that he has extracted the good sense contained in the old philosophical questions and solutions concerning the concept and definition of law: *supra* n.15, at 7. For a history of how the problem has been dealt with, see N. Bobbio, *Teoria della norma giuridica* (Turin: Giappichelli, 1958), ch.V.

20 See my "Il giurista selvaggio. Un contributo alla metodologia della descrizione social", *Sociologia del diritto* 1 (1974), 85ff.

21 This represents the underlying link between the problem of legal knowledge and that of the nature of legal interpretation. See *infra* , at 333ff.

> A legal model is not some sort of dress which can be discarded and replaced by a simple act of will; in this respect, the less moderate defenders of legal modernism recall the sarcasms and disingenuous insults against lawyers' wickedness with which modern European literature is filled ...[22]

As to the second point, we can say that contrary to astrologers, lawyers show a certain degree of agreement, at least on the central part of their own descriptions. This leads us to conclude that they may be applying inter-subjective methods after all, though they may not be very rigorous. Many people think that such methods, though non-empirical, are at least socially useful, not for any disguised ideological function, but for what they allow to do openly.

2. *An Object-Oriented Approach; Hart's Theory of Legal Discourse*

In recent times, the most acute, vigorous, and influential defence of the traditional way of speaking of positivist lawyers is not to be found in the work of continental legal theoretician occupied with problems of method. Rather one may find it in the work of the well known English legal philosopher Herbert Hart. He deals with the question as one of identifying the object of legal discourse and about the definition of the concept of law. Hart's disregard for the problem of method (though necessarily this problem springs from his own concerns) is of such proportions as to leave us in doubt whether there is any significant room left for it in his theory. Hart's contribution to our problem is implicit. Nevertheless, his work has stimulated much discussion and has been the cause of many studies on the subject.

It is not by chance that the greatest modern British legal theorist uses an objectivist approach (the problem consists in identifying the object of the legal discourse). Neither is it by chance that Hart does consider some of the traditional "continental" problems relating to legal science, but only in as far as they can be translated in questions of what is the object of law. Finally it is not surprising that such an "objectivist" approach would result in a legal theory favourable, on the whole, to the traditional discourse of lawyers.[23]

Setting aside the theoretical reasons, we can see the reasons for this

22 B. Leoni, *Il problema della scienza giuridica* (Turin: Giappichelli, 1940), 167.

23 It is best to leave this vague and to clarify it later. On this particular point, at all events, I refer to my article "Hart e l'analisi del linguaggio", *Materiali per una storia della cultura giuridica* 1 (1979), 161-230.

in the fundamental differences, which we have referred to many times already, between Anglo-Saxon and Continental European law and legal culture. First of all, as we have already seen, the judge has a much more important position in the Anglo-Saxon legal world. It is commonly believed that there are two reasons for this. Firstly, appointment as a judge comes as the last and most coveted step in a lawyers's legal career. Secondly, the importance of law "made" by judges in *common law* systems. Obviously, these two facts reduce the relative importance of academic lawyers, the "legal scientists" and their straightforward descriptions of the law are not given much theoretical attention. Furthermore, complex historical reasons going back to opposition to absolute monarchy in Great Britain, mean that law is viewed in the Anglo-Saxon world as the *law of the land*. Thus, not as an arbitrary end product of the political sovereign but as an expression and a defence of society.

Though the role of statute law in Anglo-Saxon countries today is much the same as on the continent, lawyers' approach to the description of law tends to be different according to whether law is seen a product of will or as a social fact, however normative it may be.[24] We should therefore bear in mind the differences of the legal environment both in our look at Hart and in the whole of legal theory. An enquiry into the influence of a cultural environment should not of course be conflated with a judgment as to the value of a theory.

Within such limits, therefore, the importance and prestige of judicial law and the courts' normative practice explain the small amount of interest in the institutional image of the academic lawyers. In their intellectual activity in respect of describing law. It also explains, though it certainly does not justify it theoretically, the fact that the question of legal science is not among the common questions of Anglo-Saxon jurisprudence. So much so that the expression "*legal science*" sounds strange if not incomprehensible to the ear of Anglo-Saxon theorists and lawyers. Furthermore it means that the problem of method here (surely one which cannot be by-passed) is being disregarded.

It is the general idea of law as an existing and persistent element of social reality that partly explains Hart's attempt to present legal norms straightforwardly as social facts. As abstractions from social reality, as

24 A clear analysis can be found in N. Bobbio, *Il positivismo giuridico* (Turin: Giappichelli, 1979, 2nd ed.). Anglo-saxon thinkers hostile to *common law* are among those favouring the idea of law as an expression of will (Hobbes, Bentham, Austin).

social rules. In this way then we can see Hart's theory as a faithful interpretation of two real aspects of the Anglo-Saxon legal world.

To turn to a theoretical analysis. In *The Concept of Law*, Hart explains what is the *object* of legal discourse in two parts. Firstly, as everyone knows, Hart shows how Austin's theory is unable to account for legal facts. According to Austinian theory, law consists of commands generally obeyed by a social group and stemming from an authority (the sovereign) who generally obeys no one. If one succeeds in showing that law is not always a command and that the habit of obedience is not sufficient explanation of important aspects of legal life, then, Hart concludes, law can only be a social norm or rule.[25] To say a social rule exists, means the existence of a complex reality of behaviour and of interpretations of behaviour. It is not only the regularity of external behaviour, but a complex phenomena which Hart names the "internal aspect" of rules. This consists of critical reaction to any rule's violation. And that consists in the critical language used in disapproval, and eventually even stronger reactions (sanctions).

Secondly, he comes to the second stage of his own analysis of the concept of law, what is concerned in the identification of legal discourses. Hart distinguishes *legal* social rules from all other rules. Legal (juridical) rules, at least in the central case of law, are social rules belonging to an order or system containing both primary rules and secondary rules. That is an order provided with certain complex conceptual and institutional mechanisms allowing for the identification and the modification and application of the rules.[26] In consequence, legal discourse finds its object, law, when it encounters complex systems of social rules. At this point, it appears that the problem of method has also been solved and that, according to Hart, legal science is a description of social phenomena. For Hart adds that even rules which are not effective, but legal and valid

25 Hart speaks of *rules*: the word is the one normally used in current legal English and has been usually translated in Italian by "norma", or sometimes by "regola". Anglo-saxon legal theory has recently artificially redefined "*rule*" and has seen it as a category of "*standard*", with particular characteristics attached to it (see N. MacCormick, *H.L.A. Hart* (London: Edward Arnold, 1981), 40ff. In this essay I make no attempt to distinguish between "norm" and "rule".

26 H.L.A. Hart, *The Concept of Law* (Oxford: Clarendon Press. 1961), ch.V. Hart argues that such normative systems require certain institutional realities, such as, first of all, the presence of judicial organs and, further, that of legislators, police, etc.

because, belonging to a complex system, are still, because they are part of a system, on the whole, socially effective, part of social phenomena and maintain a "vicarious" life and effectivity. However, while we would have expected here a simple methodological explanation, what we find instead in *The Concept of Law*, is the well known description of the internal legal discourse. Of internal statements, typical of whoever accepts legal rules and uses them as criterion for practical judgement of his own and other peoples' behaviour.[27]

This internal discourse is contrasted with two kinds of external discourse. The extreme external discourse, according to Hart, tries to describe and explain social behaviour regulated by rules, without taking into consideration the norms and meanings stemming from them.[28] The non-extreme external discourse describes actions through the meanings given by the (legal) rules.

We thus have, according to Hart, three models of legal discourse (internal, extreme external, non-extreme external). Where can we situate the discourses used by positivistic lawyers to describe law (Hart among them)? It is surprising that such a sophisticated theorist as Hart should not even mention explicitly the problem. This can be partly explained by the special characteristics of the Anglo-Saxon legal environment referred to above, where judges accepting and applying the law draw all the attention of legal theorists.

However, the most acute recent Anglo-Saxon commentary on Hart, by Neil MacCormick, has noticed and explained the omission. MacCormick says:

> If there is any point of view which seems to capture that which the Hartian legal theorist as such must hold, it is surely this non-extreme external point of view depicted by Hart. He does, after all, describe himself as a legal positivist, taking as his ground for that the proposition that understanding a law or a legal system in its character as such is a matter quite independent of one's own moral or other commitment to upholding that law or legal system ... Hence, precisely what the legal theorist of Hart's school must do is take as his

27 I have dealt in depth with the notion of internal discourse in *Il metodo giuridico tra scienza e politica* (Milan: Giuffrè, 1976), ch.4.

28 Hart's observation is an implied criticism of extreme behaviourism. There remains some doubt as to the methodological meaning of such criticism, as well as of Hart's appreciation of P. Winch's work, *The Idea of a Social Science and Its Relation to Philosophy* (London: Routledge and Kegan Paul, 1958), one of the most acute attacks, in recent times, against the neo-empirical conception of social sciences (see *supra* n.26, at 288).

> standpoint that of a person who understands and seeks to describe legal rules as they are held from the internal point of view regardless of any commitment he himself has for or against these rules. ... to portray the rules for what they are in the eyes of those whose rules they are.

MacCormick calls this the *hermeneutic* point of view, clearly referring to a theological tradition which has been seen for some time in the social sciences.[29] He claims Hart is not coherent when making the description of rules dependent on the acceptance of rules necessary to the internal discourse.[30]

No doubt MacCormick is right when he says that Hart should accept that a descriptive knowledge of law is possible. Such a possibility being the condition of the possibility of any other positivistic legal attitude and discourse. This includes, as a further step, the internal attitude and discourse which is the full acceptance of the rules and legal order. "The cognitive element covers the very notion of a 'pattern' of behaviour" — a capacity to conceive in general terms behavioral patterns and real or imaginary facts as well as their relationship of "conforming to, not conforming to, or irrelevant to, the pattern."[31]

MacCormick's observations are important. They show that he is able to overcome the prejudices of Anglo-Saxon theory. He sees that the stage of legal knowledge is a necessary and problematic part of every legal operation.

However, MacCormick's specific solution is both right and wrong. He is right when he completes Hart's theory of law as social rule with a minimum of addition and modification, adding only a characterisation of the project as "hermeneutic".

That he is wrong stems from some very important aspects of positivists lawyers' descriptive discourse which, as we shall see, is nearer to discourses by which we make use of legal norms. It is therefore nearer to the Hartian internal discourse than to sociological description. Therefore, even though MacCormick is right in saying that Hart is, on this point, incomplete and ambiguous to the point of incoherence, that very incoherence is paradoxically a sign that Hart is closer to the complexity of the problem of legal description. There is no doubt that his mistakes have helped and stimulated the discussion on legal knowledge better than

29 MacCormick, *supra* n.25, at 38-39.

30 MacCormick, *supra* n.25, at 40. MacCormick refers to *The Concept of Law*, *supra* n.26, at 99.

31 MacCormick, *supra* n.25, at 33.

MacCormick's coherent and simple solution (a little too simple, perhaps) could have done.

Such complex and, at first sight, incompatible aspects of legal description appear clearly in the discussion that has developed on the continent and in particularly in Italy before and after Hart's book (*The Concept of Law* has acted as a powerful stimulus). The discussion has allowed a systematic look at complex questions which are hard to solve through the objectivist approach, however sophisticated it may be.[32]

3. *The Methodological Approach to Legal Description*

We now emphasise those characteristics of positivistic legal science which make it hard to find a place for it in social sciences, even among hermeneutic ones. These have been discussed in the methodological approach current on the continent in general and in Italy in particular.

In the short space of this essay, I shall deal with the questions raised conceptually rather than give a historical exposition of the discussion. Some authors have a different significance when viewed in the light of what followed. My procedure, however is not as arbitrary as it appears, when we consider the effective unity of Italian discussion on legal science. This is mainly concentrated in the writings and discussions of the so called "Turin School" which, in a relatively short time, grew up around Bobbio.[33] The central ideas in the discussion, to which I now turn, are the following:

(1) methodological description and prescription
(2) the theory of the basic norm
(3) the theory of effectiveness

It is no coincidence that the clearest statement of the first of these ideas is by Bobbio himself (even though it is not the first but actually one of the last contributions by Bobbio to our problem).[34] To the by now traditional

32 Anglo-saxon literature still ignores most of the continental literature on the subject, and totally ignores the Italian. On the other hand, in Italy MacCormick, Raz, Finnis and Dworkin are studied and even translated.

33 One should remember in particular the Turin meeting mentioned above (see note 10) and the IVR World Congress which followed in September 1967 (Milan and Gardone Rivera). Both these events had a great impact on Italian legal theory in the following years.

34 "Essere e dover essere nella scienza giuridica", *Rivista di filosofia* LVIII (1967), 235-62, reprinted in his *Studi sulla teoria generale del diritto* (Turin:

distinction between descriptive and prescriptive jurisprudence, Bobbio adds the symmetric opposition between *descriptive and prescriptive meta-jurisprudence*. Studies of jurisprudential methodology can try to prescribe an optimal model of jurisprudential discourse. Or, they can limit themselves to describing the way in which lawyers speak. Using this distinction, Bobbio shows us a time when meta-jurisprudence prescribed that the lawyer describe law and that he be a scientist at least in the first and unavoidable cognitive part of his activities (Kelsenian positivism). Bobbio also describes a more recent period when meta-jurisprudence goes on to describe what lawyers actually do and shows that lawyers secretly prescribe innovative interpretation even though they pretend to be limited to description.

Prescriptive Kelsenian meta-jurisprudence then, prescribes that the lawyer be a "pure" scientist and that he limit himself to description, even though the method is "*sui genereris*" (describing all and only the legal norms in force within a legal system). Whereas, according to Bobbio, realistic meta-jurisprudence which followed realises that lawyers do not limit themselves to describing. In particular, that jurisprudential interpretation, whether doctrinal or judicial, does not merely and positivistically ascertain meanings but "invents" them and "innovates".[35]

In this way Bobbio has transformed our problem, and shown it to be much more complex than a merely objectivist approach would reveal. The question here is not only to see the real nature of cognitive jurisprudence but to clarify, meta-jurisprudentially, the nature of its difficult relation with methodological questions. Once Bobbio has drawn our attention on the problem of the relations between meta-jurisprudence and jurisprudence, more radical difficulties appear than even those referred to by Bobbio. Thus, the very notion of "describing" a method becomes seen as highly problematic. What facts verify of falsify a given methodological description? Looking at the real world, we can see that certain common methodological practices can be considered as errors and deviations from the correct scientific practice. Or, they can be considered orthodox and used to affirm a different type of description. The scientific model thus "extracted from the reality" will vary accordingly. In the case of

---

Giappichelli, 1970), 139-73.

35 Here (*Studi*, *supra* n.34, at 174 n.11). Bobbio mentions L. Lombardi's fundamental work, *Saggio sul diritto giurisprudenziale* (Milan: Giuffre, 1975, 2nd ed.).

jurisprudence this will be particularly true of "creative" interpretative practices which are viewed by some as mere errors and by others as characteristics of the true legal method.

In short, every methodological "description" which goes further than just re-producing the history or sociology of science includes a prescriptive or redefining component. The model under consideration must actually exist and operate, but it must also be considered a model in respect of it own internal normative relations, and not only in respect of the way in which such relations are considered by its users (they might be wrong). This shows that meta-jurisprudence, in so far as it is normative and norm descriptive, meets with the same problems as does cognitive jurisprudence.[36]

With the help of these new conceptual instruments, we can now read Hart once more. It has been noted[37] that Hart may risk mixing up description with prescription *at the meta-jurisprudential level*. The risk would be of violating "Hume's law". I do not mean here in the banal sense that Hart might use his theory to conceal his political-practical choices as to the acceptance of legal rules (adoption of the internal point of view towards law). Rather, but in the more subtle sense, that Hart might to suggest acritically that the legal internal discourse, as he characterized it, would also be justified. Hart would then pass surreptitiously from describing the method in fact followed by contemporary lawyers to his own positive approbation of it. He would thus disregard, without giving any

36 See *Il metodo giuridico, supra* n.27, at 40. In the article quoted, Bobbio favours instead, with no further arguments, a descriptive metajurisprudence in the sense of one that only describes the social functions of jurisprudential activity. Jurisprudence, therefore, is said to be descriptive or prescriptive according to the social function performed (Bobbio, *Studi*, *supra* n.34, at 163ff.). In my opinion such a stance radically eliminates the normative component which is inherent in meta-jurisprudence as methodological discourse — though it is very difficult to grasp such a normative element in descriptive methodology. Bobbio argues instead:

> A descriptive meta-jurisprudence should limit itself to producing an inventory of suggested models and to explaining their historical and ideological reasons (*ibidem*).

However, we are still dealing with *models*. It will therefore be necessary, at the very least, to develop and describe their methodological internal prescriptions as such, not only as statistically recurrent habits. With this thesis, therefore, Bobbio abandons, in reality, the methodological discussion.

37 By U. Scarpelli, *Cos'è il positivismo giuridico* (Milan: Edizioni di Comunità, 1965), 85.

reason, the methodological aspect of realistic critics like Ross, who wish, in fact, to reform present jurisprudence. The fact that lawyers' make internal statements does not prove that those statements are good science.

Scarpelli's objection supposes, of course, that Hart's internal discourse has pretensions to being an empirical science. This is made irrelevant by MacCormick's correction to Hart where cognitive jurisprudence is only a non-extreme external discourse (which he calls hermeneutics). Because of Hart's methodological silence, it is difficult, if not impossible, to know whether jurisprudence is a discourse which must be approved of because it exists and has an important social function; or because, above and beyond its effective existence, it is itself based on the principle of effectiveness in as much as it describes norms as effective and represents therefore empirical description. In MacCormick's version, it should be noted, Hart's theory would not involve a methodological alternative to legal realism. This tends to turn cognitive jurisprudence into an empirical science. As "hermeneutical", Hart would simply be a better realist, more aware of the complexity of normative legal phenomena and of the necessity to explain them by referring to social norms.[38]

In MacCormick's revision also, Hart's theory meets with another objection, already referred to several times but clearly expressed mainly by Scarpelli. As we shall see, it concerns the selection principle or basic norm.

Leaving aside once more the history of the argument, we shall refer once again to Bobbio's *Teoria della scienza giuridica*. Here Bobbio has clearly and explicitly set the methodological problem within an epistemological framework which he defines as neo-empirical and even neo-positivist. Bobbio makes two points clear:

> [...] by science, we mean a system of propositions, the initial propositions and transformation rules of which are clearly defined, and which unfolds consistently with its premises and rules. Work will be scientific then, not so much for the *truth* that it embraces, but for the *rigour* with which it is carried out.[39].

38 Such appears to be Ross's opinion. Ross's instructive confrontation with Hart shows how Ross fails to pick up the ambiguous hints to the non-empirical nature of Hart's jurisprudence (of the internal discourse). See A. Ross, "Review of the Concept of Law", *Yale Law Journal* 71 (1962), 1189. Hart's previous criticism of Ross did not make the question any clearer than *The Concept of Law* (H.L.A. Hart, "Scandinavian Realism", *Cambridge Law Journal* 18 (1959), 233ff.).

39 N. Bobbio, *Teoria della scienza giuridica* (Turin: Giappichelli, 1950), 213-14.

Bobbio's second thesis is that contemporary positivist jurisprudence follows such a scientific model, at least in the "purified" version of Kelsen's theory. We can apply Bobbio's terminology of *Essere e dover essere* (1967) to Bobbio's *Teoria della scienza giuridica* (1950) without worrying about the changes of opinions which have taken place between the two works. We are then able to say that according to the 1950 Bobbio it is well possible to translate the methodological prescriptions of a neo-Kantian Kelsen into neo-empirical terms. Bobbio (1950) thinks that the resulting jurisprudence model is not radically different from the actual descriptive activities of positivist jurisprudence. According to the 1950 Bobbio, we are of course dealing with a science which explains by way of meanings, in this case the meanings given to legal norms, as do the advanced social sciences.[40]

It seems to me that it is this latter point that is important for our discussion and worth accepting, though not in its entirety. First of all however, we must critically examine Bobbio's thesis. Our criticisms will not take us in the direction of his *Essere e dover essere*. His theoretical stance there is such as to make any further contribution to the problem of the method impossible. He takes us into the history and sociology of jurisprudence.

Scarpelli had already put these criticisms forward and used them as a starting point for his own analysis. Hints of them can also be found in the text of *Teoria della scienza giuridica* itself, where they appear incongruous. For example, when Bobbio says that legal science is "a work *based on experience*, on legal normative propositions, aiming at understanding their meanings [...]".[41]

It is clear that internal rigour and consistency are not sufficient for neo-positivist empirical science.[42] If anything, rigour might turn it into a rational discourse (in the weak sense) but not necessarily into an empirical scientific one. For this, the discourse must indeed be based on experience. It is also true that the experience based process cannot be considered conceptually simple and free of problems. It is itself the product of application of principles, such as the verification or falsification principle. It is the reference to and the application of the *appropriate*

40 *Supra* n.39, at 134-35.

41 *Supra* n.39, at 201. Italics are my own.

42 Not all neo-empiricist agree, following the much discussed thesis of the conventionality of mathematics and logic, that such formal sciences need only internal rigour.

methodological principles, that turn a rigorous discourse into an empirical science.

Can we consider the tradition cognitive discourse of lawyers, or at least the Kelsenian model, not only rigorous but also empirical? Scarpelli's considerations are, it seems to me, particularly important. They are rightly directed against Bobbio's attempt to use rigour in order to obtain a scientific jurisprudence and thus assimilating it to the formal sciences. They stand against Hart's attempt to assimilate it to a type of empirical science. If, as we shall see, Scarpelli is right in considering that jurisprudence does not match any of those two models, there does not seem to be any room left to insert positivist science into a neo-empiricist epistemology.[43]

We thus reach Scarpelli's crucial consideration of the Kelsenian basic norm and the (perhaps) analogous Hartian conception of the rule of recognition. According to Scarpelli, positivist cognitive jurisprudence cannot be a formal science, because the lawyer studies the empirical facts constituted by positive law. On the other hand, it does not match the model of empirical science, because it cannot be said that its "field of enquiry [is][...] open to the linking of the events in question with any event, under any aspect relevant for the purpose of explanation [...]". The set of legal norms which jurisprudence studies is, instead "a totally privileged datum".[44] As far as this aspect is concerned, Scarpelli compares jurisprudence to theology.[45]

The above point means that, for Scarpelli, the pragmatic argument acquires a decisive strength. In another context one could not base a judgement as to the non scientificity of jurisprudence merely by saying that the its purpose is to provide practice with the necessary means to act. Here, however, Scarpelli can argue that he has shown that limiting legal cognition by means of the Kelsenian and Hartian fundamental norm can *only* be justified pragmatically. One can only explain the reason why so

43 Scarpelli, *supra* n.37, at 43.

44 *Ibid.*

45 MacCormick, *supra* n.25, also without knowing Scarpelli's work, uses a comparison with descriptive theology to help illustrate his own "hermeneutic" interpretation of Hart's internal discourse.

The problem of "relevance" and of the selection of the material to be described is given too restrictive an interpretation by Bobbio, who reduces it to the problem of antinomies ("Essere e dover essere nella scienza giuridica", *Rivista di Filosofia* LVIII (1967), 235-62).

many bizarre characteristics are attached to the discourse of lawyers by keeping in mind the social function that it performs.

Therefore, according to Scarpelli, cognitive jurisprudence supposes a practical (political) choice and has to be evaluated by reference to that choice. With great consistency, Scarpelli then goes on to state his own political choices on the subject, giving good reasons and with an explicit prescriptive meta-jurisprudence. It is better that such choice be made on the basis of specific criteria rather than contingently. Scarpelli opts for a political choice allowing the identification of a type of basuc norm able to safeguard positivist political values, which would include respect for constitutional and democratic principles.[46] For the time being, we leave unresolved the question of whether Scarpelli is thus innovatory in relation to the practice of today's positivist lawyers.

There is in these considerations a subtle criticism of Hart. The accusation, now, is not that of concealing political choice concerning acceptance or denial of law; Hart, being a good critical positivist, certainly does not hide that. The accusation is rather that of concealing the political nature of the legal description itself. Through his meta-jurisprudence, Hart would be guilty of producing ideology, encouraging contemporary lawyers to consider as "natural" and neutral any reference to a determinate concept of law, to certain kinds of fundamental norms or recognition norms, that is effective ones.[47] From noticing that a norm or an order are socially effective, to choosing to describe, let alone to accept them, there is, says Scarpelli, a logical jump. The same would be true even if positivist lawyers were already using this method of describing and were not aware of the existence of such a jump.

4. *The Principle of Effectiveness and the Concept of Law*

However convincing Scarpelli's considerations might appear, there is at least one paradoxical consequence flowing from them. If positivist legal "cognition" can only stem from a particular political choice, such cognition can certainly not be scientific and not even, I think, true cognition. Because it lacks the presuppositions with which I referred to at the beginning of the essay, Scarpelli's positivism appears self-destructive from

46 Scarpelli, *supra* n.37, at 149-50.

47 A criticism which Hart, in his objectivist approach, was bound to find hard to appreciate.

the very start. Any distinction between existing and imaginary law (for example, just law) would be impossible and the fundamental logical presupposition of positivism would collapse. Failing objective knowledge and objective description, how would Scarpelli be able to give a positive evaluation of fidelity to the positive (though democratic and constitutional) law ?

To help us clarify this point, we must examine the principle of effectiveness. This is, according to the majority of positivist theorists, Kelsen, Bobbio and Hart among them, an essential characteristic of law in force at a certain time and in a certain place (in the objectivist approach). While in the methodological approach, it is called a basic methodological principle of legal science. We can say from the start that the methodological approach to this question has the advantage of allowing dealing with a much wider range of problems than the objectivist approach, such as Hart's. From the very start, Hart defines norm (*rule*) as a social rule or norm and thereby is unable to consider the possibility of law as something socially ineffective.

Even in an objectivist approach, however, it is difficult not to realise that what common sense calls "rules" covers a wide range of things. These, as far as their existence is concerned, have only a few characteristics in common. The spectrum covered goes from the rule or norm which exists as a linguistic object, as an occasional prescription (the setting of an order), to the permanent slice of psycho-social reality in the case of rules followed for a certain time and place by a particular social group which feels them as binding.[48] Even in this latter case, we see a continuous range of cases (with which sociology and legal sociology are well acquainted) with varying degrees of the quantity and quality of "effectiveness", for example higher or lower effectiveness of declarations, emotions and external behaviour.

Legal sociology has no fundamental methodological difficulties when facing such differences of effectivity (see however *infra*). It takes into account the fact that the concept of effectiveness is vague, and that the boundaries might need to be defined more precisely with the help of the empirical explanation. In this case, it will produce new terms and concepts able to clearly put in focus the relevant degrees of effectiveness.

48 A. Ross's remarkable book (*supra* n.1), mentioned already many times, covers this particular problem. This particular aspect of Hart's theory (the *practice theory* of normativity) is also criticised by J. Raz, *Practical Reason and Norms* (London: Hutchinson, 1975), 53ff.

It will make free use of composite terms (effectiveness of declarations, behavioral effectiveness) or newly defined individual terms (artificially distinguishing, for example, between effectiveness and efficacy).

It is clear that contemporary positivist jurisprudence does not contemplate any such procedure. This is a strong argument in favour of Scarpelli's thesis that jurisprudence is not an empirical-sociological science and that the principle of effectiveness (*one* of the principles of effectiveness) can operate as a political principle for the selection of norms so that they can be accepted. Being a political principle, the principle of effectiveness becomes one of many such possible principles. An example of an alternative principle is the one which Scarpelli prefers. This is a rather generic principle of effectiveness completed and limited by the principles of democracy and constitutionality; the element of effectiveness in Scarpelli's concept of law is found in his reference to a *dominant* political will. Scarpelli then declares himself ready to accept and describe as legal any order representative of the expression of the dominant political will within a social group, if democratic and constitutional.

Hart's principle of efficacy should therefore also be considered as a political simplification. It is produced by the resolve, only justifiable politically, to look only and exclusively at some aspects of efficacy, i.e. normative declarations made by judges and meeting with the approval of the other citizens. Finally, it is obvious that political considerations could lead us to accept or reject a principle with natural law connotations. This, on condition that the principle concerned is semiotically "functioning". This is not the case with many natural law theories which trust, unwisely, to the discriminatory power and the inter-subjectivity of totally vague principles like the reference to a common sense of morality, and/or of principles unable to discriminate among moral choices unless hidden values are added, like reference to right reason.[49]

We can therefore face, within the legal field, partially different types of criteria for the identification of legal rules or, in other words, partially different *definitions of the concept of law.*[50] Such political choices cannot be of a totally free or arbitrary nature. When that description of legal

49 Kelsen's criticism of *these* naturalistic criteria is still valid. See "What is Justice?", in *Essays in Legal and Moral Philosophy* (Reidel: Dordrecht, 1973), 1-26.

50 See U. Scarpelli, "Il metodo giuridico", *Rivista di diritto processuale* 4 (1971), 553ff.; also *Cos'è il positivismo giuridico* (Milan: Edizioni di Comunità, 1965), 30.

rules that we call jurisprudence takes place, we cannot operate outside the generic area which common sense considers as the legal one. To avoid therefore misunderstanding as to the word "law", we keep within the context of social and effective rules, however vague that might be; or within the context of complex normative systems (including primary and secondary rules); or within the context of rules regulating the use of organised coercion.

As to the first stipulation, we can see that it is common to all positivistic theories; while the second one is specific to Hart; and the third one, it is that of Kelsen which is also accepted by Bobbio.[51] If we follow Scarpelli, each of these authors is correct in using one of those criteria for the identification of the approximate legal area. They are wrong however, in considering such procedure as precise enough to provide a clear-cut concept which might solve all the problems of the choice of an object for jurisprudence. It is only political reasons, according to Scarpelli, that justify the choice within the generically legal. This is also true of Hart's criterion, his particular redefinition of the principle of effectiveness which distinguishes the legal official's role from that of the citizen, requiring from the first a full acceptance and at least a passive one from the others. Hart's definition reflects his opinion as to the importance within the law of the actual practices of the judiciary. The fact that most Anglo-Saxon lawyers would make the same choice, would not change its political nature.[52]

It can be said therefore, that the methodological problems of descriptive jurisprudence lead Scarpelli to say that what law is (or better what are its exact boundaries) results from peoples' political choice. This does not thereby mean that jurisprudence becomes a creative art. Though defining what a law is a choice, the reality on the basis of which one determines a law presents no such choice. Furthermore, what we find are normative systems, which have their own internal system of connections and self-limitations. A somehow inbuilt structure which makes them resist arbitrary division.[53]

51 Bobbio, *supra* n.19, at ch.V.

52 Hart excludes from his theory any problem of the marginal efficacity of legal norms (in relation to his own criterion) since he considers as pathological situations where this kind of efficacity (from his point of view: of non efficacity) is socially relevant. As we shall see, such a device is not enough to avoid Scarpelli's criticisms.

53 For instance, using Hartian effectiveness as a criterion for the identification of

If Scarpelli is right (and on this point I think he is), Bobbio's well known view as to the two different meanings of positivism should be reconsidered and even turned upside down. Bobbio thinks that the word is used in two quite opposite senses: positivism as a scientific and neutral approach to law, and as an ideology favourable to positive law. He calls himself a positivist in the first sense and an anti-positivist in the second sense.[54] Scarpelli, on the other hand, would appear to be a positivist in the second sense and not in the first. But things are much more complex and the differences between Bobbio and Scarpelli are not so clear-cut, particularly so when we consider Bobbio's *Teoria della scienza giuridica.*

In the end, both authors accept (and rightly so, I think) a conception of the descriptive discourse of jurisprudence as one rigorously based on explicit premises. Bobbio is after all correct in basing the descriptions of jurisprudence on rigour alone, but wrong in considering it, for that reason, a science according to the model of neo-empirical science. Scarpelli is correct in holding that among the methodological principles of jurisprudence there is one which drives it to search for norms which exist *in rebus*, but on the basis of a pre-definition of the field of enquiry (law). The effect of this is that legal cognition is incompatible with the neo-empirical model; a model with which legal sociology agrees insofar it is free from any pre-definition. Provided we bear in mind this fundamental point, we can see that Scarpelli as well is not far from considering as a fundamental characteristic of any acceptable jurisprudence the internal rigorous consistency of a discourse based upon explicit principles.

Scarpelli's thesis gives a central role to a conceptual distinction, not quite so new in the positivist theory; that between the *definition of law* and the *basic norm* (or rule of recognition). The failure to apply this distinction consistently has lead to many problems in the theory of legal knowledge, in Kelsen and Hart, for example.

The definition of law is used to identify the concept of law, which is a

---

law, could lead to the inclusion among our country's (effective) legal sources, of legal precedent. We would then meet other rules, in particular basic norms, such as our Constitution, equally effective but implicitly or explicitly denying such sources any validity. The legal system itself would resist being changed through a definition. See *infra* in the text for some problems which this question raises.

54 In reality Bobbio is not against a moderate form of positivistic ideology. See N. Bobbio, *Giusnaturalismo e positivismo giuridico* (Milan: Edizioni di Comunità, 1965), in part. ch.V.

postulate of legal thinking. The expression is Kelsen's but, if Scarpelli is correct, he is wrong in referring it to the basic norm. The basic or fundamental norms are the fundamental norms which are eventually found in various places and times, on the basis of a particular chosen criterion. Kelsen is wrong when he fails to notice that in the area, vaguely delimited, of legality it is possible to make use of different legal definitions and end up identifying a *variety of fundamental norms* within the same legal situations.[55] We can take as an example Hart's concept of law. For Hart, law is a normative system made of primary and secondary rules fully accepted and actively followed by the officials of the order and at least passively by the other citizens, that is the other subjects of the system. Hart then identifies in the United Kingdom today a basic norm (or rule of recognition) which can be summed up as follows: "Whatever the 'Queen in Parliament' says is law" where "Queen in Parliament" indicates a complex procedure. Here we can, without contradiction, refer in the concept to the beliefs of the officials (the judges) who, in terms of the British basic norm, are subordinate to Parliament and therefore to law. Even although, what the law is looks, on the basis of the definition above, to be based ultimately on what they do.[56] This is not as strange as it sounds; the definition merely holds that judicial practices are the ultimate criterion for identifying the law, while the judges are not the ultimate authorities of the legal system. The way out of the conundrum, of course, is that the judges accept a superior authority.

In Italy, the same definition would naturally result in the identification of a different basic norm, which would be something like: "What the Italian Parliament enacts ...". In any case, one should point out that Hart's definition of law refers to a complex sociological fact, though apparently in his opinion, no particular research is necessary to prove it. The best way to highlight the importance of the distinction between the concept of law and basic norms is to compare the definitions of Hart and Scarpelli at the level of descriptive jurisprudence. Which is more successful at reproducing the cognitive practices of contemporary

55 This is Scarpelli's expression ("Il metodo giuridico", *Rivista di diritto processuale* 4 (1971), 533-554, reprinted in R. Guastini, ed., *Problemi di teoria del diritto* (Bologna: Il Mulino, 1980), 261-280).

56 What appears to be a vicious circle within the definition is not really so. In the first meaning, Hart refers to a sociological notion, the existence of people who carry on particular social functions; while in the second meaning he refers to judicial organs, which exist because of legal rules.

positivist lawyers?

One should not immediately assume that Hart is right because he makes us feel that he plainly considers his a description of lawyers' practices while Scarpelli considers his theory a meta-jurisprudential prescription. If we apply Bobbio's idea of different levels, we are forced to admit that it is possible for a methodological prescription to turn out to be very much consistent with the practice. Furthermore, applying the principle of efficacy to jurisprudence is different from applying it to meta-jurisprudence. It is obvious that a method (the description of norms) can be actually used without implying that the norms themselves need be effective. On the other hand, it is not so clear that a descriptive method based on the principle of efficacy (like Hart's) would be widespread among lawyers. The only logical connection between the two levels will be the following: where certain legal norms are described by lawyers, they will have at least a minimum degree of efficacy, if only in the form of cultural and academic influence.

Scarpelli's definition of law as the predominant will could turn out to be widespread among lawyers and in the jurisprudence, even if it adopts a narrow version of the principle of efficacy. It could indeed turn out that it owes its popularity precisely to that fact that it does so.

When looking the descriptive nature of Scarpelli's meta-jurisprudential thesis in respect of lawyers' practices, we must make a difference between his global theory and his positivist political choice. As far as the whole of his theory is concerned, it is clearly not restricted to positivism. That only represents *one* possible political choice within the theory, even if it is the one which Scarpelli prefers. For this reason, Scarpelli's theory crosses the boundaries of positivism, and should be considered as a more open kind of normativism. A normativism which is also able to comprehend non-positivist positions since they would be justified by other, equally legitimate, political choices. In fact, there would be various positivisms (like those of Scarpelli and Hart) each corresponding to the partially different positions often taken by Western contemporary jurists as to the exact limits of the legal field. Even outside positivism, Scarpelli's theory could account for alternative solutions among the main modern conceptions of law — positivism, realism and natural law theory — in their different versions. They could be justified, to be sure, but they should abandon their pretentions of being the only correct solution. Therefore, looking at the history of law, Scarpelli's theory, on the whole, appears to be better suited to account for the different actual jurisprudential practices.

If we forget Scarpelli's preference for a positivist definition of law, we can see that his theory does not require law to be a system. Neither does it posit the necessity of a basic norm nor that there should always be one only basic norm and one system in each situation. To clarify this point, we should also consider Scarpelli's choice to describe and accept law as a democratic and constitutional expression of the dominant political will. That is his positivistic choice of a definition of law. Obviously Scarpelli's positivistic definition presumes that law is a system where norms are produced and identified through meta-norms, and finally, on the basis of a basic or fundamental norm. Thus Scarpelli sees law only in situations where his definition allows him to identify order (systems). It would make no sense speaking of the constitutionality and democratic quality of isolated norms, and no sense at all speaking of positivism, were it not for such a "formal" ideology. This is so clear that even Hart's definition of law, though partially different, emphasises and presumes the systemic aspect of law, made up of primary and secondary norms, while law without all the characteristics of a developed order is *primitive* law.

So far then, the theories of Hart and Scarpelli reach the same conclusions, though through different paths. We can consider, because of their presumption that it is in the nature of law to exist as system, that they are kin to jurisprudential practices of lawyers and to contemporary Western laws.

One must note however, that Scarpelli has a hidden postulate which is absent from Hart. Scarpelli requires that the lawyer begin from above, that he starts from the basic norm, when identifying the system. In fact, the requirements of constitutionality and democratic quality imply that the validity of the individual norm depends (within the system) on the fundamental meta-norm. This is identified autonomously and is not the result of an "induction" from lower norms. Thus in the case of opposition between meta-norms as to source of law (constitutional norms) and lower norms the former prevail.

All this corresponds so well to the actual practice of lawyers that anything else seems otiose. Even Hart tacitly assumes a jurisprudence which operates in the same way. However, a consistent application of the criterion of efficacy in Hart's definition of law leads us to different conclusions. How can the meta-rule of recognition, which exists because it is effective in the way which Hart points out, be identified in a given situation? Given a meta-norm, we can certainly examine whether it is effective or not by looking generally at the efficacy of the norms produced on the basis of the meta-norm. But should deviant actions, that is rule-producing actions that cannot be derived from the meta-norm, be considered as legal errors or are they to be read as the sign of, and evidence for, the existence (efficacy) of an implied different meta-norm able to justify them? For example, a given meta-norm might exclude judicial custom as a source of norms. But should the fact that such judicial norms are followed be considered as a deviation (a mere fact) or an indication that the effective meta-norm in that legal system should be modified accordingly? In this respect, Scarpelli's definition is, it seems to me, much more successful. In other aspects also, it appears much closer to the jurisprudential practices of Western contemporary lawyers than Hart's, though the former aims at being a methodological prescription while the latter, probably, a description. What leads me, more than anything else, to this conclusion is the fact that lawyers never justify their choices by looking to the efficacy of the legal rule. Neither would they accept as a satisfactory argument, and one that would lead them to modify the object of their own jurisprudence, any demonstration to the effect that the legal system was not effective, even in the way which Hart requires. I will deal with this more closely when I come to distinguish two main uses of jurisprudence.

As has been said several times, many of the differences between Scarpelli and Hart can be better explained in the context of the difference between Italian and British cultural and legal circumstances. On the one hand law is seen, through historical-juridical factors, more as a will and command from above than a social reality rising from the bottom. On the other hand in my country less prestige for law, less unity in the legal class and also (perhaps) less efficacy in the norms encourage a sceptical and problematical conception of the efficacy of the norms described by jurisprudence.

5. *Analytical Legal Theory Beyond Positivism*

With Scarpelli, fundamental differences within cognitive jurisprudence are, for the first time, included in a meta-jurisprudential theory molded on the normativistic paradigm. This can only occur when three conditions are fulfilled: 1) the "scientist" jurist must still be a jurist, he must still operate in the legal field as generally and generically identified; 2) he must still be a "scientist", in however weak a sense, which means that the material identified through the criterion of selection should be described through the proper and constant (rigorous) application of the criterion; 3) he should avoid applying an ideology at the meta-jurisprudential level, by excluding the acceptance of partially different definitions of law and justifying this exclusion by pseudo-scientific arguments rather than by political reasons. justified pseudo-scientifically and not politically.

The first condition is the most obvious one. It simply forbids any abuse of the conventional definition technique, of common sense and ordinary language when using the word "law" otherwise than in its common or approximate meaning.

The other two conditions are more important. There is at least some doubt as to whether Scarpelli fully accepts them. They are necessary, however, to the development of his thesis. It helps to prevent the self-destruction of his positivism which could follow the failure of an objective and internal knowledge of the law. By accepting them, I think that we also take a step further than Scarpelli. For they suggest that it might be useful, if not necessary, to qualify as descriptive and cognitive those operations of jurisprudence which we intend and must keep separate from the jurisprudential practice of the application of norms. This concerns in particular the operations required to fulfil the second condition, which ensure the internal rigour of the discourse. These operations concern not only the consistent application of the assumed criterion but also the correct application of norms identified *in rebus*, by means of the appropriate logical and empirical operations.[57]

In such a case, we can indeed say that, in an important sense, one who describes the norms is neutral in respect of them. Such description in fact, far from implying that they are accepted, is, on the contrary, a logically necessary condition to any ethical attitude to them; whether that be of acceptance, disobedience or indifference. If it is true that legal science is pragmatically in the service of jurisprudential practice, it is also true that this does not always and necessarily coincide with a jurisprudence which accepts a law thus described.

The third and last condition is necessary to avoid a more subtle and insidious surrender of values by cognitive jurisprudence. That of whoever argues that resorting to a specific definition of law results from an operation scientifically necessary and not from choice. Such a condition

57 I have described in more detail these kind of operations in *Il formalismo giuridico* (Milan: Giuffrè, 1980).

looks a little strange. Could the positivist lawyer not be able to fulfil it and carry on as before? Perhaps, he would only have to add his own description as an introduction, a sort of cautionary formula reading: "My conception of law is the following ... the others can do as they please" In this case methodological analysis or legal science, will end up by endorsing, in an extremely and uselessly complicated way, the existing practices of positivist jurisprudence. Scarpelli has certainly been misunderstood in this sense.

This however, underestimates the innovative scope of Scarpelli's theory, in relation to positivist practices. Such innovation concerns precisely the conditions at which a lawyer is able to claim to be totally neutral with regard to his own descriptions. For this to happen, an attitude is necessary which is scarcely widespread among contemporary lawyers. In short, they should be aware and be able to give an account of the assumptions which they used in their descriptions of the law. They should be aware that in the same legal situation it would be possible to make other assumptions. There could be widespread consensus among lawyers belonging to a particular culture as to what these choices (of the concept of law) are, but dissent will occur more frequently at the margins.

In our legal culture, for example, there is widespread controversy as to whether, under certain conditions, certain moral principles are or are not juridical. The same is the case for some social rules, customs and desuetude, above all, and for certain semiotic techniques, mainly interpretative techniques. Scarpelli's theory allows the lawyer to account for the various possible and actually existing attitudes in respect of this and other things, while still remaining neutral.

Through this Scarpelli's theory acquires a scope which was already implicit in his thesis and which goes beyond positivism. However, before the Scarpellian jurist can be said to have adopted a neutral and scientific attitude, we must develop the theory on one last important point. For Scarpelli's "scientific" jurist is wholly dependent on practice in the sense that his particular (re)definition of law can *only* be justified by reference to the particular fundamental norm which he has identified in order to adhere to and approve of it. We must now see what other justifications there are for a scientist of law (without inverted commas) for using of Scarpelli's descriptive jurisprudence in spite of being "cold" or perhaps even hostile not only towards the norms so described but also towards the definitions of law adopted.

The first answer is obvious. The most important pragmatic

justification for the existence of a jurisprudence is that it gives people a description and a knowledge of legal norms which they can then use practically. The jurist says to the world: "(given this definition of law) here are the legal norms which can be object of judgment and practical choice". Scarpelli's theory contains several arguments which can be expanded to a range of measures allowing to overcome this author's suspicions as to the politically compromised nature of this description. For legal practical choices are only constricted by jurisprudential description in so far as such description is not kept open and it selects dogmatically the norms which it describes on the basis of a specific definition of law — which is not the only possible one; if the description, that is, is based without reasons on a discriminating political hypothesis or on the dogmatic selection of a special level of effectiveness, while a different kind of effectiveness or political hypothesis could have been reasonably used as a governing principle of the description.

For example, cognitive jurisprudence can serve an individual wishing to adopt a practical, though not necessarily favourable, attitude in the face of legal norms produced by a predominant political will which operates through the forms of a modern constitutional state; or the face of the effective legal norms produced by the courts[58] or even in front of norms supplemented by respect for certain moral principles. The enormously complex description that will follow will not carry any *necessary* acceptance of the norms so described, either by the describer or by the user of the description. At this point, we can recall our initial story of the undisciplined driver. Those who describe norms and those who, as a

58 Less common criteria and definitions of law with stronger political elements are those proposed, in past years in our country, by a group of self-styled "progressive lawyers". Such criteria consist of a peculiar mixture of effectiveness and political values and generated descriptions of law made under the assumption that pacts made at the national level between unions and representative of employees have the force of law; the results were called an *inter-union legal system* (see on the subject G. Tarello, *Teorie e ideologie nel diritto sindacale* (Milan: Edizioni di Comunità, 1972, 2nd ed.).

Whoever engages in such open attempts to twitch the predominant legal conception to obtain specific results, will at least have to take the common conception into consideration, in order to obtain some of the effects aimed at. Whatever their success, the predominant conception of law persists at least as one factor of legal reality, together with the other marginal conceptions of law circulating in jurisprudence and practice and all vying for influence on the legal mind and behaviour.

consequence, come to know them, can sometimes be "bad men"[59] only preoccupied by how better to break those legal norms and to get off scot-free. Or else, they can be reformers, or even revolutionaries, intent on changing those legal norms either by methods which the norms themselves consider as admissible (legal reform) or which the norms consider as inadmissible (legal revolution).

In short, such descriptions are pragmatically justified by the fact that law can be viewed as a reason for action, do not require acceptance of the law thus described. It is legal norms' and legal orders' primary function to act as elements of possible argument aiming at justifying choices of action (reasons).[60] It should be noted that the discourse of justification is an abstraction which can also be applied *a posteriori* to actions of people unaware of the norms or reasons in question. Reasons, therefore, are not necessarily psychological motivations which are effectively behind people's actions.[61] This means it makes sense to criticise or qualify actions, by reference to norms, *objectively*, in as far as it is opposed to subjective awareness, on condition that the norms themselves do not require the agent's awareness — as is the case in many ethical systems but few legal systems. This means that we can attribute to actions normative meanings other than those given by the agent. We can, for example, qualify and condemn as crimes acts performed by people unaware that they are violating the very legal norms on the basis of which we condemn.

As we can see, we are now using Kelsenian terminology, though with a different meaning. The law gives "objective" meanings because any set of reason, and therefore of norms, gives objective meaning in the sense seen above, i.e. in the sense of a meaning not necessarily known to the agent.

A description of legal norms (according to the chosen redefinition of law) can therefore be used to accomplish such an objective operation, to estimate those norms as possible reasons for justifying actions, one's own

59 Hart, *Concept, supra* n.26, at 39 and 240.

60 Raz, in an attempt to iron out some of the problems in Hart's theory, has developed a similar conception of norms, as particular types of reasons. Raz rightly links his own conception of norms as reasons, with a criticism of Hart's thesis to the effect that legal norms are always social norms (see *supra*, n. 49). Bound to the object approach as he is, Raz does not totally realise how the two conceptions of normativity correspond to two types of discourses about rules: sociological description and practical justification.

61 On this, my *Formalismo giuridico*, *supra* n.57, at 86ff, elaborating on Raz's ideas.

or somebody else's. The same is true of any group of norms or rules. Obviously, objectivity does not imply at all that such norms should necessarily be accepted. What matters only is an intellectual commitment, the fact of *temporarily* considering those norms and not others.

There is a relation between the fact that a description of law is to be used in practical choice and the sort of definition of law which is normally used as a basis for this description. Quite naturally, those who deal with descriptions of legal norms for the purpose of practical evaluation, simplify the definition of law by the introduction of simplifying political elements. This is the only way in which we can explain Hart's cavalier treatment of the criterion of efficacy. He reduces the principle of the effectiveness of norms to a clean and simple criterion, norms followed and accepted by officials. At the same time all variations, vague elements and connections, are consigned to the residual category, the "Pathology of Legal Systems".[62]

The essential point is that Hart's use of "pathology" is far more clear-cut than a truly sociological description of law would allow. The only instance in which a phenomenon could be defined as pathological within an empirical description-explanation, would be when stating that it is "extremely rare and near to radical changes brought in by the characteristics already mentioned". And indeed, this is what Hart's examples of pathological legal situations would seem to suggest. They are examples of a country on the point of collapse and in a state of anarchy or civil war. But these examples deceive. Hart's concept of efficacy, as defined, sets very demanding requirements. Consequently, it is much easier to find non efficacious rules and legal systems in Hart's sense than he himself seems to think, even in much less dramatic situations than the social chaos of Hart's examples.

For instance, Hart's concept of law would be problematic, seriously applied to the present Italian situation. In fact, there is a risk that any situation where there were significant differences between officials behaviour and their various normative declarations would have to be called pathological according to Hart's definition, a situation where no (single) legal system exists. The same would be the case for situations where officials and citizens and various groups of officials have a pattern

62 The political criterion, which Scarpelli suggests, is equally clear-cut. He refers to the predominant political will, democratically and constitutionally interpreted, well aware that it is a political ideology, with a relatively clear-cut prescriptive content but a much more uncertain social effectivity.

of behaviour considerably different from that set in official legal norms. As I find it difficult to believe that the efficacy of legal norms in Italy today is radically different from the UK, Hart's concept of efficacy of a legal system would then lead us to conclude that such situations are pathological and lacking a legal system. This is absurd. Hart's concept of efficacy becomes plausible if we forget most of its sociological pretensions. It can primarily and more easily be justified when used to identify a very particular area of effective norms, say effective in courts' or other "official" organs' official statements. It is useful for practical choices rather than for sociological descriptions.

Scarpelli clearly see that jurisprudence is not a free-standing discourse and should, first of all, be used for the description of legal norms for practical judgment. It is therefore an auxiliary descriptive discourse, in respect of the practical (ethical, political economic, etc.) evaluation of the hidden "political manifesto" which is part of the particular criterion of identity at the base of jurisprudential description.

This is why it is helpful to use a, by now, widespread terminology, and paraphrase Hart by calling the type of normative description provided by jurisprudence, *internal description*. It can be considered a model of science *sui generis*, to be used whenever there is a need to describe and to know the norms "from the inside", i.e. to use them in practical judgment. The description is called "internal" as a reminder that it is nearer to the central instance of Hart's internal discourse (the full acceptance of norms) than to the central case of Hart's external discourse (legal sociology).[63]

There is one more lesson that Hart can teach us. It appears in his writings as an ambiguity to be clarified by adding methodological considerations to the objectivist approach and by applying Bobbio's and Scarpelli's distinctions to it. The lesson is about the relations between internal description (cognitive jurisprudence) and sociology of law. What can these relations be? I have confined myself, up to now, to emphasising that they cannot be relations of identity. I believe that Scarpelli is correct in maintaining that internal description is not a social empirical one, at least according to the empiricist model. Let us be clear that we are not trying to establish new relations. These already exist. They have been strengthened through the practice of legal culture and have produced remarkable results. One should remember that when speaking of relations between descriptive jurisprudence and empirical sciences, the latter expression should be given a wide meaning and to include not only

63 MacCormick, *supra* n.25, argues for this view.

the relatively recent discipline of *sociology of law*, but also *legal history*.

These disciplines are all about law. But often they consider that the problem is only about finding an object ("the law") and not about clarifying the relation between perhaps different methods of description. The relation, that is, between a description such as it has been traditionally provided by jurisprudence (mainly positivistic) and a sociological and historical description. We need a deeper analysis of these relations and not arrogant "legislation" on the subject. This task is not as simple as it looks. On one hand, sociologists and historians have too often been satisfied with formulas which are clearly metaphorical. Most are not analytical in the least, like those which separate official from non-official law or formal from non-formal law[64]; or law in books (on paper) from law in action (real)[65]; these are purely "objectivist", that is they neglect to say how these object must be handled, the problem of method. The distinction between the empirical science of law from metaphysical knowledge is little better. The latter obscure formula should be generally interpreted as a criticism of the legitimacy of jurisprudential description.[66]

On the other hand, while using hurried formulas when pointing to the object of legal description, empirical scholars of law sometimes take for granted the monolithic nature of jurisprudence, at least of the modern positivistic version. I hope that our discussion in these pages has shown that this is not true. If it is true that the concept of law is both complex and variable, this should not allow for any short and simple reference by empirical disciplines to a "formal law" or a "lawyers' law", which is often a fundamental starting point to their explanations. Nevertheless, such empirical explanations work very well. For example, legal sociological work is often based on the difference between an effective law and a formal law, a highly instructive difference at the sociological level.[67]

64 See for example: J. Kurczweski, "Due dimensioni del diritto: diritto positivo o intuitivo e diritto ufficiale o non ufficiale", *Sociologia del diritto* III (1976), 29-49. This article contains a clear exposition of the sociological theory of the existence of different levels of legal effectiveness (at 36).

65 R. Pound, "Law in Book and Law in Action", *American Law Review* 44 (1910), 12-36.

66 M. Weber, *The Methodology of the Social Sciences*, trans E. Shils and H. Finch (New York: Free Press, 1949). He distinguishes between the objective and formal logical determination of law which jurisprudence deals with and the study of human actions, which is the object of sociology.

67 As a recent example, one should consider the description and the explanation of the way in which "formal" norms on succession are being replaced with

Other examples can be taken from legal history. Here the particularity of, and the change in, law are often explained through the idea, not further clarified, of the inability of formal law adequately to reflect changing historical conditions. How is this possible?

Methodological difficulties cannot be avoided by the sceptical device of claiming that empirical scientists should limit themselves to seeing as mere facts the pseudoscientific opinions predominant among lawyers. In reality, historians and sociologists often manage to exploit as a powerful mean of explanation, not only the internal *inconsistencies* of law, but the internal inconsistencies in the descriptive jurisprudence relative to a legal situation. It seems evident to me that in order to reach such results, empirical legal scientists must also be able to *use* the criteria which inspire jurisprudence. This means a capacity of describing, understanding and finally applying the principles from an internal point of view. While this does not require that such principles or norms be actually accepted, it cannot correspond to the simple acknowledgement and description of the actual predominant or common application of those principles. In the latter case, the historian and the sociologist would have to abstain from observing that the correct applications of an interpretative technique do not match the interpretation advocated by jurisprudence. They would have to confine themselves to the actual predominant application and to the actual principles proclaimed, and that is exactly what they do not do. To reject the possibility of objective control of the internal description and to maintain that all that is possible is the sociological description of current opinions about this correctness is a clumsy way out.[68] Logically, any sociological description implies the possibility of an independent use of the criterion of correctness, which can only be identified through an internal description. Sociologists do this all the time, they describe widespread beliefs and opinions and claim that these are consistent or inconsistent with other beliefs and opinions, or with *systems* of beliefs and opinions. This is called "cognitive dissonance", a powerful explanatory tool.

However, the difference between internal description of normative relations and sociological explanations of opinions based on such relations

---

norms with a different content, in V. Ferrari, *Successione per testamento e trasformazioni sociali* (Milan: Edizioni di Comunità, 1972).

68 See for example the rather specious distinction between correctness (in the application of criteria internal to the law) and truth (of sociological statements about legal opinions) made by K. Olivecrona, *Law as Fact*, *supra* n.3, at 259ff.

is of the greatest importance when dealing with a complex legal system. This is because the opinions of the users are only relevant to the internal description of normative relations within a legal system when they are made relevant by a rule of the legal system itself; for instance the opinion of judge and jurors in a trial are relevant, my own private opinions are not. On the other hand, popular opinions about the law are obviously important facts for any sociological description of it.

As a consequence, reference to "formal" jurisprudence within sociological and historical discourse can only be retained with its full explanatory potential, when objective criteria allowing to identify it and control it "from the inside" are used and understood by the sociologist himself. He must be able to understand how, and if, the jurists are playing at their own game.

Furthermore, an "open" internal description of the law that admits, as advocated above, the possible coexistence of varying conceptions of law and thus of varying internal descriptions of the same situation, could be a useful tool for the sociologist or historian of law. On one hand he will have to account for the fact that in any normal society there exists a dominant and prevailing conception of law, to the point that such a conception can be presumed by legal systems. This is certainly the case with a rather generic positivist conception which prevails in our contemporary Western societies. Any would-be legislator knows that he can and must rely on this "prejudice" shared up to a point by officials, judges, and "normal" citizens in his society. Shared conceptions of what the law is are a powerful and basic factor of the effectiveness of the law itself. It is necessary for sociologists and historians to refer implicitly to such a conception when speaking of *a* formal law and *a* jurisprudence in the attempt of describing its social causes, effects and features.

On the other hand, it will be also useful for the empirical scientist (sociologist or historian) to refer to internal descriptions based on definitions of law partially diverse. Alternative, or marginal conceptions of the law are social factors as well. Usually, the empirical scientist already knows that, though he might not fully grasp all the implications. Taking these facts into account in a formal framework is made easier by the open normative theory which I have been formulating here.

Of course, sociologists and historians as such will be less interested in testing the consequences of accepting various political-juridical hypotheses than showing what legal norms there are and what is their level of effectiveness. As we have seen before, when the internal description is used for practical-political aims, there are reasons for preferring more clear-cut definitions of the concept of law. The historian and the sociologist on the contrary, will often have to use concepts of law which are vague and complex, as well as more variable, for their explanations.

In fact, the sociologist and historian often refer to different concepts of law, and often explain historical and social phenomena by emphasising the difference between legal norms and systems existing at various levels of effectiveness in the same situation. Frequently, for example, a significant difference can be discovered between the norms which actually determine officials' legal decisions and those which govern their external behaviour.[69] No doubt this is a normal and important practice in history and in sociology of law. It seems to me, that it can only be analyzed as a comparison between internal descriptions of rules and related practices assuming partly divergent definitions of law (for instance, formal "official" law vs "unwritten" law, and so on). These descriptions are actually based on partially divergent definitions of law, which refer to different "places" in the same society where law can be found, that it to different levels of effectiveness. While in a stable society a common core of effective legal rules will certainly be effective at most levels of effectiveness, marginal differences will probably be found at different levels of society and behaviour, concerning both the precise configuration of the fundamental norms (say different conceptions of the Constitution) and the status of single legal rules (say about the enforceability of blatantly unjust or useless or desuete laws). Whether these differences should be identified with more or less precision by the historian and the sociologist will depend on the explicatory requirements of the empirical discourse in each situation. In fact, in this particular case, the internal discourse is merely a tool for an historical or sociological explanation. In some cases, distinguishing between official and un-official law will suffice, say, to the sociologist, in other case, say, the legal historian will have to distinguish between rules determining what the judges do and what they say they do, what the police actually does and so on. He will have to describe the social existence of different ideologies of law.

Therefore, that jurisprudential description is based on a (partially)

69 The sociologist also has to specify what "following" the norms and norms "governing" actions mean to him. In other words, he has to provide the conditions of verification of the sociological propositions where such phenomena are dealt with.

variable concept of law does not diminish its utility for historical and social description. So called "normative facts" (i.e. rules) are a very elusive and complex phenomenon. There is a persistent uncertainty as to the sort of reality or factual existence that they might possess, and this suggests that it is varying, and refers to partially different facts; rules might be thought to exist when they influence either decisions, or emotions or external behaviour, or all of these.[70] Such variation is not due to a defect of the theory, but is itself a social fact of great importance in the explanation of social rules. It is in fact often used. Thus, a phenomenon according to which legal norms with "full" effectiveness in a group, can, after a certain time, end up by being effective only at a certain level of social reality, for example only in public decisions. I am merely trying to analyze these common aspects of historical and sociological explanations of law.

To conclude these considerations on the utility of internal descriptions of norms for empirical sciences of law. It must be said that the empirical scientist will sometimes find a legal internal description based on a "political" criterion equally useful. In fact, normative ideas or ideologies in the legal arena will be relevant and socially influential factors in themselves.

My examination of the problems inherent in the theories of legal science, so far has led me to support a conception of legal description that could be characterized as a non-positivistic "open" normativism. I believe that the resulting theoretical framework helps in the task of comparing different conceptions of law and, at the same time, might be useful to do away with some common inconsistencies internal to these theories, for instance in Hart' s theory of the existence of a legal system.

Bobbio's distinction between meta-jurisprudential prescription and description allows us to try and untangle the knot of often ambiguous questions concerning what jurisprudence does, should do or can do. The field of jurisprudential studies certainly consists in a bizarre jumble of empirical knowledge and logico-semantic operations, most strangely defined; a hotch-potch which cannot be reduced to a neo-empirical science, whether empirical or formal. Once it is accepted that cognitive jurisprudence, as internal normative description, need not be a science in the sense of the empirical or formal sciences, the question appears easier to solve. Cognitive jurisprudence can still be said to produce a description

70 See Ross's lucid analysis of T. Geiger's notion of normativity (Ross, *supra* n.1, at 81ff.).

which is neutral in the face of the opposing value-choices of giving and refusing allegiance to a legal system, and which can be controlled through objective procedures, that is arguments which produce a common core of identical results even when used by different persons.

I now turn to the two main objections to such use of internal description both in practical reasoning and within empirical explanation. They occur nowadays in sceptical theories of interpretation and normative system. As internal descriptions describe meaning relations, interpretative scepticism would make them impossible.

These are expressed by the sceptical theory of the semiotics of prescriptions and scepticism towards normative (legal) systems. The first is sceptical as to the inter-subjective nature of the meaning of legal language, claiming that it is very difficult to *describe* normative meanings, i.e. norms or rules, neutrally and at all objectively. At its most extreme, the theory would claim that in respect of the meaning of norms there could be no description. There could only be attributions of normative meanings and arbitrary, even if statistically widespread, opinions as to the content of law. The thesis of extreme interpretative scepticism is one paradoxical to the point of impossibility.[71] If normative meaning cannot be "read" relatively univocally, then the possibility of any prescriptive language functioning as a non-illusory guide in practical reasoning is destroyed from the start. This will be true not only of legal norms, but of any type of rule. If the normative internal description cannot be carried out with a certain degree of inter-subjectivity, then any description of norms for the purpose of justifying actions in general and in the abstract, becomes impossible and practical reasoning would become an illusion entirely delusive. Moreover the attribution of meaning itself is, in general, a normative operation made possible by following linguistic norms. Thus, where the knowledge and the description of norms is not possible, then the attribution of meanings is not possible either. There can be no criteria to judge linguistic use.

Such considerations do not of course mean that "legal formalism", an old-fashioned group of theories of meaning and interpretation, widespread among positivist lawyers, should be supported. They should be rejected not so much on the grounds that there is no *literal meaning*, but because such meaning is never clear-cut and never stems from a "natural" relation between words and things. Rather it comes from the way words are used

71 A criticism, in my opinion conclusive, can be seen in Hart, *supra* n.26, at ch.VII.

normatively within the linguistic community in question. All the same, even if this semiotic theory common among lawyers is wrong on this important point, their interpretative practices might, at times, be acceptable. To know how to do something and to know what one is doing are often two very different things.

Those who criticise positivist jurisprudence are, in any case, right in pointing out that very often the results of the interpretative activity of legal "scientists" is not proven by the "theories" (i.e. rules) of interpretation which they claim to be following. Often, theories of interpretation hide interpretative operations which are not admitted to.

I think that internal descriptions of the "open" variety illustrated here are particularly suited to approach those problems as inter-normative relations and not as mere facts alone, i.e. as psycho-sociological events which either go beyond jurisprudential description being instances of bad jurisprudence, or, indeed, show the illegitimacy of the entire jurisprudential description, as based on lawyers' metaphysical beliefs. It can account both for differences among marginal "theories" of interpretation held by individual lawyers and for differences among widespread and influent "theories" of interpretation which are, by themselves, important factors in legal life. Such differences amongst various interpretation "theories" within the same legal situation can be accounted for and described as partial differences in the concepts of law, constitutive of the (variable) postulates of jurisprudential "internal" normativistic description.

Such descriptions, as we have seen, can have two main functions. They can describe consequences of adopting various "theories" of interpretation in order to allow a practical-political attitude towards the rules thus interpreted. Or, they can describe the rules of interpretation effective at different levels of social reality to help social and historical scientists in their work. This may not be reassuring for lawyers in search of simple certainties, but at least it is realistic. Such divergences occur in our societies and are powerful social and political factors.

As far as differences between "theories" of interpretation and individual attributions of meaning are concerned, they can be described perfectly well by the method we have called the "internal normativistic" description of law. With this problem, we reach the second objection, scepticism as to the existence or relevance of legal systems. This thesis claims that law by itself has no order at all, that a legal "system" is just a set of disordered rules and practices. As against this objection, it is necessary to show how the post-positivist "open" internal description is able to deal with the relation between meta-norms and norms in a non-ideological way. It must be able to develop a *theory of the normative system*.[72] As I have said above, the main specific difficulty of such a theory is that the meta-norms are sometimes implicit or partially implicit or very vague, and must therefore, be "induced" of "filled up" by mean of their assumed applications. When dealing with a somehow unusual decision, how can we distinguish an unusual interpretation, representing perhaps the only case of application of an implicit meta-norm, from an error of law, where the decision is considered as invalid (not justified by any meta-norm of the legal system)? This doubt is particularly frequent when we deal with an unusual interpretation of a legal text. How can we know whether it is a case, perhaps the first ever, of application of a particular implicit meta-norm or it is a wrong interpretation unsupported by even implicit meta-norms within the system? Ground-breaking precedents in the common law have often raised these sorts of doubts and controversies.

Only an "open" internal description can fully account for the complex and sometimes uncertain relation between meta-norms of interpretation and norms which are a result of interpretation. They do so by recognizing that marginally different conceptions of law are around, each striving to prevail. For the purposes of sociological and historical explanation we must take into account all of them, for purposes of practical choice we must choose one of them, if we wish to be consistent.

An open internal description of legal rules can do this in particular through the fundamental distinction between a concept of law and the rule of recognition. This distinction applies also to the problem of interpretation. The more general parts of a conception of interpretation will usually be an essential part of the definition of law which a lawyer assumes as postulate. In this case, these parts of a "theory of interpretation" rather than being something which is found in the law, are something through which the law is found.

Whether a particular "theory of interpretation" is part of the concept of law (of legal ideology) will be a contingent question. Such a rule might, on the contrary, be a part of the legal system identified; this too will depend on legal reality and on the presence of specific legal rules about interpreting other legal rules. The question might be irresolvable. The

72 My book *Il formalismo giuridico*, *supra* n.57, attempts to deal with some general aspects of this problem.

validity of particular legal norms of interpretation depends on whether we look for them where they are, on condition, of course that they are there. The inanity of much discussion of "theories" of interpretation is mostly due to the lack of clarification as to which problem they address; the controversy might be concerned either with the postulates of jurisprudence, whether a rule or practice must be considered as part of the legal field, or with the existence of legal norms described according to one of the concepts of law.

We have seen therefore how discussion of cognitive jurisprudence can only be really neutral when it adopts a more open attitude than the positivist one. However, the solution I have presented here, especially by developing the ideas of Hart, Bobbio and Scarpelli ideas, is much nearer to the classical Kelsenian conception of legal science than appears at first sight.

Internal normative description is *sui generis* scientific and can be used in either ethico-political or empirico-explicative discourses. It thus appears like and indeed shares many of the methodological characteristics of Kelsen's legal science. This, in turn, has a distinct and intermediate position to causal sciences and to moral discourses. Both, according to Kelsen, presuppose the description of legal science and the concept of law on which that is based.

The main difference between my model and that of Kelsen is the acceptance of a certain variability in the pre-suppositions of internal legal description. This translates itself into a variability in the concept of law. The criterion identifying the scope of legal description is generated by various practical interests (for the purpose of using the law as a tool in the field of actions and practical decisions) or by the requirements of historico-social explanations. Recognizing this partial variability eliminates the main ideological element subtly hidden in positivist legal description. By operating a distinction between these two phases of each legal argument, a normativistic post-positivist conception of legal knowledge allows clearly to separate two aspects of arguments in jurisprudence. These are as to the choice, hypothesis or postulates of legal thought and as to the normative positive legal data, discovered by applying the first to the real world.

Unfortunately, it is exactly this open and dual aspect of the suggested model which is most strongly resisted by the common wisdom of positivist lawyers and judges. Contemporary lawyers and judges do not accept that differences in describing law may stem from differences in the fundamental hypotheses of their cognitive jurisprudence, not from different applications of the same hypothesis, that is from differences in the law.

They find much easier to deny that there are basic divergencies which cannot be decided by what the law is, for the very good reason that what the law is found to be depends on the solutions given to these very divergencies. Under the cloak of the "objectivist" approach, all legal problems are reduced to problems of giving a correct description of a positive legal system. This form of positivism is just defensive methodology. We can say however, at the level of descriptive meta-jurisprudence, that, past the appearances to the contrary, an element of variability and controversy as to what the law in general is, is widespread in descriptive practices of contemporary lawyers, in particular when differences appear as to "theories" of the sources of law, "theories" as to the proper function of each branch of government, and "theories" of legal interpretation.[73] To be sure, lawyers and judges are a conformist bunch and their conceptions of the law are unlikely to stray too far from received and shared ideas. If this were not the case, law would cease to exist. But marginal differences exist and are of great importance, not only in hard cases and in times of crisis.

It should be noted, therefore, that our conception of knowledge of law does not pretend to condemn or even modify the present positivist "official" model of jurisprudence. It wants simply to clarify what it is done but non recognized.

73 See on the subject L. Lombardi Vallauri, *Corso di filosofia del diritto* (Padova: Cedam, 1981), part I, ch.I.

SOME OBSERVATIONS ON THE LANGUAGE OF THE ITALIAN CIVIL CODE

by

ANDREA BELVEDERE

1. *Introduction. Legislative Terms and Legal Terms*

In looking, as we are going to, only at the language of the Italian Civil Code, and even there only at a part of it, my work will inevitably lack completeness. Looking at the code as a whole would need a computer to investigate the frequencies and the context of the terms used. However even here, our enquiry can be of interest if it succeeds in drawing our attention to the linguistic complexity of the code. Here I have in mind the problem of the meaning of the words i.e the relation between the terms and concepts used by the legislator. We need to make clear that our work here will deal with both ordinary language and so called legal language.

Legal language itself is a vague notion. We can consider it as one comprehensive unity, including legislative language.[1] But if we look at it from the point of view of the legal nature of the terms which constitute it, then there is only a partial overlap with legislative language (see *infra*).

Whatever the exact limits are, undoubtedly a large part of legal language has, from the internal point of view, a certain homogeneity. From the external point of view it can be differentiated from ordinary language. From the first point of view, it is sufficient to say that the language of the mythical legislator is also made by the same jurists who then interpret it. They are the real addressees of the «discourse» of the legislator. It is idealistic to think of legislation immediately

Law and Language, The Italian Analytical School, ed. A. Pintore and M. Jori (Liverpool: Deborah Charles Publications, 1997).

1 There would only be different "discourses" which use legal language, those of the legislator, and those of jurists: see L. Lantella, "Pratiche definitorie e proiezioni ideologiche nel discorso giuridico", in A. Belvedere, M. Jori and L. Lantella, *Definizioni giuridiche e ideologie* (Milan: Giuffrè, 1979), 132 (footnote).

comprehensible to the citizen.[2]

From the second point of view, legal language is, in relation to ordinary language a *sectorial* language. The difference between it and ordinary language is not the same as the difference between technical language and ordinary language. Technical language is more rigorous and separate.[3] As in each *sectorial* language, ordinary language constitutes the framework of legal language.[4] And since the linguistic rules are the same, the differences are in vocabulary and especially the use of words in different meanings.[5] But if a special language depends on the specificity of the terms used, or on the difference of their use, then this raises doubts (as we saw above) as to whether legislative language can be totally absorbed by legal language. The criterion by which some legislative terms are specified can only be "topographical", based on their presence in legislative texts. This is not the same as that more restrictive criterion by which the legal nature of a term is specified by its difference from ordinary language.[6] The question is made more complicated by the "open" nature of legal language,[7] which is not rigidly distinct from ordinary language and often exchanges words with it. Thus often the difference between ordinary language and legal language is not in the words used but the different meaning they have in the two languages. We therefore have to consider not only technical terms of legal language but also the technical use of terms belonging to ordinary language.[8]

2 See M. Cattaneo, *Illuminismo e legislazione* (Milan: Edizioni di Comunità, 1966).

3 See G.L. Beccaria, "Linguaggi settoriali e lingua comune", in *Linguaggi settoriali in Italia* (Milan: Bompiani, 1973), 29; on the subject see also G. Preti, "Linguaggio comune e linguaggi scientifici", in *Saggi filosofici* (Firenze: La Nuova Italia, 1976), 33ff. To achieve maximum rigour scientists sometimes try to construct so-called perfect languages: see A. Pasquinelli, *Nuovi principi di epistemologia* (Milan: Feltrinelli, 1974), 72ff.; U. Scarpelli, "Introduzione all'analisi delle argomentazioni giudiziarie", in U. Scarpelli, ed., *Diritto e analisi del linguaggio* (Milan: Edizioni di Comunità, 1976), 429ff.

4 See M. Porro, "I linguaggi della scienza e della tecnica", in *Linguaggi settoriali*, *supra* n.3, at 185, 188.

5 See G.L. Beccaria, *supra* n.3, at 33; M. Porro, *supra* n.4, at 187. See however G. Tarello, *L'interpretazione della legge* (Milan: Giuffrè, 1980), 118, who underlines the different relevance of syntactical-grammatical ambiguity in a prescriptive discourse such as that of the legislator.

6 Or other special languages: see Tarello, *supra* n.5, at 109.

7 See Scarpelli, *supra* n.3.

8 Tarello, *supra* n.5, at 108ff., speaks here of *technicalised terms*. The idea of

Taking for granted the normal ambiguity and vagueness of ordinary language, we have to ask what sort of difference is necessary before we can speak of a technical use of a term which originally comes from ordinary language.[9] All this makes clear the difficulty of not only producing a theoretical framework for characterising in a technical-legal sense the terms and their linguistic use but also to classify the particular concrete case which is often ambiguous. Thus it does not seem promising to classify the terms of the Civil Code in this way since there we will meet many different situations. Furthermore such classification demands in each case a preliminary look at the use made in the code of the terms in question, that is understanding their meaning.

2. *Preliminary Classifications*

The semantic variety of the terms in the Civil Code (and also in other laws) is remarkable, even if we limit ourselves to so called *descriptive terms*. These latter are terms which express names and predicates of various kinds; they exclude the so called logical terms ("no", "if...then", "some", "all"). There are those who claim that even logical terms can have a different meaning in legal discourse. For example "everyone" could mean "not only everyone in the world (probably the ordinary language meaning) but could have a more restricted meaning. Here the class 'everyone' would be identified by a series of legal requirements (being a citizen, being in the age of majority, living in a certain place and being not barred from public offices, and so on)".[10]

The first group of terms refers to norms or sets of legal norms.[11] It is

---

technicalisation is well suited to explain the process by which a term which originally came from ordinary language becomes specialised. It is not, however, well suited to explain the opposite process. On the relation between technical-legal terms and ordinary language see also N. Irti, "Note per uno studio sulla nomenclatura giuridica", now in *Norme e fatti* (Milan: Giuffrè, 1984), 165ff.; A. Martino, *Le definizioni legislative* (Turin: Giappichelli, 1975), 42ff.

9 Lantella, *supra* n.1, at 138ff.

10 Lantella, *supra* n.1, at 140.

11 We follow here the classification and (partially) the terminology of U. Scarpelli, "La definizione nel diritto", in *Diritto e analisi del linguaggio*, *supra* n.3, at 187ff.; *Contributo alla semantica del linguaggio normativo* (Turin: Accademia delle Scienze, 1959), 68. There is a new edition of this work (Milan: Giuffrè, 1985), with a useful introduction by Anna Pintore. The references are from the

present in the Civil Code but not much. We can (as an example) point to "diritto" (law, in the objective sense) in art. 1 Preleggi (Provisions on the law in general). The legislator in 1942 code prefers to use the term *legge* (*statute)* even in general and comprehensive expressions such as "legge dello Stato" (State statutes) "legge nazionale" (national statute)(art. 17 and ff. Preleggi). This is an expression of the ideological view that written sources prevail over others (the expression "diritto" appears other times but in a different use: see art. 1456 and f., 1924, 1932, 1939).

As we have said, the use of "legge" (statute) is frequent (art. 822, 1387, 1418, 1441), sometimes in the expression "legge speciale" (special statute) (art. 856) or in the expression "disposizione di legge"(statutory provision) (art. 428, 1324). At other times we find the term "disposizione" (provision) by itself (art. 815, 1526, 1718).

In this category also comes the term "norma" (*norm*) (art. 1555) "norma imperativa" (mandatory norm) (art. 1419), "norma corporativa" (corporative norm) (art. 1339), and also "regola" (rule) (art. 1570).

The Civil Code also uses the terms "ordinamento giuridico" (legal order) (art. 832 and 1322) "principi generali dell'ordinamento giuridico" (general principles of the legal order) (art. 12 Preleggi) and naturally "regolamento" (regulation) (art. 892) and "uso" (custom) (in the sense of art. 1 Preleggi and art. 1374).

We must also point out that in the Civil Code there are references to particular laws (for example to the Code of Civil Procedure, art. 1513) and subdivisions of the Civil Code. Some of these expressions only indicate metonymically the content of the norm in the statement, for example when one says that "the warranty for gratuitous alienations is regulated by art. 797" (art. 1547). Sometimes however, in expressions like "the provisions contained in Book" (art. 13), it is clear that "Book" does not refer to the norms but to the linguistic statements by which these norms are expressed.[12] Again other terms refer to (or at least can be interpreted as doing so) to norms or socio-ethical principles. This is the case of "buona fede"(good faith) in its objective sense as in art. 1337 and 1375 and also perhaps as in "equità" (equity), as it is used in art. 1374.[13] We can say

---

first edition.

12 On the relation between normative statements and norms, see G. Tarello, *Diritti, enunciati, usi* (Bologna: Il Mulino, 1974), 199ff., 394f.

13 Difficulties connected with good faith and equity are so great that we cannot even attempt to verify the hypothesis adumbrated in the text. Here see (also for a very complete bibliography) two entries of S. Romano, "Buona fede (dir.

this with more confidence in respect of "correttezza" (fairness) (art. 1175 talks of "rules of fairness" and of "correct behaviour in the trade" (art. 2598, n. 3 talks of "principles of correct behaviour in the trade") "buon costume" (public morals) (art. 1354).

One should say a word about the terms in the Civil Code which refer to norms created by contracts and by jurisdictional or administrative acts.[14] But we can leave this till later (see below sections 7, 16).

3. *Terms Referring to Qualifications and Legal Positions*

A second group of terms refers to possible deontic qualifications.[15] They thus express the possible relations between legal norms and reality, i.e. the normative qualification of that reality. For example "rilevante" (relevant, with reference to facts in general), "vietato" (forbidden, with reference to human behaviour) "valido" (valid, with reference to other norms which are inferior to the norm which expresses the normative qualification).[16]

The Civil Code does not make much use of these terms in relation to behaviour (here we can recall only "vietato" (prohibited) with reference to

---

priv.)", in *Enciclopedia di diritto* V (Milan: Giuffrè, 1959), 677ff. and "Principio di equità (dir. priv.)", in *Enciclopedia di diritto* XV (Milan: Giuffrè, 1966), 83ff. (on art. 1374, see also S. Rodotà, *Le fonti d'integrazione del contratto* (Milan: Giuffrè, 1969), 91ff.). In respect of art. 1124 of the 1865 Civil Code, we limit ourselves to saying that C. Grassetti, *L'interpretazione del negozio giuridico* (Padova: CEDAM, 1983), intended "good faith" in the objective sense as a positive law of loyal behaviour (at 199).

14 *Pure Theory of Law* (translation of the second edition of *Reine Rechtslehre*) by Max Knight (Berkeley and Los Angeles: University of California Press, 1967); *The General Theory of Law and State*, trld. A. Wedberg (Cambridge, Mass.: Harvard University Press, 1945).

15 We are following here the classification proposed by Scarpelli, *supra* n.3.

16 Opinions vary as to which terminology should be adopted and what should be its basis. See A.G. Conte, *Saggio sulla completezza degli ordinamenti giuridici* (Turin: Giappichelli, 1962); U. Scarpelli, "Il permesso, il dovere e la completezza degli ordinamenti normativi", in *Rivista Trimestrale di diritto e procedura civile* (1963), 1634-1656 (reprinted in *L'etica senza verità* (Bologna: Il Mulino, 1982), 221-250); N. Irti, *Introduzione allo studio del diritto privato* (Turin: Giappichelli, 1976, 3rd ed.), 60ff.; S. Castignone, R. Guastini and G. Tarello, *Introduzione teorica allo studio del diritto* (Genova: ECIG, 1984, 4 ed.), 68ff.

contractual behaviour: art. 323, 378, 388); more frequent are those terms which refer to legal acts and to their features, for example "illecito" (unlawful, art. 1343). Because the dispositions of the code look to the relations between determinate subjects, rather than characterising, as in "obbligatorio" (obligatory), the behaviour of A to B, the Code prefers to say that A "è obbligato" (is under an obligation) to conduct himself in a certain way in respect of B.[17]

We ought therefore to introduce another set of terms, which indicates the subjective legal positions, both the so-called "elementary" or "fundamental", such as "obbligo" (duty), "pretesa" (claim), "potere" (power), [18] and those "complex" such as "diritto" (right). The Civil Code makes use of the same terms that are used in general theory but obviously not with the same rigor. The use of the term "diritto" in a subjective sense (right) often designates, with the ambiguity which is common to all legal discourse, an elementary position. For example, the "pretesa" or claim of depositor, entitled to inspect the goods deposited and withdraw the customary sample (art. 1788). Sometimes it can designate a complex legal position, for example a right of "superficie" (art. 952).

The difficulties connected with the use of the term "diritto" are shown more clearly in the rubric of art. 832, "content of the right" (of ownership). There "the right to enjoy and dispose of things" appears together with "observance of the obligations established by the legal system". If we look more closely at this right of enjoyment and disposal, there we quickly see that the active position of the owner, indicated by the word "right" in reality also covers claims against other people interfering, powers (of disposition), "permessi" (permissions) and "facoltà" (options of enjoyment of the thing by the owner). [19]

17 On the relation between qualification and intersubjective normative relations, see Castignone, Guastini and Tarello, *supra* n.16, at 70ff.

18 Here we follow P. Trimarchi's clear exposition in *Istituzioni di diritto privato* (Milan: Giuffrè, 1983, 6 ed.), 56. See also W.N. Hohfeld *Fundamental Legal Conceptions as Applied in Judicial Reasoning* (Westport: Greenwood Press, 1919).

19 We use here the distinction between "permesso" (permission), in the sense of "not forbidden" and "capacity" in the sense of "not obligatory". See A.G. Conte, *supra* n.16, at 10; Castignone, Guastini and Tarello, *supra* n.16, at 70. More synthetic is the notion of "facoltà" (capacity) in Trimarchi, *supra* n.18, at 57.

4. *Substantial and Procedural Situations (continued)*

A particular use of the word "diritto" is encountered in articles 1492 and 1497 where one talks of the right of dissolution and the right to obtain the dissolution of the contract of sale. The legislator here appears to refer to an hypothesis of "diritto potestativo" (potestative right).[20] This appears to mirror that conception of "diritto potestativo" which has been identified with «the right to put in motion the duty of the judge to make a change» in a given situation by his decision.[21] The fact remains that in the above articles, the use of "right" does not correspond to the notion of claim. The duty of the judge to make a decision is only one aspect of his duty to render justice. It does not constitute an obligation in respect of the parties to the case.[22]

The "right" which is spoken of in articles 1492 and 1497 is therefore (according to the terminology we have adopted) a power of a procedural nature. The addressee is not here in a situation of direct subjection. He is submitted to the effects of the judicial decision and not to the acts of the opposing party.

The complexity of the relation between procedure and substance can also be seen in legislative language. This appears to oscillate between referring to substantive situations and the procedure to protect them. In some cases the law which provides for judicial determination is not equivocal. This is so either because it is expressly stated, as in art. 7 ("can judicially request"), or on the basis of what is requested, as in art. 1513 ("the seller or the buyer can request its inspection in the manner provided

20 This is extremely controversial in doctrine: see the stringent criticisms by Irti, *supra* n.8, at 86; Trimarchi identifies it in a power (a power to modify a normative situation by oneself) which is not part of the complex framework of subjective right but which appears "isolated" (*op. cit.*, at 57ff.); it is doubtful, however, whether this would justify the adoption of a new term.

21 See E. Allorio, *Problemi di diritto* (Milan: Giuffrè, 1957), vol I, 103ff.: he distinguishes between "diritto potestativo" (disposable right) and the situation of power, in which someone can modify normative relations by his own will. On this see. C. Ferri, *Profili dell'accertamento costitutivo* (Padova: CEDAM, 1970), 40ff.

22 Allorio, *supra* n.21, at 104, makes clear that the "diritto potestativo" as he sees it "cannot be confused with the action that takes place in the constitutive process. This action is power, abstract as always ... eventually the *diritto potestativo* should be identified with the action understood as a concrete manifestation of power", that is the power to seek a favourable decision from the courts.

by art. 696 of the code of civil procedure") or for both reasons, as in art. 49 ("they can petition the competent tribunal .... that his absence be declared"). There are also particular cases where the result produced by judicial action is described by the norm not by what is requested but by what the actor "can obtain" (art. 51, 1584).

At other times however, dispositions formulated generally according to the scheme "X can request" are more ambiguous. The addressee can be either the other party or the judge even though, in general, a prevailing processual formulation can be found in the context. Thus art. 80, in the case of the breach of a promise of marriage, says that the "person who made the promise of marriage can demand restitution of the gifts". From the second part of the article, "the demand cannot be brought after one year from the day ... " it is obvious that the legislator here refers to an action of restitution. However the power of the promisor to set the action in motion is founded on his claim in respect of a party to which there is a corresponding obligation. It is probably not possible to give a general reason why the Civil Code prefers a procedural point of view. One reason might be that it allows a more synthetic formulation in cases where the procedural aspect has to be regulated as well, or where a judicial provision is necessary.

In respect of terms used by the legislator to regulate even procedural situations, it is important to note that the term "power" is often used referring to judicial activity. The adoption by the judge of measures foreseen by the law cannot be considered simply "permitted" (permesso) or "optional" (facoltativo). It constitutes indeed the object of a duty which is linked to the public function of the judge.

In some cases the term "power" really means the power of the judge to modify a judicial situation either established by law or contract, for instance permitting the marriage of a 16 year old minor (art. 84) or reducing the indemnity established in a contract (art. 1526). This case is also similar to cases where the judge can perform an act which is normally performed by someone else (as in the case of convocation of meetings of associations, art. 20). In other cases however, the formula «the judge can» only serves to make clear the measures that the judge can take in order to ensure compliance with the law, such as sequestration (art. 1513) or publication of a decision (art. 7). But when he cannot but take a specific measure, the phrase has a paradoxical tone, as for example when art. 10 says that the court "can" order the termination of the abuse of another person's likeness.

The term power also refers (superfluously) to the principle that the judge is free to decide whether the conditions for taking those measure exist. This is sometimes expressly stated by the legislator as in art. 1526 ("according to the circumstances") and 1648 ("considering the financial conditions of the tenant").

5. *"Power", "Obligation", "Duty"*

Leaving this procedural excursus, we come now to substantive legal positions. We have already considered *right* and now turn to *power* in the relations between private individuals. The code prefers to use the verb "potere" instead of the noun "potere" (power). But it does so in different meanings. Alongside cases where it is rigorously used to show the possibility of making a change in a given legal situation (for example through the withdrawal privilege of civil servants, art. 1613), there are other cases which designate different situations.

Often the verb "potere" stands for "to be allowed to" (art. 1481, 1577, see also art. 1619 which also expresses the claim to the collaboration of the renter). Likewise the verbal expression "non potere" is equivalent to a prohibition (see art. 29 and 1582) and sometimes also to the absence of a claim (art. 1530).

Frequently then the verb "potere", when referring the parties to a contract, expresses the importance of the content of the intention of the parties and thus the validity of the corresponding clauses in the contract (art. 1487, 1500). For a related use of "non potere" see art. 1501 and 1573). Sometimes "potere" is used referring to the capacity to act, normally, however, to deny such capacity (art. 84, 774).

We have seen above how the verb "potere" sometimes refers to non obligatory and non prohibited behaviours. This can be put more precisely by using the word "facoltà" (option). This is also not without ambiguity (see note 19). The term is not unknown in the Civil Code. It is used with a wide meaning, referring both to permitted behaviour (art. 1594), and to situations of power (art. 1537), by expressing the possibility of choice among several alternatives (art. 1278; art. 1287).[23] To conclude this summary of active subjective positions, we can mention "pretesa" (claim). This is normally indicated by the term "right" but can also be indicated by the expression "is allowed to claim" (art. 1488).

23 Irti is critical of the notion of "facoltà" (option), *supra* n.8, at 96ff.

Passing to "passive" positions, we consider that position indicated by "obbligo"(obligation) in theoretical language. This term appears naturally in different forms in the code: "is under an obligation" (art. 1706), "assumes the obligation" (art. 1548), "to be released from an obligation" (art. 1557), "to be exempted from an obligation" (art. 1691), "obligations of a carrier" (art. 1741), "obligation to render account" (art. 1743). Sometimes, finally, the verb "obbligare" (to oblige) is used transitively to indicate the effects of a certain act (art. 1725).

More interesting is the legislative use of "duty". We must note that the code obscures, as do many writers, the difference between "obligation" and "duty" which depends on the presence or absence of a corresponding claim.[24]

The code also obscures the difference between the positions of obligation and "onere" (burden).[25] Thus both art. 1477 ("The seller shall deliver the deed and the documents pertaining to the ownership and use of the thing sold") and art. 1512 ("The buyer shall notify the seller of the defect in functioning within thirty days after discovering it, or he shall forfeit his remedy") are worded in the same way. In relation to "onere", there are also uses of "dovere" in norms which prescribe formal requirements ("The following must be made by public act ... under penalty of nullity": art. 1350) or the content of acts ("The founding act and bye-laws must contain...": art. 16). Here the grammatical subject is not the author of the act but the act itself. This formulation also occurs frequently in those norms establishing obligations and in which reference is made either to the behaviours which must be adopted (art. 1679: "Transportation shall be provided in accordance with the order of requests") or to the object of the performance (art. 1658: "the materials necessary to perform the work shall be furnished by the independent contractor"). Finally one can note the frequent use by the legislator of the expression "E' tenuto" (is required to) as a synonym of "deve" (shall ...). Sometimes both expressions are used in the same article, perhaps for stylistic reasons (art. 1479 and 1483).

6. *Factual and Normative Terms*

We can now introduce a further distinction, that between *factual*

24 See here Trimarchi, *supra* n. 18, at 57.

25 For a critique of this notion see Irti. *supra* n.8, at 93ff.

terms and *normative* terms. This, from the theoretical point of view, is possibly most important and most productive. The name given to this second category is a clear indication that it covers terms which refer (also) to legal norms. Any descriptive term examined in the previous sections are therefore fully entitled to be included in that category. We can now add to these the most interesting group, those terms which refer not only to norms but to both facts and norms.[26]

Let us start by pointing out which terms can be said to be *factual*. As their name clearly indicates, these terms designate facts and, we could add, facts only. They look at reality considered in itself, independently from any possible consideration or evaluation given to it by the legal order. We are thus correct in using a factual term when confronted with something real in the external world, the existence of which can be empirically ascertained by our daily experience or, if necessary, through methods worked out by science.

What the reality that allows us to use the word correctly is, depends on the rules governing the use of that word. Often we will be able to see this by looking at ordinary language. But the way it is used might also be formed within the framework of a specific scientific language. Though not likely, such rule could also be our personal rule, different from the one (or from those) which others apply to the use of that word. The problem of the origin of such rules — to which we revert in section 9 *infra* — has no relation to that of the more or less factual nature of a certain term.

The distinction between factual and normative terms does not rest on the nature of the origin of the rule, but on what it consists of. Whatever the origin of the rule, a term is factual if it can be used in respect of phenomena which are not juridically qualified. More precisely, in respect of phenomena the possible legal qualification of which is irrelevant for the purpose of using the term. It is most important that the source and content of the rule be kept separate in order to determine whether a term is factual. The meaning attributed by the legislator to certain words, though different from the other ways the word is used, still remains factual.

A paradigm case is that of the rule for the use of the term "*immovable property*", described in art. 812 c.c. Here the legislator departs from the ordinary language and extends its use to objects commonly considered as

26 Though it may be true to say that some of the terms examined in the previous sections refer also to both norms and facts (e.g. "subjective right"), we prefer to leave this point for now and return to it at section 8.

"movable" such as "floating buildings".[27] Though, in establishing the list of property considered as immovable, he still describes physical reality from which any legal characterisation is totally absent.

The purpose of any law is to introduce discipline into a reality which is external to it and which is made of concrete social and economic relations. Clearly, therefore, factual terms must be present in the Civil Code. They concern human beings ("people": art. 1049; "person": art. 1681); relations, events, situations relating to persons ("consanguinity": art. 74; "death": art. 246; "mental infirmity": art. 414; "pregnancy": art. 89; "deaf-mute": art. 415; "deceased": art. 456); animal ("animal": art. 1496; "livestock": art. 1643; "rabbit": art. 926); plants ("tree": art. 895; "plane": art. 892; "grass": art. 933); things ("water": art. 1117; "smoke": art. 844); events relating to things ("fire": art. 1589). Other factual terms can refer to more abstract things: "market price" (art. 1474), "crop year" (art. 1627), "time" (art. 1183); or indicate numbers ("one tenth": art. 1664) and a unit of measurement of water (art. 1081).

In some cases, however, it is not easy to determine the category in which a term should be classified. For example, "age" (art. 2, par. 2) could be considered a factual term but for two obstacles. The first concerns the so-called "civil" calculation of the age against the so-called "natural" calculation.[28] The second lies in the lack of a perfect coincidence between the astronomical or solar calendar (year) and the civil calendar, on the basis of which the passage of years is computed. The artificial (and authoritative) character of the criteria which are adopted both for computing the number of years and determining the completion of the age year might lead us to conclude that the term is not factual. This conclusion would be wrong and would stem from confusion between the source of the rule (and that of its differences with other possible rules) and that of its content. Such content, in the case of "age" and "year" — even by a "civil" calculation — would still be linked to the passing of time. The later is certainly hard to define theoretically, but it has no legal character whatsoever. The difference in the case of a "civil" calculation is the

27 Under certain conditions. Nor do we take into account the introductory words "are considered", on which see *infra*, par. 18.

28 The difference lies in the fact that according to the first criterion, a given age is considered to be reached not in the hour corresponding to the hour of birth — a "natural" calculation — but at midnight of the previous day: see C. Ruperto, "Età (diritto privato)", in *Enciclopedia del diritto, XVI* (Milan: Giuffrè, 1967), 85-92.

system of measurement. The fact, for example, that the length corresponding to one "metre" has been established authoritatively within the framework of law concerning modes of measurement does not turn "metre" and "length" into normative terms.[29]

The same can be said for "age of majority" — which points only to an age equal to (or greater than) eighteen years. There is here an important difference. Though "age of majority" is a factual term, it is always (even in the most current and non-technical discourse) used according to a rule belonging to a legal order. Such a rule will set an equivalence between "age of majority" and a (any) minimum number of years.[30] This example is a further confirmation that qualifying a term as "legal" does not characterise it as factual or normative.

7. *Factual and Normative Terms (continued)*

We now turn to normative terms. These are terms which cannot correctly be applied to a fact before its correspondence with one or more norms has been established. And this qualifies it in a certain way which represents a necessary condition for the use of those terms.

The following is not the best example because of its polysemic nature (we shall turn to this in section 16 *infra*); let us however take the word "contract", in the meaning it has in the sentence of the first paragraph of art. 1372 c.c.: "A contract has the force of law between the parties". By looking at the law, art. 1372 means by "contract" the ordering of relations between parties, negotiated by them and accepted by the legal order.[31] But it is that reception by the legal order which makes it impossible to use the term "contract" in a concrete situation on the basis of purely factual information.

In order to say that A and B are bound by law because of the contract that they have concluded it is not sufficient to make sure they have agreed on a text from which it is possible to extract (through interpretation) rules

29 See A. Amorth, "Misure et pesi (diritto amministrativo"), in *Enciclopedia del diritto* XXVI (Milan: Giuffrè, 1976), 610-616.

30 How relevant is, within such legal order, the fact of reaching the "age of majority" is a different problem: see A.G. Conte, "Variationen über Wittgensteins Regelbegriff", in R. Haller, ed., *Sprache und Erkenntnis als soziale Tatsache* (Wien: Holder-Pichler-Tempsky, 1981), 70ff.

31 On this meaning of the word "contract", see P. Schlesinger, "Complessità del procedimento di formazione del consenso ed unità del negozio contrattuale", in *Studi in onore di P. Greco* (Padova: CEDAM, 1965), II, 1003ff.

of behaviour which they have addressed to themselves. It is also necessary to compare step by step the facts with the legal norms relating to consent and to the form and content of a contract. It is only then that we can reach a conclusion as to the validity and efficacy[32] of the contractual transaction between A and B.

It could be objected that the above example is not very meaningful. In this case the word "contract" points to some precepts (even if autonomous and private). They should therefore be likened to those terms which refer to sets of norms (see *supra*, section 2) and which clearly have not only a factual meaning. There are arguments against this objection. For example, it is based on the idea that "norm" always equals "valid norm" — though to speak, as we often do, of "invalid norms" would then be a contradiction.

Let us however try to find further examples where the factual element is stronger. For example, it is evident that "abuse of another person's likeness" (art. 10) indicates a situation which cannot be ascertained on the basis of factual data alone. In order to distinguish "use" from "abuse" it is furthermore necessary to be aware of cases in which the exhibition and the publication of the likeness "is permitted by the law".

In the same way, we cannot use the term "possession" in relation to any situation of effective power over a thing because the highly criticised[33] art. 1140 compels us to make sure that the presumed possessor's activity corresponds "to the exercise of ownership or other real right". This requires a comparison with the relevant norms. Again in respect of possession it is not possible to select "things outside commerce" (art. 1145) merely on the basis of their physical characteristics. One must refer to those things "of which ownership cannot be acquired". Once more, this requires a comparison with legal norms.

More generally then, not everything which we can consider physically a "thing" can be considered "property". Art. 810 declares that for the term to be used it must be a thing which "can form the subject matter of rights". Here we must recall that we had previously considered (section 6) "immovable property" to be a factual term, on the basis of the definition of art. 812. Because of the link between art. 810 and 812 we must now acknowledge that there is in "immovable property" an element that is not

32 We avoid examining further the hypothesis of a voidable contract which can produce temporary effects.

33 V.A. Fedele, *Possesso ed esercizio del diritto* (Turin: Giappichelli, 1950), 37ff., 65ff.; R. Sacco, *Il possesso* (Milan: Giuffrè, 1950), 13ff.

merely factual.

"Default" (referring to the creditor, art. 1206) is also a normative term because there is no default when there is a "legitimate cause" to the non-acceptance of the payment.

The adjective "legitimate" clearly expresses a qualification based norms and turns into "normative" any expression which includes it (for ex.: "legitimate children" art. 566), or any expression helping to define it (for ex.: "natural son", meaning "not legitimate").

Also normative is the term "public act" (art. 2699), which indicates a document drawn "with the required formalities" by a notary or by another public official "authorised", etc. "Notary" and "Public official" are also normative terms because they indicate positions and roles specific to the legal organisation of the State, attributed according to procedures regulated by norms. The same can be said, for instance, of "guardian" (art. 343).

Different, though still relating to the legal position of a person (this time relating to the phenomenon of succession for reason of death) is the term "heir" (art. 533).

Any term referring to legally organised procedures must be considered as normative, for example, "transcription". This must be so at least when the terms relate to procedures which fulfil every condition legally required for them to be relevant (as in art. 2666).

In conclusion, it might be of interest to compare the two terms "missing" (art. 48) and "absentee" (art. 50). The first one is a factual term because it applies to a person in a certain situation ("When a person has disappeared from the place of his last domicile or of his last residence and is no longer heard of .. "), which is described, and can be verified by way of purely factual criteria. The term "absent", on the other hand, cannot be simply applied to the missing person "after the lapse of two years from the day on which the person has last been heard of" (art. 49) as the use of the term is conditioned by the tribunal issuing a (valid) decree. In order to verify the fulfilment of such condition is necessary to make legal judgments and draw conclusions from a series of norms.

8. *Norms and Facts in Some Normative Terms*

To complete our survey of normative terms, we have now to refer to a group of norms which presents great theoretical difficulty. I refer to words such as "property" or "owner" (art. 832), "obligation" (art. 1173), "debtor" (art. 1180), to words designating various minor real rights, and so on. I refer to all those words which refer to legal relations, and to the position of those involved in such relations, both in an active and passive way.

There is no doubt whatsoever that these are normative terms. Any tentative definition would naturally use expressions such as " ... it is the right (the obligation) of ...", " ... whoever has the right (the obligation) of ...". We can here refer back to section 3 which dealt with the relation between qualification by precepts and elementary intersubjective positions. How the latter join up into more complex legal situations which correspond exactly to the various subjective rights with which we are dealing here.

There is no doubt, therefore, that the meaning, for instance of "property" can (and must) be analyzed in terms of capacity, power, claim, and obligations of the owners and third parties. Such terms can, in their turn, be analyzed with the help of qualifying terms ("allowed", "prohibited", etc.) referring to legal norms. The real difficulty is elsewhere. Do such terms as "property" etc. besides designating norms (as we have just seen) also indicate facts in the same way as the other normative terms examined in the previous section?[34]

Facts involved in the use of such terms could be those to which the legal order links the acquisition of the right. However, the meaning of owning something and that of acquiring a property are two different questions in the legal language (as well as in the Civil Code: see art. 832 and 922). These two questions might get conflated should a reference be made in the conditions for using, for example, the term property, to its "modes of acquisition".[35]

Continuing with the example of "property", another factual point of reference could be the behaviour of the owner and that of third parties in relation to the thing. Those facts, though, are not necessarily "actual". They could be eventual, possible, and would be somehow qualified by the

34 The question has been widely debated in studies of general legal theory. For references see A. Belvedere, "Aspetti ideologici delle definizioni nel linguaggio del legislatore e dei giuristi", in *Definizioni giuridiche ed ideologie*, *supra* n.1, at 383ff.

35 See Scarpelli's comments in *Contributo*, *supra* n.11, at 89ff., with a critical reference to A. Ross's well known views in *On Law and Justice* (Berkeley: California University Press, 1959). According to Ross, terms such as "property" express nothing other than a systematic link between a series of different cases and a cumulative series of legal effects.

legal order should they happen.[36]

It is doubtful whether possible behaviour can represent a factual point of reference comparable with behaviour (or other actual situations) which has already taken place. It might therefore be better, from the theoretical point of view, not to classify the terms which we are now examining, together with those which indicate facts normatively qualified. Rather we should consider them together with terms expressing normative qualification of behaviour (or the consequent legal position of the subjects of the behaviour) including possible behaviour (see section 3).

The same conclusion can be reached for the expression "legal person". Such an expression, according to the best current legal thought, designate a complex set of relations (established between physical persons), made of a series of norms which qualify facts and behaviour. These latter are not necessarily actual.[37]

Finally, the "normative" character of a term's use subsists in spite of it being anomalous and even wrong according to the rules set by the legislator and the lawyers. I refer here to terms which are used in ordinary language. And, though given a different meaning than the one given by the legislator or by the lawyers, maintain the reference to norms. What we have in mind is the frequent use of "compromesso" (compromise) instead of "preliminary contract" (art. 1351) or the use of "delega" instead of "procura" (letter of attorney). Alongside (uses of) factual, though "legal" terms (see above section 6, *in fine*), there are also normative, though "non-legal", terms.

9. *Rules For Use and Definitions*

On several previous occasions we have mentioned how the source of the rules for the use of a word can differ from the rules themselves. In ordinary language we mostly use the words according to rules historically laid down. This means we face a large measure of uncertainty (when we

36 If, for instance, the owner behaves in a certain way in relation to the thing, such behaviour is legal. See Scarpelli, *Contributo*, *supra* n.11, at 68ff. 107ff., 123ff.

37 See F. Galgano, *Delle persone giuridiche*, in *Commentario del codice civile*, ed. A. Scialoja and G. Branca (Bologna-Rome: Zanichelli, 1969), 3ff.; F. D'Alessandro, "Persone giuridiche e analisi del linguaggio", in *Studi in memoria di T. Ascarelli* (Milan: Giuffrè, 1969), 243ff.; U. Scarpelli, *Contributo*, *supra* n.11, at 109ff.

are confronted with a non-paradigmatic situations) in the use of a word (this is the problem of the "vague" meaning). Another consequence is that often, uses (meanings) which are sometimes extremely different are envisaged for the same word (this is the problem of "ambiguity").

In the context of various scientific disciplines, as we have already mentioned (see *supra*, section 1), ordinary language is still widely used. There has been a felt need however, to eliminate (or to reduce as far as possible) vague meanings and ambiguities (or at least of some of them) in the words used. The solution has consisted in the introduction of new symbols and in ensuring that known terms are more precise. In both cases this has been done by formulating the rule for the use of the word. The greater is the agreement, within a given scientific environment, on the meaning to be given to the various terms the more helpful such a procedure will be. The definition of a word by one single scholar (or on one occasion) also makes comparisons and verifications easier. And anyway, it is better than verbal uses which (deliberately or not) differ, but in a covert way, from the most common uses[38].

The proposition which expressly describes the meaning of a word represents a definition.[39, 40] Following an established terminology,[41] definitions introducing a new symbol or giving a new meaning to a word already in use are called "stipulative" (a word which underlines their agreed character). Whereas "lexical" definitions aim at recording the meaning or, more often, the meanings of a word; either in general language, as in the language dictionaries where several meanings are given for the same word, or within a more or less restricted context (legal language, Civil Code). Finally, there is a further intermediary category comprising definitions which neither wish totally to exclude past uses of

38 On rigour as an essential characteristic of scientific language, see N. Bobbio, "Scienza del diritto e analisi del linguaggio", in *Rivista Trimestrale di Diritto e Procedura civile* 4 (1950), esp. at 350ff.

39 At least if we take it as a "nominal" definition (i.e. as an answer to the hypothetical question "what is the meaning of word "X"?) and not as a "real" definition" (which answers the question "what is "X"?). On the latter notion see. L. Lantella, *supra* n.1, at 6ff., 10ff., 26ff.

40 The literature on definition is too vast and cannot be mentioned here, even briefly. We shall only mention the fundamental work of R. Robinson, *Definition* (Oxford: The Clarendon Press, 1972) and U. Scarpelli, *Contributo*, *supra* n.11, at 15ff. Further bibliographical references in Belvedere, *supra* n.1, at 349, and A. Peruzzi, *Definitions* (Milan: Angeli, 1983).

41 See Lantella, *supra* n.1, at 20ff.

the word (as in stipulation) nor wish passively to reflect them (as in definition). Though one wishes to stay within the context of meanings already attributed to the word, the aim is to eliminate as far as possible its ambiguity and its lack of vagueness. This is done by rigorously determining a linguistic use which would make the word a precise and trustworthy instrument, helping in the formulation and solution of the cognitive problems at hand. Such definitions are called "explicatory definitions" or "redefinitions".

10. *Legal Definitions*

However useful definitions are in discourse which has claims to rigour (see *supra,* section 9), lawyers have always been wary of definitions (though more on the level of principle than practice). This was as true at the time of Javolenus (*Dig*. 50.17.202: *Omnis definition in iure civili periculosa est)* as it is today.

The reasons of such attitude are not easy to understand. As far as the present legal culture is concerned, polemical attacks have been aimed mainly at the legislator's definitions.[42] There are in fact various reasons which should take into account of the various types of definition.[43] Here, I think it is possible (and necessary) to mention (even briefly) at least one (perhaps the most important) presupposition for such an unfavourable attitude. This is the idea that by laying down a definition one performs a task of a different quality. A task more important and more exacting than that of giving a meaning to a word and, as a consequence, than the interpretative activity of the lawyers and, sometimes, of the legislator himself.[44]

This idea can become so extreme as to lead to identify the concept of definition with that of "real" definition. That is of a proposition which does not concern words and meanings but things (or "concepts" considered as things), having an autonomous "existence" from that of the words which identify them. Furthermore, not all descriptions are considered to be definitions. A definition must seize the "true" nature of the thing by

42 For a history of this see G. Tarello, *L'interpretazione della legge*, *supra* n.5, at 157ff.

43 Cf. Lantella's study on the ideological aspects of the alternative between defining and not defining. See Lantella, *supra* n.1, at 191ff.

44 On the problem of interpretative laws, see G. Tarello, *L'interpretazione*, *supra* n.5, at 241ff.

indicating its necessary, its "essential", attributes.[45]

Let us transfer such an idea of definition to law and think of fundamental "concepts" in legislation and "legal science" (such as "contract", "donation", "property") — which was what the debate was really about. If we do so we are lead to think that to define means to outline the "essential" features of an "institution" through a synthesis of all norms which refer to it; sometimes also by a classifying comparison with other "concepts" and "institutions". A definition seen in those terms represents a difficult and fearsome task to be avoided by the legislator. Any mistake — always possible and even likely in view of such an ambitious aim- would produce, within the law itself, inextricable contradictions between normative syntheses and synthesised norms.

The pernicious influence of the doctrine of "real" definition is also seen when a definition which admittedly concerns words is given the function of capturing the "true" meaning of a word, or at least "the minimum common meaning" underlying its use or its various uses. Lawyers who see definition in those terms fail to realise that they cannot succeed because of the high degree of vagueness and ambiguity of nearly all the words in both ordinary and legal language. They are conscious of the difficulty of the task; they fear the obstacles which could ensue and stand in the way of a pliable interpretative activity aiming at capturing the various meanings which terms might have in different (or new) norms. Such obstacles would of course be much greater in case of definitions made by the legislator.[46]

We can see from what has been said so far that such stands are based on logical-linguistic doctrines which nowadays cannot be defended. Further arguments will be adduced from the examination of a meaningful "sample" of legal definitions from the Civil Code.[47]

45 On the history of real definition, see Tarello, *supra* n.5, at 182ff.

46 The idea that it is possible to give one definition only for each word (and that such is the task of the doctrine) is linked to not seeing the dialectic character of the relations between the various levels of the legal discourse. See M. Jori, "Definizioni e livelli di discorso giuridico", in *Definizioni giuridiche e ideologie*, *supra* n.1, at 483ff.

47 For a critical examination of the various positions against the presence of definitions in the law, see A. Belvedere, *Il problema delle definizioni nel codice civile* (Milan: Giuffrè, 1977). See particularly chapters I and II for an examination of the most profound argument here, that of C. Grassetti, "Le definizioni legali e la riforma dei codici", in *Studi in onore di G. Pacchioni* (Milan: Facoltà di Giurisprudenza dell'Università di Milano, 1938), 299ff.

11. *Definitions in the Civil Code*

In 1942 prevailing doctrines were against defining dispositions. Under this influence, the legislature tried to soften the theoretical and didactic character of many of the definitions in the 1865 code. It also tried to avoid the series of definitions and classifications which this code had, in its turn, inherited from the Napoleon code.[48]

All that could have been eliminated was not always eliminated. For example, it was not noticed that the definition of "consanguinity" at art. 74 was rendered superfluous by art. 75 which defines relatives in a direct line and relatives in a collateral line. Art. 900 is pointlessly complex. It does give the definition of "lights" and "views" and at the same time it considers both as species of the *genus* "windows" which, in their turn, do not have an autonomous character (on the relationship between definitions and classifications, see *infra*, sections 12, 18).

The tendency towards simplification is however evident, particularly in some parts of the code, like the one on property . Here, there is only the definition of "property" (art. 810) and "immovable property"(see art. 812 which in its last paragraph also defines, by exclusion, "movable property"), other than that of "universality of movables" and "appurtenances" (art. 816 and 817). The same can be said of servitudes, still in the third book of the code. Here one definition only, that of "non-apparent servitudes" (art. 1061) has replaced the distinctions and the definitions of the 1865 code (art. 617 and 618) relative to continuous and interrupted, apparent and non apparent servitudes. Similarly, in the fourth book, the definition of "contract" of art. 1321 is no longer followed by the definition of bilateral, unilateral, onerous, gratuitous and "aleatori" (hazardous) contracts as in the 1865 code. Definitions of various types of contracts are numerous. But in comparison to the 1865 code, one can detect a desire to describe each type of contract without linking them in a complex classification. The same can be said, in the fifth book, of various types of companies which are defined according to the types of companies included in the code of commerce. This eliminates the complex classifications of art. 1699 and ff. of the previous Civil Code.

The 1942 code differs from the previous one in another important

---

Grassetti's argument has had much influence.

48 On the abundance of definitions in these two codes, see Belvedere, *supra* n.1, at 22ff., 26ff.

aspect. This concerns the presence in the code of a definition of the right of ownership. If we compare it with art. 436 of the 1865 code, which uses the traditional defining scheme ("Ownership is the right to enjoy and dispose of etc."), art. 832 is shaped as a disposition attributing rights and powers to the owner. In itself, the way the legislative rule is laid down is not decisive. A definition of "owner" as being "one who has the right to enjoy etc." could easily be made out. Such a definition would still represent an improvement on that of art. 436 c.c. 1865. It shows that natural law considerations, the idea of the ownership as a reality existing in itself and as the presupposition for the powers of the person entitled to the right, have been left behind.[49]

Looked at as a definition, art. 832 should allow the word "owner" to be replaced by the expression "the person who has the right of etc." in all legislative rules where the word appears. A survey of those rules the interpretation of which art. 832 should help, does not however confirm this view. In most cases, in particular in the case of norms attributing special rights or setting limits to the owner (for example art. 833 and 841), such substitution would produce propositions which would not make sense.

Art. 832, therefore, does not include a definition of "owner". One could however speculate, whether that article could not be seen as an example of those "normative syntheses", sometimes called definitions (in a "real" sense). Apart from the fact that it would be improper to speak of definitions in such cases, once more the answer here must be negative. For the fact is that if we examine the subsequent norms in the matter of "ownership" (i.e. those which art. 832 is supposed to synthesize), we see that dispositions limiting the owner's rights are in the majority. Even the few dispositions which art. 832 could refer to when mentioning the "right to enjoy", give the right to the owner at and the same time limits it (for example art. 840 and 909). It is difficult to see art. 832 as a mere summary of these few norms, nearly all relating to ownership of land.

If leaving aside the "right to enjoy", we go to "limitations" and "duties" mentioned at art. 832, it appears clearly that this disposition does not sum up but refers to other norms.[50]

We must therefore conclude that art. 832 does not sum up the regulatory order laid down by other norms. Rather it contributes to its

49 See S. Rodotà, "Proprietà (diritto vigente)", in *Novissimo Digesto Italiano* (Turin, Unione Tipografico-Editrice, 1967), XIV, 128f.

50 See N. Irti, *Proprietà ed impresa* (Napoli: Jovene, 1965), 9f.

formulation by giving a fundamental part of it. It does this by attributing to the owner any right which is not excluded by the legal order.[51] Art 832, however specifically relevant, is not an isolated example of how difficult it is to determine which legal dispositions are of a defining character. But an examination of the problem requires an analysis of the legislator's methods of definition.[52]

12. *Defining Techniques and Formulation of Precepts in the Civil Code*

Spotting definitions might be easier when they are drafted *per genus et differentiam* as in art. 810. Here the reference of the word "property" is described by means of a general characteristic (being a "thing") and a specific characteristic (in this case the legal ability to become an "object of rights"). This helps to differentiate, within the *genus*, the *species*, that is the sub-class which corresponds to the word defined.

The form of the disposition should not, however, be over-estimated. For example, going back again to art. 832., one can still conclude that its function is that of attributing privileges and powers etc, to the owner and not that of defining, even if the article were drafted as follows: "Ownership is the right (generic characteristic) to enjoy and to dispose of etc. (specific characteristic)".

One can understand, however, the (culturally) conditioned reaction which considers the above formulation as a definition because such a technique has been considered for centuries as the defining method *par excellence*. The only method liable to catch the "essence" of what is to be defined. But it is this connection, historically established between definition per *genus and differentiam* and so-called "real" definition which can be source of equivocation. It means we must take great care in the appraisal of laws so drafted and we should not forget, also, the possible cultural conditioning of the legislator. Such formal elements, however, should not be over-valued. With the definition *per genus et differentiam* one simply chooses how to indicate what the defined word refers to, emphasising relations of similarity and difference in relation to other objects.

51 R. Sacco, *La proprietà* (Turin: Utet, 1968), 59, sees art. 832 as a "framework for ownership".

52 For a preliminary examination of the distribution of the definitions in the civil code as well as a slightly deeper analysis of art. 832 and other similar laws (art. 1021, 1022, 981), see Belvedere, *supra* n.1, at 101ff., 128ff.

But it is also true that this type of definition (though not only this one: see *infra* on the subject of extensional definitions) supposes a classification. That is to say, the selection of classes and sub-classes where various possible references of words are to be grouped.[53] From the laws drafted in the way we have seen, it might not be immediately clear whether it is a definition of terms corresponding to the objects classified or a classification of objects corresponding to those terms (the meaning of which, in this case, is presumed known).

In any case, the importance of this kind of definition in the Civil Code is without doubt, if only from its weight in numbers. The fact that they sometimes appear linked to each other in a series of chains clearly reveal a classifying procedure. For example, take the sequence: "A contract is the agreement (general remark) ... to establish etc. (specific remark)" (art. 1321); "A mandate is a contract (general remark) whereby one party etc. (specific remark)" (art. 1703); "A forwarding contract is a mandate (generic remark) by which a forwarding agent etc. (specific remark)" (art. 1737).

The *per genus et differentiam* definition is not the only one which mirrors, at the level of nouns, a classification of objects to which specific terms relate. Just as, within a classification, a process of embodiment of the *species* in the *genus* takes place, the reverse can also happen and there can be a disaggregation of the *genus* from the *species* which constitute it. Such a process, called "logical division", also has an effect at the level of the modality of definition. This can happen when it is applied to determine the meaning of the word indicating the *genus* with words indicating the constituent *species*. In such a case the terms indicating the *species* are known while the meaning of the term indicating the *genus* is unknown — or at least should be clarified or "determined" conventionally. For *per genus et differentiam* definitions the procedure is reversed.

There is a great difference between these two types of definition. With the *per genus and differentiam* definition, the different characteristics specific to the *species* together with the characteristics common to all the components of the *genus* (which is assumed to be known) tell us the set properties which an object must have in order to be designated with a certain word. The technical name given to this set of properties is the *intension* of the word and constitutes the "concept"

53 Tarello, *L'interpretazione*, *supra* n.5, at 194ff., considers definitions *per genus et differentiam*, extensional and by exclusion as being "based on classifications".

corresponding to the word.[54]

It is different with those definitions which explain the meaning of a word indicating a *genus* by listing the *species* within it. Here one indicates the set of all the objects (or sub-classes of objects) to which the term refers. Nothing however is said of the common characteristics justifying the objects' inclusion into the *genus* (and the subsequent use, for each of them, of the term referring to the *genus*). The set of entities which the term designates is called the *extension* of the term and definitions which refer to it are called extensional.[55]

Extensional definitions could help us to a faster understanding when terms indicating sub-classes are well known. They could also help in avoiding the use of a more general and dangerously abstract word (indicating the *genus)* than the one to be defined. They could also be helpful when it is difficult to express synthetically and clearly the criterion of attribution of the word. But this would disappear whenever an extensional and an intensional definition is given at the same time.

Such is the case with the definition of "immovable property" in art. 812. Here after mentioning that "The soil, water sources and water courses, trees, buildings and other constructions, even if joined to the soil for a temporary purpose ... are immovable property" (extensional definition), there is the additional statement «and in general everything that is artificially or naturally annexed to the soil» (intensional definition). Here however, it must be noted that the intensional definition concerns constructions and plantations only and therefore could not totally replace the extensional one. The legislator could have said more simply, "the soil and everything which is annexed to the soil are immovable property", though even so a clear reference to water courses would be missed out. What art. 812 help us to understand is how useful it is, for some definitions, to use an extensional criterion, as an alternative to or cumulatively with an intensional criterion.

Sometimes, the contemporaneous presence of an intensional definition might lead us into thinking that what appears to be an extensional definition is in fact a classification of objects within the *genus* indicated by that word (the meaning of which is established through the specific intensional definition). A similar doubt can occur when the enumeration of the sub-classes constituting the *genus* and which exemplify it, appears incomplete.

54 See Lantella, *supra* n.1, at 44f.

55 See Tarello, *L'interpretazione* , *supra* n.5, at 202ff.

This latter observation might conceal a *petitio principii* The only time we can consider an enumeration linked with a word as being incomplete is when the meaning of this word is considered already established and corresponding to a wider *genus* than the one resulting from the given enumeration. Otherwise — that is if one considers that the meaning of the word should result from the enumeratio — it will be possible to argue about the "quality" of the definition (whether it correspond to its lexical use, or, whether it is a proper a re-definition). But that will not be sufficient reason to deny its character as a definition or to claim that we are dealing with an incomplete extensional definition.

On the other hand, we cannot exclude the possibility of statements which at the same time present themselves as giving definitions and (clearly) only examples, such as the following: "legal acts are, for example, contracts and wills". In such cases however we can only agree with the opinion[56] that exemplifications cannot in any way be considered as definitions. Having excluded the hypothesis examined previously that a list of examples is a classification and not a definition, we must conclude that such laws are aborted attempts at definitions.

There are not many extensional definitions in the Civil Code (as opposed to those *per genus et differentiam).* It is even difficult to find examples which could be anything else but classifications. Such is the case of art. 601 indicating various forms of wills, or of art. 900 which sub-divides "windows" into "lights" and "views"; the fact that the legislator considers the meaning of "window" to be known appears also from the reference in the division between lights and views to any other "opening" (on the land of the neighbour). This classification is linked to successive intensional definitions of "light" and "view". Therefore art. 900 — which to a (very) superficial reader would appear to contain an extensional definition of "window" — has in reality two *per genus et differentiam* definitions: "lights (views) are windows which...".

A final observation on art. 900 and on the (inevitable) lack of precision in legislative language. Art. 900 sub-divides "windows or other openings on the land of the neighbour" into lights and views. This could imply that something opening on someone's land is part of the intension of both "light" and "view". More simply, it could be seen to imply that these terms could only be used with reference to openings (provided with some further characteristics) on someone's land. But then art. 901 points to characteristics required by "lights that open on the land of the neighbour".

56 Tarello's opinion in *L'interpretazione* , *supra* n.5, at 202ff.

This introduces the contrary hypothesis that there could be lights which do *not* open on the land of the neighbour but which could yet be called lights.

Going back to the real extensional definitions, apart from art. 812, we can mention the one included in art. 1429 listing the four cases of "essential mistake", provided we consider such a list as mandatory.[57] As opposed to art. 812, there is no indication in art. 1429 as to what are the attributes shared by the four cases justifying their common heading — logicians would say that it is the intension which determines the extension.[58] Study of the doctrine has not lead to any clear result. One should not forget also how difficult it is to prove, in all four cases, that the same relation exists between mistake and consent[59] (supposing that any legislative policy whatsoever lays behind the various wordings used in the text of the four numbers of the article).

13. *Defining Techniques and Formulation of Precepts in the Civil Code (continued)*

Obviously, *per genus et differentiam* and extensional definitions are not exclusive to legislative language, nor are they limited to particular "styles" and legislative techniques.[60]

Things are a little different with those definitions, frequently found in the Civil Code, which can be obtained by analyzing the relation between the rubric and text of an article. For instance, a comparison between rubric and text of art. 833 shows that by "emulative acts" the legislator means "acts that have no other purpose than that of harming or causing annoyance to others".

It might happen that the defined word is not in the rubric of the

57 See R. Sacco and G. De Nova, "*Il contratto* ", in *Trattato di diritto civile diretto da Pietro Rescigno* (Turin: UTET, 1982), vol.10, p.145.

58 See for references to all of them I. Copi, *Introduction to Logic* (New York: MacMillan, 1972).

59 On all these problems, see Sacco, *supra* n.33, at. 145ff.

60 The same can be said of the so called parenthetical definitions, to be found not so much in the civil code as in special legislation and in German and Anglo-Saxon legislative texts. In this type of definition the description of a fact or of a phenomenon is followed by the name of that fact or phenomenon in brackets. On such definitions see Tarello, *L'interpretazione* , *supra* n.5, at 206f. On the *Klammer-Definitionen* of the BGB, see also Belvedere, *supra* n.1, at 35.

article but in the titles of the internal divisions of the code (Chapters, sections, etc.). Its meaning however might be described in the text of one of the articles (the first) in that division. The text of art. 1647 for example, tells us what the legislator means by (lease to) "the farmer who cultivates personally". This name figures only in the title of the paragraph which begins with art. 1647. The rubric of which is "Notion" with a clear reference to the title of the paragraph.

It might be possible to find similar definitions in non-legislative documents, provided they contain sections with their own specific titles. These definitions are however, typical of legislative documents. This is so because of the important role played by such documents with those formal characteristics (rubrics of articles and titles in internal divisions) which are required by our definition.

Definitions of this kind present a few problems which are worth analyzing. Briefly, we can say that it is sometimes difficult to locate the word (which is supposed to be defined) within the rubric which might include more than one word, or the proposition which defines it within the text. For example, under the rubric "Effects of the mandate to grant credit" art. 1958 lays down that "if a person directs another to extend credit to a third person in the name and for the account of the person thus directed, and the latter binds himself to act accordingly, the person so directing is answerable as a surety for a future debt". While it might be easy to locate, in the rubric, the word to be defined in the text, it might be less easy to spot exactly which proposition defines it (in the text). So much so that there is an ongoing argument as to whether the obligation of the directing person to answer as a surety is part of the definition. In this case such an obligation should be included in the "mandate to grant credit" agreement between the parties. In the other case, the obligation is only one of those "effects" of the agreement mentioned in the rubric. Thus an agreement failing to include such an obligation would still be treated as a mandate to grant credit.

All in all, it can happen that such definitions should be *reconstructed*, rather than *discovered* by the interpreter, something requiring a certain effort.

We are therefore at the limits of the notion of definition meaning a specific attribution of meanings. Beyond those limits lays the land of so-called "implicit" definitions, those which can be obtained by a survey of the word's use in any context.[61] A notion so wide takes all specificity away

61 On the necessity of also taking into consideration implicit definitions, see Jori,

from the problem of the evaluation definitions in the legal context. It is thus of no advantage to an analysis of legal texts.

To end our panoramic enquiry into modes of definition,[62] we can (as a curiosity) mention one not used in the code but which is interesting as an instrument of analysis and as a comparison with the definitions of the 1942 legislator. This is a sophisticated technique, that of the so-called *contextual definitions*. These definitions do not select, for a given word, a semantic equivalent and allow a substitution wherever it appears. Instead they outline the meaning taken by a word in a specific context with the help of a sentence equivalent (and therefore replaceable) to that specific quotation in which the term appears, but not to others. What is given is not an expression which, for example, can at all times be a substitute to the word "brother". Rather a phrase is given which does not comprise the defined term any more (for example "A and B have the same parents"). This is able to replace for example the phrase "A is B's brother" but not other phrases where the term appears (for example "A has many brothers"). In this latter instance, a definition of "brother" would require a different contextual definition (for example "A's parents have many other children").

Contextual definitions have an undoubted disadvantage. They do not always make the elimination of the defined term possible. They are however necessary when such term requires more than one definition because of the varied syntactical statuses it assumes according to its context. For example, a term can refer either to a quality of an individual ("B is a parent") or to a relation between individuals ("B is A's parent"). In this case a definition making possible its elimination from the first sentence ("parent" = person having (had) at least one child") does not, at the same time, allow its elimination from the second.

In general we can say that the direct definitions which we have up till now considered are not suitable to define terms which express relations. Contextual definitions can do this much better. A good example can be in family relations. In trying directly to define "consanguinity", art. 74 is forced to use the metaphoric expression of "connection". This gives credit to the idea that there is indeed in this world something called consanguinity, the truth being that there are only people and reproductive

---

supra n.1, at 491.

62 On definitions "by heading" or "by title", see Tarello, *L'interpretazione* , *supra* n.5, at 207ff.

events concerning them.

The 1942 legislator must have sensed it possible, and even desirable, to avoid such direct definitions. When defining consanguinity in a direct and in a collateral line the art. 74 scheme has been avoided. The legislator does not say that «consanguinity in a direct line is the connection between persons who descend from one another», and in art. 75 he has preferred to speak of "relatives". This is undoubtedly a step forward in relation to the definition of art. 74, though failing to solve every problem.

It is true that art. 75 also still includes a direct definition allowing the substitution of "relative" in texts such as "A and B are relatives in a direct line" but not in others such as "A is a relative of B in a direct line". To be exact, art. 75 should be re-worded bearing in mind a series of contextual definitions which can be taken from it such as: "A and B are relatives in a direct line" = "A descends from B or B descends from A" (this definitions can also be used for other texts such as "A is a relative of B in a direct line", and, of course, "B is a relative of A in a direct line"). A (contextual) definition of "relative in a collateral line" is more complex: "A is a relative of B in a collateral line" = "A and B descend from the same person; A does not descend from B; B does not descend from A". The same definition can also be used in texts such as "A is a relative of B in a collateral line".

14. *The Ambiguity of Legal Terms*

That words are ambiguous is an experience common to anyone, renewed every time a dictionary is consulted. It should be banished from any language requiring rigor. Nevertheless, getting rid of ambiguity is most likely an unattainable ideal for languages without the formal element provided by logical-mathematical symbols. It is definitely a very distant ideal for legal language in general and legislative language in particular.

Above, we have seen examples of ambiguity when talking of terms which can refer both to qualities and relations. We now turn to ambiguity more specifically. Ambiguity is most dangerous not when it reflects a variety of meanings clearly distinct one from the other but when the different meanings relate to different aspects of the same, more complex, reality, or to phenomena somehow interconnected. This is only superficially paradoxical, as the danger of mistake and misunderstanding is much greater in the latter case than in the former.

Therefore we are not worried when we find out that the Civil Code speaks, at art. 1342, of contracts made by means of "moduli" (forms) after having found, at art. 1081, that the "modulo" is "the unit of measure of running water". Nor has anybody ever considered the definition of "modulo" in the last paragraph of the art. 1081 wrong.

More care, on the other hand, should be used when dealing with the word "condition". This can indicate either the clause by which the parties make the contract dependent upon a future and uncertain event (as in art. 1354 which speaks of "attached" condition) or the event itself (as in articles 1359 and ff., which speaks of "fulfilment of condition"). The same is true of "onere" (burden) which sometimes designates the clause and sometimes the obligations deriving from it (art. 793, 2nd paragraph) — so much so that some writers specifically warn of this.[63]

We cannot, of course, deal with all the ambiguities in the Civil Code. Here we will draw attention to those more closely linked with legal problems. In particular, with the relation between facts and norms, both in respect of the qualification of facts and of the legal consequences of certain facts.

Beginning from the latter we can say briefly that the problem stems from the same name being used to indicate both a specific occurrence and the succession of legal events determined by it. For example, it has been noted[64] that the words "cessione del credito" (assignment of claims) (art. 1260) can indicate either the succession to a credit claim, or the corresponding contract. Here the ambiguity comes from the word "assignment" which refers (even in ordinary language) both to the act and effect of assigning.[65] Furthermore, because of its content, the contract in question cannot be called anything other than a "contract of assignment of credit" and thus, owing to a common ellipsis, "assignment of claims". In general, it is understandable that such an exchange of terms should take place between contracts, where parties figure out specific effects, and their effects themselves.

The phenomenon is not limited to contractual cases. In art. 1241 and ff., for example, the word "compensation" is used to designate both the

63 For example U. Carnevali "*Le donazioni*", in *Trattato di diritto privato* (Turin: Utet, 1982), VI.491.

64 For example by M. Allara, *Le fattispecie estintive del rapporto obbligatorio* (Turin: Giappichelli, 1952), 45ff.

65 See N. Zingarelli, *Vocabolario della lingua italiana* (Bologna: Zanichelli, 1983, 11th ed.).

extinguishing of debts and the events which determines it.[66] This continuous change of meaning is particularly conspicuous in art. 1242 which, because the rubric "Effects of compensation" would appear to refer to an event. And in fact its first paragraph, which states "Compensation extinguishes both debts ..." is consistent with the rubric. But in its second paragraph, stating that «compensation is not barred by prescription» the word "compensation" clearly refers to the extinguishing of a debt.

In the matter of compensation, the problem of ambiguity of words is related to that of legislative definitions. From the comparison between heading and text in art. 1241 it is possible to obtain (see above section 13) a definition of "compensation" as being "coexistence of reciprocal debts". This definition though, only concerns one of the two meanings of the word as it only refers to the event which extinguishes a debts.

A similar phenomenon arises in matter of novation where, when using the term, some dispositions (art. 1233 and 1234) refer to "fattispecie" (a set of events) while others (art. 1231) refer to the extinguishing of a debt (vicenda).[67] It should be noted that, compared with "compensation", it is more difficult here to identify a definition, even with the help of the rubric. The article to be considered would be art. 1230 ("Objective novation") which seems to refer to novation as the extinguishing of debts.

The presence in the law of such ambiguities does not necessarily represents a major obstacle towards the understanding of legal phenomena. Some scholars even appear to relish them.[68] However easy to overcome, it is still a deficiency of legal (and legislative) language. It makes it harder to get a clear view of the problems. All the more so because ambiguity can not only be the cause of a confusion in interpretation but can also be seen as a symptom of the confusion of the legislator.

Other situations demonstrate that the 1942 legislator is a "prisoner" of the language. Here I do not have in mind cases where the ambiguity is generated, as in the examples above, by the attribution of the same name to phenomena effectively distinguishable one from the other, each performing a specific function within a particular legal discourse. Rather,

66 See P. Schlesinger, "Compensazione (diritto civile)", in *Novissimo Digesto Italiano* III (Turin: UTET, 1959), 722; P. Perlingieri, "Dei modi di estinzione delle obbligazioni diversi dall'adempimento", in *Commentario, supra* n.37, at 256-399.

67 See Perlingieri, *supra* n.66, at 59.

68 See Perlingieri, *supra* n.66, at 256.

I have in mind ambiguity generated by a pointless conceptual proliferation resulting in legal phenomena being presented in an artificially complicated and twisted manner. Thus art. 467, stating that "Representation substitutes legitimate or natural descendants ..." leads us into thinking that there exists a use of "representation" referring to a case by which descendants are substituted in the place and degree of their ascendants. If we analyse representation we can easily show that the law does not require any intermediary thing, between the impossibility or refusal to accept the inheritance from an heir and the substitution in their place of the descendants (if the conditions of the law are fulfilled). It is clear therefore, that representation does not *induce* but *is* (the) substitution of the descendants. Thus the only correct use of the term is in reference to a change of legal relations, such as appears from the text of the second paragraph of art. 467 and the following articles.

Art. 280 gives us another example of apparent ambiguity (just as dangerous and even more misleading than actual ambiguity). By stating that "Legitimation attributes ... the status of legitimate child" it gives the impression that the word "legitimation" refers to a legal "entity" which is both the consequence of the marriage of the natural son's parents (or the judge's measure) and the reason for the attribution of the quality of legitimate son. The truth is that no intermediate "entity" is foreseen by the law. Legitimation consists precisely in the acquisition by natural children of the quality of legitimate children in the manner foreseen by law.

Similar examples of such equivocations are at the origin of some legislative classifications (for example that of art. 922 on the modes of acquisition of ownership, where "fattispecie di acquisto" (set of events producing the acquisition of ownership, such as contract, occupation, etc.) are assimilated to conveyances of rights (succession at death).[69] One could explain this differently, and could base it, more simply, on the generality of the expression "modes of acquisition" and on the need for the legislator to indicate each mode in a clear and concise manner. We can imagine how difficult it would be, however, to turn the reference to the succession at death into a reference to a set of events which might be the cause of the succession. At the most, one could question the legislator's choice (of a rather scholastic character) of listing the various modes of acquisition. A choice which carries the need to give specific names (occupation, invention, etc.) to phenomena governed by the provisions which follow in that part of the code.

69 See Allara, *supra* n.64.

15. *Factual / Normative Ambiguities (continued)*

We now turn to consider the second case of legal ambiguity. Our starting point must be the distinction, seen above (section 6) between factual and normative terms. In some cases the same term may be used both in a factual and in a normative sense. Let us take the word "testamentary provision" and compare the following texts (included respectively in art. 588 and in the rubric of art. 590): "Testamentary provisions...attribute the status of heir, if ..."; "Confirmation ... of void testamentary provisions".

In the first, the word refers to provisions formally and substantially laid down in accordance with the law. There cannot be attribution of the status of heir if the provisions are not written in testamentary form or if, for example, the provision benefits the notary who receives the will (art. 597). The term therefore cannot be used for all declarations aiming at disposing of one's own property after death, but only for those conforming to all the rules concerning wills.

In this text then, the word does not refer to situations which can be verified on the basis of purely factual criteria (concerning the historical existence of someone's last will in favour of someone else). It refers instead to a state of affairs considered complete only when all the facts match the pattern set by the norms. This would then allow us to qualify the fact in respect of its validity and effect (to simplify, we restrict our distinction to that between valid and void acts). In conclusion, "testamentary disposition" is used in the first text not as a factual term but as a normative term since it is equivalent to "*valid* testamentary disposition".

When we now examine the second text, dealing with void testamentary provisions, it is evident that we have not got the same meaning here unless we want to deal with an utterly contradictory expression: "void valid testamentary disposition". Nor could the problem be solved were we to consider it equivalent to "non valid testamentary provision". The term would still have a normative use though expressing the opposite qualification. The legislative expression "void testamentary provision" would cease to be inconsistent. It would instead be pleonastic as the normative qualification would be expressed both by the noun ("testamentary provision") and by the adjective ("void"). It is then evident that in the heading of art. 590, "testamentary provision" does not designate a legally qualified fact (the qualification comes from "void") and its use is therefore only a factual one.

On the other hand, the word "will" in art. 587 is defined on the basis of this use. This definition tells us in which circumstances we are dealing with a will but does not enable us to know whether we are dealing with a valid will. Its function is not the nearly impossible one of summarizing the requirements of validity laid down in several norms. Rather, it tells us what actual transactions in the world are to be matched against these norms as opposed to the norms, for example, which determine marriage or contract.[70]

16. *A Particular Case: The Notion of Contract*

We have thus far examined two types of ambiguity, that between the factual and the normative sense and that based on the change of meaning between cause and effect, between the whole and one of its parts (see above section 14. For the sake of brevity, I shall call the latter "metonymic"). We can find both types affecting the use of the same term. The word "contract" gives a good example of this.

For a long time already the best doctrine has acknowledged the variety of its meanings.[71] When speaking, for example, of formation of contract (art. 1326 and ff.), the word "contract" indicates the mutual agreement between parties. A second use of "contract" relates the word to the text of the agreement itself, for example, when it is a matter of interpretation of the contract (articles 1362 and ff.). A third use of the word, "contract" refers to the contractual order laid down by the parties, as it appears from the interpretation of the text. This meaning is the one assumed by notions such as "partial nullity of the contract" (art. 1419), or "integration of contract" (art. 1374). Finally, "contract" designates the contractual order which binds the parties when it has been accepted by the legal order, after control and possible modification. Thus art. 1372 states that "A contract has the force of law between the parties" and art. 1375 declares that "The contract shall be performed according to good faith".

What are the connections between these various meanings of the word

70 On this systematic function of many legislative definitions, see Belvedere, *Le definizioni*, *supra* n.1, at 88f., 169, 150ff.

71 See P. Schlesinger, "Complessità del procedimento di formazione del consenso ed unità del negozio contrattuale", in *Studi in onore di P. Greco* (Padova: CEDAM, 1965), II,1003-1021.

"contract"? In relation to the first three it is possible to detect a "metonymic" ambiguity. On the other hand things are different if we are dealing with the connections between the third and fourth meanings and with the difference between the regulatory order laid down by the parties and the one which is then binding. Here we find a factual/normative ambiguity. The difference remains even when the regulatory order arranged by the parties is totally accepted into the legal order, without any modification. The set of rules is identical in both cases; however, it is one thing to deal with rules already expressed, whose existence can be historically proven; it is something else to deal with rules which are valid because of their conformity with a complex set of legal norms (and therefore binding the parties).

When using the word "contract" in the third of the above meanings, we presume the existence of a set of rules ordering the transaction but saying nothing about their validity. In its fourth meaning, we presume that the characterisation as legal of those rules has already (successfully) taken place: "contract" is not equivalent then to "contractual regulations" (as in the third case), but, more precisely, to "valid contractual regulations".

Comparing this analysis with the definition of art. 1321, we can see that definition matches well the first meaning but also can be referred to the third. The reason being that not every agreement constitutes a contract but only the agreement with a given content (according to the text of the same art. 1321). In any case the meaning of "contract" in the definition of art. 1321 corresponds to a use in a factual sense since we can use it to know whether we are dealing with a contract but not whether it is a valid one. The factual character of the definition in art. 1321 concerns both the content and the "procedural" aspects of the agreement. A situation could perfectly well correspond to such a definition but could still not be turned into a valid contract. Either because the content is unlawful or because an agreement which though factually existing does not conform to the criteria of articles 1326 and ff. on the procedure for establishing contracts (for example, when the acceptance has been given in a different form from that required by the offeror).

Therefore, even without referring to content, the word "agreement" also appears ambiguous. It can indicate both an agreement which cannot be legally classified, and a "valid" agreement (according to articles 1326 and ff.). Thus we have two renderings of the first meaning of "contract".[72]

72 Whereas the second of those meanings still belongs to the realm of the facts

17. *The "Existence" of Contract as a Systematic Category*

Following on from the above interpretation of art. 1321, it might be of some interest to examine the possibility of a link between that definition and the antithesis existent/non existent contract.

It might be imagined that only when the requirements of art. 1321 are absent that the "non-existence" of contract could be spoken of. On the other hand, their presence would allow a contract to be considered "existent", even though, on the basis of other norms, it would be void.

Reference in the definition of art. 1321 to rigorously factual requirements might appear to clash with the dominant doctrinal tendency to view the question as being one of "legal" and not simply one of "material" existence/non-existence.[73]

In fact, the distinction itself is not properly set out or, at the most, is ambiguous. We would hesitate as to which of the two notions would apply in the absence of factual requirements which are also legal requirements, because legally required for a certain purpose. The fact of using, as adjectives with a factual or legal meaning, categories which indicate always, and only, the presence or the absence of something, is misleading. It would be wiser to better distinguish and classify the kind of objects of which we wish to establish the presence or absence of.

If what we are looking for is, essentially, a valid act, our search cannot be a purely factual one. What we need is a comparison between the facts and a very complex set of norms stating what requirements are needed for a specific act to be valid. Should just one requirement be missing, we would conclude that there is no valid act within the segment of reality under consideration. Unless that is, we say that there "exists", for example, a void act. That one act (even a void one) should exist results from the logical necessity to find out the thing which is object of the legal qualification (in terms of voidness).

A legal qualification of non-existence would still have to refer to an act which, in any actual instance, we would have to consider as "existent". This paradox shows that existence is not a quality (Kant would call it a predicate) of the act, equal to its validity. It shows that non-existence and nullity are logically so different that one cannot compare one to the other.

---

only (contract equals text). We have already covered the character, respectively factual and normative, of the last two meanings.

73 See G. Filanti, *Inesistenza e nullità del negozio giuridico* (Napoli: Jovene, 1983), and my review in *Quadrimestre* (1985), 308ff.

In a sense, it is far more correct to speak of the existence/non-existence of an act, rather than existent/non-existent act).

The same conclusions can be reached using the prosaic reasoning of the positive law. The qualification of an act (it does not matter whether as valid or invalid) requires the identification of the set of norms to be used as its basis. The more so because norms are different according to the various types of act. An act which could be void as a testament because of formal requirements, could be valid as an act *inter vivos*. First of all then, it is necessary to assess the concrete case and match it with one of the forms of transaction specifically foreseen and regulated by law (for the sake of simplicity, we leave aside the question of atypical transactions). Possible legislative definitions like those of articles 1321 and 587 might help us to do this (and bind us, though we cannot deal here with this aspect of the question). Once we have decided that we are dealing with a contract, and not a will, we assess whether the act is regular as to its form according to articles 1350 and ff. (and not according to articles 601 and ff.) and reach conclusions as to the validity of the act.

But let us go back to the previous stage; here, having acknowledged that the act might be a contract, we are still unable to say whether it is valid or not. At this stage, we can speak of the existence of a contract and leave its validity or its voidness undecided.

The latter alternative would not arise if we were to deny the "existence" of a contract. What might eventually remain undecided is the question of whether it would be possible to refer the behaviour in question to a different form of transaction. Seen in this way, the categories of existence/non-existence neither express a legal qualification nor have legal relevance seen as the ability to produce legal effects. They do reflect the ability to be taken into account by (some specific norms of) the legal order.

In conclusion, it is evident that this notion of "existence" has nothing to do with the question of legal effects produced by acts void but existent.[74] It fulfils instead a systematic function by reflecting the sphere of application of a series of norms. The same function must also be attributed to possible legislative definitions helping to determine its requirements.

74 According to a common way of seeing the problem, correctly criticised by Filanti, *supra* n.73; in particular chapter II where he denies any usefulness to the notion of "existent transaction" when interpreting isolated hypothesis of effectiveness of a void transaction.

18. *Legislative Conceptualisations and Similar Figures*

Our analysis of the language of the code has followed two main paths. Firstly, classification of the adopted terms — and therefore also of the corresponding "concepts", if we mean these as the (intensional) meanings of the various words and of their synonyms. Secondly, the ways in which the (1942) Italian civil legislator drafts the rules for using some of those terms or, if one prefers, endeavours towards the formation of some of the concepts used.

To conclude, I would now like to say something about how this activity of defining relates to certain figures which have sometimes been compared to them. Undoubtedly there is a relation between definitions and "fictions".[75] So much so that "defining fictions" have been mentioned[76] in relation to definitions drafted as the one found in the second paragraph of art. 812. While there is no doubt that these are definitions, it is doubtful whether they can be said to be fictions.

Some indication of this can be found in the introduction of the second paragraph of art. 812 "are considered immovables" (instead of simply "are immovables"), though the argument is not decisive because similar expressions can occur in normal definitions such as in art. 816 ("...is considered a universality of movables").[77] Furthermore, in art. 812, the expression used could also be justified by the fact that floating buildings are considered immovables only when they are "securely" and permanently attached to the bank or the bed of a waterway.

There are reasons, though, as to why such definitions should be treated differently. And these have well motivated the legislator in drafting. The reason for using a more vague expression might have been the wish (the illusion, perhaps) to avoid a conflict between the legislative use of the term and its ordinary language use. According to the latter, in the example above floating buildings would not be "immovables".

One should note however, that such a contrast could be seen as

75 See on the subject S. Pugliatti, "Finzione", in *Enciclopedia di diritto* (Milan: Giuffrè 1968), XVII, 658-673, and "Conoscenza", *ibid.* (Milan: Giuffrè, 1961), IX.85-130. See also A. Ross, "Le finzioni giuridiche", in *Critica del diritto e analisi del linguaggio* (Bologna: Il Mulino 1982), 177ff., and R. Guastini, "Problemi di analisi del linguaggio normativo", in Ross, *ibid.*, at 55ff.

76 Pugliatti, *Conoscenza*, *supra* n.75, at 88.

77 A similar set of problems arises in the BGB with the expression "*als ... gilt*". See on this subject Belvedere, *supra* n.1, at 34f. and note 51.

problematic and to be avoided only if one remains tied to the wrong idea that for each word there is only one meaning and thus only a single definition can be given for it. In a conception that accepts stipulative definitions and redefinitions (cf 9 above), the affirmation that floating buildings are immovables would not appear paradoxical. It would merely be a method of extending to floating building the discipline of the various rules which apply to immovable property.

The same result could be obtained by the different technique of adding a specific reference to floating buildings in all the norms which refer to immovable property. Still another alternative would consist in establishing a category and a name comprehending all immovable property and floating buildings to which the various norms could then refer. The problem of a correct approach does not appear to be in any way modified or, even less, solved by the adoption of a (transparent) "fictional" wording.

In conclusion, identifying a separate category of definitions at the cognitive level is of doubtful utility. This results from a "contamination" between the two figures, definition and fiction. These two figures are the expression of deeply heterogeneous mental operations.

With definition, we operate at the level of names, giving them meaning. We cannot speak of "pretending" attribution of meaning or of attribution of a "pretend" meaning.

Fiction does not concern names but the reality to which names refer. It consists in considering as existing a certain reality which does not exist or (the same thing) considering that a determinate phenomenon presents characteristics which it does not have. The legislator considers, for determinate legal purposes, that situation A (characterised by certain elements) is identical with situation B where some or all of these elements are missing. There is fiction only when what is required is a real identity between the two situations and not a pure equivalence of their effect.[78]

We can thus consider the provisions of art. 1340, "Customary terms are deemed to be included in the contract" as the result of a fiction (provided it is not a presumption see *infra*). But what is found in the last paragraph of art. 1326 is certainly not a fiction. It is only the provision of equal effects so that "an acceptance that does not conform to the offer is equivalent to a new offer". The same is probably true of art. 1359,

78 To say that cats are equal to dogs as far as the obligation of vaccination against rabies is concerned does not imply that cats are dogs and even less a definition of "dog" where the word applies also to cats.

according to which "a condition is considered fulfilled when it fails for a cause imputable etc.";[79] and art. 1431 is a definition rather than a fiction when it states "a mistake is considered recognisable" using a wording not unlike that of art. 1429, which determines when "mistake is essential".

Arts. 1354, second paragraph (an impossible resolutive condition "is treated as non-existent") and 1344 ("the *causa* is also considered unlawful" when the contract evades the law) are more problematic (the "causa" of a contract in Italian civil law is usually considered the socio-economical function of the contract). One can be confident that as art. 1354 is not a case of fiction. One must go beyond the wording and capture the meaning of the disposition which nullifies only the conditional clause and not the whole contract, following the rule *vitiatur sed non vitiat*.

As for art. 1344, there is a fundamental objection to the fiction thesis. It is doubtful whether the fiction can be referred not only to the events stipulated but also to its legal qualification. In other words, the question arises as to whether it is correct to state that in art. 1344 the "causa" of the contract "is considered by the law as if it were unlawful, whereas it is not so".[80] The answer can only be that the fact of considering a "causa" as being unlawful is equivalent to qualifying it as such.[81] This is because the legal qualification derives exclusively from the legislative will and there is no possibility of conflict with the nature of thing, the historical reality or previous linguistic uses.

Why is there this difference between art. 1344 and art. 1343? It could be linked to the fact that the legislator considers the "causa" as unlawful not only when the function of the transaction, viewed alone, conflicts with the legal order. But also (the importance of "also" in art. 1344 should not be overlooked) when the function taken by the contract, when looked at in a wider transactional context, is directed at evading the application of a norm.[82]

In so far as presumptions operate not at the verbal level but at the level of reference of a word,[83] they do represent, though, a figure

79 For view which runs counter to the widely held thesis of a fiction of fulfilment, see C.M. Bianca, *Diritto Civile* (Milan: Giuffrè, 1984), 527f.

80 See L. Carraro, "Frode alla legge", in *Novissimo Digesto Italiano,* VII, (Turin: UTET, 1961), 649.

81 See G. Giacobbe, "Frode alla legge", in *Enciclopedia del diritto* XCII (Milan: Giuffrè, 1969), 81.

82 See Giacobbe, *supra* n.81, at 83f. and Bianca, *supra* n.79, at III, 587.

83 Even if sometimes definitions starting with the expression "si considera" are

contiguous to that of fictions. Presumption also, helps to establish an equivalence between a situation which generates certain effects (though difficult to verify) and another situation involving lesser or different requirements and in any event easier to ascertain. While with a fiction it is accepted from the very start that there can be no actual identity between the two situations, a presumption is based instead on a possible, and even likely coincidence between them. For example, it is for this reason that art. 231 says that "the husband is the father of a child conceived during the marriage" and, according to art. 599, the spouse and other near relatives of the person lacking capacity to benefit from testamentary dispositions "are treated as interposed persons".[84]

Anyway the alternative is quite clear. A definition describes the necessary and sufficient requirements needed for a certain phenomenon to be indicated with that word. A presumption gives no indication as to which reality corresponds to the word (the meaning of which is supposed to be known). It tells us instead which elements need to be checked in order that the legislator consider such reality as existing (about which the presumption gives no information).

The greatest difficulty in distinguishing between definitions and propositions relative not to nouns but to their references is to be found in the comparison between classifications (or logical divisions) on one side and *per genus et differentiam* (or extensional) definitions on the other. We have already seen (above, section 12) how these definitions, as far as nouns are concerned, reflect specific classifying procedures (in a wide sense) and how only by examining the context of the disposition we can therefore ascertain its function; whether such a function is to describe that part of reality which the legislator wants to indicate by using a certain word, or whether it is to compare two realities (objects) already known.

The problem is easily solved only in a few cases. For example, when the subdivision of a *genus* in sub-classes is not able to perform the function of describing the *genus* itself, because of the way it is worded. Or else, when such function has already been performed by another (undoubtedly) defining proposition. Both these possibilities can be found

---

interpreted as presumptions, as pointed out by Tarello, *supra* n.5, at 222.

84 On the difference between fiction and presumption, see V. Andrioli, "Presunzioni (diritto civile e diritto processuale civile)", in *Novissimo Digesto Italiano,* XIII, (Turin: UTET, 1966), 766-772.

in art. 2730, second paragraph ("A confession is judicial or extra-judicial"), where the two sub-classes are indicated with a distinction which says nothing of what constitutes the *genus*. Besides, we know from the first paragraph what facts corresponds to the word "confession".

How unsuitable a sub-division is as a definition is also shown by of art. 900 (see above section 12). We could add a further argument here. To try to identify a definition of "window" would be useless, since the legislator subsequently gives his views on each specific sub-class with no reference to the wider figure which includes it. This is, though, a misleading argument. It tends to confuse the problem of determining whether something is a definition with the actual usefulness of the definition in the law.

BIBLIOGRAPHY

In addition to writings cited in the book, this bibliography includes other works of the following Italian analytical jurists: Giampaolo Azzoni, Mauro Barberis, Norberto Bobbio, Patrizia Borsellino, Gaetano Carcaterra, Silvana Castignone, Alfonso Catania, Mario Cattaneo, Bruno Celano, Pierluigi Chiassoni, Paolo Comanducci, Amedeo Conte, Paolo Di Lucia, Enrico Diciotti, Luigi Ferrajoli, Giacomo Gavazzi, Letizia Gianformaggio, Riccardo Guastini, Mario Jori, Giorgio Lazzaro, Eugenio Lecaldano, Mario Losano, Claudio Luzzati, Tecla Mazzarese, Maurizio Mori, Gianpaolo Parodi, Enrico Pattaro, Anna Pintore, Giuliano Pontara, Uberto Scarpelli, Giovanni Tarello, Michele Taruffo, Giulio Ubertis and Vittorio Villa.

Aarnio, A., *On Legal Reasoning* (Turku: Turun Yliopisto, 1977).

Abbagnano, N., "Sul concetto del diritto", *Rivista di Filosofia* LIII (1962), 63-68.

Agazzi, E., "Il problema della caratterizzazione conoscitiva della normalità e della devianza", in Orazio Siciliani, Piergiorgio Muzi, Mariano Bianca, eds., *Normalità e devianza* (Milan: Angeli, 1981), 19-38.

Agazzi, E., "The Presence of Values in the Social Sciences", *Epistemologia* V (1982), 5-26.

Alchourrón, C. and Bulygin, E., *Normative Systems* (New York and Vienna: Springer Verlag, 1971, Library of Exact Philosophy).

Alchourrón, C. and Bulygin, E., "The Expressive Conception of Norms", in R. Hilpinen, ed., *New Studies in Deontic Logic* (Dordrecht: Reidel, 1981), 95-124.

Alchourrón, C. and Bulygin, E., *Sobre la existencia de las normas jurídicas* (Valencia: Oficina Latino-americana de investigaciones jurídicas y sociales, 1979).

Allara, M, *Le fattispecie estintive del rapporto obbligatorio* (Turin: Giappichelli, 1952).

Allorio, E., *Problemi di diritto* vol. I (Milan: Giuffrè, 1957).

Amorth, A., "Misure e pesi (diritto amministrativo")", *Enciclopedia di diritto* (Milan: Giuffrè, 1976), XXVI, 610-616.

Amselek, P., "Le droit dans les esprits", in P. Amselek and C. Grzegorczyk, eds., *Controverses autour de l'ontologie du droit* (Paris: PUF, 1989), 27-49.

Amselek, P., *Méthode phénoménologique et théorie du droit* (Paris: R. Pichon et R. Durand-Auzias, 1964).

Andrioli, V., "Presunzioni (diritto civile e diritto processuale civile)", *Novissimo Digesto Italiano* (Turin: Unione Tipografico-Editrice Torinese, 1966), XIII.766-772.

Ascarelli, T., "Giurisprudenza costituzionale e teoria dell'interpretazione", *Rivista di diritto processuale* 12 (1957), 351-64.

Austin, J.L., "Performative Utterances", in *Philosophical Papers*, ed. J.O. Urmson and G.J. Warnock (London: Clarendon Press, 1961), 237-239.

Austin, J.L., "Truth", in *Philosophical Papers*, ed. J.O. Urmson and G.J. Warnock (London: Clarendon Press, 1961), 85-101.

Austin, J.L., *How to do things with Words*, ed. J.O. Urmson (London: Clarendon Press, 1962).

Azzoni, G.M., "Condizioni costitutive", *Rivista internazionale di filosofia del diritto* LXIII (1986), 160-195.

Azzoni, G.M., "Regola tecnica tra ontico e deontico", *Rivista internazionale di filosofia del diritto* LXIV (1987), 297-321.

Azzoni, G.M., "Validità semantica in deontica", *Rivista internazionale di filosofia del diritto* LXIX (1992), 166-177.

Azzoni, G.M., *Cognitivo e normativo. Il paradosso delle regole tecniche* (Milan: Angeli, 1991).

Azzoni, G.M., *Il concetto di condizione nella tipologia delle regole* (Padova: CEDAM, 1988).

Baratta, A., "Il positivismo e il neopositivismo", in R. Orecchia, ed., *La filosofia del diritto italiana nel XX secolo, Atti dell'XI Congresso Nazionale della Società di Filosofia Giuridica e Politica* (Milan: Giuffrè, 1977), vol. II, 21-57.

Barberis, M., "Bobbio su scienza e giurisprudenza: una rilettura", *La difesa penale* I (1983), 147-160.

Barberis, M., "Kelsen e la giustizia costituzionale", *Materiali per una storia della cultura giuridica* XII (1982), 225-242.

Barberis, M., "La giurisprudenza nello specchio della scienza. In margine a un libro di Vittorio Villa", *Materiali per una storia della cultura giuridica* XV (1985), 275-283.

Barberis, M., "La norma senza qualità. Appunti su «validità» in Hans Kelsen", *Materiali per una storia della cultura giuridica* 11 (1981), 405-438.

Barberis, M., "Tarello, l'ideologia e lo spazio della teoria", *Materiali per una storia della cultura giuridica* XVII (1987), 317-356.

Barberis, M., "Universal Legal Concepts? A Criticism of "General" Legal Theory", *Ratio Juris* 8 (1996), 1-14.

Barberis, M., "Vincoli e strumenti. Sulla filosofia analitica del diritto", *Analisi e diritto* 6 (1995), 7-26.

Barberis, M., *Benjamin Constant. Rivoluzione, costituzione, progresso* (Bologna: Il Mulino, 1988).

Barberis, M., *Il diritto come discorso e come comportamento* (Turin: Giappichelli, 1990).

Barberis, M., *Introduzione alla storia della filosofia del diritto* (Bologna: Il Mulino, 1993).

Barberis, M., *Sette studi sul liberalismo rivoluzionario* (Turin: Giappichelli, 1989).

Barbero, D., "Empirismo e dogmatica nel diritto", *Rivista trimestrale di diritto e procedura civile* III (1949), 310-31.

Barker, S.F., *Philosophy of Mathematics* (Englewood Cliffs, N.J.: Prentice-Hall, 1964).

Barrere Unzueta, M.A., *La escuela de Bobbio. Reglas y normas en la filosofía jurídica italiana de inspiracíon analitica* (Madrid: Tecnos, 1990).

Beccaria, C.B., *On Crimes and Punishments* (Indianapolis: Bobbs-Merrill: 1963); italian translation: *Dei delitti e delle pene*, ed. G.D. di Pisapia (Milano: Giuffrè, 1964).

Beccaria, G.L., "Linguaggi settoriali e lingua comune", in *Linguaggi settoriali in Italia*, ed. G.L. Beccaria (Milan: Bompiani, 1973), 29-59.

Belvedere, A., "Aspetti ideologici delle definizioni nel linguaggio del legislatore e dei giuristi", in *Definizioni giuridiche ed ideologie,* ed. A. Belvedere, M. Jori and L. Lantella (Milan: Giuffrè, 1979), 349-480.

Belvedere, A., "Definizioni", in *Digesto delle discipline privatistiche. Sezione civile* (Turin: UTET, 1989), V.1-14.

Belvedere, A., "Il linguaggio del codice civile: alcune osservazioni", in *Trattato di diritto civile diretto da Pietro Rescigno*, vol.21 (Turin: UTET, 1985), 1-44.

Belvedere, A., "Le clausole generali tra interpretazione e produzione di norme", *Politica del diritto* XIX (1988), 631-653.

Belvedere, A., *Il problema delle definizioni nel codice civile* (Milan: Giuffrè, 1977).

Belvedere, A., *Il problema delle definizioni nel codice civile* (Milano: Giuffrè, 1978).

Belvedere, A., Jori, M., and Lantella, L., *Definizioni giuridiche e ideologie* (Milano: Giuffrè, 1979).

Bergmann, G., "Two Cornestones of Empiricism" (1953), reprinted in F. Zabeeh, E.D. Klemke, A. Jacobson, eds., *Readings in Semantics* (Urbana: University of Illinois Press, 1974), 612-639.

Bernstein, R.J., "Professor Hart on Rules of Obligation", *Mind* 73 (1964), 563-566.

Bianca, C.M., *Diritto civile* (Milan: Giuffrè, 1984).

Blackshield, A.R., "Hart's Concept of Law," *Archiv für Rechts und Sozialphilosophie* XLVIII (1962), 329-341.

Blanché, R., *L'axiomatique* (Paris: PUF, 1955).

Bobbio, N., "Ancora sulle norme primarie e secondarie", *Rivista di Filosofia* LIX (1968), 35-53.

Bobbio, N., "Considerazioni in margine", *Rivista di Filosofia* LVII (1966), 235-246.

Bobbio, N., "Diritto e logica", *Rivista internazionale di filosofia del diritto* XXXVIII (1961), 119-119.

Bobbio, N., "Diritto e scienze sociali", in N. Bobbio, *Dalla struttura alla funzione. Nuovi studi di teoria del diritto* (Milan: Edizioni di Comunità, 1977), 43-61.

Bobbio, N., "Essere e dover essere nella scienza giuridica", *Rivista di filosofia* LVIII (1967), 235-62, reprinted in his *Studi sulla teoria generale del diritto* (Turin: Giappichelli, 1970), 139-73.

Bobbio, N., "Francesco Carnelutti, teorico generale del diritto", in *Giurisprudenza italiana* IV (1949), 113-127, repr. in: *Studi sulla teoria generale del diritto* (Turin: Giappichelli, 1955), 1-26.

Bobbio, N., "Intervento di Norberto Bobbio", in *Tavola rotonda sul positivismo giuridico (Pavia, May 2, 1966)* (Milan: Giuffrè, 1967), 69-73.

Bobbio, N., "Kelsen et les sources du droit", *Revue internationale de Philosophie* 138 (1981), 474-486 (issue on *Kelsen et le positivisme juridique*).

Bobbio, N., "La funzione promozionale del diritto rivisitata", *Sociologia del diritto* XI (1984), 7-28.

Bobbio, N., "Law and force", *The Monist* XLIX (1965), 321-341.

Bobbio, N., "Per un lessico di teoria generale del diritto", in *Studi in memoria di Enrico Giucciardi* (Padova: Cedam, 1975), 125-146, reprinted in R. Guastini, ed., *Problemi di teoria del diritto* (Bologna: Il Mulino, 1980), 47-55.

Bobbio, N., "Reason in Law", *Ratio Juris* 1 (1988), 97-108.

Bobbio, N., "Scienza del diritto e analisi del linguaggio", *Rivista Trimestrale di Diritto e Procedura civile* IV (1950), 342-367, reprinted in U. Scarpelli, ed., *Diritto e analisi del linguaggio* (Milan: Edizioni di Comunità, 1976), 287-324, and in U. Scarpelli and P. Di Lucia, eds., *Il linguaggio del diritto* (Milan: Ledi, 1994), 87-93.

Bobbio, N., "Scienza e tecnica del diritto", in *Memorie dell'istituto giuridico dell'università di Turin*, series II, Memoria XXIX (Turin: Istituto della Regia Università, 1934).

Bobbio, N., "Scienza giuridica tra essere e dover essere", *Rivista internazionale di filosofia del diritto* XLV (1968), 475-486.

Bobbio, N., "Sul ragionamento dei giuristi" (1955), in P. Comanducci and R. Guastini, eds., *L'analisi del ragionamento giuridico. Materiali ad uso degli studenti* (Turin: Giappichelli, 1989), vol. 2, 161-179.

Bobbio, N., "Teoria sociologica e teoria generale del diritto", *Sociologia del diritto* I (1974), 9-15.
Bobbio, N., *Contratto sociale, oggi* (Napoli: Guida, 1980).
Bobbio, N., *Dalla struttura alla funzione. Nuovi studi di teoria del diritto* (Milan: Edizioni di Comunità, 1977).
Bobbio, N., *Diritto e potere. Saggi su Kelsen* (Napoli: ESI, 1992).
Bobbio, N., *Giusnaturalismo e positivismo giuridico* (Milan: Edizioni di Comunità, 1965).
Bobbio, N., *Il futuro della democrazia. Una difesa delle regole del gioco* (Turin: Einaudi, 1984).
Bobbio, N., *Il positivismo giuridico* (Turin: Giappichelli, 1961; 2nd ed. 1979).
Bobbio, N., *Il problema della guerra e le vie della pace* (Bologna: Il Mulino, 1979).
Bobbio, N., *Introduzione alla filosofia del diritto* (Turin: Giappichelli, 1948).
Bobbio, N., *L'analogia nella logica giuridica* (Turin: Istituto Giuridico dell' Università, 1938).
Bobbio, N., *L'età dei diritti* (Turin: Einaudi, 1990).
Bobbio, N., *La consuetudine come fatto normativo* (Padova: CEDAM, 1942).
Bobbio, N., *La teoria delle forme di governo nella storia del pensiero politico* (Turin: Giappichelli, 1976).
Bobbio, N., *Lezioni di filosofia del diritto* (Turin: Giappichelli, 1946).
Bobbio, N., *Quale socialismo? Discussione di un'alternativa* (Turin: Einaudi, 1976).
Bobbio, N., *Saggi sulla scienza politica in Italia* (Bari: Laterza, 1977).
Bobbio, N., *Stato, governo, società. Per una teoria generale della politica* (Turin: Einaudi, 1985).
Bobbio, N., *Studi hegeliani. Diritto, società civile, stato* (Turin: Einaudi, 1981.
Bobbio, N., *Studi per una teoria generale del diritto* (Turin: Giappichelli, 1970).
Bobbio, N., *Studi sulla teoria generale del diritto* (Turin: Giappichelli, 1955).
Bobbio, N., *Teoria dell'ordinamento giuridico* (Turin: Giappichelli, 1960).
Bobbio, N., *Teoria della norma giuridica* (Turin: Giappichelli, 1958).
Bobbio, N., *Teoria della scienza giuridica* (Turin: Giappichelli, 1950).
Bobbio, N., *Una guerra giusta? Sul conflitto del golfo* (Venezia: Marsilio, 1991).
Borsellino, P., ""La questione animale": a proposito di un recente contributo al problema", *Rivista internazionale di filosofia del diritto* LXIII (1986), 265-271.

Borsellino, P., "L'analogia nella logica del diritto: un contributo di Norberto Bobbio alla metodologia giuridica", *Rivista internazionale di filosofia del diritto* LXII (1985), 3-39.

Borsellino, P., "Norberto Bobbio e l'empirismo logico: una analisi con riguardo alla tesi divisionistica", *Rivista internazionale di filosofia del diritto* LXIV (1987), 322-366.

Borsellino, P. and Mori, M., "Riviste di filosofia pratica: rassegna di un decennio", *Rivista internazionale di filosofia del diritto* LXI (1984), 128-150.

Borsellino, P., *Norberto Bobbio metateorico del diritto* (Milan: Giuffrè, 1991).

Borsellino, P., *Norberto Bobbio e la teoria generale del diritto. Bibliografia ragionata 1934-1982* (Milan: Giuffrè, 1983).

Braithwaite, R.B., *Scientific Explanation* (Cambridge: Cambridge University Press, 1953).

Broad, C.D., "Filosofia critica e speculativa", in *Filosofi inglesi contemporanei,* ed. J.H. Muirhead (Milan: Bompiani, 1939), 253-283.

Bulygin, E., "An Antinomy in Kelsen's Pure Theory of Law", *Ratio Juris* 3 (1990), 29-45.

Bulygin, E., "Enunciados jurídicos y positivismo: respuesta a Raz", *Análisis filosófico* 1/2 (1981), 49-59.

Bulygin, E., "Norms and Logic: Kelsen and Weinberger on the Ontology of Norms", *Law and Philosophy* 4 (1985), 154-163.

Bulygin, E., "Norms, Normative Propositions, and Legal Statements", in *Contemporary Philosophy. A New Survey, III. Philosophy of Action*, ed. G. Floistad (The Hague: Martinus Nijhoff, 1982); Italian translation: "Norme, proposizioni normative, e asserti giuridici", in P. Comanducci and R. Guastini, eds., *L'analisi del ragionamento giuridico. Materiali ad uso degli studenti* (Turin: Giappichelli, 1987), vol. 1, 7-37.

Bulygin, E., "Sobre la regla de reconocimiento", in *Derecho, filosofía, y lenguaje. Homenaje a Ambrosio L. Gioja* (Buenos Aires: Astrea, 1976), 31-39.

Bulygin, E., "Time and Validity", in A.A. Martino, ed., *Deontic Logic, Computational Linguistics, and Legal Information Systems* (Amsterdam: North-Holland, 1982), vol. 2, 65-81.

Bulygin, E., "Validez y positivismo", in *Segundo Congreso Internacional de Filosofía del derecho. Comunicaciones* (La Plata: Asociación Argentina de Filosofía del derecho, 1987), vol. 1., 241-55.

Bulygin, E., *Normas y logica. Kelsen y Weinberger sobre la ontologia de las normas*, in C.E. Alchourrón and E. Bulygin, *Análisis lógico y Derecho* (Madrid: Centro de Estudios Constitucionales, 1991), 249-265.

Carcaterra, G., "Analogia (I) Teoria generale", *Enciclopedia giuridica* (Rome: Istituto della Enciclopedia italiana, 1988), vol. II, 1-25.

Carcaterra, G., "Certezza, scienza, diritto", *Rivista internazionale di filosofia del diritto* XXXIX (1962), 377-394.

Carcaterra, G., *Il principio di normatività. Riflessioni sul normativismo* (Rome: Bulzoni, 1984).

Carcaterra, G., *Il problema della fallacia naturalistica. La derivazione del dover essere dall'essere* (Milan: Giuffrè, 1969).

Carcaterra, G., *La forza costitutiva delle norme* (Rome: Bulzoni, 1972).

Carcaterra, G., *Le norme costitutive* (Milan: Giuffrè, 1974).

Carcaterra, G., *Norme giuridiche e valori etici. Saggi di filosofia del diritto* (Rome: Bulzoni, 1991).

Carnap, R., "Carl G. Hempel sulle teorie scientifiche", in *La filosofia di Rudolf Carnap*, Ital. transl. by M.G. de Cristoforo Sandrini (Milan: il Saggiatore, 1974), vol. II, 938-45.

Carnap, R., "Formal and Factual Science", in Herbert Feigl and May Brodbeck, eds., *Readings in the Philosophy of Science* (New York: Appleton-Century-Crifts, 1953), 121-28.

Carnap, R., "Il carattere metodologico dei concetti teorici", in *Analiticità, significanza, induzione*, ed. A. Meotti and M. Mondadori (Bologna: il Mulino, 1971), 263-313.

Carnap, R., "Linguaggio osservativo e linguaggio teorico", in *Analiticità, significanza, induzione*, ed. A. Meotti and M. Mondadori (Bologna: il Mulino, 1971), 49-62.

Carnap, R., "Überwindung der Metaphysik durch logische Analyse der Sprache", *Erkenntnis* II (1932), 219-241.

Carnap, R., *Foundations of Logic and Mathematics*, International Encyclopedia of Unified Science, vol. I, n.3 (Chicago: University of Chicago Press, 1939); Ital. trans. by G. Preti (Turin: Paravia, 1956).

Carnap, R., *Introduction to Symbolic Logic and its Applications* (New York: Dover Publications, 1958).

Carnap, R., *The Logical Syntax of Language* (London: Routledge and Kegan Paul, 1937).

Carnap, R., *The Logical Syntax of Language*, English trans. Amathe Smeaton (London: Kegan Paul, Trench, Trubner & Co. Ltd., 1937).

Carnevali, U., "*Le donazioni*", in *Trattato di diritto privato* (Turin: UTET, 1982), VI.491-538.

Carraro, L., "Frode alla legge", in *Novissimo Digesto Italiano* (Turin: Unione Tipografico-Editrice Torinese, 1961), VII.647- 651.

Carriò, G.R., "Principi di diritto e positivismo giuridico", *Rivista di Filosofia* LXI (1970), 127-148.

Carriò, G.R., "Sobre la interpretación en el derecho" (1965); Italian translation "Sull'interpretazione giuridica", in P. Comanducci and R. Guastini, eds., *L'analisi del ragionamento giuridico. Materiali ad uso degli studenti* (Turin: Giappichelli, 1989), vol. 2, 127-151.

Carriò, G.R.,"Sul concetto di obbligo giuridico", *Rivista di Filosofia* LVII (1966), 141-155.

Castignone S., "Il diritto internazionale pericolo di morte per i popoli?", *Sociologia del diritto* V (1978), 1-12.

Castignone, S., "«Il re è nudo». La critica dei realisti americani alla nozione di sovranità", *Materiali per una storia della cultura giuridica* XVII (1987), 385-402.

Castignone, S., "«Le parole del fare»: Austin, Olivecrona, Ross e la «fallacia performativa»", *Materiali per una storia della cultura giuridica* XI (1981), 439-458.

Castignone, S., "Coazione e coercibilità", in *Digesto delle discipline privatistiche. Sezione civile* (Turin: UTET, 1988), vol. II, 416-417.

Castignone, S., "Legittimazione e potere. Elementi per una riflessione analitica", *Sociologia del diritto* XI (1984), 15-20.

Castignone, S., "Naturalismo o emotivismo? Un dilemma dell'etica humeana", *Rivista di Filosofia* LXII (1971), 3-21.

Castignone, S., "Punto di vista interno ed efficacia", in U. Scarpelli, ed., *La teoria generale del diritto* (Milan: Edizioni di Comunità, 1983), 9-20.

Castignone, S., and Guastini, R., eds., *Realismo giuridico e analisi del linguaggio* (Genova : ECIG, 1989).

Castignone, S. and Lanata, G., eds., *Filosofie e animali nel mondo antico* (Pisa: ETS, 1994).

Castignone, S., *Diritto, linguaggio, realtà. Saggi sul realismo giuridico* (Turin: Giappichelli, 1995).

Castignone, S., ed., *I diritti degli animali* (Bologna: Il Mulino, 1985).

Castignone, S., ed., *L'opera di Giovanni Tarello nella cultura giuridica contemporanea* (Bologna: Il Mulino, 1989).

Castignone, S., *Giustizia e bene comune in D. Hume* (Milan: Giuffrè, 1964).

Castignone, S., *La macchina del diritto. Il realismo giuridico in Svezia* (Milan: Edizioni di Comunità, 1974).

Castignone, S., Guastini, R., and Tarello, G., *Introduzione teorica allo studio del diritto. Lezioni* (Genova: ECIG, 1978; 4th ed., 1984).

Catania, A., "Carl Schmitt e Santi Romano", *Rivista internazionale di filosofia del diritto* LXIV (1987), 545-575.

Catania, A., "Hobbes e Kelsen", *Rivista internazionale di filosofia del diritto* LXVI (1989), 407-423.

Catania, A., "Il diritto come organizzazione della forza", *Rivista internazionale di filosofia del diritto* LI (1974), 371-397.

Catania, A., "L'accettazione nel pensiero di Herbert L.A. Hart", *Rivista internazionale di filosofia del diritto* XLVIII (1971), 261-279.

Catania, A., "Sovranità e obbedienza", *Rivista internazionale di filosofia del diritto* LXVII (1990), 219-229.

Catania, A., *Analisi del diritto. Studi di teoria generale* (Napoli: Jovene, 1992).
Catania, A., *Argomenti per una teoria dell'ordinamento giuridico* (Napoli: Jovene, 1996).
Catania, A., *Decisione e norma* (Napoli: Jovene, 1979).
Catania, A., *Il diritto tra forza e consenso. Studi sulla filosofia giuridica del novecento* (Napoli: ESI, 1987).
Catania, A., *Il problema del diritto e l'obbligatorietà. Studio sulla norma fondamentale* (Napoli: ESI, 1983).
Catania, A., *Introduzione allo studio del diritto* (Salerno: Gentile Editore, 1989).
Catania, A., *Lezioni di filosofia del diritto* (Salerno: Gentile Editore, 1992).
Catania, A., *Manuale di filosofia del diritto* (Napoli: ESI, 1995).
Cattaneo, M.A., "Analisi del linguaggio e scienza politica", *Rivista internazionale di filosofia del diritto* XXXVI (1959), 296-308.
Cattaneo, M.A., "Austin et l'utilitarisme", *Archives de philosophie du droit* XXVI (1981), 121-132.
Cattaneo, M.A., "Diritto e società nel pensiero di Herbert L.A. Hart", *Sociologia del diritto* I (1974), 61-84.
Cattaneo, M.A., "Il diritto naturale nel pensiero di H.L.A. Hart", *Rivista internazionale di filosofia del diritto* XLII (1965), 673-694.
Cattaneo, M.A., "Introduzione a Hart, Il concetto di diritto", in V. Frosini's Italian translation (Turin: Einaudi, 1965).
Cattaneo, M.A., "John Austin", *Materiali per una storia della cultura giuridica* VIII (1978), 13-95.
Cattaneo, M.A., "La retribuzione penale nell'interpretazione e nella critica di H.L.A. Hart", *Materiali per una storia della cultura giuridica* IV (1974), 639-699.
Cattaneo, M.A., "Positivismo giuridico", *Novissimo Digesto Italiano* (Turin: UTET, 1957), XIII.315-322.
Cattaneo, M.A., "Sul significato dell'espressione «i giudici creano diritto»", *Rivista internazionale di filosofia del diritto* XLIII (1966), 250-257.
Cattaneo, M.A., *Il concetto di rivoluzione nella scienza del diritto* (Milan: Istituto Editoriale Cisalpino, 1960).
Cattaneo, M.A., *Il positivismo giuridico inglese* (Milan: Giuffrè, 1962).
Cattaneo, M.A., *Illuminismo e legislazione* (Milan: Edizioni di Comunità, 1966).
Celano B., "L'interpretazione del conflitto fra norme nell'ultimo Kelsen [1]", *Rivista internazionale di filosofia del diritto* LXVII (1990), 13-50.
Celano, B., "Consuetudini, convenzioni", *Analisi e diritto* (1995), 35-88.
Celano, B., "Giustificazione di norme e procedure ideali", *Analisi e diritto* (1992), 31-84.

Celano, B., "Grande divisione e teoria degli atti linguistici", *Analisi e diritto* (1993), 41-64.

Celano, B., "Il problema delle norme autonome", in L. Gianformaggio, ed., *Sistemi normativi statici e dinamici. Analisi di una tipologia kelseniana* (Turin: Giappichelli, 1992), 333-366.

Celano, B., *Dialettica della ragion pratica* (Turin: Giappichelli, 1994).

Celano, B., *Dover essere e intenzionalità. Una critica all'ultimo Kelsen* (Turin: Giappichelli, 1990).

Cerroni, U., *Marx e il diritto moderno* (Rome: Editori Riuniti, 1972).

Chiarloni, S., "Diritto di azione e diritto di difesa nel procedimento preliminare per la dichiarazione giudiziale di paternità e maternità naturale", *Giurisprudenza costituzionale* X (1965), 865-881.

Chiassoni, P., "Ackerman e il fantasma della libertà", *Materiali per una storia della cultura giuridica* XIV (1984), 539-554.

Chiassoni, P., "Dworkin's Skeptical Jurisprudence: Paradoxical Remarks", *Annali della Facoltà di Giurisprudenza di Genova* (Genova: Giuffrè, 1989), 331-340.

Chiassoni, P., "L'antiscetticismo panglossiano di Ronald Dworkin", *Materiali per una storia della cultura giuridica* XVII (1987), 213-236.

Chiassoni, P., "L'interpretazione della legge: normativismo semiotico, scetticismo, giochi interpretativi", *Materiali per una storia della cultura giuridica* XX (1990), 119-159.

Chiassoni, P., "Natura e artificio nella dottrina dello stato di Robert Nozick", *Materiali per una storia della cultura giuridica* XV (1985), 233-256.

Chiassoni, P., "Precetti non logicamente strutturati. In margine alla teoria della norma giuridica di Giovanni Tarello", *Materiali per una storia della cultura giuridica* XVII (1987), 403-440.

Chiassoni, P., *Law and Economics. L'analisi economica del diritto negli Stati Uniti* (Turin: Giappichelli, 1992), 360.

Cohen, L.J., Review of H.L.A. Hart, *The Concept of Law*, *Mind* 71 (1962), 395-412.

Comanducci, P. and Guastini, E., eds., *L'analisi del ragionamento giuridico. Materiali ad uso degli studenti* (Turin: Giappichelli, 1987-89, 2 vols.).

Comanducci, P., "Aarnio ed il problema della certezza del diritto", *Analisi e diritto* (1994), 111-130.

Comanducci, P., "Allocare e punire. Note sul ruolo del diritto nelle utopie socialiste dell'Ottocento", *Materiali per una storia della cultura giuridica* XI (1981), 325-338.

Comanducci, P., "Di un approccio multiprospettico in teoria del diritto", *Analisi e diritto* (1991), 111-126.

Comanducci, P., "Diritti vecchi e nuovi: un tentativo di analisi", *Materiali per una storia della cultura giuridica* XVII (1987), 95-128.

Comanducci, P., "Joseph Raz e la teoria generale del sistema giuridico", *Materiali per una storia della cultura giuridica* VIII (1978), 359-422.

Comanducci, P., "La costituzionalizzazione americana: un capitolo nella storia della cultura giuridica europea", *Materiali per una storia della cultura giuridica* XVII (1987), 441-468.

Comanducci, P., "Sul problema della tolleranza", *Analisi e diritto* (1993), 249-260.

Comanducci, P., *Assaggi di metaetica* (Turin: Giappichelli, 1992).

Comanducci, P., *Contrattualismo, utilitarismo, garanzie* (Turin: Giappichelli, 1991, 2nd ed.).

Comanducci, P., *Settecento conservatore: Lampredi e il diritto naturale* (Milan: Giuffrè, 1981).

Conte, A., "Parerga leibnitiana", in A. Martino, E. Maretti and C. Ciampi, eds, *Logica, informatica e diritto* (Florence: Le Monnier, 1978), 217-255.

Conte, A.G. and Mazzarese, T., "Founding Rules on Rules", in C. Faralli and E. Pattaro, eds., *Reason in Law* (Milan: Giuffrè, 1988), II.283-288.

Conte, A.G., "Décision, Complétude, Clôture. A propos des lacunes en droit", *Logique et Analyse* 33 (1966), 1-18.

Conte, A.G., "Deontica aristotelica", *Rivista internazionale di filosofia del diritto* LXIX (1992), 178-252.

Conte, A.G., "Erkenntnis von Regeln und Erkenntnis durch Regeln", in R.M. Chisholm, J.C. Marek, J.T. Blackmore and A. Hübner, eds., *Philosophie des Geistes. Philosophie der Psychologie. Akten des 9. Internationalen Wittgenstein-Symposiums* (Kirchberg and Wien: Hölder, Pichler, Tempsky, 1984), 577-579.

Conte, A.G., "Fenomeni di fenomeni", *Rivista internazionale di filosofia del diritto* LXIII (1986), 29-57.

Conte, A.G., "In margine all'ultimo Kelsen" (1967), in: R. Guastini, ed., *Problemi di teoria del diritto* (Bologna: Il Mulino, 1980), 197-208.

Conte, A.G., "Incoerenza costitutiva", *Rivista internazionale di filosofia del diritto* LXIX (1992), 507-518.

Conte, A.G., "L'enjeu de régles", *Droit et Societé* 17-18 (1991), 121-143.

Conte, A.G., "Materiali per una tipologia delle regole", *Materiali per una storia della cultura giuridica* XV (1985), 345-368.

Conte, A.G., "Minima deontica", *Rivista internazionale di filosofia del diritto* 65 (1988), 425-475.

Conte, A.G., "Phénoménologie du langage déontique", in G. Kalinowski and F. Selvaggi, eds., *Les fondements logiques de la pensée normative. Actes du Colloque de Logique Déontique de Rome (29-30 avril 1983)* (Rome: Pontificia Università Gregoriana, 1985), 179-193.

Conte, A. G., "Regola costitutiva, condizione, antinomia", in U. Scarpelli, ed., *La teoria generale del diritto* (Milan: Edizioni di Comunità, 1983), 21-40.

Conte, A. G., "Ricerca di un paradosso deontico", *Rivista internazionale di filosofia del diritto* LI (1974), 1-42.

Conte, A. G., "Studio per una teoria della validità", *Rivista internazionale di filosofia del diritto* XLVII (1970), 331-354.

Conte, A.G., "Un saggio filosofico sopra la logica deontica", *Rivista internazionale di filosofia del diritto* XLII (1965), 564-577.

Conte, A.G., "Variationen über Wittgentsteins Regelbegriff 1.3.2", in R. Haller, ed., *Sprache und Erkenntnis als soziale Tatsache* (Wien: Holder-Pichler-Tempsky, 1981), 69-78.

Conte, A.G., *Filosofia del linguaggio normativo. I. Studi 1965-1981; II: 1982-1994* (Turin: Giappichelli, 1995, 2 vols.).

Conte, A.G., *Nove studi sul linguaggio normativo (1967-1978)* (Turin: Giappichelli, 1985).

Conte, A.G., *Primi argomenti per una critica del normativismo* (Pavia: Tipografia del libro, 1968).

Conte, A.G., *Saggio sulla completezza degli ordinamenti giuridici* (Turin: Giappichelli, 1962).

Copi, I., *Introduction to Logic* (New York: Macmillan, 1972).

Crisafulli, V., "Disposizione (e norma)", in *Enciclopedia del diritto* (Milan: Giuffrè, 1964), vol. 13, 195-209.

Crisafulli, V., "Gerarchia e competenza nel sistema costituzionale delle fonti", *Rivista trimestrale di diritto pubblico* 10 (1960), 775-809.

Crisafulli, V., "Le sentenze "interpretative" della Corte costituzionale", in *Studi in memoria di Tullio Ascarelli* (Milan: Giuffrè, 1969), vol. 5, 2871-2894.

Crisafulli, V., "Questioni in tema di interpretazione della Corte costituzionale nei rapporti con l'interpretazione giudiziaria", *Giurisprudenza costituzionale* 1 (1956), 929-49.

Crisafulli, V., *Lezioni di diritto costituzionale* (Padova: CEDAM, 1984, 5th ed.).

Crisafulli, V., *Stato, popolo, governo. Illusioni e delusioni costituzionali* (Milan: Giuffrè, 1985).

Cuocolo, F., "Gli atti dello Stato aventi 'forza di legge'", *Rivista trimestriale di diritto pubblico* XI (1961), 97-198.

D'Alessandro, F., "Persone giuridiche ed analisi del linguaggio", in *Studi in memoria di T. Ascarelli* (Milan: Giuffrè, 1969), 243-343.

D'Entrèves, A.P, "Intorno all'obbligo politico", *Rivista di Filosofia* LVII (1966), 156-164.

D'Entrèves, A.P., *Obbedienza e resistenza in una società democratica* (Milan: Comunità, 1970).

Di Lucia, P., *Deontica in Von Wright* (Milan: Giuffrè, 1992).

Di Lucia, P., ed., *Normografia* (Milan: Giuffrè, 1995).

Diciotti, E., "Giustificazioni della tolleranza", *Analisi e diritto* (1993), 261-284.

Diciotti, E., "I conflitti normativi e l'etica del discorso", *Rivista internazionale di filosofia del diritto* LXXII (1995), 187-217.

Diciotti, E., "Interferenze paternalistiche", *Rivista internazionale di filosofia del diritto* LXV (1988), 748-756.

Diciotti, E., "Paternalismo", *Materiali per una storia della cultura giuridica* XVI (1986), 557-586.

Diciotti, E., "Vaghezza del diritto e controversie giuridiche sul significato", *Analisi e diritto* (1992), 97-138.

Dworkin, R., *Taking Rights Seriously* (London: Duckworth, 1978, 2nd ed.).

Eckmann, H., *Rechts-positivismus and sprachanalystische Philosophie: der Begriff des Rechts in des Rechtstheorie H.L.A. Harts* (Berlin: Duncker & Humblot, 1969).

Esposito, C., *La validità delle leggi* (1934; reprint Milan: Giuffrè, 1964).

Faralli, C. and Pattaro, E., eds., *Reason in Law* (Milan: Giuffrè, 1985-88, 3 vols.).

Farrell, M.D., *Hacia un criterio empírico de validez* (Buenos Aires: Astrea, 1972).

Fassó, G., *Storia della filosofia del diritto*, vol. III (Bologna: Il Mulino, 1970).

Fedele, V.A., *Possesso ed esercizio del diritto* (Turin: Giappichelli, 1950).

Ferrajoli, L., "Guarantees and Truth in judicial Decisions", in C. Faralli and E. Pattaro, eds., *Reason in Law* (Milan: Giuffrè, 1987), vol. I.301-311.

Ferrajoli, L., "Interpretazione dottrinale e interpretazione operativa", *Rivista internazionale di filosofia del diritto* XLIII (1966), 290-304.

Ferrajoli, L., "L'America, la conquista, il diritto. L'idea di sovranità nel mondo moderno", *Meridiana. Rivista di storia e scienze sociali* 15 (1992), 17-52.

Ferrajoli, L., "La formazione e l'uso dei concetti nella scienza giuridica e nell'applicazione della legge", *Materiali per una storia della cultura giuridica* XV (1985), 401-422.

Ferrajoli, L., "La semantica della teoria del diritto", in U. Scarpelli, ed., *La teoria generale del diritto* (Milan: Edizioni di Comunità, 1983), 81-130.

Ferrajoli, L., "Linguaggio assertivo e linguaggio precettivo", *Rivista internazionale di filosofia del diritto* XLIV (1967), 514-545.

Ferrajoli, L., "Reato (profili teorici)", "Reato (profili reali)", "Pena (principi teorici)", "Pena (profili reali"), "Processo penale (principi teorici)", "Processo penale (profili reali)", in C. Donati, ed., *Dizionario critico del diritto* (Milan: Savelli, 1980).

Ferrajoli, L., "Saggio di una teoria formalizzata del diritto", *Rivista internazionale di filosofia del diritto* XLII (1965), 55-105.
Ferrajoli, L., "Sulla possibilità di una teoria del diritto come scienza rigorosa", *Rivista internazionale di filosofia del diritto* XL (1963), 320-363.
Ferrajoli, L., "Tolleranza e intollerabilità nello stato di diritto", *Analisi e diritto* (1993), 285-293.
Ferrajoli, L., *Diritto e ragione. Teoria del garantismo penale* (Rome-Bari: Laterza, 1989).
Ferrajoli, L., *La sovranità nel mondo moderno* (Milan: Anabasi, 1994).
Ferrajoli, L., *Teoria assiomatizzata del diritto. Parte generale* (Milan: Giuffrè, 1970).
Ferrari, V., "L'analisi funzionale in sociologia del diritto. Problemi terminologici e problemi metodologici", *Sociologia del diritto* 1 (1980), 43-70.
Ferrari, V., *Successione per testamento e trasformazioni sociali* (Milan: Edizioni di Comunità, 1972).
Ferri, C., *Profili dell'accertamento costitutivo* (Padova: CEDAM, 1970).
Filanti, G., *Inesistenza e nullità del negozio giuridico* (Napoli: Jovene, 1983).
Frege, G., *Grundgesetze der Arithmetik* (Jena: Pohle, 1903; repr. Hildesheim: G. Olms, 1962).
Frosini, V., "H.L.A. Hart, The Concept of Law", *Rivista internazionale di filosofia del diritto* XXXIX (1962), 532-535.
Frosini, V., trld., *H.L.A. Hart, Contributi all'analisi del diritto* (Milan: Giuffrè, 1964).
Galgano, F., *Delle persone giuridiche*, in *Commentario del codice civile*, ed. A. Scialoja and G. Branca (Bologna-Rome: Zanichelli, 1969), 3-101.
Gavazzi, G., "Il discorso dei giuristi: descrizione o prescrizione?", *Rivista internazionale di filosofia del diritto* XLIV (1967), 443-458.
Gavazzi, G., "In difesa (parziale) di una concezione predittiva dell'obbligo giuridico", *Rivista di Filosofia* LVII (1966), 165-174.
Gavazzi, G., "L'interpretazione giuridica in H. Kelsen", *Rivista internazionale di filosofia del diritto* XXXIV (1957), 217-227.
Gavazzi, G., "La motivazione delle leggi", *Il Politico* XXXIX (1974), 173-193.
Gavazzi, G., "Le sanzioni nel diritto. Problemi vecchi e nuovi", in R. Orecchia, ed., *Problemi della sanzione. Società e diritto in Marx, Atti del XII Congresso nazionale della Società di Filosofia politica e giuridica (Ferrara, 2-5 ott. 1978)* (Rome: Bulzoni, 1978), 101-122.
Gavazzi, G., "Sul concetto di «moralità critica»", *Rivista di Filosofia* LVI (1965), 56-74.

Gavazzi, G., "Validità ed effettività", in C. Roehrssen, ed., *Hans Kelsen nella cultura filosofico-giuridica del novecento* (Rome: Istituto dell'Enciclopedia Italiana, 1983), 77-86.

Gavazzi, G., *Delle antinomie* (Turin: Giappichelli, 1959).

Gavazzi, G., *Elementi di teoria del diritto* (Turin: Giappichelli, 1970; 2nd ed., 1984).

Gavazzi, G., *L'onere. Tra la libertà e l'obbligo* (Turin: Giappichelli, 1970).

Gavazzi, G., *Norme primarie e norme secondarie* (Turin: Giappichelli, 1967).

Gavazzi, G., *Studi di teoria del diritto* (Turin: Giappichelli, 1993).

Geymonat, L., "La crisi della logica formale", in *Fondamenti logici della scienza* (Turin: F. De Silva, 1947), 111-113.

Giacobbe, G., "Frode alla legge", in *Enciclopedia di diritto* (Milan: Giuffrè, 1969), XCII.81.

Gianformaggio, L., "Ancora su la logica e le norme", *Materiali per una storia della cultura giuridica* XVII (1987), 251-262.

Gianformaggio, L., "Hans Kelsen on the Deduction of Validity", *Rechtstheorie* XXI (1990), 181-207.

Gianformaggio, L., "Il gioco della giustificazione. Osservazioni in margine ad una teoria procedurale dell'argomentazione giuridica", *Materiali per una storia della cultura giuridica* XIV (1984), 475-503.

Gianformaggio, L., "L'interpretazione della costituzione tra applicazione di regole ed argomentazione su principi", *Rivista internazionale di filosofia del diritto* LXII (1985), 65-103.

Gianformaggio, L., "La guerra come negazione del diritto", *Democrazia e Diritto* XXXII (1992), 271-298.

Gianformaggio, L., "Legal Certainty, Coherence and Consensus: Variations on a Theme by MacCormick", in P. Nerhot, ed., *Law, Interpretation and Reality* (Dordrecht: Kluwer, 1990), 402-430.

Gianformaggio, L., "Modèle Deductif, modèle inductif et modèle rhetorique de raisonnement juridique", *Rechtstheorie* XVII (1986), 39-46.

Gianformaggio, L., "Morale critica e riforma della morale", *Rivista internazionale di filosofia del diritto* XLIV (1967), 770-789.

Gianformaggio, L., "On Moral and Legal Justification", *Archiv für Rechts- und Sozialphilosophie* LXXVI (1990), 145-157.

Gianformaggio, L., "Significato e forza", *Rivista internazionale di filosofia del diritto* XLIV (1967), 459-464.

Gianformaggio, L., "Sul senso della giustificazione morale e giuridica", in L. Gianformaggio and E. Lecaldano, eds., *Etica e diritto* (Roma-Bari: Laterza, 1986), 151-172.

Gianformaggio, L., ed., *Hans Kelsen's Legal Theory. A Diachronic Point of View* (Turin: Giappichelli, 1990).

Gianformaggio, L., ed., *Le ragioni del garantismo. Discutendo con Luigi Ferrajoli* (Turin: Giappichelli, 1993).
Gianformaggio, L., ed., *Sistemi normativi statici e dinamici. Analisi di una tipologia kelseniana* (Turin: Giappichelli, 1991).
Gianformaggio, L., *Filosofia e critica del diritto* (Turin: Giappichelli, 1995).
Gianformaggio, L., *Gli argomenti di Perelman: dalla neutralità dello scienziato all'imparzialità del giudice* (Milan: Edizioni di Comunità, 1973).
Gianformaggio, L., *In difesa del sillogismo pratico ovvero alcuni argomenti kelseniani alla prova* (Milan: Giuffrè, 1987).
Gianformaggio, L., *Studi sulla giustificazione giuridica* (Turin: Giappichelli, 1986).
Gianformaggio, L. and Lecaldano, E., eds, *Etica e diritto* (Milan: Angeli and Bari: Laterza, 1986).
Gianformaggio, L. and Paulson, S., eds., *Cognition and Interpretation of Law* (Turin: Giappichelli, 1995).
Giannini, M.S., "Alcuni caratteri della giurisdizione di legittimità delle norme", *Giurisprudenza costituzionale* 1 (1956), 902-28.
Giannini, M.S., "L'illegittimità degli atti normativi e delle norme", *Rivista italiana per le scienze giuridiche* 7 (1954), 39-71.
Gorla, G., "I precedenti storici dell'articolo 12 delle disposizioni preliminari del codice civile del 1942", *Foro italiano* XCII/5 (1969), 112-32.
Grassetti, C., "Le definizioni legali e la riforma dei codici", in *Studi in onore di G. Pacchioni* (Milan: Facoltà di Giurisprudenza dell'Università di Milano, 1938), 297-314.
Grassetti, C., *L'interpretazione del negozio giuridico* (Padova: Cedam, 1983).
Grzegorczyk, C. and Studnicki, T., "Les rapports entre la norme et la disposition légale", *Archives de philosophie du droit* 19 (1974), 243-256.
Guastini, R., "A Framework for the Analysis of Judicial Discourse", in C. Faralli and E. Pattaro, eds., *Reason in Law* (Milan: Giuffrè, 1987), vol. 1, 281-300.
Guastini, R., "A Tentative Analysis of Two Juristic Sentences", in A. Peczenik, L. Lindhal and B. van Roermund, eds., *Theory of Legal Science* (Dordrecht: Reidel, 1984), 571-581.
Guastini, R., "A Theory of Derogation", in A.A. Martino and F. Socci Natali, eds., *Automated Analysis of Legal Texts. Logic, Informatics, Law* (Amsterdam: North Holland, 1986), 495-514.

Guastini, R., "Cognitivismo ludico e regole costitutive", in U. Scarpelli, ed., *La teoria generale del diritto. Problemi e tendenze attuali. Studi dedicati a Norberto Bobbio* (Milan: Edizioni di Comunità, 1983), 153-176.

Guastini, R., "Concetti e criteri di validità", *Rivista trimestrale di diritto e procedura civile* XLIII (1989), 867-878.

Guastini, R., "I briganti e lo Stato. Un enigma nella dottrina pura del diritto", *Rivista trimestrale di diritto e procedura civile* XXXVIII (1984), 655-665.

Guastini, R., "I giuristi alla ricerca della scienza (Rileggendo Bobbio)", *Rivista internazionale di filosofia del diritto* LXIV (1987), 179-195.

Guastini, R., "Introduzione", in *H. Kelsen, La teoria politica del bolscevismo e altri saggi*, ed. R. Guastini (Milan: Il Saggiatore, 1981), 7-32.

Guastini, R., "Kelsen critico del marxismo", in C. Roehrssen, ed., *Hans Kelsen nella cultura filosofico-giuridica del novecento* (Rome: Istituto dell'Enciclopedia Italiana, 1983), 135-148.

Guastini, R., "Metateoria degli atteggiamenti normativi", *Materiali per una storia della cultura giuridica* XII (1982), 167-186.

Guastini, R., "Norberto Bobbio: analisi del linguaggio e teoria formale del diritto. (I) 1949-1960", *Materiali per una storia della cultura giuridica* VIII (1978), 293-356

Guastini, R., "Norberto Bobbio teorico del diritto. (II) 1961-1965", *Materiali per una storia della cultura giuridica* IX (1979), 523-541.

Guastini, R., "Norberto Bobbio teorico del diritto. (III) 1966-1980", *Materiali per una storia della cultura giuridica* X (1980), 483-508.

Guastini, R., "Norme che sono condizioni sufficienti del loro oggetto?", *Materiali per una storia della cultura giuridica* XVI (1986), 213-222.

Guastini, R., "Norme, giudizi di validità e scienza giuridica nell'ultimo Kelsen", *Materiali per una storia della cultura giuridica* XXI (1991), 441-454.

Guastini, R., "Problemi di analisi logica della motivazione", *Contratto e Impresa* II (1986), 104-128.

Guastini, R., "Problemi di analisi logica delle decisioni costituzionali", in P. Comanducci and R. Guastini, eds., *Analisi e diritto 1990. Ricerche di giurisprudenza analitica* (Turin: Giappichelli, 1990), 77-97.

Guastini, R., "Production of Rules by Means of Rules", *Rechtstheorie* 17 (1986), 295-309.

Guastini, R., "Redazione e interpretazione dei documenti normativi", in S. Bartole, ed., *Lezioni di tecnica legislativa* (Padova: CEDAM, 1988, Pubblicazioni dell'ISAPREL), 37-117.

Guastini, R., "Six Concepts of «Constitutive Rule»", in *Annali della Facoltà di Giurisprudenza dell'Università di Genova* (Milan: Giuffrè, 1982-83), 487-495.

Guastini, R., "Some Remarks on the Conceptual Framework of "Law's Empire"", *Ratio Juris* 1 (1988), 176-180.

Guastini, R., "Sui principi di diritto", *Diritto e società* 4 (1986), 602-623.

Guastini, R., "Sulla validità della costituzione dal punto di vista del positivismo giuridico", in *Scritti in onore di Angelo Falzea, vol. I, Teoria generale e filosofia del diritto* (Milan: Giuffrè, 1991), 331-346.

Guastini, R., "Teoria delle regole costitutive", *Rivista internazionale di filosofia del diritto* LX (1983), 548-564.

Guastini, R., *Dalle fonti alle norme* (Turin: Giappichelli, 1990; 2nd ed., Turin: Giappichelli, 1992).

Guastini, R., ed., *Problemi di teoria del diritto* (Bologna: Il Mulino, 1980).

Guastini, R., *Il giudice e la legge. Lezioni di diritto costituzionale* (Turin: Giappichelli, 1994).

Guastini, R., *Le fonti del diritto e l'interpretazione* (Milan: Giuffrè, 1993).

Guastini, R., *Lezioni di teoria analitica del diritto* (Turin: Giappichelli, 1982).

Guastini, R., *Lezioni sul linguaggio giuridico* (Turin: Giappichelli, 1985).

Guastini, R., *Produzione e applicazione del diritto. Lezioni sulle «Preleggi»* (Turin: Giappichelli, 1989, 2nd ed.).

Guastini, R., *Quindici lezioni di diritto costituzionale* (Turin: Giappichelli, 1991).

Hacker, P.M., "Sull'uso di 'dovere'", *Rivista di Filosofia* LVII (1966), 175-192.

Hare, R.M., *The Language of Morals* (Oxford: Oxford University Press, 1952).

Hart, H.L.A., "Il concetto di obbligo", *Rivista di filosofia* LVII (1966), 125-140, engl. transl.: *Legal Duty and Obligation,* in *Essays on Bentham* (Oxford: Clarendon Press, 1982), 127-161.

Hart, H.L.A., "Kelsen's Doctrine of the Unity of Law", in *Ethics and Social Justice,* ed. Howard E. Kiefer and Milton K. Munitz (New York: State University of New York Press, 1970), 171-199.

Hart, H.L.A., "Legal and Moral Obligation", in *Essays on Moral Philosophy*, ed. A.I. Melden (Washington: University of Washington Press, 1958), 82-107.

Hart, H.L.A., "Legal Duty and Obligation", in *Essays on Bentham* (Clarendon Press: Oxford, 1982), 127-161.

Hart, H.L.A., "Positivism and the Separation of Law and Morals", *Harvard Law Review* 71 (1958), 593-629.

Hart, H.L.A., "Scandinavian Realism", *Cambridge Law Journal* 18 (1959), 233-240).

Hart, H.L.A., *Definition and Theory in Jurisprudence* (Oxford: Clarendon Press, 1954), inaugural lecture reprinted in *Law Quarterly Review* 70 (1954), 37-60.

Hart, H.L.A., *The Concept of Law* (Oxford: Clarendon Press, 1961).

Hempel, C.G., "Riflessi dell'opera di Carnap sulla filosofia della scienza", in P.A. Schillip, ed., *La filosofia di Rudolf Carnap,* Ital. transl. by M.G. de Cristoforo Sandrini (Milan: il Saggiatore, 1974), vol. II, 659-84.

Hempel, C.G., *Fundamentals of Concept Formation in Empirical Science*, Ital. transl. by A. Pasquinelli (Milan: Feltrinelli, 1961).

Hernández Marín, R., *Teoría general del derecho y de la ciencia jurídica* (Barcelona: PPU, 1989).

Hohfeld, W.N., *Fundamental Legal Conceptions as Applied in Judicial Reasoning* (Westport: Greenwood Press, 1919).

Husserl, E., *Logische Untersuchungen* (Tübingen: Niemeyer, 1968, 5th ed.).

Irti, N., "Note per uno studio sulla nomenclatura giuridica", reprinted in *Norme e fatti* (Milan: Giuffrè, 1984), 165-178.

Irti, N., *Introduzione allo studio del diritto privato* (Turin: Giappichelli, 1976, 3rd ed.).

Irti, N., *Proprietà ed impresa* (Napoli: Jovene, 1965).

Jackson, B.S., *Law, Fact and Narrative Coherence* (Merseyside: Deborah Charles Publications, 1988).

Jackson, B.S., *Semiotics and Legal Theory* (London: Routledge & Kegan Paul, 1985).

Jori, M. and Pintore, A., *Manuale di teoria generale del diritto* (Turin: Giappichelli, 1988, 2nd ed. 1995).

Jori, M., "Abrogazione, validità, atti linguistici", in C. Luzzati, ed., *L'abrogazione delle leggi* (Milan: Giuffrè, 1987), 47-64.

Jori, M., "Definizioni e livelli di discorso giuridico", in *Definizioni giuridiche ed ideologie,* A. Belvedere, M. Jori and L. Lantella (Milan: Giuffrè, 1979), 483-530.

Jori, M., "Definizioni giuridiche e pragmatica", *Analisi e diritto* (1995), 109-144.

Jori, M., "Hart e l'analisi del linguaggio", *Materiali per una storia della cultura giuridica* 1 (1979), 161-230.

Jori, M., "I princìpi nel diritto italiano", *Sociologia del diritto* X (1983), 7-33.

Jori, M., "Il concetto di norma nella scienza empirica del diritto", *Rivista internazionale di filosofia del diritto* XLIX (1972), 55-78.

Jori, M., "Il giurista selvaggio. Un contributo alla metodologia della descrizione social", *Sociologia del diritto* 1 (1974), 85-108.

Jori, M., "Karl Olivecrona e il problema della scienza", *Rivista trimestrale di diritto e procedura civile* XXX (1976), 732-760.

Jori, M., "Oggetto e metodo della scienza giuridica", in U. Scarpelli, ed., *La teoria generale del diritto* (Milan: Edizioni di Comunità, 1983), 177-230.

Jori, M., "Paradigms of Legal Science", *Rivista internazionale di filosofia del diritto* LXVII (1990), 230-254.

Jori, M., "Razionalità e ragionevolezza del diritto", *Sociologia del diritto* II (1975), 438-442.

Jori, M., "Revolutions in Legal Science: Back to the Concept of Law?", in N. MacCormick and Zenon Bankowski, eds., *Enlightenment, Rights and Revolution. Essays in Legal and Social Philosophy* (Aberdeen: Aberdeen University Press, 1989), 337-363.

Jori, M., "Scienza giuridica e scienze naturali", *Materiali per una storia della cultura giuridica* XV (1985), 423-440.

Jori, M., "Tendances en sémiotique juridique", *Revue Internationale de Sémiotique Juridique* 2 (1989), 277-300.

Jori, M., ed. *Legal Positivism* (Aldershot: Dartmouth, 1992).

Jori, M., ed., *Ermeneutica e filosofia analitica. Due concezioni del diritto a confronto* (Turin: Giappichelli, 1994).

Jori, M., *Il formalismo giuridico* (Milan: Giuffrè, 1980).

Jori, M., *Il giuspositivismo analitico italiano prima e dopo la crisi* (Milan: Giuffrè, 1988).

Jori, M., *Il metodo giuridico tra scienza e politica* (Milan: Giuffrè, 1976).

Jori, M., *Saggi di metagiurisprudenza* (Milan: Giuffrè, 1985).

Kalinowski, G., "Il significato della deontica per la filosofia morale e giuridica", in G. Di Bernardo ed., *Logica deontica e semantica* (Bologna: il Mulino, 1977), 251-289.

Kalinowski, G., "Théorie, métathéorie ou philosophie du droit. Réflexions sur "The Concept of Law" de H.L.A. Hart et "On Law and Justice" d'Alf Ross", *Archives de philosophie du droit* XV (1970). 179-195.

Kalinowski, G., *Disputa sulla scienza normativa*, Ital. transl. by G. Ferrari (Padova: Cedam, 1982).

Kalinowski, G., *Querelle de la science normative* (Paris: R. Pichon et R. Durand-Ausiaz, 1990).

Kant, I., *Grundlagen zur Metaphysik der Sitten* (Leipzig: Modes and Baumann, 1938).

Kaufmann, F., *Methodenlehre der Sozialwissenschaften* (Wien: Julius Springer, 1936).

Kelsen, H., "Derogation" (1962), Italian translation "La derogazione", in H. Kelsen, *La teoria politica del bolscevismo e altri saggi*, ed. R. Guastini (Milan: Il Saggiatore, 1981), 189-206.

Kelsen, H., "Professor Stone and the 'Pure Theory of Law'", *Stanford Law Review* 17 (1965), 1120-57.

Kelsen, H., "Recht und Logik" (1965), Italian translation "Diritto e logica", in P. Comanducci and R. Guastini, eds., *L'analisi del ragionamento giuridico. Materiali ad uso degli studenti* (Turin: Giappichelli, 1989), vol. 2, 65-98.

Kelsen, H., "The Pure Theory of Law and Analytical Jurisprudence", *Harvard Law Review* 55 (1941), 44-70.

Kelsen, H., "What is Justice?", in *Essays in Legal and Moral Philosophy* (Reidel: Dordrecht, 1973), 1-26.

Kelsen, H., "Zur Theorie der Interpretation" (1934), Italian translation "Sulla teoria dell'interpretazione", in P. Comanducci and R. Guastini, eds., *L'analisi del ragionamento giuridico. Materiali ad uso degli studenti* (Turin: Giappichelli, 1989), vol. 2, 107-120.

Kelsen, H., *Allgemeine Theorie der Normen* (Wien and Mainz: Manzsche, 1979), Italian translation by M.G. Losano, *Teoria generale delle norme* (Turin: Einaudi, 1985).

Kelsen, H., *Die philosophischen Grundlagen der Naturrechtslehre und des Rechtspositivismus* (Charlottenburg: Pan Verlag Rolf Heise, 1928).

Kelsen, H., *Hauptprobleme der Staatrechtslehre. Entwickelt aus der Lehre vom Rechtssatz* (Tubingen: Mohr, 1911).

Kelsen, H., *Pure Theory of Law*, translation of the second edition of *Reine Rechtslehre* by Max Knight (Berkeley: University of California Press, 1967).

Kelsen, H., *Reine Rechtslehre* (1960. 2nd ed.), Italian translation *Dottrina pura del diritto*, by M.G. Losano (Turin: Einaudi, 1966).

Kelsen, H., *Reine Rechtslehre. Einleitung in die rechtswissenschaftliche Problematik* (Leipzig and Vienna: Deuticke, 1934).

Kelsen, H., *The General Theory of Law and State*, translated by Anders Wedberg (Cambridge, Mass.: Harvard University Press, 1945).

King, B.E., "The Basic Concept of Professor Hart's Jurisprudence, the Norm out of the Bottle", *The Cambridge Law Journal* 22 (1963), 270-303.

Kneale, W.C. and Kneale, M., *The Development of Logic* (Oxford: Clarendon Press, 1962).

Kurczweski, J., "Due dimensioni del diritto: diritto positivo o intuitivo e diritto ufficiale o non ufficiale", *Sociologia del diritto* III (1976), 29-49.

Lantella, L., "Pratiche definitorie e proiezioni ideologiche nel discorso giuridico", in *giuridiche ed ideologie,* ed. A. Belvedere, M. Jori and L. Lantella (Milan: Giuffrè, 1979), 5-346.

Larenz, K., "Der Rechtssatz als Bestimmungssatz", in *Festschrift für Karl Engisch zum 70. Geburstag* (Frankfurt: Klostermann, 1969), 150-160.

Lavagna, C., "Sulle sentenze additive della Corte costituzionale", in *Scritti in onore di Gaspare Ambrosini* (Milan: Giuffrè, 1979), vol. 2, 1131-1144.

Lavagna, C., *Istituzioni di diritto pubblico* (Turin: UTET, 1985, 6th ed.).

Lazzaro, G., "Come legiferare?", *Analisi e diritto* (1992), 175-202.

Lazzaro, G., "Diritto e linguaggio comune", *Rivista trimestrale di diritto e procedura civile* XXXV (1981), 140-181.

Lazzaro, G., "Diritto, scienza giuridica e varie interpretazioni di un celebre passo di Paolo", *Rivista internazionale di filosofia del diritto* XLIV (1967), 754-764.

Lazzaro, G., "Imperativismo e responsabilità civile", *Rivista internazionale di filosofia del diritto* XLI (1964), 780-790.

Lazzaro, G., "La funzione dei giudici" (1971), in R. Guastini, ed., *Problemi di teoria del diritto* (Bologna: Il Mulino, 1980), 299-313.

Lazzaro, G., "Realtà sociale e amministrazione della giustizia", *Rivista internazionale di filosofia del diritto* XLVII (1970), 468-470.

Lazzaro, G., "Reciprocità e consuetudine", in U. Scarpelli, ed., *La teoria generale del diritto* (Milan: Edizioni di Comunità, 1983), 231-248.

Lazzaro, G., "Sul diritto come forma", *Rivista internazionale di filosofia del diritto* XXXIX (1962), 636-655.

Lazzaro, G., "Teoria generale e interpretazione nel concetto di «fattispecie»", *Rivista italiana di diritto e procedura penale*, new series, X (1967), 40-61.

Lazzaro, G., *Entropia della legge* (Turin: Giappichelli, 1985).

Lazzaro, G., *L'interpretazione sistematica della legge* (Turin: Giappichelli, 1966).

Lazzaro, G., *Storia e teoria della costruzione giuridica* (Turin: Giappichelli, 1965).

Lecaldano, E., "Limiti e natura della giustificazione razionale in morale da un punto di vista metateorico", in L. Gianformaggio and E. Lecaldano, eds., *Etica e diritto* (Bari: Laterza, 1986), 59-90.

Lecaldano, E. and Veca, S., eds., *Utilitarismo oggi* (Bari: Laterza, 1986).

Lecaldano, E., *Etica* (Turin: UTET, 1995).

Lecaldano, E., *Etica e significato: un bilancio delle teorie etiche contemporanee* (Turin: Boringhieri, 1990).

Lecaldano, E., *Introduzione a Moore* (Bari: Laterza, 1972).

Lecaldano, E., *L'illuminismo inglese* (Turin: Loescher, 1985).

Lecaldano, E., *Le analisi del linguaggio morale* (Rome: Ateneo, 1970).

Lee, K.K., "Hart's Primary and Secondary Rules", *Mind* LXXVII (1968), 561-64.

Leoni, B., "Il valore della giurisprudenza e il pensiero di J.H. von Kirchmann", *Rivista internazionale di filosofia del diritto* XVIII (1940), 343-59; XIX (1941), 64-95.

Leoni, B., "On a Recent Theory of the 'legal obligation'", *Il Politico* XXXI (1966), 535-539.

Leoni, B., *Il problema della scienza giuridica* (Turin: Giappichelli, 1940).

Liebman, E.T., "Contenuto ed efficacia delle decisioni della Corte costituzionale", *Rivista di diritto processuale* 12 (1957), 507-25.
Lloyd, D., *Introduction to Jurisprudence* (London: Stevens and Sons, 1965, 2nd ed.).
Lombardi Vallauri, L., *Corso di filosofia del diritto* (Padova: Cedam, 1981).
Lombardi, L., *Saggio sul diritto giurisprudenziale* (Milan: Giuffrè, 1967; 2nd ed., 1975).
Losano, M.G., "Diritto e logica in Hans Kelsen", *Il Politico* XXXI (1966), 812-821.
Losano, M.G., "Il problema dell'interpretazione in Hans Kelsen", *Rivista internazionale di filosofia del diritto* XLV (1968), 524-545.
Losano, M.G., "Il rapporto tra validità ed efficacia nella dottrina pura del diritto", *Sociologia del diritto* 2 (1981), 5-23.
Losano, M.G., "Per un'analisi del "Sollen" in Hans Kelsen", *Rivista internazionale di filosofia del diritto* III (1967), 546-568.
Losano, M.G., "Una teoria marxistica dell'interpretazione", *Rivista internazionale di filosofia del diritto* XLIII (1966), 518-533.
Losano, M.G., *Forma e realtà in Kelsen* (Milan: Edizioni di Comunità, 1981).
Losano, M.G., *Sistema e struttura nel diritto. I: Dalle origini alla Scuola storica* (Turin: Giappichelli, 1968).
Luzzati, C., "Le definizioni implicite dei giuristi", *Analisi e diritto* (1992), 215-224.
Luzzati, C., "Vaghezza, interpretazione e certezza del diritto", *Analisi e diritto* (1990), 133-178.
Luzzati, C., ed., *L'abrogazione delle leggi. Un dibattito analitico* (Milan: Giuffrè, 1987).
Luzzati, C., *La vaghezza delle norme. Un'analisi del linguaggio giuridico* (Milan: Giuffrè, 1990).
MacCormick, N., "Contemporary Philosophy: the Rediscovery of Practical Reason", *Journal of Law and Society* 10 (1983), 1-18.
MacCormick, N., *H.L.A. Hart* (London: Edward Arnold, 1981).
Mally, E., "Formalismus I", in *Logische Schriften* (Dordrecht: Reidel, 1971), 189-199; "Formalismus II", *ibid.,* at 200-207; "Formalismus III", *ibid.,* at 208-218.
Mally, E., *Grundgesetze des Sollens. Elemente der Logik des Willens* (Graz.: Leuschner und Lubensky, 1926).
Mally, E., *Logische Schriften* (Dordrecht: Reidel, 1971).
Martino, A., *Le definizioni legislative* (Turin: Giappichelli, 1975).
Mazzarese, T., "'Norm Proposition': Epistemic and Semantic Queries", *Rechtstheorie* XXII (1991), 39-70.

Mazzarese, T., "Antinomie, paradossi, logica deontica", *Rivista internazionale di filosofia del diritto* LXI (1984), 419-464.
Mazzarese, T., "Deontica kelseniana", *Materiali per una storia della cultura giuridica* XVIII (1988), 429-457.
Mazzarese, T., "Dubbi epistemologici sulle nozioni di «quaestio facti» e «quaestio juris»", *Rivista internazionale di filosofia del diritto* LXIX (1992), 294-320.
Mazzarese, T., "Metanorme e linguaggio deontico. Un'analisi logica", *Materiali per una storia della cultura giuridica* XII (1982), 409-445.
Mazzarese, T., "Negazione e abrogazione in deontica (A proposito d'un saggio di Alchourron e Bulygin)", *Materiali per una storia della cultura giuridica* XI (1981), 205-216.
Mazzarese, T., "Negazione e linguaggio giuridico. Contributo per una critica della logica deontica", *Materiali per una storia della cultura giuridica* XVIII (1988), 163-208.
Mazzarese, T., "Scoperta vs giustificazione. Una distinzione dubbia in tema di decisioni giudiziali", *Analisi e diritto* (1995), 145-198.
Mazzarese, T., *Logica deontica e linguaggio giuridico* (Padova: CEDAM, 1989).
McBride, W.L., "The Acceptance of a Legal System", *The Monist* 48 (1965), 377-396.
Messineo, F., *Manuale di diritto civile e commerciale* (Milan: Giuffrè, 1957).
Modugno, F. and Nocilla, D., "Stato d'assedio", in *Novissimo Digesto Italiano* XVIII (Turin: UTET, 1971), 273-291.
Modugno, F., *Appunti per una teoria generale del diritto. La teoria del diritto oggettivo* (Turin: Giappichelli, 1988).
Modugno, F., *L'invalidità della legge* (Milan: Giuffrè, 1970), 2 vols.
Modugno, F., *Legge. Ordinamento giuridico. Pluralità degli ordinamenti. Saggi di teoria generale del diritto* (Milan: Giuffrè, 1985).
Monateri, P.G., "Giurisprudenza", in *Digesto delle Discipline Privatistiche. Sezione civile* (Turin: UTET, 1993), 150-167.
Montesano, L., "Le sentenze costituzionali e l'individuazione delle norme", *Rivista di diritto processuale* 18 (1963), 20-54.
Montesano, L., "Norma e formula legislativa nel giudizio costituzionale", *Rivista di diritto processuale* 13 (1958), 524-39.
Mori, M., "Il diritto alla vita e il paradosso della posizione antiabortista: un'analisi filosofica", *Rivista internazionale di filosofia del diritto* LVI (1979), 172-221.
Mori, M., "Il problema della giustificazione nella filosofia pratica recente: una disamina e una proposta", in L. Gianformaggio and E. Lecaldano, eds., *Etica e diritto* (Bari: Laterza, 1986), 91-116.

Mori, M., "Recenti sviluppi nella filosofia pratica di lingua inglese", *Rivista di Filosofia* LXXI (1980), 139-156.

Mori, M., ed., *Questioni di bioetica* (Rome: Editori Riuniti, 1988).

Mori, M., *La fecondazione artificiale: questioni morali nell'esperienza giuridica* (Milan: Giuffrè, 1988).

Mori, M., *Utilitarismo e morale razionale. Per una teoria etica obbiettivista* (Milan: Giuffrè, 1986).

Morris, H., Review of H.L.A. Hart, *The Concept of Law*, *Harvard Law Review* 75 (1962), 1452-61.

Mullock, P., "Professor Bernstein on Rules of Obligation", *Mind* Volume (1967), 435-436.

Murdoch, I., *The Sovereignty of Good* (London: Routledge and Kegan Paul, 1970).

Nagel, E., *The Structure of Science: Problems in the Logic of Scientific Explanations* (Indianapolis: Hackett Publishing Co., 1961).

Neurath, O., "Protocol Sentences", in *Logical Positivism*, ed. A. J. Ayer (Glencoe: The Free Press, 1959), 199-208.

Nino, C. S., *La validez del derecho* (Buenos Aires: Astrea, 1985).

Olivecrona, K., "L'imperativo della legge", *Jus* (NS) V (1954), 451-467.

Olivecrona, K., "Legal Language and Reality" in *Essays in Jurisprudence in Honor of Roscoe Pound,* ed. Ralph A. Newman (Indianapolis-New York: The Bobbs-Merrill Co., 1962), 151-91; Italian translation: "Linguaggio giuridico e realtà", in U. Scarpelli, ed., *Diritto e analisi del linguaggio* (Milan: Comunità, 1976), 239-283.

Olivecrona, K., *Law as Fact* (London: Oxford University Press, 1939; 2nd ed. London: Stevens and Sons, 1971).

Pace, A., "Identità o differenza tra la questione di costituzionalità della norma e la questione di costituzionalità della interpretazione?", *Giurisprudenza costituzionale* 10 (1965), 1650-1656.

Parodi, G., "Aspetti della metagiurisprudenza tarelliana", *Materiali per una storia della cultura giuridica* XVII (1987), 555-588.

Parodi, G, "Sul concetto di "norma giuridica" nell'Allgemeine Theorie der Normen di H.Kelsen", *Materiali per una storia della cultura giuridica* XV (1985), 153-231.

Parodi, G., *Tecnica, ragione e logica nella giurisprudenza amministrativa* (Turin: Giappichelli, 1990).

Pasquinelli, A., *Introduzione alla logica simbolica* (Turin: Boringhieri, 1965).

Pasquinelli, A., *Nuovi principi di epistemologia* (Milan: Feltrinelli, 1974).

Pattaro, E., "Contributo al seminario «Se la logica si applichi alle norme»", *Materiali per una storia della cultura giuridica* XVI (1986), 511-519.

Pattaro, E., "Criteri e credenze sull'uguaglianza", *Il Mulino* XXXII (1983), 151-161.

Pattaro, E., "Diritto oggettivo, norme e precetti", *Rivista trimestrale di diritto e procedura civile* XXXII (1978), 686-710.
Pattaro, E., "Diritto, morale e concezione realistica del diritto", *Rivista trimestrale di diritto e procedura civile* XXIV (1970), 986-999.
Pattaro, E., "Il Positivismo giuridico italiano dalla rinascita alla crisi", *Politica del diritto* III (1972), 821-852, reprinted in U. Scarpelli, ed., *Diritto e analisi del linguaggio* (Milan: Edizioni di Comunità, 1976), 469-76 (Special issue of *Il Politico*).
Pattaro, E., "Il realismo giuridico come alternativa al positivismo giuridico", *Rivista internazionale di filosofia del diritto* XLVIII (1971), 61-126.
Pattaro, E., "La completezza degli ordinamenti giuridici e i «princìpi generali dell'ordinamento giuridico dello stato»", *Materiali per una storia della cultura giuridica* XVIII (1988), 145-162.
Pattaro, E., "La realtà del diritto e la sua conoscenza (A proposito di Alf Ross)", in A. Tarantino, ed., *Scienza e politica nel pensiero di A.Ross* (Milan: Giuffrè, 1984), 103-146.
Pattaro, E., "Models of Reason. Types of Principles and Reasoning. Historical Comments and Theoretical Outlines", *Ratio Juris* 1 (1988), 109-122.
Pattaro, E., "Per una critica della dottrina pura", in E. Pattaro, ed., *Contributi al realismo giuridico* (Milan: Giuffrè, 1982), I. xi-lxxxvi.
Pattaro, E., "Per una mappa del sapere giuridico", in U. Scarpelli, ed., *La teoria generale del diritto* (Milan: Edizioni di Comunità, 1983), 249-279.
Pattaro, E., "Presupposti metafisici e metaetici di un'etica della responsabilità", *Rivista di filosofia* LXXIV (1983), 117-41.
Pattaro, E., "Reason, Law and History", in A. Peczenik et al., eds., *Theory of Legal Science* (Dordrecht: Reidel, 1984), 363-372.
Pattaro, E., "Validità o verificabilità del diritto?", *Rivista trimestrale di diritto e procedura civile* XX (1966), 1005-1056.
Pattaro, E., "You Cannot Do Things with Words (The Concept of a Legal Transaction According to Axel Hägerström)", in P. Trappe, ed., *Conceptions Contemporaines du Droit. Actes du 9 Congrès Mondial. Part 2* (Wiesbaden: Franz Steiner, 1982), 153-161.
Pattaro, E., ed., *Contributi al realismo giuridico* (Milan: Giuffrè, 1982).
Pattaro, E., *Introduzione al corso di filosofia del diritto* (Bologna: CLUEB, 1986-87).
Pattaro, E., *Lineamenti per una teoria del diritto* (Bologna: CLUEB, 1985).
Pattaro, E. and Faralli, C., eds., *Reason in Law* (Milan: Giuffrè, 1987-1988, 3 vols).

Peczenik, A., "Non-Equivalent Transformations and the Law", in W. Krawietz, K. Opelak, A. Peczenik and A. Schramm, eds., *Argumentation und Hermeneutik in der Jurisprudenz* (Berlin: Duncker & Humblot, 1979), 163-176 (*Rechtstheorie*, Beiheft 1).

Peczenik, A., *The Basis of Legal Justification* (Lund: Lund University Press, 1983).

Perelman, Ch. and Olbrechts-Tyteca, L., *Traité de l'argumentation* (Paris: Presses Universitaires de France, 1958).

Perlingieri, P., "Dei modi di estinzione delle obbligazioni diversi dall'adempimento", in *Commentario del Codice Civile*, ed. A. Scialoja and G. Branca (Bologna-Rome: Zanichelli, 1975), 256-399.

Perlingieri, P., *Il diritto civile nella legalità costituzionale* (Napoli: ESI, 1984).

Perlingieri, P., *Scuole tendenze metodi. Problemi di diritto civile* (Napoli: ESI, 1989).

Peruzzi, A., *Definizioni: la cartografia dei concetti* (Milan: Angeli, 1983).

Pintore, A., "Il concetto di persona giuridica nell'indirizzo filosofico analitico", *Quaderni Fiorentini per la storia del pensiero giuridico moderno* 12 (1983), 1982-83.

Pintore, A., "La teoria generale del diritto in Italia. Problemi e tendenze attuali", *Materiali per una storia della cultura giuridica* XV (1985), 543-556.

Pintore, A., "Law and Hypocrisy", *International Journal for the Semiotics of Law* 4 (1991), 191-204.

Pintore, A., "Law as Fact? MacCormick's Institutional Theory of Law: Between Legal Positivism and Sociological Jurisprudence", *International Journal for the Semiotics of Law* 4 (1991), 233-253.

Pintore, A., "Nozick e il rischio dello Stato", *Sociologia del diritto* IX (1982), 143-156.

Pintore, A., *Il diritto senza verità* (Turin: Giappichelli, 1996).

Pintore, A., *La teoria analitica dei concetti giuridici* (Napoli: Jovene, 1990).

Pintore, A., *Norme e principi. Una critica a Dworkin* (Milan: Giuffrè, 1982).

Pizzorusso, A., "La motivazione delle decisioni della Corte costituzionale: comandi o consigli?", *Rivista trimestrale di diritto pubblico* 13 (1963), 345-407.

Pizzorusso, A., *Delle fonti del diritto* (Bologna: Zanichelli, 1977).

Pizzorusso, A., Volpe, G., Sorrentino, F. and Moretti, R., *Garanzie costituzionali*, in *Commentario della Costituzione*, a cura di Giuseppe Branca; [poi] fondato da Giuseppe Branca e continuato da Alessandro Pizzorusso (Bologna: Zanichelli and Rome: Foro Italiano, 1981).

Pontara, G., *Se il fine giustifichi i mezzi* (Bologna: Il Mulino, 1974).

Pontara, G., "Il presupposto teorico del razionalismo etico", in L. Gianformaggio and E. Lecaldano, eds., *Etica e diritto* (Bari: Laterza, 1986), 117-150.
Pontara, G. and Bobbio, N., "Vi sono diritti fondamentali?", *Rivista di Filosofia* LXXI (1980), 455-463.
Popper, K.R., *The Logic of Scientific Discovery* (London: Hutchinson, 1959).
Porro, M., "I linguaggi della scienza e della tecnica", in *Linguaggi settoriali in Italia*, ed. G.L. Beccaria (Milan: Bompiani, 1973), 181-206.
Pound, R., "Law in Books and Law in Action", *American Law Review* 44 (1910), 12-36.
Preti, G., "Linguaggio comune e linguaggi scientifici", in *Saggi filosofici* (Firenze: La nuova Italia, 1976), 127-220.
Pugliatti, S., "Conoscenza", *Enciclopedia di diritto* (Milan: Giuffrè, 1961), IX.85-130.
Pugliatti, S., "Finzione", *Enciclopedia di diritto* (Milan: Giuffrè, 1968), XVII.658-673.
Quine, W.V.O., "La teoria e l'osservazione", *Rivista di filosofia* I (1975), 1-19.
Quine, W.V.O., "Two Dogmas of Empiricism" (1951), reprinted in F. Zabeeh, E.D. Klemke, A. Jacobson, eds., *Readings in Semantics* (Urbana: University of Illinois Press, 1974), 583-610.
Rawls, R., "Two Concepts of Rules", *The Philosophical Review* LXIV (1955), 3-32.
Raz, J., "Legal Validity" (1977), in J. Raz, *The Authority of Law. Essays on Law and Morality* (Oxford: Clarendon Press. 1979), 146-159.
Raz, J., *Practical Reason and Norms* (London: Hutchinson, 1975).
Raz, J., *The Concept of a Legal System* (Oxford: The Clarendon Press, 1970; 2nd ed. 1973); Italian translation: *Il concetto di sistema giuridico*, ed. P. Comanducci (Bologna: Il Mulino, 1977).
Reinach, A., *Sämtliche Werke*, ed. Karl Schumann und Marry Smith (Munchen-Hamden-Wien: Philosophia, 1989, 2 vols.).
Robinson, R., *Definition* (Oxford: The Clarendon Press, 1972).
Rodotà, S., "Proprietà (diritto vigente)", in *Novissimo Digesto Italiano* (Turin: Unione Tipografico-Editrice, 1967), XIV.125-146.
Rodotà, S., *Le fonti d'integrazione del contratto* (Milan: Giuffrè, 1969).
Romano, S., "Buona fede (dir. priv.)", in *Enciclopedia di diritto* (Milan: Giuffrè, 1959), V.677-699.
Romano, S., "Principio di equità (dir. priv.)", in *Enciclopedia di diritto* (Milan: Giuffrè, 1966), XV.83-106.

Ross, A., "Definition in Legal Language", *Logique et Analyse* 3-4 (1958), 139-49; Italian translation "La definizione nel linguaggio giuridico", in U. Scarpelli, ed., *Diritto e analisi del linguaggio* (Milan: Comunità, 1976), 199-214.

Ross, A., "Le finzioni giuridiche", in *Critica del diritto e analisi del linguaggio* (Bologna: Il Mulino, 1982), 177-194.

Ross, A., "Review of the Concept of Law", *Yale Law Journal* 71 (1962), 1185-90.

Ross, A., "Tû-Tû", *Harvard Law Review* 70 (1957), 812-825; Italian translation: "Tû-Tû", in U. Scarpelli, ed., *Diritto e analisi del linguaggio* (Milan: Comunità, 1976), 165-181.

Ross, A., "Validity and the Conflict between Legal Positivism and Natural Law", *Revista Juridica de Buenos Aires* (1961), 46-93; Italian translation "Il concetto di validità e il conflitto tra positivismo giuridico e giusnaturalismo", in A. Ross, *Critica del diritto e analisi del linguaggio*, ed. by A. Febbrajo and R. Guastini (Bologna: Il Mulino, 1982), 137-158.

Ross, A., *Directives and Norms* (London: Routledge and Kegan Paul, 1968).

Ross, A., *Om ret og retfærdighed* (København: Busck, 1953).

Ross, A., *On Law and Justice* (London: Stevens & Sons, 1958; Berkeley: California University Press, 1959).

Ruggeri, A., *Gerarchia, competenza, e qualità nel sistema costituzionale delle fonti normative* (Milan: Giuffrè, 1977).

Ruperto, C., "Età (diritto privato)", in *Enciclopedia di diritto* (Milan: Giuffrè, 1967), XVI.85-92.

Sacco, R., *Il possesso* (Milan: Giuffrè, 1950).

Sacco, R. and G. De Nova, *Il contratto* (Turin: UTET, 1982; *Trattato di diritto civile diretto da Pietro Rescigno*, vol.10).

Sandulli, A.M., "Legge (diritto costituzionale)", in *Novissimo digesto italiano* 9 (1963), 630-651.

Sandulli, A.M., *Il giudizio sulle leggi* (Milan: Giuffrè, 1967).

Sandulli, A.M., *Manuale di diritto amministrativo* (Napoli: Jovene, 1964).

Sartorius, R., "The Concept of Law", *Archiv für Rechts- und Sozialphilosophie* LII (1966), 161-193.

Sauvel, T., "Histoire du jugement motivé", *Revue du Droit Public et de la Science Politique en France et à l'Etranger* 71 (1955), 5-53.

Savigny, F.C. von, *Vom Beruf unserer Zeit für Gesetzgebung und Rechtswissenschaft*, in J. Stern, ed., *Thibaut und Savigny* (Darmstadt: Wissenschaftliche Buchgesellschaft, 1959).

Scarpelli, U., "Auctoritas non veritas facit legem", *Rivista di Filosofia* LXXV (1984), 29-43.

Scarpelli, U., "Dalla legge al codice, dal codice ai princìpi", *Rivista di Filosofia* LXXVIII (1987), 3-15.

Scarpelli, U., "Dovere morale, obbligo giuridico, impegno politico", reprinted in U. Scarpelli, *L'etica senza verità* (Bologna: Il Mulino, 1982), 165-175.

Scarpelli, U., "Filosofia e diritto", in F. Tessitore, ed., *La cultura filosofica italiana dal 1945 al 1980* (Napoli: Guida editori), 173-199.

Scarpelli, U., "Gli orizzonti della giustificazione", in L. Gianformaggio and E. Lecaldano, eds., *Etica e diritto* (Bari: Laterza, 1986), 3-44.

Scarpelli, U., "Il diritto pubblico italiano di Santi Romano", *Materiali per una storia della cultura giuridica* XIX (1989), 143-150.

Scarpelli, U., "Il metodo giuridico", *Rivista di diritto processuale* 4 (1971), 533-554, reprinted in R. Guastini, ed., *Problemi di teoria del diritto* (Bologna: Il Mulino, 1980), 261-280.

Scarpelli, U., "Il permesso, il dovere e la completezza degli ordinamenti normativi", *Rivista Trimestrale di diritto e procedura civile* (1963), 1634-1656 (reprinted in *L'etica senza verità* (Bologna: Il Mulino, 1982), 221-250.

Scarpelli, U., "Il positivismo giuridico rivisitato", *Rivista di Filosofia* LXXX (1989), 461-475.

Scarpelli, U., "Introduzione all'analisi delle argomentazioni giudiziarie" (1970), reprinted in U. Scarpelli, ed., *Diritto e analisi del linguaggio* (Milan: Edizioni di Comunità, 1976), 407-450.

Scarpelli, U., "L'educazione del giurista", *Rivista di diritto processuale* (1968), 1-33.

Scarpelli, U., "L'interpretazione. Premesse alla teoria dell'interpretazione giuridica", in U. Scarpelli and V. Tomeo, eds., *Società norme e valori. Studi in onore di Renato Treves* (Milan: Giuffrè, 1984), 141-165.

Scarpelli, U., "La bioetica: alla ricerca dei principi", *Biblioteca della Libertà* 99 (1987), 7-32.

Scarpelli, U., "La critica analitica a Kelsen", *Rivista di filosofia* LXXII (1981), 481-490.

Scarpelli, U., "La definizione nel diritto", *Jus* IV (1959), 496-506, reprinted in U. Scarpelli, ed., *Diritto e analisi del linguaggio* (Milan: Edizioni di Comunità, 1976), 183-198.

Scarpelli, U., "La filosofia. La filosofia dell'etica. La filosofia del diritto di indirizzo analitico in Italia", Introduzione a U. Scarpelli, ed., *Diritto e analisi del linguaggio* (Milan: Comunità, 1976), 7-35.

Scarpelli, U., "La teoria generale del diritto: prospettive per un trattato", in U. Scarpelli, ed., *La teoria generale del diritto* (Milan: Edizioni di Comunità, 1983), 281-340.

Scarpelli, U., "Le "proposizioni giuridiche" come precetti reiterati", *Rivista internazionale di filosofia del diritto* XLIV (1967), 465-482.

Scarpelli, U., "Per una sociologia del diritto come scienza", *Sociologia del diritto* I (1974), 266-274.
Scarpelli, U., "Riflessioni sulla responsabilità politica. Responsabilità, libertà, visione dell'uomo", *Rivista internazionale di filosofia del diritto* LVIII (1981), 27-79.
Scarpelli, U., "Risposta di Uberto Scarpelli", in *Tavola rotonda sul positivismo giuridico (Pavia, May 2, 1966)* (Milan: Giuffrè, 1967), 77-86.
Scarpelli, U., "Scienza, sapere, sapienza", *Rivista internazionale di filosofia del diritto* LXIII (1986), 245-258.
Scarpelli, U., "Semantica giuridica", *Novissimo Digesto Italiano* XVI (1969), 978-999.
Scarpelli, U., "Scienza del diritto e analisi del linguaggio", *Rivista di Diritto Commerciale* 46 (1948), 212-16.
Scarpelli, U., "Società e natura nel pensiero di Hans Kelsen", *Rivista internazionale di filosofia del diritto* XXXI (1954), 767-780.
Scarpelli, U., "Teoria formale o teoria strutturale del diritto. Per la dissoluzione della metafora formalistica", in *Studi in onore di C. Grassetti* (Milan: Giuffrè, 1980), 1669-1675.
Scarpelli, U., "Validità", in *Gli strumenti del sapere contemporaneo* (Turin: UTET, 1985), 928-32.
Scarpelli, U., *Contributo alla semantica del linguaggio normativo* (Turin: Memorie dell'Accademia delle Scienze di Turin, 1959; 2nd edition: Milan: Giuffrè, 1985).
Scarpelli, U., *Cos'è il positivismo giuridico* (Milan: Edizioni di Comunità, 1965).
Scarpelli, U., ed., "La logica e il dover essere", *Rivista di Filosofia* LXVII (1976).
Scarpelli, U., ed., *Diritto e analisi del linguaggio* (Milan: Edizioni di Comunità, 1976).
Scarpelli, U., ed., *La teoria generale del diritto. Problemi e tendenze attuali* (Milan: Edizioni di Comunità, 1983).
Scarpelli, U., *Filosofia analitica e giurisprudenza* (Milan: Cisalpino, 1953).
Scarpelli, U., *Filosofia analitica, norme e valori* (Milan: Edizioni di Comunità, 1962).
Scarpelli, U., *Il problema della definizione e il concetto di diritto* (Milan: Istituto Editoriale Cisalpino, 1955).
Scarpelli, U., *L'etica senza verità* (Bologna: Il Mulino, 1982).
Scarpelli, U., *Semantica, morale, diritto* (Turin: Giappichelli, 1969).
Scarpelli, U. and Luzzati, C., "Filosofia del diritto", in P. Rossi, ed., *La filosofia* (Turin: UTET, 1995), 221-312.
Scarpelli, U. and P. Di Lucia, eds., *Il linguaggio del diritto* (Milan: LED, 1995).

Schlesinger, P., "Compensazione (diritto civile)", in *Novissimo Digesto Italiano* (Turin: UTET, 1959), III.722-731.
Schlesinger, P., "Complessità del procedimento di formazione del consenso ed unità del negozio contrattuale", in *Studi in onore di P. Greco* (Padova: CEDAM, 1965), II.1003-1021.
Schlick, M., "Über das Fundament der Erkenntnis", *Erkenntnis* IV (1934), 79-99.
Searle, J.R., "How to Derive 'Ought' from 'Is'", *The Philosophical Review* LXXIII (1964), 43-58.
Searle, J.R., "What is a Speech Act?", in Max Black, ed., *Philosophy in America* (London: Allen and Unwin, 1964), 221-39.
Searle, J.R., *Speech Acts. An Essay in the Philosophy of Language* (Cambridge: Cambridge University Press, 1969).
Singer, M.G., "Hart's Concept of Law", *The Journal of Philosophy* 60 (1963), 197-220.
Sorrentino, F., *Le fonti del diritto* (Genova: ECIG, 1985, 2nd ed.).
Stevenson, C.L., *Ethics and Language* (New Haven: Yale University Press, 1945).
Stevenson, C.L., *Facts and Values. Studies in Ethical Analysis* (New Haven and London: Yale University Press, 1963).
Stoljar, S., *Moral and Legal Reasoning* (London: Macmillan, 1980).
Summers, R.S., "Toward a Better General Theory of Legal Validity", *Rechtstheorie*, 16 (1985), 65-83.
Tarello, G., "Discorso assertivo e discorso precettivo nel linguaggio dei giuristi", *Rivista internazionale di filosofia del diritto* XLIV (1967), 419-435.
Tarello, G., "Due interventi in tema di deontologia", *Materiali per una storia della cultura giuridica* XII (1982), 207-218.
Tarello, G., "Il concetto di diritto: una teoria generale 'analitica'", *Annali della Facoltà di Giurisprudenza dell' Università di Genova* I (1962), 141-155.
Tarello, G., "Il diritto come ordinamento", in R. Orecchia, ed., *Il diritto come ordinamento, Atti del X Congresso nazionale (Bari, 3-5 ottobre 1974)* (Milan: Giuffrè, 1976), 49-82.
Tarello, G., "Kelsen e la cultura europea", in C. Roehrssen, ed., *Hans Kelsen nella cultura filosofico-giuridica del novecento* (Rome: Istituto dell'Enciclopedia Italiana, 1983), 53-60.
Tarello, G., "L'autonomia dell'interprete", *Rivista internazionale di filosofia del diritto* XLII (1965), 159-165.
Tarello, G., "L'interpretazione della legge", in *Trattato di diritto civile e commerciale*, ed. A. Cicu, F. Messineo and L. Mengoni (Milan: Giuffrè, 1980).

Tarello, G., "La nozione di diritto positivo nella cultura giuridica italiana", *Sociologia del diritto* IV (1977), 315-324.

Tarello, G., "La nozione di diritto: un approccio prudente", in U. Scarpelli, ed., *La teoria generale del diritto* (Milan: Edizioni di Comunità, 1983), 341-360.

Tarello, G., "La sociologia nella giurisprudenza", *Sociologia del diritto* I (1974), 40-51.

Tarello, G., "«Obbligo» e «Conflitto di obblighi»", *Rivista di Filosofia* LVII (1966), 214-234.

Tarello, G., "Orientamenti analitico-linguistici e teoria dell'interpretazione giuridica", in U. Scarpelli, ed., *Diritto e analisi del linguaggio* (Milan: Edizioni di Comunità, 1976), 375-396.

Tarello, G., "Studi sulla teoria generale dei precetti, I, Introduzione al linguaggio precettivo", in *Annali della Facoltà di giuriprudenza di Genova* (Milan: Giuffrè, 1968), reprinted in *Diritto, enunciati, usi* (Bologna: Mulino, 1974), II.135-269.

Tarello, G., *Cultura giuridica e politica del diritto* (Bologna: Il Mulino, 1988).

Tarello, G., *Diritto, enunciati, usi. Studi di teoria e metateoria del diritto* (Bologna: Il Mulino, 1974).

Tarello, G., *Dottrine del processo civile. Studi storici sulla formazione del diritto processuale civile* (Bologna: Il Mulino, 1989).

Tarello, G., *Il realismo giuridico americano* (Milan: Giuffrè, 1962, repr. 1995).

Tarello, G., *L'interpretazione della legge* (Milan: Giuffrè, 1980).

Tarello, G., *Storia della cultura giuridica moderna I: Assolutismo e codificazione del diritto* (Bologna: Il Mulino, 1976).

Tarello, G., *Teorie e ideologie nel diritto sindacale* (Milan: Edizioni di Comunità, 1972, 2nd ed.).

Tarski, A., *Introduction to Logic and to the Methodology of Deductive Sciences* (New York: Oxford University Press, 1941).

Tarski, A., "The Semantic Conception of Truth and the Foundations of Semantics" (1944), reprinted in H. Feigl and W. Sellars, eds., *Readings in Philosophical Analysis* (New York: Appleton-Century-Crofts, Inc., 1949), 52-84.

Taruffo, M., "Aspetti della giustificazione delle decisioni giudiziarie", in L. Gianformaggio and E. Lecaldano, eds., *Etica e diritto* (Bari: Laterza, 1986), 271-276.

Taruffo, M., "Cassazione e revisione: un problema nella storia delle istituzioni giudiziarie", *Materiali per una storia della cultura giuridica* XII (1982), 41-60.

Taruffo, M., "Elementi per un'analisi del giudizio di fatto", *Rivista trimestrale di diritto e procedura civile* XLIX (1995), 785-821.

Taruffo, M., "La giustificazione delle decisioni fondate su standards", *Materiali per una storia della cultura giuridica* XIX (1989), 151-174.
Taruffo, M., "Le prove scientifiche nella recente esperienza statunitense", *Rivista trimestrale di diritto e procedura civile* XLX (1996), 219-249.
Taruffo, M., "Presunzioni, inversioni, prova del fatto", *Rivista trimestrale di diritto e procedura civile* XLVI (1992), 733-756.
Taruffo, M., "Ragione e processo: ipotesi su una correlazione", *Ragion Pratica* I (1993), 49-60.
Taruffo, M., *La motivazione della sentenza civile* (Padova: CEDAM, 1975).
Taruffo, M., *La prova dei fatti giuridici* (Milan: Giuffrè, 1992).
Taruffo, M., *Lezioni sul processo civile* (Bologna: Il Mulino, 1995).
Thomae, J.K., *Elementare Theorie der analytischen Functionen einer complexen Verändlichen* (Halle an der Saale: L. Nebert, 1880, 2nd ed. 1898).
Tönnies, F., *Community and Society*, trans. C.P. Loomis (Michigan: Michigan State University Press, 1957).
Treves, R., *Il diritto come relazione. Saggio critico sul neokantismo contemporaneo* (Turin: Tip. Accame, 1934).
Trimarchi, P., *Istituzioni di diritto privato* (Milan: Giuffrè, 1983, 6th ed.).
Troper, M., "Kelsen, la théorie de l'inteprétation et la structure de l'ordre juridique", *Revue internationale de philosophie* 138 (1981), 518-529 (issue on *Kelsen et le positivisme juridique*).
Troper, M., "Les théories volontaristes du droit: ontologie et théorie de la science du droit", in P. Amselek and C. Grzegorczyk, eds., *Controverses autour de l'ontologie du droit* (Paris: PUF, 1989), 53-68.
Tugendhat, E., "Zur Entwicklung von moralischen Begründungsstrukturen im modernen Recht", in *Archiv für Rechts und Sozialphilosophie, Beiheft N.F.* 14 (1980), 1-20.
Twining, W. and Miers, D., *How to do Things with Rules* (London: Weidenfeld & Nicolson, 1976).
Ubertis, G., ed., *La conoscenza del fatto nel processo penale* (Milan: Giuffrè, 1992).
Ulrich, M., *Thetisch und kategorisch* (Tübingen: Narr, 1985).
Urmson, J.O., *Philosophical Analysis* (Oxford: Clarendon Press, 1956).
Villa, V., "Hermeneutic point of view e analisi delle norme", *Rivista internazionale di filosofia del diritto* LIX (1982), 721-731.
Villa, V., "Implicazioni meta-teoriche nella teoria del diritto di Alf Ross", *Rivista internazionale di filosofia del diritto* LVI (1979), 258-288.
Villa, V., "La coerenza normativa e i presupposti epistemologici della giustificazione", *Rivista internazionale di filosofia del diritto* LXV (1988), 567-597.
Villa, V., "La formazione dei concetti e delle teorie nella scienza giuridica", *Materiali per una storia della cultura giuridica* XV (1985), 371-400.

Villa, V., "La metagiurisprudenza analitica e la dicotomia descrittivo/prescrittivo", in *Studi in memoria di Giovanni Tarello, II: Saggi teorico-giuridici* (Milan: Giuffrè, 1990), 617-665.

Villa, V., "La metodologia di Ross", in A. Tarantino, ed., *Scienza e politica nel pensiero di A.Ross* (Milan: Giuffrè, 1984), 67-78.

Villa, V., "La scienza giuridica fra scienze naturali e scienze umane", *Materiali per una storia della cultura giuridica* XIV (1984), 401-459.

Villa, V., "Legal Science and Hermeneutic Point of View", in A. Peczenik et al., eds., *Theory of Legal Science* (Dordrecht: Reidel, 1984), 509-520.

Villa, V., "Sulla nozione di "filosofia analitica"", in M. Jori, ed., *Ermeneutica e filosofia analitica. Due concezioni del diritto a confronto* (Turin: Giappichelli, 1994), 163-181.

Villa, V., "Truth and Acceptability in Legal and Empirical Science", in C. Faralli and E. Pattaro, eds., *Reason in Law* (Milan: Giuffrè, 1987), II.361-369.

Villa, V., *Conoscenza giuridica e concetto di diritto positivo. Lezioni di filosofia del diritto* (Turin: Giappichelli, 1993).

Villa, V., *Teorie della scienza giuridica e teorie delle scienze naturali* (Milan: Giuffrè, 1984).

Volpe, G., *L'ingiustizia delle leggi. Studi sui modelli di giustizia costituzionale* (Milan: Giuffrè, 1977).

von Wright, G.H., *Explanation and Understanding* (London: Routledge, 1971).

Walter, R., "Der gegenwärtige Stand der reinen Rechtslehre", *Rechtstheorie* I (1970), 69-95.

Weber, M., "R. Stammlers 'Überwindung' der materialistischen Geschichtsauffassung", in *Archiv für Sozialwissenschaft und Sozialpolitik* XXIV (1907), 94-151; new edition in Max Weber, *Gesammelte Aufsätze zur Wissenschaftslehre* (Tübingen: Mohr, 1968), 291-359.

Weber, M., *The Methodology of the Social Sciences*, trans E. Shils and H. Finch (New York: Free Press, 1949).

Williams, G., "Language and the Law", in *Law Quarterly Review* 61 (1945), 71-86, 179-195, 293-303, 384-406; 62 (1946), 387-406.

Winch, P., *The Idea of a Social Science and its Relation to Philosophy* (London: Routledge and Kegan Paul, 1958).

Wittgenstein, L., *The Blue and Brown Books* (Oxford: Blackwell, 1958); Ital. ed. by Amedeo G. Conte: *Libro Blu e Libro Marrone* (Turin: Einaudi, 1983).

Wright, G. H. von, *Norm and Action. A Logical Enquiry* (London: Routledge & Kegan Paul, 1963).

Wright, G. H. von, *Practical Reason* (London: Routledge & Kegan Paul, 1983).

Wróblewski, J., "La normatività della scienza giuridica", Ital. transl. by G. Lombardi, in U. Scarpelli, ed., *Diritto e analisi del linguaggio* (Milan: Edizioni di Comunità, 1976), 325-44.

Wróblewski, J., "Tre concetti di validità", *Rivista trimestrale di diritto e procedura civile* 36 (1982), 584-595.

Wurzel, K.G., *Das juristische Denken* (Wien: Perles, 1904).

Zagrebelsky, G., *Il sistema costituzionale delle fonti del diritto* (Turin: UTET, 1984).

Zagrebelsky, G., *La giustizia costituzionale* (Bologna: Il Mulino, 1988, 2nd ed.).

Zingarelli, N., *Vocabolario della lingua italiana* (Bologna: Zanichelli, 1983, 11th ed.).

Znamierowski, C., *Podstawowe pojecia teorji prawa. I. Uklad prawny i norma prawna* (Poznan: Fiszer i Majewski, 1924; 2nd ed.: Poznan: Górski i Tetzlaw, 1934).

INDEX